LOVE IN EXILE

LOVE IN EXILE

AN AMERICAN WRITER'S MEMOIR
OF LIFE IN DIVIDED BERLIN

EDITH ANDERSON

STEERFORTH PRESS
SOUTH ROYALTON, VERMONT

For information about permission to reproduce selections
from this book, write to: Steerforth Press L.C.,
P.O. Box 70, South Royalton, Vermont 05068.

Library of Congress Cataloging-in-Publication Data
is available from the Library of Congress

ISBN 1–883642–67–1

Photograph of Noel and Herta Field is reprinted by courtesy of
Werner Schweizer, author of *Noel Field: The fictitious spy*.

Manufactured in the United States of America

FIRST EDITION

PART I

*My mother went on in her forthright way,
"By habit and inclination you, Herr Doktor,
are an incorrigible aristocrat. I can't
imagine you in a society where everyone
is equal."*

*"Neither can I," said Karl Marx. "Such a
time will come, but we had better be out
of the way when it does."*

— FRANZISKA KUGELMANN,
daughter of Marx's close friend
Dr. Ludwig Kugelmann,
from *Mohr und General* (Moor and General)

Toward morning, in a dream, I see my parents. They are visiting me in my home in Berlin. I go over to their bed, a sort of baby crib. Mother is at one end, Dad at the other, but it is so small that they are almost touching. I gather their heads to mine and we hold our cheeks together tenderly.

There are no rights and no wrongs in this dream of continuity and reconciliation. In it I am as much the parent of my parents as I am their offspring. My grandson's toys lie on the dresser where my daughter's had briefly been kept when she and I had visited Dad after Mother's death.

Dad asks me a question about my life, and it does not strike me that this is the first time in decades that he has shown concern for me without condemnation. I tell him that my life has been torn right through the middle.

I N NOVEMBER, 1946 a group of mostly left-wing German exiles, among them my husband Max Schroeder, was given a good riddance present by the U.S. State Department. They had requested repatriation and were sent back to the remains of their country on the *Marine Flasher*, a no longer seaworthy troop-transport vessel that was due to be scrapped. Not too surprisingly it broke down mid-Atlantic, circled about in quiet waters for two days like a celluloid fish in a bathtub, and was then nearly ripped apart by a storm. Canadian papers reported it lost, but no search parties were sent. Eventually its feeble emergency motor got it moving at four knots until it reached Ponta Delgada in the Azores.

There the Germans soaked up sun and enjoyed a blessed respite from anxiety and the *Flasher*'s dreadful food until another hulk, the *Marine Marlin*, picked them up. Nearly a month after they left New York they disembarked in Bremerhaven and their new life among the ruins began.

Max and I were not living together at the time of his departure. I did not see him off at the pier, it would have been too painful, but we had not relinquished one another. We wrote each other careful letters in which our yearning was barely hinted at.

His first letter, posted from the Azores to reach me by my birthday, ended: "I am loving you with heart and mind." That was a present, wasn't it, I asked myself. Enclosed in his next letter, from Bremerhaven, were three dollars "for a pint of rum" at Christmas. He had been chary of the porous sop "I love you" long before our troubles began.

> I am in good health and spirits [he wrote in March]. Happy? Yes, sometimes, and with reason, but it would be exaggerating to say I was happy. The happiness of feeling needed and appreciated here, of finding I can do things I wanted to do all my life and never had the chance — this is not just superficial happiness, but I know its limits very well. The other more personal sector of happiness is quite empty at the moment, and I am very careful in this regard. I saw Rosl in Hannover, where her husband has an assignment. I was very much attracted by her, but something "deep down," as you say, tells me to stay alone for a while. I think I am not as pathetic as I was when we met, I am sure I am not. I am questioning myself about things of the past and the future.

I too was questioning myself about things of the past and the future. If he was no longer as "pathetic" as when we met, neither was I as blind. Now, in his absence, with memory uninterrupted, I could study him like the bud of a flower and see the petals open slowly one by one. Further illumination came with extraordinary letters from the wilderness of Berlin. The last, longest, and most moving of these, which began simply "Dear Edith," and ended "So long," contained not one calculated word of love. It contained a full-grown man. I longed to be good enough for him.

As to my feelings about my own country, they are crystal-
lizing more and more into a conviction that it is my house
and my home which for decades or even centuries was
governed by lackeys and parasites to keep me and all the
true owners of this good old house in the basement and let
us starve. If God or some other obscure divinity gives me
the time to live, then like old Fontane I hope to start
writing real books at sixty. Now there is still too much to
do to cleanse the house of roaches. They are still in the
majority.

Max crossed devastated Germany slowly, weighing job offers. In Berlin
he accepted the post of editor-in-chief of a literary publishing house, at
that time the largest in Germany. The Aufbau Press was an arm of the
Kulturbund (The League for the Cultural Revival of Democratic Germany). Its headquarters were in the British Sector, but the actual publishing offices were in the Soviet Sector. It was a period of political
puss-in-the-corner and the freedom of sixes and sevens. Max found it in-
vigorating.

"Is it a good project to come over here?" He raised and answered the
question with the dispassionate mien of a professor advising a student on
a course of study. "I think it is," he wrote, "and I mean in itself. Not in
the way — understandable as it is — that many people long for Paris.
Here is a point from which one can acquire perspective. Come and see.
I think it is worthwhile."

He agreed that despite everything our relationship had not ended and
he offered me support in Berlin — a room or small apartment of my
own, spending money, and a cleaning woman because, as he said, he
wanted me to have time to write. I deserved this in return for all he
"owed" me: "By this I do not mean so much the material support I got
from you, as the treasures of your mind with which you opened worlds to
me that I had not seen before or had neglected." But if I preferred a job,
he wrote, he was sure he could find me one.

I wrote back: "I will move heaven and earth. I am determined to come."

Non-German civilians were not permitted in occupied Berlin. Senator Wagner of New York State arranged a personal interview for me with
Ruth Shipley, the head of the Passport Division of the State Department
in Washington. She proved to be a benighted fanatic in a housedress.

Certainly not, she snarled, "we" would have to "chase the Russians out of Berlin" first. But there was hope; she for one thought this could be accomplished within a year.

Christina Stead and her husband, William Blake, wrote from Antwerp advising me to lie low for a while, then apply in an ordinary New York passport bureau for a schoolteacher's summer jaunt to Paris (teaching being my nominal profession). Things pronounced impossible in Washington could be managed from Paris, they said; quite different people were running American affairs there. Bill's former wife and daughter would help me find a job — they had contacts. Bill, who knew all about banking though he never had any money, gave me the address of a basement exchange in lower Manhattan where francs could be bought at the most favorable rate.

My parents had a romantic portrait photo of me at eighteen, large-eyed, soft-lipped, in an expensive draped dress which I now realize was a kind of investment, like my college education. I was thirty now and had not yet shown any awareness of what harvest a girl's bloom could reap. Slowly and sadly Dad and Mother were resigning themselves. Dad opened a separate savings account for me. It would not be in my name, he explained, but when real need overtook me, as it obviously must, the money would be at my disposal.

I sold my piano and asked Dad if I might have the money in the new savings account. "Not for that purpose," he said curtly. He would not go to the country of the Nazis, he said, meaning: How can *you*? And what do you want with a penniless German Communist who is much too old for you, why do you throw every chance of your youth away?

Chris and Bill sent me a hundred which I could pay back, they joked, when I was rich. Other friends provided shorter-term loans, Paris addresses, and a trunkful of provisions which would last me and Max a year.

Into shiny white Tampax tubes I stuffed my contraband francs, thinking myself extremely cunning. Any young female would have struck on this obvious idea, but fortunately my baggage was not opened. This assured me a few weeks of minimum subsistence in a maid's room at the top of a hotel near the rue Haussmann while I got my bearings.

We may think we have no definite plan. Plans form themselves in a region of the brain which the brain knows nothing of. While I was still agonizing over the decision to leave all that was precious to me for one man, my astute friend Helen Cole asked, "Are you afraid you'll be happy?"

This startling formulation was like the shot of brandy that settles the stomach. The title of Wendell Willkie's end-of-the-war book, *One World*, was still in the foreground of people's minds. I could always come back. And the teeter-totter began.

When the ship actually moved out of New York Harbor with three hoarse, prolonged blasts of farewell and I saw the towers of my past shrink and fade into blank sky, sobs convulsed me and would not subside. Yet again, when I rose from my berth next morning I was unexpectedly transformed, light as man on the moon. The swell of the ocean uplifted me, my spirit flew with the gulls still following our ship. How was that? Had America itself, which I loved to distraction, been the millstone around my neck? Should I not have been worried sick about going to Europe with money for only three weeks, stumbling school French, no German?

There were answers, but at the moment I did not require them, nor would I have understood them.

Soon after Max left the United States I heard a woman at a party in Greenwich Village ask, "Who did you say her husband was?" and the ardent, artless reply of the hostess, a young dancer named Lily, "Oh, you know, you met him, Max Schroeder — that tall, wonderful man?" So stricken was I by her infatuated tone that all further recollection of the party ceases there, as if an earthquake had rocked the place and all the guests fled into the street.

Lily hardly knew Max, yet she recognized his transcendence, and a terrible insight wrung me, not a new one but painfully perceived anew: that intimacy is not knowledge of the other but actually works against such knowledge. All I knew of Max was what I saw. I had no more grasp of his origins than Elsa of Lohengrin's. Before the Nazis came to power I had taken little notice of Germany. I was not familiar with the language or the nation's history or (with a very few exceptions) the German literature with which Max was unceasingly involved. It was not ignorance alone; it was a total lack of curiosity. My mind was too preoccupied with my own country to make room for other people's.

At a meeting of the League of American Writers early in 1942 a stranger rose at the other side of the sparsely lighted hall to say a few words. He leaned forward across heads like a long tattered streamer in the wind and spoke haltingly in what seemed to be German, but was English. I realized that this must be one of the rare brave human beings who had resisted Hitler openly, and my heart went out to him. I did not connect him with the shabbily dressed man in an oversized coat, stained felt hat, and gold-rimmed spectacles who used to pass me, always in a hurry, on Horatio Street a year or so later. He was very gaunt and squinted against the sun, which wrinkled the bridge of a mountainous nose and made his glasses slip. He seemed pitiable, so obviously uncared-for.

His occupation as chief editor of an anti-Nazi periodical, *the German American*, was better than respectable, for he had persuaded the most illustrious of the exiles to write for it, but his name did not appear on the masthead, and he received no salary. Instead, like countless other Germans on their list of the deserving, he got eighty dollars a month from the Joint Anti-Fascist Refugee Committee. No one could live on that.

I had a humbler but similar job, though it had come to me, as the Germans say, like the infant to the virgin. Hastening down Broadway to my Marxist analyst who charged only five dollars a session because I was unemployed (he too was still young) I bumped into a former college crony named Milton. He hailed me joyously, "You're just the person I need!" He told me he was the cultural editor of the *Daily Worker* but had just been drafted into the army and must find a replacement by the weekend.

"Oh, Milton, I would scrub floors for the *Daily Worker*," I said fervently, "but I have no newspaper experience."

"I'll break you in."

"In three days?"

"Less."

I didn't even ask what they paid. The question for me was how I could have the gall to pass myself off as a cultural editor, an arbiter of taste, an authority, to readers fed up with the preciosity and rudderlessness of other papers.

My analyst brushed these scruples aside. He was delighted that I had a real challenge to bite into; life, as Marx said, was a struggle, and I was no more a fraud than anyone else. As to the "right" way to do a thing, there were no blueprints valid for all.

They paid fifteen dollars a week. That is, they paid me fifteen, which was less than Max's alms. I never did learn what they paid Milton. Alvah Bessie, the successor chosen by the higher-ups, was to get forty-five, the

Party's maximum (so one heard), but he changed his mind when summoned by Hollywood.

The union minimum was twenty-seven. When I found this out a couple of months later, I demanded and got it. I was no longer quite so blue-eyed about scrubbing floors. The cultural page itself was an Augean stable and my Marxist struggle a running battle with managing editor Louis Budenz to prevent his squeezing all the culture off it.

"This will end up as a fart on the cultural page," a callous colleague in the city room remarked in my presence as she tossed aside a release.

Mike Gold, author of *Jews without Money*, provided page seven's one reliable ornament, his column "Change the World." It was insulted by movie ads that staggered up the sides of the page like dislocated staircases, ruining every layout, and by photos of Hollywood bosoms, thighs, and the opulent parted lips of women trying to look as stupid as possible. These were musts, or we would lose the ads. An inept poem by a shnook or a drama review spun off in a hack's spare time at least had some relation to the page's function, but slag from other departments, anything at all that was free and a deadly bore was dumped in the culture corner.

Once Louis brought me a screed by some worthy union organizer that forced everything else off the page. "Nobody will look at such an unbroken mass of type," I said. "There's got to be room for subheads, white space, at least a picture!"

"All right, put in a picture," Louis agreed with his usual phlegm.

Hoist with my own petard, I ransacked the photo file. We had one steel cut that went with anything, a head of Lenin, but it was rather large. I was just slashing lines to accommodate it when Louis reared his ugly head from behind a linotype machine and said no, every word counted. He dragged the printer, Dave, into a corner, and presently the screech of sawed steel went through my marrow. "He made me cut off Lenin's beard," Dave moaned. Dave was the only comrade in the shop.

"What? Destroy the *cut?*"

"And part of the chin," Dave said.

My wails mingled with his moans. Steel cuts were expensive, they were like gold, they had to be returned to the file immediately so as not to get lost. We had no other cut of Lenin!

I unburdened myself to V. J. Jerome in the offices of the National Committee on the ninth floor. Jerome was known unofficially as the cultural commissar of the party. A learned, rabbinical-looking man with moist brown eyes and a weakness for young ladies, he put his soft paw on my arm and in his Polish-tinged English accent jested, "You must see things historically, my dear. The cultural page in itself represents progress. A few years ago our comrades hadn't even heard of culture."

A lady in a pert hat visited me at my apartment on Horatio Street and introduced herself as Janet Stevenson. Wasting no time on chitchat she sat down in my maple rocker and tackled me about the malevolent review of *Counterattack* which had appeared on page seven. It was an anti-Nazi play with a Soviet hero, so of course she and her husband Phil, the authors, had counted on our support. Instead we had irresponsibly wrecked its chances.

The byline of our theater critic was Ralph Warner. He saved his real name for paying jobs. It impressed my bosses mightily that a man who made his living on the slicks would deign to bother with us. Fearful of losing a pearl, they instructed each new cultural editor that Warner's copy was taboo — no red-penciling from the likes of us. He never greeted me, just glared out of ringed, baleful eyes, threw his dilations down on my desk like the glove preceding a duel, and stumped back to the rat race. Occasionally I heard him stop in the corridor outside my door to hobnob with someone of status.

Janet listened to my apologies courteously and pointed out that if something was not done on the spot, *Counterattack* would close.

"I'll go myself," I said. "I'll write my own review."

She gave me a ticket. More cordial now, she told me that the key character in the play, a German miner, was absolutely authentic; she and her husband had sought advice from someone who must know. The denouement required a Wehrmacht soldier taken prisoner on the eastern front to turn against his fellows and save the life of their exhausted Russian captor. Dreaming him up was not good enough, there had to *be* such a man incognito among the Nazis — but could there be? Max Schroeder did not doubt it. It was he who in the end made flesh and blood of the character and wrote his speeches.

"You know Max, of course?" No. "But you have seen him, he lives in this house on the floor below?" I hadn't noticed a German. "You'd like him," Janet said. "Why don't you knock at his door?" She also dropped a word to him, but for one reason and another we did not meet while I was on the *Daily Worker.* Which was not to be much longer.

Most of the staff came in around eleven. I arrived at eight like a one-man orchestra with a harmonica in my teeth, cymbals strapped to my hands, a ukulele draped around my neck — I was editor, reporter, rewrite man, layout man. After putting the page to bed downstairs I sometimes went back to the city room, whither I had recently been demoted, to knock off one more filler for next day. One night I found myself coughing into eerie silence, and panicked. I didn't want to be caught alone again in an air-raid drill and have to cower on the back stairs wondering whether this time it was for real. I had been in the building sixteen hours that day. By morning I was down with the new viral pneumonia that was filling the army hospitals.

I went back to the office after six weeks — too soon, tottering, but how could the paper manage without me — and found my desk drawer full of strange property. A voice behind me stopped my feeble rummaging: "Louis wants to see you."

He fired me on the spot. Not for my review of *Counterattack,* of course, or the many other instances of insubordination that challenged his indifference to the Party's welfare, but because a colleague on maternity leave had returned, he said, and there wasn't enough money for us both. I was the last hired. As I burst into tears Louis instructed me sternly, "A good Communist doesn't cry!"

The two or three people in the city room at that early hour looked away as I passed through with red eyes. My pal on the staff, a rewrite man named Singer, came to my apartment that evening with a note from Mike Gold that said, "Don't take it to heart, it happens to all of us."

For a moment it was balsam. I looked up to Mike Gold as a great writer. He could be a Gorky, I thought, if he didn't continually undermine his talent in the daily grind. Couldn't *he* make them undo this injustice? Hadn't he told me I edited his columns better than anyone ever before? He received the maximum salary, so they obviously set great store by him. I kept rereading the note, but resignation was all it expressed. *Why* must it happen to all of us? Was this some immutable law of Party life? What was the matter with Mike Gold?

He was sick, Singer reminded me. In the lunch bar across University Place he never touched the potato latkes the rest of us devoured so lustily. He was not allowed coffee. Someone said alcohol would kill him.

He was not yet fifty and there was already ash in his flaming eyes. His swarthy pugilistic face had a yellowish cast.

Still. Could a mere physical disorder take the fight out of a fighter? I was not yet equipped to understand how. I hoped never to be so equipped. Were we not to go down — if we had to go down — fighting?

Maybe he thought this too trifling an issue to waste his substance on. "It happens to all of us" meant that not even he mattered in the perspective of the revolution. His one novel ended with the words:

> O Workers' Revolution, you brought hope to me, a lonely, suicidal boy. You are the true Messiah. You will destroy the East Side when you come, and build there a garden for the human spirit.
>
> O Revolution, that forced me to think, to struggle and to live.
>
> O great Beginning!

But if "it" happened to all of us, and we let it, how could the Great Beginning take root?

A month later an inexperienced young man was hired in my place, but no one was fired on that account.

I landed a war job as a railroad trainman, a position to which American women had not hitherto been admitted, and nothing would have induced me to give it up. I thought it was romantic.

So did Max. The sight of the DW's cultural editor rushing down Horatio Street in a dark blue uniform with matching cap and silver buttons puzzled and greatly intrigued the editor of the *German American*. For a time he remained diffident about approaching. Although I wore glasses and looked rather earnest, I seemed to be occupied with a different man every time he passed me on the stairs. Eventually he invited me to dinner at a moment when my face was covered with sweaty grime. I washed it, changed my shirt, and went down the block with him to a Spanish bistro I hadn't even known was there.

Over paella and red wine he praised my stimulating country, its jazz, its skyscrapers, its poets. His enthusiasm touched me, though I understood very little of the guttural English in which it was expressed. Seen close up, his face rosy with animation, he looked no more than thirty-five. To my mind thirty-five was old, so the news that he was forty-three appalled me. I had never known an interesting and interested man so advanced in years.

All the same our two apartments soon became a zigzag duplex and Max's English improved rapidly. Upstairs, overlooking the rackety crossing at Hudson Street, was the master bedroom, my one-room kitchenless "studio" with fake, dark-stained rafters and arty latticed casement windows. Downstairs in his indefinable dump at the back was the fireplace stuffed with waste paper — there was no room around it, just space to pass by — and the kitchenette with cot, sink, and two-burner gas stove. The single sliding window faced a flat roof to which we might jump in case of fire, though hardly escape, for all around it were higher inflammable buildings. We each paid twenty-five dollars a month and together possessed two baths.

Awake in the small hours, Max sometimes lit a cigarette and told me stories of his former life, his various lives, and the great chunks lost from them, the narrow escapes and the times when he was caught, the jails and the concentration camps. He told me of Till, the sweetheart left behind in '33, and of Rosl, the all-but-wife from whom he became separated when they fled through occupied France to Marseilles and the Western Hemisphere. He told me about Ali, an Arab shoeshine boy in Casablanca whom he taught to read and whose face he saw in mine. Worry about close friends in Germany with whom communication was impossible preyed on his mind. There was no way to reassure himself about them, and the western Allies were doing nothing to relieve the Soviet Union and speed the end of the war.

Rosl was in Mexico. His ship had also been bound there, but when it made a scheduled stop in New York the day after Pearl Harbor, all Germans were taken ashore. They were interned, as it was called, within the city limits — not imprisoned, but subject to surveillance and forbidden to leave town.

When he took a drag of his storytelling cigarette, the glow lit up promontories and caverns of a countenance from some carved medieval altarpiece or roadside crucifix. The undiscerning considered it ugly — he knew this and it wounded him — but especially in those illuminated seconds of reminiscence the oddly matched, changeful features had an irresistible fascination.

For twelve of his best years this man existed hand to mouth in virtual anonymity. In me he at least found temporary roots and someone to watch with him as he projected his past on the darkness. By dawn it had sifted apart with the first bluish clouds and I was striding to Penn Station, losing the thread, forgetting the names.

Max was surprisingly extroverted for a high-strung, poetic man. His own psyche interested him not at all, and neither did other people's, including mine. This fazed me. It is hard to pry Americans away from their psyches.

He was an excellent, foresighted organizer of life strategies, although he could assume when necessary, as under police questioning, a vague deranged look, like a harmless imbecile. He crossed and re-crossed European borders without papers during the spreading Nazi occupation and escaped from a new concentration camp in Vichy France by simply walking away before the barbed wire was put up. He was practical as a peasant. Though skinny he had the toughness of cartilage.

The spectacles he wore for astigmatism made his eyes look large and beautiful. The great nose jutting from a tapering face was like a powerful rudder on a frail ship, signaling absolute confidence in his own navigation. Behind the brow were library stacks of encyclopedic knowledge. Modestly he placed it at the disposal of anyone who asked.

In order to kiss his rounded, innocent, choirboy lips I had to look up, although tall myself. Being fifteen years younger than he, I felt the physical act of looking up as perfectly appropriate. While convinced of the inborn equality of the sexes, I rejoiced in not being equal to Max. For his part he derived particular pleasure from educating my ignorance.

He was born of an upper-class Hansa family similar to the Buddenbrooks, in 1900. His grandfather had been a banker and senator of Lübeck and his father a well-to-do attorney. On the distaff side he was descended from the Polish Potockis, nobles notorious for their pogroms, but his mother's father had been a decent German apothecary in Pasewalk. This was the only ancestor he was glad to own, though he remembered his father, an excellent pianist, with considerable tenderness.

A family photograph dated 1920 shows Max as an attenuated youth resting languidly in a white-painted armchair near his somber mother and gallantly smiling sister, also in white chairs, on the lawn of their twenty-room mansion. At their feet lies the old Alsatian, Bella. The mansion is no longer entirely theirs. The mother dressed in black is facing down the camera; it is not her duty to smile. The father had died suddenly the year before during the wild inflation and turnip regimen that followed World War I. Left penniless, the widow began dedicating the long remainder of her life to self-pity. To keep her home she had to rent out its rooms, an unthinkable degradation. Max escaped her scepter soon after the picture was taken. He entreated his sister, to whom he was much attached, to break out of her enslavement as assistant landlady and join him, but she was already as helpless as the half-eaten meal of a tiger.

In the effervescent bohemia of Munich and Berlin he wrote surrealist poetry, experimental plays, and art reviews that somehow kept body and soul together. The precious photo collection of Lotte Pritzel, a queen of that bohemia, includes one of Max wearing a black velvet smoking jacket and lying on someone's sofa, perhaps hers, in a state of blissful inebriation. In 1932, incomprehensibly to her and Dr. Pagel, her husband, Max joined the Communist Party. They assumed it was a passing mania. Then one day he was gone.

Max had no use for marriage, he said. He spoke sarcastically of what he called the American marriage terror. I thought I knew what he meant. My own recently dissolved marriage had lost its meaning because it *was* a marriage, to whose legality I had originally objected; but then I allowed myself to be talked over, and at once idiotic obligations to new relatives sprang up in every corner of our still fragile privacy and blighted it.

Even then I wanted babies, but Norman said no, he was a professional revolutionary and so should I be. Now in my late twenties, I had to fight down tears when I saw other people's. Mine, if I ever got any, must be protected and have a garden to play in.

So I listened to Max's views with sympathetic reserve. He was not a possibility for me; he would be going back to Germany in any case. Once, however, when he spoke dreamily of the garden he meant to have after the war, I felt a pang.

He proposed from a telephone booth instead of waiting to get home. He thought it would amuse me, and it did, but it also upset me. Max was still a stranger to whom I had few clues. Germany was unthinkable. And what was to become of Rosl?

It appeared that a woman from the refugee committee had recently gone to Mexico, met Rosl among others, and brought Max a verbal message from her. Having written to him repeatedly for three years and heard nothing, with a heavy heart she stopped believing. She married.

One day Max found out where their letters had gone. Entering the FBI office for his regular grilling he saw them in her writing and his scattered over the desk of the inquisitor. The bureau's assumption that such an outrage would make the victim lose his head and betray his political connections was disappointed. Max's eyes floated unseeing as soap bubbles over the cruel display. Neither he nor the agent referred to it. For the rest Max knew nothing, as usual.

"But I'm not in love with you," I said at some point before dawn.

"You will be," said Max. He spoke as if stating a simple truth written across the sky. It affected me powerfully.

Our relationship was in a category so different from any previous ones that I knew no name for it. I thought of my last "great love" for the unattainable Waldo, who wrote me from a battleship in the Pacific, "Shall I make a terrible confession to you? I despise all women." And this complacent boast which he was pleased to call a confession made me ache with pitying tenderness for him, as if he had shown me a wound. It became my wound and it was still festering.

Max did not speak of what festered in him except indirectly, as a storyteller in the night. He could not help mounting each tale, whether about himself or others, within a perspective he conveyed only by a faraway look and a tone of artistic gratification. He would gesture widely, indicating some backdrop as a painter's brush sweeps the long line of a horizon behind figures-to-be. "*That* was a story," he would say at the end, savoring its literary potential like the first sip of a vintage cognac, until I protested indignantly, "Those are not 'stories'! They happened! People suffered! And you smile. . . ."

Long afterward I found the following undated memorandum in his jagged handwriting:

> In this war I lost everything I ever had of love and friendship, I lost the fruits of invaluable experience, all I had written and a few negligible worldly goods as well.
>
> In France I lost a child that came into being one night when a certain decision deprived me of my freedom. The previous evening a friendly prison official let me go on the understanding that I report at the Colombe Stadium by noon the next day. I would not have done it, but R. told me that our friends [euphemism for the German Party in exile]

had decided we should all obey the ruling of the French government.

Not until early spring did I hear what that night in autumn had wrought. R. had to see everything through by herself, the hope and the renunciation. Our rotten papers counted for too little in France to let us marry, so she could not visit me in camp. By illegal contrivances we met for one more night in a village near the camp.

R. lost more than I did. She wanted the child more. We reveled in that one day's stolen freedom as if it were a lifetime's. Devout as the faithful looking to kingdom-come we talked of what had been and what would be. How should I console her loss? On the way back across freshly plowed fields I stumbled and fell, blinded by headlights from the road where I dared not be seen. For a while I took care not to rise. Our primitive ancestors evolved the strength to walk upright, but we have reverted to the status of worms eating dirt and throttling the life we beget.

Over a year passed and we each put many miles behind us before we met again.

I was waiting in a village near Marseilles for passage to Mexico. R.'s visa could not be issued in my name and she had to wait for another ship. The law of the underground railroad forbade me to wait. So I lost R. too.

The zigzag duplex was exchanged for a long narrow apartment at the top of a five-story walkup on West Twentieth Street. As before, each of us paid twenty-five dollars, but now we had a bright bed-sitter with a tall mirror between the windows and a view of green lawns around the theological seminary. That room was the observation car, so to speak, just emerged from a tunnel and waiting for the go-ahead while the five little cars behind it, each with just one window, were stuck forever between a dim shaft and a hall that weirdly ended nowhere. Once the hall had reached the kitchen its job was done: kitchen opened into dining room and dining room into bed-sitter. The hall groped forward in darkness, breeding nightmares.

Though cramped and roach-ridden, the kitchen was not to be despised. It became the scene of great and unexpected culinary triumphs.

Max turned out to be a cook by divine right, adept at combining inge-
niously whatever was at hand. He needed no recipes and never repeated
a dish, nor would he disclose how he made it. It was his only arrogance.
"Be glad you are getting it," he would say, and I was. Being on twenty-
four-hour call like a soldier, I was as likely to arrive home before dawn
as any other time, but an exquisite meal always awaited me.

It might be delayed for a few minutes if Max was having an editorial
meeting in the dining room with Gerhart Eisler and Albert Norden.
Although rather gloomy, being on the shaft, it was the only room with a
table big enough to spread manuscripts over.

Norden was a distant man with no words to spare for an American
mistress, but round little Eisler was irresistibly jolly and cordial. I had no
idea what special significance, if any, these men might have in their own
country, but neither did I know Max's. I took everything at face value.

"Do you go to the dentist?" Gerhart Eisler asked me out of a clear sky.
When I hesitated, he admonished me that a Communist should have
regular checkups to make sure he was in fighting form. He was smiling,
but not joking.

I was touched. Why should he care about my teeth? I went to the
dentist. Gradually I came to understand that Gerhart was Max's superior
in an invisible hierarchy of the German Party. He had a perky little red
headed wife with a lisp who worked somewhere, I believe, as a secretary.
What Norden did all day I never knew; for that matter, where did Gerhart hang out? I myself was always in such a rush that I had no time to be
curious.

A friend of Max I saw more of was Alfred Kantorowicz, called Kanto,
a sort of intellectual without portfolio. He dispensed a seignorial charm,
invented amusing anecdotes out of whole cloth, and had many of the
American literati eating out of his hand. A journalist and critic of sorts,
he had survived the war in Spain with an aplomb now enhanced by discreetly hung spangles of self-advertisement. He monitored Nazi broadcasts for CBS, a dull job in an airless cubbyhole, but he made it sound
more prestigious than what other exiles did. There was an air of ease
about him, as if he had a prosperous relative in the offing; his suits were
good and sat well; he laughed through his nose with an agreeable and
rarefied haw-haw.

Since Max had chosen me, Kantor assumed my social equality with
himself and was aghast when he heard me describe the latest round in a

fight for women's seniority rights on the railroad. I was out of breath from running up the stairs and plunged into my "I sez he sez" style of narrative without regard to a guest's presence. "How can you lower yourself to the level of such people?" he remonstrated.

Max laughed. He was addicted to this daily serial from a native in the thick of things. I was his ringside seat at the American scene.

"Funny sort of Communist, your pal Kanto," I remarked afterward, but Max only made a considering, noncommittal sound.

The best man at our wedding, if one can speak of a best man at a two-dollar ceremony in the Municipal Building, was a human whirligig with the nom de guerre of Alexan. Technically he was just one of the two required witnesses and may have been picked because his time was flexible. His constantly pumping energy and a beautiful, hospitable wife predestined him to a central role among those exiled German and Austrian intellectuals who meant to return home after the war. They were by no means all Communists; nor was he. The loosely organized group called itself The Tribune.

It was Alexan's mercantile family (if I understood correctly) that staked him to the bilingual bookshop he owned, also named The Tribune, at Forty-second Street and Sixth Avenue in the subway mezzanine. It was a dingy, rumbling location, but central and a magnet for all sorts of casual booklovers. Even if they bought nothing they might pick up the latest pink or green mimeographed bulletin of news about Nazi-banned art and artists and Tribune-sponsored cultural events. The homely, enthusiastically sputtering little Alexan wrote or compiled those bulletins on his own. If the business broke even, it was probably thanks to his wife Masha who could not leave the store to attend a wedding, who at thirty-eight spared a half hour for labor pains and gave birth to her one child with the ease of a cow dropping a calf, and whose parties for the Tribune crowd included, in the course of time, just about every distinguished representative of the exile scene on the East Coast. Her kindness and stunning legs and Alexan's bubbling optimism were momentary antidotes to depressing news; their comfortable living room provided a forum for people who not only liked to hear themselves talk but also seemed to have something to say.

"Seemed," only because my impressions were no more dependable than those of a TV viewer when the sound is turned off. I saw, rather than heard, Hermann Budzislawsky, who worked for columnist Dorothy Thompson as an adviser-amanuensis, holding people spellbound while his wife vehemently smoked a pipe. I saw, and loved, the actor Alexander Granach, though I no longer know how many words of German or pidgin English we exchanged. Perhaps none. He was a distinctly *mucho* but not *macho* hombre, he had the frame of a wrestler and the tenderness of a mother. Two weeks later he broke my heart by dying of a burst appendix, unattended, in his hotel room.

The marriage ceremony, at which Alexan signed a name we had not heard before, was pragmatism pure and simple. It was undertaken only to ease my admission to Germany. Distant and unreal as that prospect still appeared, Max had learned from the Rosl disaster that one could not be too farsighted.

All the same we celebrated the occasion with an all-day-and-half-the-night party attended by a continuously flowing mob of Max's friends, my friends, assorted acquaintances, the FBI for all I know, and some total strangers, one after midnight in a sari with a red dot on her forehead and eyes ashine like moonlight in the pool of Agra.

I chiefly remember from that party the prodigious beer marathon of Oskar Maria Graf, the Bavarian novelist who never learned English. Twice I ran down to the corner with George, the young son of publisher Wieland Herzfelde, to buy another case and lug it up our five flights. All that happened to Oskar Maria was that English began coming out of his mouth. "You are great lyric," he kept telling my poet friend Deborah, following her about with a large, generous smile. Not that he could read her poetry, but she was so beautiful. She had shy animal eyes and straight black hair that would not hold a part and swung like heavy silk against one tender, transparent, faintly flushed cheek.

And I remember Gerhart Eisler coming up close to me and saying in a low voice with frightening sharpness though with his never-failing smile, "You want to go to Germany? You're crazy." The persistence of that smile stemmed, I think, from a balanced view of things, a skilled weighing of events which always allowed the possibility of a good outcome. In this case, however, it was clear that he did not anticipate a good outcome, and I resented his elbow in my private life.

Hans Meyer was not at our wedding party because he was almost always in Washington. Of the many thousands of Hans Meyers, Mayers, Myers, and Maiers who helped populate the Germanic and German-Jewish world, Max's Hans was the only one related to Albert Einstein. Einstein was his uncle. This would have carved out a privileged niche for Hans in America even if he had not been a uniquely charming, witty, and knowledgeable man. A stutter which he bore with the utmost nonchalance compounded his attraction, for it made him seem vulnerable and more in need of love.

Incredibly, to me, his wife became frigid in their marriage and went to stay with relatives on a farm in New Jersey. He led a bachelor's life in their comfortable Greenwich Village flat. It had a large fireplace that really drew and made conversation leap and crackle along with the flames. I took little part in it. Even when the two men spoke English I failed to catch many of their laughing, learned allusions. Being under thirty I got away with naiveté by being an ornament, a fact I only half understood and got little satisfaction from. I was chagrined to discover the insularity of an American education. When Hans laughed caressingly at one of my mistakes I felt mortified.

He was the only friend of Max with whom I felt an affinity. After Max returned to Germany it was in him I confided. Hans was a chameleon who could assume American coloration as readily as any, so that when alone with him I felt comfortable and understood. This happened just once, when he asked me to dinner at Billy the Oysterman's.

"It isn't easy to be married to *you*, my dear girl," he pointed out.

"How would *you* know!"

"It's written all over you. You're a p-p-pest."

He could say that without giving the slightest offense, as if it was a kind of compliment. I laughed with delight and the gratitude one feels on hearing certain truths. I had long realized I must be a pest and tried to mend my ways, if I had only known which ones.

"Max is the most remarkable man I ever met," Hans said.

We went to his apartment and drank some excellent cognac before the fire. He said it was the same kind he and Max stole from a bistro in Paris once when they were broke.

"The thing is," I said, "relationships never end. We keep negotiating with our memories and with dreams. Someone you've lost for whatever reason keeps coming back, always in a new guise, growing older with you."

Hans said it was like listening to a symphony on the radio and being interrupted when the telephone rang; and afterward you tried to imagine the possibility that would never be realized, and you couldn't.

That wasn't what I meant. "My point is that relationships simply do not end. *Do not end.* Separations don't separate people They may perform some other useful function. . . . A flower may grow out of a stone," I added, and he looked at me without understanding; how could he understand when I didn't myself.

At the end of the evening he said, "Let me know what you de-de-decide about M-M-Max." There was a look of hard-edged complicity in his eye. The hard edge told me: "I am honorable. I'm not sure about you."

I did not let him know. When we spoke again it was in Berlin under embarrassing, ambiguous, and disquieting circumstances.

Max's messy study on Twentieth Street was the pigeonhole opposite the apartment door. Late one night when I unlocked it I saw him in there folded like a collapsed shed over a gallon jug of California red wine. It was about three-quarters empty. Most of his half-rotted upper teeth, the result of malnutrition during two wars, had been removed that afternoon. The money was raised by Gerhart.

Because of a conservative Jewish upbringing I had never before seen the effects of drunkenness on a person close to me. Max shockingly resembled an ancient Bowery derelict crouched in a doorway. The hurting mouth was caved in, the head hung unconscious of its appearance. Peering half-blinded over the top of his glasses he nevertheless registered my horror, was offended by it, and waved me to a chair with elaborate politeness. I sat down gingerly.

"You are not really sitting," he pointed out with remarkable clarity. "You are not here."

I moved back until I felt the hard slats against my vertebrae.

"Would you like some wine?"

"Not now, thanks."

He studied me as if at last the scales had fallen from his eyes. "You are very ambitious," he said.

The accusation gave me a fright. "How?" I asked.

A pause ensued. It lengthened.

"You want to tell me —" I ventured.

"Don't rush me," he said.

I waited, wooden with weariness. He was too Spartan to utter a moan, so my own discomfort was more obvious to me than his. The maximum free time granted by the crew dispatcher was ten hours, but usually a trainman without a regular run got only eight. I had no regular run then.

Max seemed to lose track of my presence. He rambled incoherently about literature, blinked and squinted at dissolving images in his mind. When the shaft wall outside his window became visible, I struggled to my feet and left the room. For a long time I lay in bed too exhausted and resentful to fall asleep.

After I met Rosl I knew how she would have reacted. She would have knelt at his side and put her arms around him. She would have cajoled and supported him to bed. If he told her she was ambitious she would have asked with infinite humility, "I?"

There were times when squalor spread about us like damp creeping up plaster walls. Roaches multiplied behind the jars on our kitchen shelves. Mice kept me awake by scrabbling in the uncovered garbage can (it was covers that made garbage smell, Max insisted) until, though it made his heart ache, he poured water on the poor things and drowned them to protect my sleep. We drove out bedbugs with bug powder, but the neighbor's bug powder drove them back. Max found two little nail kegs in the gutter and stood them next to armchairs as coffee-table substitutes. I curtained off the corridor's dead end to make a walk-in closet we forgot to walk into, and everything in it became impregnated with dust and rotted. As a birthday surprise Max painted the dining-room floor migraine green. "It looked better on the label," he apologized.

When I undressed I turned aside so he shouldn't see the holes in my winter underwear, but he protested tenderly, almost on the verge of tears, "Don't hide — I love them!" How, I wondered, could a man be touched by holey underwear?

> *Every one of us*
> *Who with torn shoes walks through the crowd*
> *Bears witness to the shame which now defiles our land,*

Stephen Spender translated from Brecht (*Über die Bezeichnung Emigranten*), whose poetry I could not yet read; and that may have been the explanation. To the exile in cast-off clothes I was the apposite partner, the Raggedy Ann of a Claire Bloom to my plucky German Chaplin.

Mother defied Dad by visiting us and looked about the apartment with her large romantic eyes. There was, after all, a precedent for my unsuitable relationship with Max. Hadn't Jo, in *Little Women*, after failing to get the boy next door, ended up most happily with an oldish German professor? Still, when Max was out of the room she said, standing on that frightful floor, "You were two poor, lonely creatures, that's what it was."

Max had rescued his father's gold watch through every vicissitude, but as it didn't go I took it to a watchmaker. I never had the six dollars to recover it, or rather, when I had six dollars I forgot and took Max to a jam session with Eddie Condon at the Village Gate, or we went to the Vanguard where Leadbelly still struck fierce thunder out of his twelve-string guitar and his old wife sat nearby and kept an eye on him. Max never mentioned the watch. The guilt of losing it stabs me to this day.

Shiftlessness is the recreation of the poor. "Come to the Mardi Gras," wrote Jack and Gina, and I cleaned out what I had left in the bank. Of course Max wasn't allowed to leave town, which made it more fun. Two could ride free on my railroad pass as far as Washington and half-fare return from there to New Orleans, so we could afford a Pullman berth and a bottle of Southern Comfort to swig as we gazed at the passing scenery. Stepping out of Jack and Gina's patio we joined the drunken populace, I a gypsy in satin rags, Max rakish in one of my earrings. Jack carried a jug of martinis from which we all sipped as we strolled in the summery February sun. Naughty Catholic Gina stopped a priest and kissed him on the mouth, and I saw with a pang that Max was enchanted by her.

Once by the fitful light of his cigarette he told me of a luxury brothel in Paris to which a well-heeled friend had treated him. The girl assigned to him was a marvel, she "danced love." Anxious to learn, I asked how this was done, but he must have sensed that he had said enough. His memories, even only reveries, of incomparable women, made me feel like a hulking hobbledehoy. At such moments I acted like one. In my confusion I bought an unbecoming dress, I walked clumsily.

All the more, I insisted within myself, did it behoove me to "understand" or at least make room. Jealousy was ignoble and I was proud to think I was overcoming it. I didn't know what real jealousy was. What babes in the woods we both were!

We had been together for about a year when the *New York Times* published on its front page a letter from Louis Budenz proclaiming his "return to the bosom of Mother Church." Soon afterward the man who told me that good Communists didn't cry laughed all the way to the House Un-American Activities Committee and started selling names.

I crowed, I shouted, I had been right about him the whole time! Then I began to burn. "To think he had the whole editorial board eating out of his hand! They let him fire me, they covered up for him. *Why?* Something's rotten there! Who knows how high up it goes!" I thought of Earl Browder.

Max appreciated the way I felt, but saw nothing suspicious in the board's support of Budenz. "They're overworked," he said. "They're not psychologists."

He looked at me warningly when I continued erupting in the presence of a strange woman. We were lunching with his immaculate friend Friedl, Kanto's wife, an actress with a face as pure and withheld as a lily, and an American acquaintance she introduced. Virginia's clothes and quiet self-assurance suggested ladies' Ivy League, but her mind seemed accessible and Friedl had thought fit to bring her, so despite the unmistakable message in Max's eyes I fired another round or two before subsiding.

"How do we know who Friedl's friend is?" Max rebuked me. "You can't wash the Party's dirty linen in public!"

"Then let them not dirty their linen," I retorted.

He pointed out that the people I called "them" included ourselves.

Though it stung to have my ears boxed like a bad boy's, if only metaphorically, I did recollect myself and was vaguely ashamed. At least Earl Browder was not boring, he was a wit. I still savored his bon mot about a lying newspaper report "as thin as the homeopathic soup made by boiling the shadow of a pigeon that was starved to death." He had lifted it from Abraham Lincoln, but I didn't know that yet.

However, Browder was soon to startle us with a brainstorm of his own. His book *Teheran and After* was hailed by the Party as a great new theoretical breakthrough. The smoothly functioning wartime cooperation between American business and workers suggested to Browder that the millennium was at hand. Overlooking one little detail — that the workers alone had brought about this truce by renouncing their right to strike for the duration of the war — he anticipated an imminent and permanent burying of the hatchet. As a preliminary peace pipe he now proposed that the name Communist Party be changed to something less blunt (The Communist Political Association). This was quickly accomplished through "democratic centralism," a form of top-to-bottom ideological hypnosis by which members were persuaded to believe whatever the National Committee declared correct. Its dicta gathered mass and irresistibility as they snowballed down through the district to the section organizations and at last to the Jimmy Higginses and FBI infiltrators in the branches.

Even so, most of us were bewildered. The better Marxists were appalled. Bill Blake started a seminar in his apartment for the preservation of imperiled theory in time of crisis. Others quietly dropped out of the ex-Party.

After the war the *Daily Worker* published an astounding letter from Jacques Duclos of the French Communist Party censuring the Browder line of fraternization with the capitalists. It was unheard-of that one Party should publicly take another to task, with the culprit writing "I have been bad" a hundred times on page one of its own paper. It made a resounding sensation in the international press that day. A conference was called to cleanse the Party leadership, although there was no one else to call it but the Party leadership. For some reason the railroad branch, which had only about seven members from three railroads, delegated me to represent it at the conference.

The honorary patron of our diminutive branch was Party Chairman William Z. Foster, an ex-railroader. On one of his birthdays we presented him with a cake, but he only excoriated us bitterly for never recruiting anybody and went off, leaving the cake untouched and us crestfallen but none the wiser about recruiting the unrecruitable.

As a group the railroaders were virulently anti-Communist, antiforeign, anti-black, anti-Semitic, and anti-woman. They looked down on workers too, considering themselves of finer cloth. It seemed hardly necessary for the companies to take the additional precaution of forcing an anti-"totalitarian" oath on employees, but they did. This meant that for every railroader the Party recruited (a purely arithmetical hypothesis for the sake of argument) two would be kicked off the railroad, unless the recruit was a company stooge. The branch would shrink to nothing.

Admittedly we were useless, but I bought a black and white striped conference dress of soft, sheer voile that clung or billowed with the breeze and a shining black straw hat with an immense dipping brim.

Max was proud that my comrades had chosen me. He and his friend Berthold Viertel, the Austrian poet, whose old black eyes sparkled with tender perceptions, accompanied me as far as the subway station at Twenty-third Street and Eighth Avenue. They talked shop in German all the way, but the glances they exchanged referred to me. They made that fine summer day memorable whatever else happened.

The election of a new National Committee proved to be a game of musical chairs without music and with only one round. As soon as the last former member's lame excuse was verbosely concluded, his resignation offered, and Browder unanimously expelled from the Party, the same National Committee plumped right down again on the chairs just vacated, though not exactly in the same order. Each ended up with a title that had been someone else's before.

The delegates murmured and stirred in their places, but before they could collect themselves the conference chairman announced cancellation of tomorrow's discussion. The day was over, we must clear the hall; rent for the scheduled second day had not been raised. The delegates were enjoined to approved the slate with dispatch — as yet the functionaries on the chairs were only a slate — and transform it into the new National Committee before our collective coach turned into a pumpkin.

Hot and limp, brains steaming like a sauna from the long day of repetitious mea culpas, with a dim sense of having had their chairs pulled out from under them while the manipulators still sat, the delegates raised their right hands. I among them.

Did I say "without music?" No, we sang the "International," but by then the game was over.

Although pained by dissonances in the Party, most of us explained them to ourselves in Lenin's terminology as infantile disorders. We could understand people who discreetly stopped coming after it abandoned its name, but we did not make common cause with renegades who denounced the Party in publications of the class enemy. Richard Wright, for example, whose telephone number Deborah virtually forced on me when I left for Paris.

During my first weeks there in August, 1947, I was too busy to give Wright or any other possible contact a thought, but on Saturdays and Sundays I was so lonely I could have howled. Repeatedly I scanned my dwindling list of addresses and passed over his name each time. I could not believe I would ever be sufficiently far gone to use it.

Neither sawdusty rationed bread nor twilight hours without electricity detracted from the bracing medicinal quality of postwar Paris. On the contrary, a little austerity quickened the step and made me long to match mine with that of genuine Parisians, but none would have me. Americans were not acceptable unless they spoke charming French. Mine must have sounded to the native ear like the braying of a donkey or a G.I. People stared when I asked for directions. The nice French journalist who found me my hotel room and asked me to tea with his mother and aunts, all trying not to titter aloud, prudently dropped me. The shoemaker bellowed at me to go home and take the American army with me. G.I.s were no longer seen as saviors but as yahoos battening on depleted France without a care for the distress of its people.

With a certain malice, Mme. Vidonne, the proprietress of my Right Bank hotel, confided that the German officers quartered on her during the occupation had been perfect gentlemen in comparison; indeed she would gladly accommodate any one of them again. She considered me rather a joke; what could be more preposterous than an American without even money? To save the lovely suit I had bought in a sale on Fifth Avenue I wore my railroad uniform on cool days, with navy-blue leather toggles replacing the silver buttons and a Paris hat to match. Mme. Vidonne congratulated me effusively when I appeared in the hat and inquired if it came from a *grand maison.*

Not perceiving the irony, I said yes.

She was astonished, examined the hat more respectfully, and asked which one.

"The Samaritaine," I replied, and she went into convulsions. Big, *bien sûr,* a house, *mais oui,* the cheapest department store in Paris! She was still in stitches as I stepped into the *hydraulique,* hatted head held high, and let myself be transported with an ancient wheezing hum and the slowest of slow motion up, up, up to my cubbyhole under the roof.

In that garret I wrote half a novel and innumerable letters during lunch hours when I had no pupil for an English lesson and on evenings when I was not required at Agence France Presse. Three evenings a week I went there to telephone news in English to Tel Aviv. Days I was a filing clerk for a Jewish philanthropy, the Joint Distribution Committee, commonly known as "The Joint." These three sources of income paid for the room and one restaurant meal a day, with a bit left over for stamps and sausage and the trip to Germany. If there was ever to be a trip.

It transpired that the American embassy in Paris, a branch of the State Department, had no jurisdiction over travel to the occupied zones of Germany. The State Department was a civilian agency. I might as well have applied to my vegetable man as to Mrs. Shipley. The embassy receptionist sent me to a Major Secouta of the American military permit office in the rue Greuze, but I was not allowed upstairs; he did not receive civilians. My husband, so I was told, could apply at the military permit office in Berlin, but since an actual princess had just been denied a visa I could imagine — said the unfriendly woman behind the glass — what *my* chances would be.

Germans were not permitted to get phone calls or telegrams from abroad, this was a part of their collective punishment, and the urgent letters I wrote to Max moved no faster than the *hydraulique*. Some never arrived. His to me were weeks out of date. See the Rodins if you do nothing else, he urged, visit my old hangout the Café Bonaparte, ask for Tristan Tzara in the Deux Magots. Did Max know he should go to the military permit office? Had he already been? There was no way to find out.

And Berlin was so tantalizingly close, by American standards. Why couldn't he drop everything and come for just one day? I dreamed fervently of finding him in my room when I got home from work. He would call me a brave girl and take me in his arms; all problems would be solved in a moment. *Then* we could see Rodins and old hangouts, and I would take him to my own discovery, an excellent restaurant I could afford in the rue des Batignolles. Frenchmen in horn-rimmed glasses sat there, each at his own table soberly reading a newspaper with his meal, and the cook prepared the most delicious green beans I ever ate. It was difficult for me to grasp that a *good* German could not travel. His soiled scrip, still known as marks, was worthless on the world exchange. His civil rights were forfeited.

I decided to join the American army and get myself stationed in Berlin. "Who do I have to see?" I asked the receptionist at the embassy.

"Major Secouta," she said, and pointed to a gray-haired man sitting quite unguarded by dragons at a normal desk. He was a Mediterranean type with intelligent and kindly black eyes, his age somewhere between mine and Max's. "Are you sure you want to be in the army?" he asked.

"Yes, as long as it's near my husband."

"I don't really see you in the army," he said.

He was about to dismiss me; there was no higher authority I could appeal to; I wept; he rummaged in his desk and pulled out a visa application form.

"Oh thank you – oh *thank* you!"

There was a large space to fill out why my husband had wanted to go home, and under the decent human gaze of this anachronism, an official who could not bear to see a woman cry, I solemnly penned a small essay on Max's desire for a new democratic Germany that should arise with his passionate assistance from the ashes of the old.

Major Secouta forwarded my application to the military permit office in Berlin. The military permit office objected that "care of the Kulturbund" was not a home address; where in the American Sector did my chosen one live? I besought him to send the address by return mail. He had, in fact, sent it twice. Weeks passed. I began to feel I would die for want of human contact.

At some point Christina Stead made a flying visit to her dentist Fred (she would see no other) and, incidentally, me. I was proud to find a reasonably priced room in my hotel for the woman I worshiped and hear her praise my bistro around the corner as "the real Paris." An unceasing writer, she despised rickety little portables and traveled everywhere burdened by a ponderous office machine with a mile-long carriage, even on a brief trip like this one. She was strong. She became ill only when prevented from writing. That year she was forty-five, broad-shouldered, keen-sighted. When the pale hawk eyes she inherited from a seafaring ancestor were not focusing benevolently on a friend, they held a strange visionary glitter. Her mouth was like a beast in her face, living its own life, a double serpent.

The oasis of her visit to Paris soon seemed a mirage. How long I endured my own arid company before principle crumbled, I don't know exactly. Subjectively it felt like months, but I remember what I was wearing the day I found a rationalization for telephoning Richard Wright — no coat, no sweater, only a white cotton summer dress printed with little smears of color like a painter's brush strokes. A diary entry of his suggests that it was the third Saturday in September. Five or six weeks I had held out, no more. He cordially invited me to come over at once. As I rang his doorbell I felt denuded of all shame and decency.

It hurts now to speak of Richard Wright. In our encounter there was an arrow pointing, but it was concealed from me. He was a spiritually wounded man, lost on earth. He was a lamb strayed from its flock, never to find another.

His welcome betrayed a boyish pleasure, yet something sad hovered about the smile. He said apologetically, "My wife and little girl have gone for the weekend," as if I might find something exceptionable in this.

Off the entryway was a clean kitchen where a Frenchwoman with a disapproving mouth was just putting on her hat to go home. She was the cook. Wright introduced us in French even worse than mine, and after the door clicked shut behind her remarked with a helpless laugh that she had probably smuggled out another half pound of butter in her bag.

He was still preoccupied with this problem as he ushered me into an immense salon where a shaft of sunlight lay across the floor. The cook was incensed, he explained, that his five-year-old daughter went into the kitchen and played with food unrebuked, punching butter in its bowl as if it were plasticene, sifting sugar between her fingers like sand in a sandbox while her mother only laughed.

"Well, I can't interfere. It's Ellen's business," he said, although in his diary entry of the day before he had written, "All this in front of people who are almost starving. I had to have an end to it, as it is rather shameful."

Perhaps his being left alone for the weekend was Ellen's way of punishing him for laying down the law in her department. Laughing unhappily he said, "In the end she'll fire the woman."

The Wrights did not live on the French economy; they bought all food as well as the gasoline for their car in the American Post Exchange. So they were not subject to rationing, only to the envy and hatred of a servant.

It was a peculiar position for the grandson of a slave to find himself in. At home in the South the black girls he knew stole from white kitchens as a matter of course. He surely sensed, too, how the grandeur of his salon with its stained-glass windows framed in wrought iron must have affected me. I hope I looked unaware of my surroundings, but his nerve endings were preternaturally sensitive. It was plain that he himself regarded his setting with irony, though he probably felt no more out of place there than he did anywhere else.

We sat down in the two nearest armchairs like tourists striking up an acquaintance in a hotel lobby, which indeed this room resembled. It was just as long and two stories high. At the far end a narrow stair led up to a small gallery with two doors side by side. No doubt the handsome furnishings were let with the apartment, for they gave no clue to personal idiosyncrasies.

He asked me about myself, and I explained the bare facts of my stay in Paris. Was I a poet too, like Deborah? But I did write? Ah, he thought so. What was the theme of the novel? His questions were not casual; his interest proved never to be feigned. I hesitated to answer.

"Don't, if it's going to inhibit your writing," he said.

"It's not that."

"Then tell me!" He was bending forward, looking keenly into my face.

"It's about love between women," I admitted.

To my amazement he seemed delighted to hear this. He saw connections between the oppression of black people, women, and Jews and thought my topic immensely important. I had thought it immensely trivial.

"If it forces you to sit down and write about it, no subject can be trivial," he said. "Not when you dig deep down into it without fear and explore its real meaning." He began to pace about the room. "I'll tell you something, girl, every writer has one theme," he said. "No matter how many novels he writes, no matter how different they appear."

But I was not aware of writing about oppression. That, in fact, was the reason for my shame. I was only writing about love. Had I dug deep down into it? Wasn't I still worriedly tiptoeing about the rim? I had not noticed the bridge, if there was one, between my love story and women's second-class human status.

My silence may have made Dick feel he was being remiss as a host. He seized a pair of binoculars from a sideboard and came to me beaming. "Ever try one of these?" he asked with that eager, bashful, laughing embarrassment he could never shake off.

He went to an open window, saying, "You'd be surprised what you can see in other people's apartments," and leveled the binoculars across the wide avenue. "I could watch for hours," he cried gleefully. "Oh! Look at this! Come here! Try them!"

I knew that game. I had played it as a child, using my parents' mother-of-pearl opera glasses, but they were too weak for the distance from our kitchen window to the house behind the elevated tracks. All one could see was an arm reaching for a towel, then disappearing, or a bulb without a shade hanging over a table where dim forms were sitting.

But now I stiffly declined to look. I was shocked that a grown-up, brilliant man, the author of such a blockbuster as *Native Son*, demeaned himself to the level of a silly Peeping Tom. His own life among the newly rich was as shadowy to me as anything I could descry through my parents' opera glasses. I did not grasp the fact that a man without a childhood was now indulging himself in one for the first time. He was playing the baby games and giving himself the presents he had been denied as a little boy. Fleeting pleasure faintly ruffled his sadness.

In fact I was doing the same thing he was doing, only without binoculars. I was trying to make sense of what I saw in this apartment and in that different room, still vivid in my memory, where I had first met him.

In 1939 Norm and I had answered an ad in the *Daily Worker* for a room on the edge of Harlem. Only Communists advertised a room in that paper, assuming only Communists would apply and they would be among themselves. A statuesque white woman of about thirty answered the door and brought us into the parlor no bigger than an anteroom. In an armchair by a fake marble fireplace sat a Negro man.

"This is my husband, Richard Wright," the woman said, and though her voice was not raised the announcement broke the sound barrier.

We were confronted for the first time not only with a writer who had made the news but with marriage between a black man and a white woman, a handsome white woman, boldly proclaimed. Such a relationship was still mind-boggling to the bumpkins most Americans were in those days, including most Communist Americans. We tried not to stare, that was the best we could do.

In a moment the house-owner, an elderly woman who was Wright's mother-in-law, came in and took us upstairs to see the room. We liked it, paid our deposit, and went away childishly rejoicing: we were going to live in the same house with a wonderful writer! We were wrong, we never saw him or his wife again, but his facial expression and bodily posture in that armchair, not his own armchair, haunted me in a way I could not define until much later. He sat there like a captive. An invisible leash was looped about his neck. He barely acknowledged the introduction; he was miles away.

"Oh, that must have been Dhima," Dick said when I mentioned the incident. She was clearly not a subject he cared to pursue, so I precipitately changed it. That may have been the moment when I confessed that I had almost not phoned him. I had to get out from under my niceness and false pretenses.

He smiled at my confession with a singular lack of animosity, almost with gratitude, for now the curtain was raised on the problem that obsessed him. Patiently, insistently, he set out to prove that I was wrong. It was a complex task, because he had not only my ignorance to contend with but guilt feelings of his own that would not lie down and die.

Once the Party condemned an author's politics, especially those of an ex-Party member, it threw out the baby with the bath. Books written prior to the apostasy could still be mentioned politely, though not in the Party press, and hindsight revealed hitherto unnoticed weaknesses in his earlier work. Books written after the fall were so thoroughly shredded by Communist reviewers that the ordinary member, like myself, was put off reading them. No exception was made for an author of Richard Wright's stature and racial significance. So I did not bother to read his autobiographical *Black Boy* or his bitter recantation in the *Atlantic Monthly*. I knew virtually nothing about his life or his motives. Everything he told me that day was new to me.

Dick was looking for a home which did not exist for him on this planet. Not in his lifetime. He started the search from the moment he could think, and when he found the Communists he believed he was there. Five years had passed since his final break with the Party, but he was still outraged and bleeding.

The youthful author of *Uncle Tom's Children* came up from the South to Chicago, applied for Party membership, and was almost immediately catapulted to a position of extraordinary prestige as chairman of the John Reed Club, the writers' branch. It was the Party's policy to maneuver new members from some populous but fairly impenetrable group into leading functions, so as to attract others of their kind into its ranks. The policy was not notably successful. It too often happened that a novice was flattered into officious conceit and drove people away.

Obviously Dick was not of that stamp. His human and intellectual equipment more than qualified him, but he was still a novice; he became not conceited but overly elated, seeing himself honored for the power of his writing and assuming in each member of his new family an honesty equal to his own. When he saw them making mistakes he took them in hand as a brother would a sister.

"The Party," I said, "who do you mean by 'the Party'? Are a few schmucks the Party, or even a lot of schmucks? Capitalism formed those people, it's a wonder any of them are any good."

He studied me kindly. No argument I could raise had not already wrestled its way through his mind and been dealt with. It was I who needed to be dealt with. "Don't you see, girl, that for opportunist reasons the Party is holding back the fight for full emancipation of the Negroes?"

No, I did not. I was flabbergasted by such a claim. The Party went on and on about Negro rights, white comrades fought and sometimes died for them. On the front page of the *Daily Worker* the words "Black and white, unite and fight" were printed every day.

"Oh girl, we have a lot of talking to do," Dick said.

During the war the Party's reluctance to move on Negro issues disturbed him seriously. Negroes were expected to fight for a country that would not even grant them army commissions, and the Party mildly looked on. The very blood banks were segregated; a Negro with a minor wound could bleed to death if no "black" blood happened to be available, but when the Brotherhood of Railway Porters called a march on Washington to protest these injustices, the Party refused to support it. Dick went to the National Committee and was told that "the war effort" had priority. How, he challenged them, could equal rights for black Americans help the Axis? Didn't they see that the formula "war effort" was becoming a cloak for racism, conscious or otherwise?

Dick could be very persistent when he took someone in hand. He buzzed around the National Committee like a angry hornet until Ben Davis, a black member of it, a towering and intimidating figure I used to see occasionally in the *Daily Worker* city room, advised him to "go back to his writing and leave the politics to the Party."

Dick went back and wrote *Native Son*, the story of a black youth at the bottom of society who murders a white girl near the top of it and is defended by a Communist lawyer. Ben Davis hit the ceiling and demanded Dick's expulsion. Earl Browder disagreed, and as the book rapidly rose to world fame and even the Soviet Union telegraphed congratulations, the controversy behind the scenes was laid to rest. Not for Dick, however. When the *Daily Worker* condemned still another lynching in the South as "an obstruction of the war effort" his cup of gall ran over.

My own squabbles with the Party seemed almost farcical beside issues of such magnitude, but I could not help recalling the drubbing it gave Ruth McKenney. At first embracing her as a great catch, author of the amusing bestseller *My Sister Eileen*, in the end the Party pilloried her in the *Daily Worker* for her well-meant novel *Jake Home* about a larger-than-life working-class hero, a sort of Communist Paul Bunyan, but with faults. Communists did not have faults. Overnight she found herself ostracized, homeless, like an orphan in the snow.

Why, I wondered, suffering as I listened to Dick, did the Party do this habitually? They bowed and scraped to "bourgeois writers" who wouldn't touch them with a ten-foot pole (all unaffiliated writers were described as bourgeois writers), but turned viciously on people who were ready to die for them.

With his characteristic helpless laugh and nothing to laugh at, Dick said, "It's like a love affair you never get over."

"Why did you choose the *Atlantic Monthly* to confide in?" I asked.

He did not take this in at all. Whether swan song or drumroll the noise made by his departure was irrelevant. Pain was all he felt. He had had to leave the one emotional and intellectual haven he had ever found. There was no substitute for the hope lost, the solidarity, the thrill of struggle shoulder to shoulder. It appalled him that comrades were still risking bread and life in it. *For what?* Believing, actually *believing!* — in a devouring chimera.

"We have no right to drive others from their salvation," I said. "As individuals we're not that important."

"Who is important, girl?"

"We have no right to weaken the movement."

"It's not we who weaken it but those sitting on top of it."

"We won't get better leadership by simply walking away."

He smiled at me with a sad, tender tolerance, as if hearing echoes of an extinct self.

He drove me back to my hotel, arguing all the way. It surprised me that a man of such renown took the trouble to argue with a nobody like myself. I had the profound sense of nonentity typical of most women. It went so far that I thought only oddballs could love me. Max was an oddball. I was a lesser oddball. Whatever little virtue I possessed came to me, I believed, through that greater thing to which I was committed and which Dick was still trying to tear from his skin—like the fiery poisoned cloak of Dejanira.

He asked to see my room. There was only one spot under its sloping ceiling where he could stand upright without striking his head. Stooping, he moved along the wall to examine my photos and art postcards. I quickly turned down the manuscript pages and he placed a book on them like a paperweight, saying; "I brought this for you to read." It was *The Twentieth Century Novel* by Joseph Beach. "It may help you. I wish I could give it to you outright, but I still need it and it's out of print."

I could tell as he looked about the room that he was comparing my circumstances with his own. "We'll have you to dinner and feed you up," he said with a gentle smile. In the doorway he admonished teasingly, "Now you think of what I told you today, girl. Hear? You might just be wrong about a thing or two."

As our friendship grew it seemed to me it was absolution he was seeking. He lay tossing in his heresies like an insomniac in sweated sheets. He was trying to make me concede that the hope he lost had been based on illusion, that a struggle led by people who changed their line from one day to the next was doomed, that it was insane to expect equity on a world scale from people so fond of punishing their nearest and dearest.

He had plenty of friends who thought he was right, distinguished friends: Sartre, de Beauvoir, Camus. Gertrude Stein had driven to the airport to welcome him to Paris. So why the to-do when the first zealot who walks in off the street doesn't agree? Absolution can be had only from a believer — the last person on earth in a position to grant it. Ruefully, affectionately, desperately, tenaciously he set out to wrest it from me.

"There was a gentleman to see you," said Mme. Vidonne. "Vree–vreesh—" She unearthed a slip of paper on which Dick had printed his one-voweled surname, a hopeless conundrum for the French eye. By the following day she had found a solution: "Monsieur Richard awaits you," and he was just behind me, coming over with a big smile and another book, this time Conrad's *Lord Jim*.

"You said you hadn't read it." It sounded like an apology.

He was self-taught and I had dreamed away four years and my father's hard-earned money in an "experimental" college. *Lord Jim* dazzled me. It was so consummate a demonstration of the writer's art that one could not learn from it, one could only fall on one's knees and worship. In *An American Tragedy* and *Crime and Punishment*, both read in Paris courtesy of Dick, I recognized cardinal strains of his literary origins. Not that he meant in any way to call attention to himself, he never did that. He only wanted to edify and give me pleasure, and he did. If only we could have dispensed with Sunday dinner in the avenue de Neuilly!

It was a ghastly occasion. The little girl having been packed off somewhere, I found myself in her place at the middle of an endless table with Ellen at the head and Dick at the foot and a shouting silence in between. It was broken by practical references to the food, which Ellen doled out in first helpings and seconds. Thirds would have been welcome, but no more were forthcoming. The butter remained near her plate and was not passed. After dinner she retired to a sofa at the far north end of the salon, adjusted and readjusted herself with sensuous rustling sounds in the plush fittings, said something about just adoring Dostoyevsky, and made even the opening of a book an acoustic performance.

In our original two armchairs Dick and I were graciously left to whatever conversation we could make under the circumstances. I have no recollection of it, only the occasional whisper of Ellen's page turning. Neither can I recall what she looked like that one and only time we met. She was a white woman of about thirty-five with dark hair. Deborah once mentioned that she had been chairman of her Party branch in Brooklyn. Dick never discussed her.

Seeing that I was about to leave, she put aside her book. "I think we ought to give Edith some cheese," said Dick in the tone of a prompter.

A small high-legged table near the door to the entryway turned out to be a food chest with a hinged lid. After a moment's awkward hesitation Ellen wrenched at the lid as if it might otherwise resist, snatched out a wrapped lump, and dropped the lid in a hurry lest I see how crammed the chest was with exciting whole cheeses (but I had seen) and thrust the lump at me with a belated air of impulsive charity. She almost knocked me down with it.

As it was tacitly understood that such a visit could not be repeated, Dick pressed me to accept money from him. It was stupid, it was pigheaded of me to refuse, he said, I was as thin as a rail, I wouldn't owe him anything, I had seen he could spare it, there were no strings attached! I felt that if I took his money I would be condoning infidelity to the movement. I didn't say this, I repeated only, "I can't. I can't," but he knew without any explanations why I couldn't.

I was elated when a recently dated letter from Max announced Anna Seghers' imminent arrival in Paris with a message for me. Puzzlingly, he again failed to mention his address, though he described the apartment and the difficulties of getting it repaired. Perhaps, I thought, this was some deeply ingrained caution from the days of "the illegality," as German

Communists called those twelve years of grim hide-and-seek. In any case the mystery would soon be cleared up by Anna Seghers.

More weeks passed, and although it was only October Paris grew dark and bitter cold. The French coal miners struck, I wrote wrapped in a blanket. The water workers struck, halting the *hydraulique* completely. Nobody collected garbage, but thick fog veiled it and presently snow swirled about the street lamps and pedestrians tried to cross streets they could not see. No mail came. No Anna Seghers came. Then one evening when I returned from the office Dick got up from a table in the lobby and hurried toward me with an anxious look. He was the bearer of good tidings, but they had a flaw.

"Anna Seghers is here," he said. "I'll drive you over."

"Oh, when did she get here?" I cried, following him out the door.

"Few days ago, I think." He spoke in an embarrassed mumble.

"*Days?*" I should have thought hours! She had an important message for me! But I pulled myself together and asked Dick how he knew of her arrival.

"Brecht," he mumbled. "He gave me her address."

She was staying in a seedy hotel on the Left Bank with almost transparent carpets and scratched woodwork. At the door of her room, behind which voices could be heard, Dick slipped away.

Among my treasures I kept an item clipped from the *New York Times* the previous April when Anna Seghers returned to Berlin from Mexico. It ran in part:

> Frau Seghers said she felt no particular emotion on returning. "No, I expected all this," she said, "or rather, yes, something has caused me emotion. Look at this one here (indicating Max Schroeder, editor-in-chief of the Aufbau Press). Max is still the same. Germany is full of Maxes, I am sure."

I knocked diffidently at her door, was not heard, and rapped louder.

The room was so small that it seemed jammed, but the only other guests were a young man and a younger girl sitting on the bed. The one chair, beneath the window, was occupied by Anna.

Her simple matronly grace did not suggest a writer but an ennobled peasant woman, all soft curves and fullnesses like a Maillol. The entire charm of her plain dress with its round white collar was that it fitted her. She had exquisite features with a faintly Chinese cast, the cheeks were pink as garden roses, the startling snow-white hair (she was only forty-seven) was drawn back in a bun held firm by a silver comb. The facets of a minute observation glanced from her eyes. Something in the irises darted like the lightning moves of a dragonfly and made them appear blue.

But as soon as she grasped that I was Max's American wife she sprang at me verbally, first from one ambush, then from another, as if to learn just what sort of interloper I was.

"Sit down," suggested the girl on the bed, and both young people made room, but Anna did not confirm this and I remained standing.

"A message? I know of no message," she said. "Max did not give me a message."

I was in an agony of mortification and shock. How should I suspect that this great woman was extremely nearsighted and too vain to wear glasses? I was a blur to her; the lightning moves of her irises were probably an attempt to see me without squinting.

"Perhaps he only meant that you would tell me his address," I said.

"He told me *your* address," Anna corrected. "It seems I have lost it. I do not know where he lives."

There was nothing for me to do but go. This Anna could see, or sense, and it was not her intention — she had had no intention, so she introduced me to her children Ruth and Peter, both studying in Paris; they were the reason for her visit. After a quick consultation in German they decided I must go to dinner with them; they were meeting old friends in a restaurant around the corner. No, no, I said, I'll come another time, but Anna shooed this aside impatiently and I found myself trailing in her wake as the third grown-up child down a dimly lit stair into the dark street.

I could hardly make out who else was at our table, which seemed very long. Candles flickered in the depths of the establishment, there were marbled columns, perhaps they were real marble, and arches with vague carvings above them of fruit or cherubs. It all looked grander than even Dick's living room, so I ordered almost nothing.

One of the shadows in the party was Brecht, who had just left the House Un-American Activities Committee behind him; as yet he meant little to me. He had been waiting about in Paris since the first of November just to see Anna before flying on to Zürich. His diary entry of the fourth clarifies her circumstances at the time and partially explains her tension and touchiness.

> anna seghers, white-haired, but the beautiful face fresh, berlin a witches' sabbath without so much as a broomstick. to retain her mexican passport she doesn't live in the russian sector, so gets none of the preferential treatment without which writing is impossible. she would like her books to be read in the non-russian zones as well. she seems frightened by the intrigues, suspicions, spying . . .

Ruth took the chair at my side, probably to put me at ease. Across the table next to Anna sat Ella Winter, a woman in her forties with bold, handsome features. I knew her from Lincoln Steffens' autobiography where she appears near the end as his very young pregnant wife. Beside her was her second husband Donald Ogden Stuart, wearing a bowtie. Anna was shining, joyous over the reunion with friends and children, and grew so mellow that at some point she invited me to come again and have dinner with her alone.

The second evening began more auspiciously, though it was equally bewildering. The moment she saw me at her door Anna began laughing like a schoolgirl. She tugged me through the corridor to the room of Helene Weigel, Brecht's actress wife, who had just arrived from California, and presented me as a hilarious find. Weigel had a likable lean brown face and was exuberant at the prospect of getting back into theater work. She apologized for her "kitchen English," all she could pick up in America as Brecht's cook and bottle-washer. The only job offered her there was the bit part as a janitress in Hollywood's filming of *The Seventh Cross*. Surprisingly, *she* had a message for me, love from Deborah, who had moved to California; Deborah was one of the first to translate poems by Brecht.

No sooner were we out of the hotel, however, than Anna became somber. Across the table in a bistro she gave me a forbidding picture of the Berlin I would find. "Of course if you love a person you will go to him anywhere," she said, impaling me on the judgment of her eyes. Did she think me some sort of adventuress? I wondered. In *Transit*, her protagonist, a young man in whom she disguised herself, speaks of his irritation with people who go off half-cocked in life, stepping into obvious traps, skidding their way to disaster. I tried not to care what she thought of me. I needed her as an emissary and begged her to visit my hotel room so that she could describe it to Max.

"What good will that do?" she asked, astounded at so much fatuity; but she did come.

Anna was the wise virgin who was always being pestered for oil from her own lamp because the foolish ones had rushed out without any. First she would give them a tongue-lashing, but then she dispensed drops of oil.

When I told Dick of an international writers' conference to be held soon in Berlin he was extremely excited about going and so were his friends. He asked me to find out whether he and Carson McCullers, then also living in Paris, were on the list of invitees. He drove me to the Café Flore where Simone de Beauvoir interrupted her writing in a back room to say how eager she was to meet "the new German intellectuals." Only thirty-nine, she looked not old but exhausted and had an unsightly rash on her bare arms. She had not yet recovered from the nervous ordeal of the occupation and was probably hungry as well. I wrote to Max at once and assured Dick that authors of their reputation could scarcely have been overlooked. *Native Son* and Carson's book *The Heart Is a Lonely Hunter* were on Aufbau's list of priority titles, and both authors had granted permission; still, considering the erratic mail situation it might be well to restrain undue impatience.

It never occurred to any of us that deliberate sabotage was the reason no invitation arrived. The authors' association, based in the Soviet Zone, had to submit its roster of proposed guests to the four-power Allied military authorities, who were getting along like cat and dog. The Americans were already making endless difficulties about the publication of Dick's and Carson's books by a house under Russian aegis. A representative American writers' delegation would be seen as another feather in the Russian cap. So in the end the only American writer to get through the sieve was a Mr. Melvin Lasky who had not even been asked for. No one in Berlin had heard of him. A representative of the *New Leader* and the *Partisan Review*, he used his floor time to attack the Soviet Union, after which, Max wrote me, "many America-right-or-wrong admirers came to our club and asked for a vodka." Whose sieve excluded Simone de Beauvoir, and for what reason, we never learned.

Deep in the dumps, Dick put the blame for all his disappointments on the unrelieved damp cold of Paris. "To hell with it, let's go to Monte Carlo," he said and laughed. We were sitting in his parked car. "No, I mean it," he insisted, still laughing. "It's warm down there. It's supposed to be beautiful."

Although he put forward the "let's" like a wacky inspiration of the moment and kept laughing, the idea may have been longer in the hatching.

At first I thought he was kidding. I laughed too. Of all the bizarre places on earth that didn't attract me, Monte Carlo took the cake. What would we do there beside the obvious that was out of the question? Stupidly lose Dick's money at the gaming tables? Gawk at diamonds nestling between the folds of fat necks?

"We could walk and talk," Dick said.

"I can't just wander off somewhere and lose my job."

"Then come for a weekend. I'll get your air ticket."

"I might miss the call I'm waiting for from the military permit office."

"It's because of my color, isn't it?"

"No!" I exploded.

In that split second I was not a hundred percent sure. One automatically felt guilty. I had never been intimate with a black man. There had neither been opportunity nor interest in creating a relationship. Even if some nasty sneaking remnant of prejudice was behind this, Dick was not the man I could test it with, nor was this the moment in my life to test it with anyone. I was saving myself frantically, like a hot-blooded virgin. There were times when I was so desperate that I felt like sitting on a curbstone with a sign around my neck: Take me. I was not desperate for any particular man, it was the wild, galloping, blind, and uncritical voracity of certain dreams. Least of all did I desire or have the slightest physical curiosity about Dick. The political taboo was insurmountable. But I could not tell him this, he was such a sweet friend, and I was sick and tired of that futile argument.

"It *is* about color," Dick probed, trying to read the truth in my face, and I saw that nothing I said would dispel his doubt. I felt so beleaguered that I wept.

So he went south by himself, and I missed him.

"I've such a deep-seated pattern and complex of rejections," he wrote me, "that when I see or smell one coming I try to get ready for it."

As to Monte Carlo itself, I was wrong; it was not at all what I pictured. He described winding streets up a pale gray-green mountainside and the light blues and tans of the freshly painted houses that climbed it. A five-thousand franc note for the air fare one way was enclosed in the letter. That was half my monthly wage at the Joint. He lured me with the misty blue sea, the bright flowers, the olive and lemon trees, red-knobbed cacti twice as tall as a man, and still higher palms with sheltering fronds to sit under.

I wrote back like some sort of automaton with rusted joints, "The implications of such a trip are too foreign to my chief desires."

He telephoned in desperation, "Why do you use such queer words to say no? You'd think you were one government and I was another! But at least keep the money if you're not coming. Use it for yourself."

No, I said, I would give it back. Then he wrote:

> You did not ask me for that money. It was I who thought of giving it to you. Remember? And I said that you were to take it with no thought of strings tied to it; and I still mean that, girl. You must accept it. The mere fact that you can accept it proves that there is more in this world between people than business, buying and selling, etc. It is an act of freedom, something which breaks in upon our daily lives which are determined by give and take, by counting and weighing; and when such as that comes, then don't narrow life down by saying no, I'll give it back. In that way you kill something in life which ought to exist much more than it does. Do you see? To give this to you is MY WAY OF BEING FREE, my way of LEAPING BEYOND THE BURDENS AND CARES THAT DRAG AT ME. Someday you will feel that you ought to do that for somebody; and if you do, then pass on to them what I've tried to give you.

How could I not keep it then? I kept it.

Sad, tragic it was, not to be able to go down and just talk and talk in the sun with the man who wrote such a letter, as he thought we could and intended we should. How we might have enriched one another with our literary speculations if Dick's unconscious driving purpose had not been to overflow the banks of my disapproval and thereby magically become right — for half an hour? — after which the corpse of our interrupted discussion about "the novel of will" would have begun to stink.

As it was, it only smelled neutrally of the paper it was written on. It was halting and lacked the spark of each other's immediate objections.

"I'm trying to make a bridge from the novel of experience to the novel of will," he wrote.

I didn't understand what he meant by the novel of will. I still don't. I thought the novel was about people's real lives. And how far does will take them? It was a contradiction in terms.

"In that story of mine, 'Bright and Morning Star,' I was toying with the notion of will," he went on. "I want to make the Negro project himself in human terms. If I can do this, then my novel about the Negro will say something not only about Negroes but about mankind. You too, if you carry out your notion of doing the story, will be skirting this problem —" (*What* problem, Dick?) "— for to show what happened will be depicting how a person goes straight against all convention. And in that area of life there is a wealth of unknown land to be explored."

No (I continued the sterile argument with someone who wasn't there), convention is not the point at issue. The point is loving one's fellow creature passionately. As if she suddenly found herself perched on some unexplored planet in the universe, one woman — absolutely unexpectedly! never having looked for it! — falls in love with another. Through this other woman, a creature only biologically like herself but different in all other ways, she becomes united to her kind instead of being pitted against it in animal competition for men. It is a one-time experience which illuminates for her all the relationships obtusely labeled "Lesbian" and thus narrowed to label size and written off. The experience arises and subsides like a tidal wave, leaving behind an infinitesimal but decisive alteration of her life.

Could I really have said this, or something like it, to Dick? I was none too clear in my own mind then about my motivation in pursuing this story; any more than he was clear about what *he* was pursuing. One has only to look at what he published subsequently: and my novel ended as an unfertilized egg.

Perhaps, Dick reflected, walking about Monte Carlo alone, it would be better to return to the United States after all and buy a plot of land on Long Island. Or no, why not settle right here in Monte Carlo for good? "Here one would not have to make a fire and buy coal," he mused in a letter to me. "And how high the sky is! I sat in the warm sun and looked at clouds of pigeons circling and wheeling, with the light of the sun gleaming through their sheer wings. I just took my temperature; I'm normal for the first time in two weeks."

Dick's temperature was the barometer of his isolation — from his country, from whites, from blacks. A happy thought could bring it to normal, but not for long. His isolation was a burden he could never lay down, only shift its weight and ease the ache of one shoulder by transferring it to the other. He was seeking a *Weltanschauung* like a big comfortable tent that would cover him and have four corners pinned dependably to earth. For a while he thought he could find it in Sartre. He made friends with Nkrumah, the father of Ghana. But his own "strange and separate road," as he called it, condemned him to resist blanket identification with any group, race or philosophy. He refused to be ghettoized in any sense, and became a one-man ghetto.

In his last letter from Monte Carlo he wrote:

> Did you see where Gide got the Nobel Prize? And I was just defending him against Ella Winter, and they were ready to say, What does it matter what becomes of Gide? I'm convinced that Gide got that prize as a gesture to the world to look at the kind of man he is today when the world is more and more willing to say, To hell with people, with individuals . . . Really, some way must be found in which individuals can live in this world. The two countries with the least understanding of people and the least traditions of culture – the USA and the USSR — are dominant on earth and are getting ready to clash. Countries like France no longer count; men like Gide will be the last of their line for hundreds of years to come. The old world is dying; all agree to that; but a new one is not being born. That is the terrible thing.

As it happened, the military permit office in the rue Greuze did get in touch with me while Dick was in Monte Carlo. The bureaucratic ball, more like a cube, had started its bumpy ricocheting roll in Berlin and I could expect news in a few weeks.

Max went to the Allied Combined Travel Board and thence to native functionaries, first the mayor, then one petty official after another in the labyrinths of Schöneberg Borough Hall. The power of the German *Beamter* to obstruct for obstruction's sake was monstrous, considering that they were supposedly defeated and doing the bidding of their victors. Wherever Max went he had to listen to maddening twaddle such as, "Let her *get* here first. *Then* we will stamp the certificates!" — without which I could not get there.

Stalin never spoke a truer word than when he opined, "The Hitlers come and go, but the German people remain," and right out front the bureaucratic *Beamter*, a species of crabbed, morally stunted civil servant whom no political system has altered. He spends his various incarnations in an everlasting dogged huff under duchies and princedoms, kings, Bismarck, Kaisers, presidents, Hitler, probably Wotan, and now the Allies, only changing his costume and knocking from door to door and back again those same hallowed and misshapen bowling balls, lest they arrive at the ninepins with unbecoming dispatch, for the cardinal rule is always: The public must not be pampered!

For the doubtful privilege of importing a wife Max had to waste many working days standing about in corridors that smelled of rancid sweat. Or, having graduated to a seat on a bench worn concave by thousands of behinds in different eras, waiting to hear his name called once again and see still another office door open; after which he could watch for an unconscionable time the sacrament of the *Beamter* (looking rather like the Mad Hatter in the court scene drawn by Tenniel) slowly munching at a slice of rationed bread held in one hand while sipping at a cracked cup of chicory held in the other as if there were nothing else to do.

I know this so precisely because later it was I petitioning for every conceivable trifle in those catacombs, so that Max could go to work and earn the money with which to pay reparations.

At last, of course — they do give in at last, if one hasn't dropped dead of aggravation, and they have always known they would give in — Max managed to get the two stamped documents out of them. One stated that the wife of a Berlin resident was also entitled to reside there and receive food rations. The other was Max's notarized oath that he, *nebbich*, was willing and able to support me.

Major Secouta for his part delayed my departure for romantic reasons. His charming secretary, a mature lady who I hoped was his mistress (we were all romantic), handed me a visa that specified I must arrive in Berlin on Christmas Day, not an hour sooner or later. They wanted to be good fairies and give me and Max back to each other like Christmas presents. The secretary was radiant at being the herald of a happy end, and I didn't mind the additional fortnight. There was much to arrange.

I bought presents with some of Dick's money, and a one-way railroad ticket, and gave notice at the Joint. Annette Barouk, an Egyptian Jewess in the shipping department, may she live 120 years, had the trunk of provisions from New York dragged out from under my bed and loaded onto one of the agency's trucks to Berlin without asking her superiors. Donald Ogden Stuart got word to Max announcing the time and terminal of my arrival. The rest of Dick's controversial five thousand francs went off by post to Chris and Bill in Switzerland, at their suggestion, so that they could send us food or clothing whenever need arose.

But Dick phoned to say he would not be able to drive me to the station, he was hospitalized. I visited him immediately in the American Hospital. It was our first sight of one another since he had gone to Monte Carlo. He was subdued and would not tell me what was wrong with him. "Just tired," he said with no voice. It was strange to find him inert and uncommunicative, with his head on a pillow. He seemed to have blocked me out, or he felt I had blocked myself out.

Writing of Dick I take leave of him one more time, and it is harder now. Thirteen years later he died of mysterious causes in another Paris hospital. He knew more than I did in 1947. He was fated to know still more, but then he lost the trail. A few letters would flap like disoriented seagulls across the immeasurable divide between East and West, a mere border, and they would even arrive, but we were not to meet again, either in the letters or anywhere else.

It was Herta, Max's art-critic friend — mine too by then, and very dear — who came from her slum flat in Belleville to see me off with a basket of food she could not afford. No, she repeated, smiling with tears in her faded blue eyes, I should tell Max she would not, no, never again come back to Germany, it didn't matter how lucrative the jobs he swore she could get; we would have to meet again in Paris.

"Oh we will! We will!" I cried, not having the faintest idea what I was talking about, leaning out the compartment window and waving; and she waved and waved and was gone, the station was gone, Paris was gone, and the northward jogging and clattering of the train took the place of thought. I was as thickly girt in cheerful ignorance as Tweedledum and Tweedledee in their armor of bolsters and blankets, dish-covers and coal-scuttles.

The French military train was an additional thickness, a citadel of good breeding which shut out all consciousness of ugly reality. No civilian trains traveled from France to Germany, so for my own protection and at no extra cost I was placed in a first-class carriage with three respectable married officers. Their stiff round hats reposed as staidly on the baggage rack above them, peaks to the fore, as they themselves sat erect with gallantry on the plush seats. They even avoided leg-crossing at first. Few words were exchanged until two grizzled brakemen off duty took the empty seats.

Still an American ingenue, I whipped out my four years of Pennsylvania Railroad passes, each a different shade, to demonstrate that during and after the war I too had been a brakeman. "Not only allies: brothers," I proclaimed, ignoring France's ambiguous status as an *ex post facto* victor. I showed them my union card from the Brotherhood of Railroad Trainmen and explained that the traveling costume I had on was my former uniform. They responded several degrees more warmly than Mme. Vidonne, and the officers began to unbend.

Slowly, ever more slowly we rolled northward. I became drowsy. When I awoke the brakemen were gone and there appeared in the falling darkness a cracked old sign in Gothic lettering over a slowly passing dilapidated station: SAARBRÜCKEN. These were the first Gothic letters I saw in their native surroundings. They seemed to spell, ABANDON HOPE, ALL YE WHO ENTER HERE.

Not a soul stood on the desolate platform. German farmhouses slid past in nearly total darkness, though it was Christmas Eve. The next time I opened my eyes the moon had come out of clouds. We were crossing a river on whose banks stood the jagged shells of bombed buildings. Their reflections shuddered in the moonlit water. Nothing more could be seen of Frankfurt am Main from the railroad. I closed my eyes and slept on.

For breakfast I was invited by the conductor into the officers' dining car. The tables gleamed with spotless white linen. Upon each plate was a festive orange. When had I last seen oranges? I pocketed mine for Max.

By the time we dawdled through drizzle into the wooded outskirts of Berlin, only one of my compartment mates remained. I got up to arrange my hat before the mirror over an empty seat, but as soon as I sat down it felt wrong and I stood before the mirror again to readjust it.

"Grunewald," the officer mentioned, and I forgot the hat and started gathering my belongings together in a panic. "We have at least half an hour to Tegel," he pointed out. I paid no attention, I had never heard of Tegel. Grunewald was the terminal according to American Express and Grunewald was the information sent through to Max.

The train was definitely slowing, but no station was visible on our side. I burst into the corridor and saw rows and rows of empty track and a distant passenger platform already slipping away to the rear. There was a lone figure on it, age and sex indistinguishable. I pulled down the window, hung out and yelled, "HEY!" The figure did not react. "Ma-a-a-ax!" I bawled at the top of my voice.

"Here I am," he said at my elbow.

Fresh-faced and all aglow, he seemed to me the handsomest man I had ever seen. Dear resourceful chap! He had simply sprinted across the rails and asked the flagman if an American woman was on board. Just one, said the flagman. That's my wife, said Max.

"And he let me get on! I tell you, no German trainman would have!"

The French officer withdrew at once to leave us alone together in the compartment and we sat down side by side, looking at each other shyly, dumb with joy. And hope; some fear; but all the good intentions that guarantee living happily ever after in Inferno, over whose gates Gothic lettering is but one of many styles.

PART II

The house is built of the stones
that happened to be there.

— BERTOLT BRECHT
"SCHLECHTE ZEITEN" (Bad Times)

A GREAT DAMP AND DIRTY winding sheet seemed to cover the area around the railroad terminal. Puddles reflected lifeless low houses in need of repair. Moisture fingered one's face, though the rain had stopped. It was not cold. Human ragbags, bent under sacks of firewood from the nearby forest, were making slow progress toward the city. The fires were out, the color gray, the meaning nil. The last French military men from the train climbed into a truck and were driven away.

There was no such thing as a taxi at the station. No cars, no gasoline were provided anywhere for civilians. Apart from trams in some districts, Berlin's public transport consisted mainly of underground and elevated trains that were forever halting between stations. It was toward one of these that we were heading.

Despite the dreary scene I scudded along by Max's side in a state of sweet completion. I had no consciousness of being stiff from sitting up all night. It even thrilled me to lug my share of the bags.

Suburb turned to city. The spires of gutted apartment houses seen from the train windows became a dense forest of destruction in which here and there the melancholy miracle of an unhit house stood out. Not that it made me melancholy, or glad either. I felt nothing for the Germans, dead or living, unless they were like my German. I doubted there were many of that sort. Viewing the center of Berlin, surely as shattering a sight as Hiroshima, my mind stood apart as if it had quit its job. The Germans have an expression for this ugly phenomenon: It's not my beer.

The people in the *S-Bahn* remained immovable as waxworks on the spot where they first planted their feet. As if nailed to the floor, not one stepped aside for a fellow human trying to get on or off the train. They did not seem to regard each other as fellows or human, but as insensate obstacles. Not one considered another's distress. Ruthlessly shoved, bumped, and jabbed at every station, they seemed to prefer an elbow in the gallbladder to yielding half an inch. The train was not even particularly crowded—there was space to turn aside.

Were they always so mean to each other? I asked Max. The question startled him. He thought not. A few knocks as the price of being rolled on wheels to their destination may have been a matter of indifference after the far worse blows they had received. They had lost family, home, "Fatherland," dignity, belief. Many had no change of clothes, all were hungry and sick, too drained of energy for waste motion.

The presence of a carefree foreigner with halfway decent baggage probably made them feel still worse, if they noticed. They knew the world detested them; that was written in their faces and they wanted to hear no more about it. Only the collective sentence passed on them seemed to throb insensibly in their skulls: Live on.

You had it coming to you, I thought.

Max's street was almost undamaged, except for the self-esteem of the inhabitants. They had the look of royalty who have been dragged out of bed and kicked downstairs by the servants.

Russian artillery and infantry having taken the whole city, building by building, floor by floor, literally room by room and from cellar to attic, every outer wall was pocked by machine-gun fire. Only one heap of rubble at the end of the block testified that a Western bomber had gone astray. We were fairly close to the suburb selected by OMGUS (Office Military Government United States) for its own living quarters and offices. An American consulate was within easy walking distance.

The heavy, curved balconies of the house opposite ours suggested breastplates of slightly bunged Valkyrie, their bulges embossed with chipped garlands and fruits. Fat-faced amoretti gaped with blind eyes out of niches. All was begrimed and dingy. Cardboard covered broken windows. In place of central heating, holes had been knocked through the masonry for stovepipes with turned-up snouts. Only rarely did a whiff of smoke arise from one of them.

Our apartment at the top of the house had once been a sculptor's dwelling, no part of it habitable when Max got it. At great expense of time and money he had had the panes of the shattered north light replaced and the worst gaps in the roof mended. He was immensely proud of these and all his other domestic achievements, and as he showed them off I too was filled with an admiration far out of proportion to their intrinsic worth.

In a drafty cave called the kitchen he cried with the zest of an art collector, "Look, the water runs!" and turned on a faucet over a gray, belly-like sink set at knee level in the smoke-stained plaster wall. Smartly he turned it off again while I, with a delicious, irresponsible sense of excitement, looked on as if he had just whipped a silk scarf out of an egg. To think he could live amid this devastation in a house with its roof on, with actual floorboards and cooking facilities! Invisible at first in its dusky corner, a one-ring electric burner soon materialized on top of a coal stove. A perfectly normal electric meter hung by the front door.

As we came out onto a balcony overlooking a court I saw about two dozen sparrows perched side by side on the neighboring red roof, all staring as if our appearance had been announced in advance and they were expecting the gala of the year. Such unwavering concentration on the part of sparrows alarmed me slightly.

"Look! Only one roof is a skeleton!" Max cried. "See that steeple back there? Perfectly intact," he exulted, waving his arms like a child's drawing of a frisky matchstick man.

A bold sparrow with swelling breast and natty business-suit markings suddenly took off and flew straight at us like a missile.

"Hey," I threatened, but clutched at Max.

It hesitated in midair, changed its mind, and returned to the others.

"They're hungry," Max explained. "They're desperate. They can't even find any manure to pick at. The people ate up all the horses."

"Shouldn't we put out bread for them?"

"I already made that mistake. They brought their friends and haven't left since."

They didn't look desperate to me, just abnormally interested. They were obviously doing better for themselves than the people. Quite unlike the humble little gray-brown specimens that used to hop anxiously, each on his own, in the gutters of the Bronx, these sparrows were an organized pack.

"You don't remark on my tomato boxes," Max said rather archly.

"Oh, is that what they are?"

They were at our feet, lining the base of the thick parapet and painted dark green.

"If you knew what they represent, the organization, the effort! First to get the boxes. Then to get the dirt. Did I write to you about Ilse? I couldn't tell you how many times she climbed the five flights with pails of humus. She was indispensable."

"Oho, got the women working for you! Why didn't *you* carry any up?"

"We both carried it up, dear feminist. But without Ilse we wouldn't have any good dirt. She's a gardening teacher."

"I guess she didn't figure I was coming."

He looked thoughtful. "I hoped she did it out of friendship. I *think* she did. Imagine, we'll have tomatoes next summer! And you'll be able to sunbathe nude. This balcony catches all the sun, but no one can see over the wall. It's my greatest treasure. Now do you see why I took the flat?"

As we went back inside he remarked, "This door is broken. There's nothing to fix it with."

The balcony door was attached only by a lower hinge. The upper one hung loose, rusted and lacking screws. "You just can't get screws," he explained, pushing the top of the door into the jamb. It immediately fell out of place again, admitting a damp draught.

In the atelier various pieces of furniture stood about irresolutely, as if waiting for the movers, but Max hurried me past to exhibit his second-greatest treasure. In a narrow bathroom which included all the usual fixtures he stood back deferentially from a bath boiler enameled in gleaming pale blue. A chromium plaque was mounted on its middle with directions in German.

"A New Yorker has never seen such a thing," he declared proudly; in my case this was true. "It cost fifteen hundred marks, but that's nothing! *Getting* it was the thing!"

I tried to read the plaque.

"Don't worry," he said, "all you have to remember is never to start the fire unless the boiler is filled with water," and he went on to demonstrate the use of a hooked window pole standing in the corner. The tiny window was located just under the ceiling.

Max had not yet invited me to take off my coat, and for good reason. The temperature inside was the same as outside, although the center of the atelier was dominated by an immense green-tiled stove. It occupied not only floor but air space with a pipe put together in sections and running every which way like a roller-coaster, upward, sideways, at an angle, straight, and with a final swoop obliquely down into the wall under the north light. The irregular hole around its exit into the street was stopped with plaster, some of which had fallen out.

"It doesn't work," Max apologized. "We won't be able to use this room until spring."

The only furnishing whose tonnage and position against a wall made it look permanent was a carved oak buffet of formidable hideousness. One corner was partially chopped away and a hatchet lay on top. The former tenant had abandoned his heirloom and Max was using it for firewood.

"I wrote you about that count and countess, I think," he said.

He had written, but only now did the story take on some relevance for me. The couple had been members of a famous resistance group and were responsible for the safekeeping of its illegal radio transmitter. They were caught. The baby was torn from its mother, who was imprisoned and ultimately guillotined. The count was sent to the eastern front in a punishment battalion. He survived.

She had been about my age, a beautiful, impeccably Aryan blond, so Max heard.

I tried to believe that only yesterday — what were four years? — in unthinkable conditions a girl I might have known had crossed this floor, had played with her baby, perhaps on the very spot where I was standing, laughed and tossed it in the air, sung to it, hugged it, and yet gone ahead and taken the chances open only to impeccable Aryans.

My imagination balked. The walls were repainted, remembered nothing, accepted anybody. The fogs of my own destiny let nothing in but this one bony man with his exhilarating faith.

"Now, I will show you where we really live," he said.

He ushered me into a short dark passage, swiftly closing the door behind us and switching on a light. "Not here. Maybe this was once a model's dressing room." There was just space to pass through without bumping into an army cot and a dresser. At the other end he opened the final door.

"*Bitte schön!* Go in!"

The hoarded warmth of the fire he had made early that morning flowed about us like peace itself. We were in the cozy chamber formed by a gable with a dormer window. Slanting wooden supports to the roof

on either side of it left little headroom, yet the space contained everything needed for daily life: a rectangular table, two straight-backed
chairs, an étagère that held a few books, a little brown stove, a single bed.

On the table in a flowerpot stood a baby fir tree. Max had cut it down in
Grunewald "with a penknife and patience," as he said. It was decorated with
four baubles, and on the soil lay an orange, his Christmas present to me.

"But I brought *you* an orange," I murmured.

He laid a few more coal briquettes on the grate, then slipped the coat
from my shoulders and threw it on the bed. I tossed the hat after it and
gazed up into the unutterably kind face of the creature, half gargoyle,
half leprechaun, to whom I was entrusting my life. Our cheeks were still
cool and we were still shy. We separated slowly, overcome. I asked for my
small bag. Taking my hat and coat Max went out to fetch it, carefully
closing the door.

I squeezed between table and bookcase to look out of the window. A
woman in a homemade turban was just emerging from a doorway with
a bundle on her back. She had neither age nor color. As she plodded toward the corner another erased individual recognizable as a male came
out of the next house and walked straight into her as if blind. She staggered and kept going, like a dray horse inured to beatings. The man was
scrutinizing the sidewalk.

"Another advantage of this place," said Max, coming in briskly with
the small bag, "is that we don't see any ruins from our windows."

"Just the people," I said.

"Yes. They are the worst. But they will recover."

"Will they?"

"It will take time."

A second man was now bending over the pavement.

"What are they looking for?"

Cigarette butts, Max told me, not bothering to check. People were always looking for cigarette butts.

I squeezed back into the open space before the stove, knelt down and
snapped open my bag. The half-size bottle of Martell was on top.

"My God," Max whispered. He held it high, gazing up with reverence into its amber lights.

"Look! A breakfast set!" It was only for two, I couldn't pour out Dick's
precious money like water. It wasn't even china, just earthenware, but it
looked like china and was bought at Printemps.

"You just can't imagine what this means . . ." He was in raptures. The set was finished in a glossy beet-red faced with glossy white, too thick for beauty but jolly and festive. He unwrapped and placed each piece on the table as I handed it up.

"Here! A pack of Gauloises Bleues from Herta. Your orange. Bacon. Oh, and some lovely *rillettes d'oie.*"

We sat down side by side on the bed, gazed at our Christmas, and lit up — he his first Gauloise, I my last Chesterfield. The stove soughed. We had so much to tell that it wouldn't come out, so Max went to cook dinner.

Despite the three closed doors between us I heard his familiar footsteps, the occasional clearing of the throat that was not quite a cough, the rattle of utensils. The heat of the stove radiated about me and I stretched out on Max's good old faded green bedspread from Horatio Street, savoring the unique sensation of being cared for and having nothing on earth to worry about. By the time he returned with a tray I was asleep.

We talked all day and into the night. Max explained the political situation. My soft-hearted major in the rue Greuze was a fluke of history, he said, a last relic of the Roosevelt administration. We had been incredibly lucky. In six months the Bizone, an American-British combination, would be rid of soft hearts. There were still tiny loopholes and a pretense of East-West alliance. In some places German war plants were being dismantled, in others they were being rebuilt. American and British cartels had no intention of sacrificing their German interests. He would show me, when he found time, the war plant untouched by a single bomb while all around it the slums were reduced to dust.

He was not likely to find time. Every antifascist with professional skills staggered under multiple burdens. Max worked literally day and night, hurrying from the publishing house to theater and then home to type out his review. Berlin's theaters were among the first buildings restored and they all played repertory and added to it frequently. When there was no new play he wrote prefaces, pamphlets, and lectures to train his gifted but benighted young staff who had gone to school under Hitler. Whenever he thought he had a moment to breathe, unexpected chores cropped up in his path like nettles invading a garden.

"You'll have to take some of it off my hands," he said. "Thank God you got here!"

At some point he told me of the fateful visit to his mother and sister on the New Year's Eve following his return to Germany. To protect them Max had never written from exile, and they did not know until shortly before his arrival that he was living.

The mansion looked much the same from outside, but his mother warned him on the doorstep that it was occupied by British officers. They had expelled all tenants, permitting only their landlady and her spinster daughter to remain.

"As servants!" the mother commented bitterly, leading him into the kitchen. It was now their only sitting room. The sister kissed him joyfully, but even at first greeting the mother had been stiff and expressed no curiosity about how her son spent the past fourteen years.

Did the Nazis harm you, Max asked. No, of course not, she replied, why should they, she had simply ignored them, but the British officers had broken some of her best china and glassware. Shortly before midnight Max asked whether, by some utterly improbably chance, she had a bottle of wine hidden away somewhere. As a matter of fact she did, said his mother, only she was saving it for a great occasion.

I had never seen Max's face looking so hard, so embittered.

"You don't mean she didn't get out the bottle?"

"She never in her life gave away anything, except alms to domestics on Christmas. I wasn't eligible for that."

"But what would your mother consider a great occasion?"

He didn't know. Maybe the return of the Kaiser. He swore never to go back to Lübeck, never to see her again, never to write.

"And your sister?"

His face did not relax. She had thrown her life away for a totem. What could pity do now?

When our daughter was born he relented to the extent of sending a printed announcement to Lübeck. Three years later his mother subtracted one knife, fork, and spoon engraved with her maiden initials from the family silver and sent them without a note to the child of her son.

I don't know when she started writing. Among Max's effects I discovered a stack of letters on pale blue paper in matching envelopes. Only the top three or four had been opened. The handwriting was a stalking, rigid German script. Each letter began "My dear, dear boy" and ended "Mutter." There were twenty to thirty of them. At random I slit open a sealed one. "My dear, dear boy," she had persevered. I slit open another. "My dear, dear boy . . ." And he had not been able to part with a single one.

But it is still Christmas night 1947 and the late hour has compelled Max to broach the problem we were both skirting.

"I promised you a flat of your own, a job and a cleaning woman—"

I didn't want to hear it. I was frightened.

"I've only made good on the cleaning woman. We can't get a second flat as things are now in Berlin, not even a room. I'll sleep on the army cot." He indicated the door to the passage.

"Please, what is this nonsense," I protested, but could hardly hear my own voice.

"You know why I wanted you to come. To give you a chance to write that you never had before," he said. "At least a year in which to think and not have to worry about money."

He was holding out the greatest gift one human being can offer another, an honest self-renunciation that concealed no secret hope of an escape hatch, and I feared that he had nothing in mind but the discharge of some imagined debt.

It took all my courage to say, "I came to be with you. I'll go back if you don't want it that way."

But fortunately or unfortunately he did want it that way.

That night Max must have felt like a pioneer starting westward from Pennsylvania who, after long and complicated preparations, has just lifted the last load onto his covered wagon. Forty-seven years old, having survived two wars, the depression, concentration camps, jails, and exile, he had finally attained the moral and financial security to start a family. He clasped me in a spasm of emotion. Tight — tighter! The journey could begin.

The day after Christmas is a legal holiday in Germany known simply as Second Christmas. (Reluctant to part with it, many Germans speak of Third Christmas, even though they have gone back to work.) The holiday's value to me was having Max all to myself.

He too looked forward to devoting Second Christmas to me, but we didn't see eye to eye on what this meant. "We mustn't be selfish," he explained gently. "Didn't you say you want to meet the good Germans?"

I admitted it.

So after breakfast we crossed the court to visit Greta Kuckhoff, the widow of Max's friend Adam, a man of parts who had fought Hitler from inside Germany and been beheaded in 1943 along with our young countess. Through the intervention of one judge on the panel, Greta's death sentence was commuted to hard labor.

No one knew for certain what motivated the judge. At Nuremberg he testified that his mercy plea was based on "human considerations"; Greta had abetted her husband like any wife in blind conjugal fidelity. Probably Stalingrad had shown him the writing on the wall and he hoped one good deed would save his skin when the time came. Something did.

She lived below the eaves on which our sparrows habitually perched. The stairs wound around an unused elevator shaft like the one in our house. All elevators were unused.

Later to be president of the state bank in a German political entity not dreamed of in 1947, Greta was a lady of consummate though not intimidating dignity. Her prominent light eyes shone benevolently on Max's happiness. Then in her early forties, slightly built, with a brainy forehead, she was far from being a prototype of blind fidelity. Though blanched by years of nightmare, she preserved a humorous habit of understatement and lightly spoke an excellent American-tinged English she had learned during postgraduate work at the University of Wisconsin.

Her apartment astounded me after our naked barn. I had expected everyone's home to be half empty. Brown as a Rembrandt, the living room contained rather more than the full complement of mementos and overstuffed, scraped leather furniture. The windows were curtained, the floors carpeted, the darkened buff walls covered with pictures and framed photos. No trace remained of the Gestapo family who moved in after Greta and Adam were arrested.

Two other housemates were introduced to me: Greta's subdued seven-year-old son Ule and a heavy-shouldered, large woman with a booming voice and a shaven face who said little and treated the mistress of the apartment with bluff deference.

As long as Ule could remember he had been shifted from pillar to post in the successive care of grandmother, friends, and concerned strangers. He last saw his father in handcuffs and was still suspicious about the transformation into a full-time protective mother of that pale auntie (was she really his mother?) who used to wave good-bye so cheerily from behind bars as his grandmother led him away.

A quiet, teasing understanding between the two women made me assume a friendship since youth, but they had met only the year before when Grete (final "e") Wittkowski was sent by a newspaper to interview the resistance heroine. Wittkowski had spent several of the war years in England as an undercover agent for the German Communist Party. Eventually she succeeded Greta Kuckhoff as president of the state bank and later rose to the highest post a woman could hold in Germany, deputy prime minister.

Years later, on television, I sometimes caught sight of the powerful figure hunched doggedly in the East German People's Chamber, a hall without windows or ventilation system, listening all day long to the droning of other members and storing up the heart condition that would kill her. Everyone knew exactly what everyone else was going to say, so why, I wondered, couldn't a brilliant woman like Wittkowski make them abolish those masochistic rituals. She should have been striding through the green forests of Thuringia, where she had a rough cabin, and airing her valuable organs.

Greta Kuckhoff said to me kindly as we were leaving, "Drop in whenever you like! Don't be lonely!" It sounded so American! Wittkowski nodded. I knew they meant it, but their quality so overwhelmed me that only a life and death emergency would have driven me back to their door.

Afterward, when an unbridgeable, protocol-filled chasm separated members of the government from everyone else, I was glad I had met them as unpretentious neighbors. It was consoling to think that if two of that anonymous bunch were human, others might be. One saw them normally only as impersonal news photos in a straight row of solemn faces and dark suits. Even the few women were jammed into those rectangular suits.

Once in the early sixties, happening to meet Greta Kuckhoff in Karl Marx Allee (it was no longer called Stalin Allee) I invited her upstairs and she asked, "May I bring my chauffeur?" The chauffeur was Wittkowski. With refreshing spontaneity they examined my rooms, leaving out nothing. Wittkowski stopped before a photo of Patrice Lamumba over my desk and rumbled, *"Sehr anständig,"* very decent of me, for wasn't I a mere scribbler, yet I apparently had some notion of right and wrong. Kuckhoff twinkled at me and made no comment.

They were living together in a Pankow villa which was not a part of the government compound. I envied them their long companionship. I chronically ached for a friend superior to the battle of the sexes. Yet in the end they gave up the house and took two separate apartments.

"It is apparently easier for many people to look death in the eye than the truth," Greta Kuckhoff wrote. She did not mean Grete Wittkowski or anyone else of that caliber, but her formidable friend would probably — if asked — have advised striking out that generalization. Who knew how the enemy might misuse it? "Tell it not in Gath, publish it not in Askelon" was the wisdom of the old guard.

Immediately after the count and countess were arrested, a young woman from a flat two floors below had moved into the apartment to take care of their baby. She was barely on nodding terms with them. Two years later, the war over, she opened the door to a weary and confused veteran. The child trying to hide behind her skirt did not recognize him.

The count had always suspected this young woman of having a fringe connection with the Red Chapel, but for mutual protection members of the network kept such conjectures to themselves. For a long time not even Greta Kuckhoff and the countess had been sure about one another.

Max referred to the young woman as "the second countess." I shall call her Walburga, which was not her name.

During a period when every Communist was asked to bring his curriculum vitae up to date, the count falsified his slightly by omitting any mention of his marriage to Walburga. Laundering one's personal history was a serious offense in the Party, but he was not expelled. As a member of the NSDAP (Nazis) since 1933, Walburga may have rated less consideration than his third and last wife, a Communist all along, who lost her best years in a Hitler penitentiary.

"Walburga is very eager to meet you," Max reminded me in the sleepy afternoon of Second Christmas. "Do you feel rested? She's waiting in great suspense. I made her promise to leave after an hour." He hurried downstairs to fetch her.

Greta would have taken a dim view of exhibiting Walburga as a good German, a fact Max was careful not to tell me until later.

She burst into our small room ahead of him, beaming and bobbing like a schoolgirl on her best behavior and spurting geysers of German mixed with school English. Having shaken my hand with great warmth and fervor she made for the bed, which served as two seats at the table, and settled herself over it like a fogbank on a meadow.

It was evident that this was her habitual landing place and style of landing, for she lay propped on one elbow and faced us in total innocence of any indecorum. Her curves flopped or were heaped into a prominence the more piteous as her eyes kept narrowing to chinks of merriment in a wan, sickly face. Bangs curled with a curling iron did not successfully conceal the forehead that was too high for prettiness.

Young as she was — my age — she already resembled one of those old-fashioned spinsters who, having lived only in books, make a great jolly show of being experienced; except that in Walburga's case the sprightliness was only a mask of good manners. Even as dimples winked in and out like neon signs, tears were brimming from her eyes. Gaily she struck them away with the side of her hand.

Her awkward English used up, she was telling me her life story in high-gear German, which she tried to sell with encouraging nods that meant, "German is such a *clear* language, is it not?" She paused only when Max put in an admonitory remark. Then her face became grave and she let him translate. It surprised me with what humility she acquiesced in being treated as a minor.

She was seventeen when she joined the NSDAP. After a year she received a chilling shock. Her favorite professor, who happened to be a Jew, was fired from the university. She saw that she had made a macabre mistake. Getting off the bandwagon would not be as simple as getting on. She stayed out, which made her useful to the underground. The Nazis did not suspect her. The underground did. It never ceased to regard her warily, never entrusted her with jobs that might have endangered others.

As Max piled the dishes and I smoothed the bed I mused, "She doesn't seem to realize how it looks when she lies around exhibiting her figure like that, does she."

"I sometimes wondered," Max admitted, and blushed.

In certain circumstances, I realized, Walburga's error of judgment in 1933 could have happened to anyone, myself included — all other things being equal. In Germany it had happened to almost everyone. Fine distinctions between major and minor guilt, minor and no guilt, were already fading like thumbprints in the pudding. At first the Western occupying powers "denazified" people individually in the courts, then finding the mummery too protracted for a list of offenders longer than the telephone book they resorted to denazifying them en masse and on paper.

In our district the names of miraculously cleansed NSDAP dupes, idiots, loudmouths, opportunists and worse were posted up at Schöneberg borough hall. Whether any of them were personally notified, I don't know, I only know that Walburga and her sister Welta were not. A year later and quite by chance they heard that they had been cleared.

But this did not help Walburga as far as Red Chapel survivors were concerned. Her gullibility at seventeen might have been forgiven by them if she had not, twelve years later, deliberately set out (as they saw it) to entrap a man still mourning a worthier woman. They would not have been interested to hear that she never quite outgrew her childhood, those carefree days without a Hitler when the grown-ups made a fuss over her dimples, freckles, still snubby nose, the cute grin that made her eyes disappear, and the smart little rattling tongue. It made them sick that even now she ghoulishly (as they saw it) draped herself in the title *Gräfin*, the only relic of a great love, hers if not his, that could not be taken from her. Legally she was a countess for the rest of her life. It sweetened the family disgrace and consoled her own battered ego with a nimbus of the extraordinary.

It also proved quite handy when she was arrested at Communist demonstrations in the American Sector after Berlin was divided. The police were always flustered when they read her identity card. By the next morning at the latest they would let her out of the cell, sorrowfully shaking their heads: "How could you get yourself mixed up with such riffraff, *Frau Gräfin?*"

It took several days before my eyes focused on the pencil drawing tacked up over the étagère. It was a naked, somber face indifferent to the onlooker. I began to wonder why Max bothered hanging it up.

"She is the only one with whom I was unfaithful to you," Max confessed. He seemed eager to confess. "Not technically," he said, "but I can't take credit for that."

"Good thing I got here when I did," I replied cheerfully, but he did not enter into my levity.

"Time and space can blur the most important things on earth," he said. "Thank God for that mediocre teacher of hers. Out of loyalty to him she refused to have anything to do with me."

There were actually tears in his eyes.

For a moment I felt an intimation of catastrophe, as when one hears of a narrowly averted accident to one's beloved; but it didn't happen and soon one has forgotten all about it.

The subject of the self-portrait was the daughter of a former sweetheart, also an artist, who had been killed in the strafing of that Dresden park where so many people sought refuge from the bombing. They thought their homes were the targets, not themselves. When Max heard that the girl he remembered as a baby was back in Berlin, he went to visit her. She had been with her mother in that park and seen her die.

The girl's teacher, Max said, was a doddering fool, clinging to her as his last hold on life. She was too young to know how to break with him. It was destroying her.

"How old is she?"

"Twenty-one. Poor thing, *she* is a good German." He hesitated. "Would you be willing to meet her?"

Of course I was willing. I neither understood what attracted Max to me nor how an alien attraction could dissolve it.

The studio was in a building on Kreuznacher Straße that before 1933 housed a whole community of leftist writers, from Arthur Koestler to Erich Weinert. Stormtroopers honored them with a special book-burning in front of the door.

"My old place is in the other wing," Max remarked as we entered.

"Why didn't you get it back?"

"I went there with that intention, but little children came to the door. I didn't have the heart to drive out children. The parents gave me back my peasant cupboard and the kitchen cabinet in such good condition, I thought that was enough."

Between Cornelia and the people in her oil paintings there was only an inward resemblance. All were as pale and stark and empty-eyed as the penciled head she arbitrarily called a self-portrait. Their rigidly angular bodies were seen against broken walls. The colors were black, white, olive. Speaking English out of courtesy, but really only addressing Max, she said, "I'm trying groups now. It's harder than I thought."

She had a quality of not being born yet, as if enclosed by a transparent membrane. Like a doe emerging soundlessly from a glade, she brought a tray of coffee out of the kitchen and paused, a wild and gentle creature amid faded furnishings which were only accidentally hers. Then she set the tray down on a paint-stained sideboard. She did not produce much of a smile, rather her face lit up almost imperceptibly, a masked bulb in a sickroom, as she handed us each a cup. The coffee smelled powerful. "Father sent it," she said. "I have any amount, drink as much as you like."

Formally, to Max, she said, "I have decided. I told you Father gave me this chance. I will go to America. I need not live with him there. I will study."

He looked dismayed.

"It is better so," she hurried on. "It solved all my problems. All." Her eyes were lowered in order not to see his opposition.

"I will not try to influence you," he said, and started doing so. "Think in terms of coming back. A German painter must not try to be an American painter." It sounded rather sententious. He talked about national traditions.

Arguing, they fell into their own language. He's being possessive, I thought, he's trying to impose his way on her. That's how he shows his love. One mustn't let him. All that death in her heart. She needs joy. She needs sunbursts, Georgia O'Keeffe, New Mexico.

At home I discovered that I had lost my aversion to the self-portrait, but Max, misunderstanding my long look at it, said, "Ach, why should that picture always hang just there! Let's change the exhibit." He removed the thumbtacks. "Before you came I had a different picture on that spot. I used to look at it when I was in bed. It reminded me of you."

He took away Cornelia's drawing and returned with an old print. "Perhaps the greatest drawing ever made. Dürer. From the Apocalypse. *St. John Eating the Book.*"

I had no idea which book was meant or why St. John eating one could remind Max of me, and I tactlessly said so. He fell silent.

"Why don't we invite Cornelia?" I asked him one day.

"Oh, she left. Didn't I tell you?"

"Why, that's too bad!" I went over to him. "Gee. . ." I wanted to console him, but how?

He stared out of the window and stroked my head. His hand was warm and heavy, as if he didn't know what was under it.

If Max ever heard from Cornelia, he didn't say. I refrained from asking. I didn't ask about Ilse of the tomato boxes either.

We did, however, learn one day with astonishment and pride that Cornelia had sold a painting to the Metropolitan Museum. The news did not come from her but from my parents, who clipped it out of Dad's morning paper, revealing what minute attention they gave every little item I wrote them — even to the girl's surname.

Ration tickets were honored in Berlin every ten days, known as a *Dekade*. There was a huge difference between the maximum rations assigned to miners and leading intellectuals and the No. 2 card for ordinary job-holders. The bottom rations for housewives and the unemployed, in-cluding pensioners, were abysmally inadequate, providing only 800 calories a day. This barely kept alive people already debilitated from years of hunger. Children were in a special category, being entitled to some powdered milk and the odd apple or onion.

Max and I did splendidly on his No. 1 card. It provided so much bread that he could easily keep me on it and also share with Walburga and our cleaning woman. It was delicious, honest bread, not like the baked sweepings of Paris, and at first I made an orgy of it. The other items were meager, but we were food aristocrats with our CARE packages and a monthly Russian *payok* for antifascists that included a great hunk of prime beef and perhaps half a pound of butter. Then my trunk arrived from Paris packed with Nescafe, chocolate, and a can of Spam two feet long that lasted a year under Max's stewardship. In addition we enjoyed the incomparable privilege of ration-free meals at the Kulturbund Club.

If I digress for a moment, it is not to evade the subject of food, our con-stant preoccupation at that time, but in thanksgiving for the faun in Max, whose innate grasp of nature, whether plant or animal, made him such an inspired cook.

I had a horror of blundering night moths and would shriek and just as blunderingly try to get my face out of the moth's way. "It's only a poor *Schöps*," Max crooned, a tuneless lullaby to me or the moth. I thought for years that *Schöps* meant moth, but finally learned that it was an af-fectionate regional word for sheep, that foolish, harmless creature whose wool is such a comfort to us. Without favoritism Max protected me from creatures and creatures from me; every living thing had its way of being, and he seemed to know intuitively what it was.

He would not even violate a vegetable. He never cooked one with thoughtless haste, as I did. "You are brutal," he said once. "You know you are brutal, don't you?"

No matter how much work was waiting for him after supper, he would tell me in the kitchen what the carrot or the leek "wanted," and he would woo it until it yielded itself, stretching and curling in its bit of fat like a grateful woman.

In suspense and some apprehension I would watch his swift, surprisingly stumpy, nicotine-stained fingers conjuring the evening meal. I was the scullery boy who would afterward have to corral the discards, the peelings, gristle, liquid that flew in all directions, sometimes even sticking to the ceiling, and clean up the mess — insofar as I could reach it — with cold water; but it was a willing service in view of the meal to come.

Our first onion in Friedenau was a present from Max's adorable friend Pagy, our doctor, whom we now both dearly loved. Pagy got the onion as his fee from a patient with a garden plot.

I had to laugh at the way Max held it up to the twenty-five-watt bulb that hung from the ceiling, turning and twisting it as if admiring the facets of a diamond.

"Slaughter it," said the brute.

"It will not be a slaughter, it will be fulfillment," he said, and operated on it with a treasured New York vegetable knife. "At least this onion will be better off than the one with the green face," he said.

I didn't know that story.

"Oh, there was once upon a time an onion with a very beautiful green face," he said, "but no one could see it because it was inside." As he talked he deftly set up the utensils and ingredients he would need for his dish, and was soon surrounded by a promising disorder.

"The other vegetables all laughed at the onion with her brown, dried-out exterior and top-knot of stiff hairs. They didn't believe her when she said that was not her face. They said, 'Well, then *show* us your face,' and jeered."

He plugged in the one-ring electric stove and cut a hunk of lard into a spotty black saucepan which had been manufactured out of a Wehrmacht helmet.

"So the poor onion in her desperation to be recognized peeled off one layer and then another layer, and another, until—"

He shrugged. *"Tya"* he said, a German utterance that expresses with a philosophical inner smile every incurable sadness that defeats words.

Fulfilling itself, the onion was sending up a delicious smell from the sizzle in the saucepan.

"That was a very short story," I said.

"It was only the synopsis. When I wrote it, it was longer. I left it with everything else in my room at the Hotel Helvétie before reporting to the Colombe Stadium. I told the landlady I would be back, but I never made it. How about setting the table?"

I drifted off to the gable room, dreamy and hungry, wondering at so much peace. Happily married. Just like in the *Ladies' Home Journal.*

After a while I flung open the dressing-room door and bawled, "When do we eat, for God's sake?"

"In a few minutes," came the answer. "The ingredients have to marry. Patience . . ."

Pablo Neruda, another faun, anticipates Max in his poem "Apogee of Celery":

> *At midnight with wet hands*
> *someone knocks at my door in the mist,*
> *and I hear the voice of the celery, a deep voice,*
> *a harsh voice of imprisoned wind,*
> *complaining wounded of waters and roots,*
> *sinking its bitter rays into my bed . . .*

Walburga's food situation would have been less disastrous if she had not been so honorable and pooled with three jobless relatives. Some people fought like animals over rations, stole coupons from helpless parents or children, even murdered to get food. The Profts were a devoted family and scrupulously divided up whatever they had. The first day of each *Dekade* was an excruciating test of willpower. The fat that people craved, always handed over by the grocer in its pitiful entirety, could have been gobbled up on two slices of bread.

Chatting with me outside her apartment door (one was never asked in) Walburga told me what they had eaten for supper the previous evening: artificially colored and flavored water with four kidney beans floating in each bowl. It had been the fag end of the *Dekade*, but now all was well, they had their new rations. "Oh, is it not terrible," she cried vivaciously. "One thinks only of food, one talks always of food, one dreams each night of food!"

By then I too was dreaming of food, although we had only recently been to a dinner reception at the Club for the French writer Vercors where the *pièce de résistance* was two scrambled eggs from actual chickens, not in powder form, courtesy of CARE.

I dreamed I went into the grocery downstairs and saw an avocado. None of the German customers seemed to notice it. "Could I please have that?" I asked quietly, to avoid attracting their attention to it, and the woman placed it on the counter before me. It was pebbly-skinned and just right to the touch, neither hard nor soft. Emboldened, I demanded a pound of butter and she fished it out from somewhere, neatly wrapped in grease-proof paper. High up out of reach was a bottle of Borden's milk, the kind the milkman used to put on our porch in the Bronx. She climbed up and got it for me. Shall I ask for Helen Harrison's French Dressing, I wondered, but decided this would be too expensive. I paid, almost hysterical in my haste to rush home and devour all this graft.

As I awoke I still felt the lovely oval weight of the avocado in the palm of my hand and tried to outwit the thieving dream god by closing my fingers over it before it could disappear.

Walburga listened sympathetically enough to my explanation of an avocado, but confided with a faraway look, "I just dream of rye bread thickly smeared with lard!"

It was not only the Profts who did their neighborly chatting outside the apartment door. Almost everyone was ashamed of exposing shabbiness and neediness to public view. The habit persisted long after an uneven prosperity returned and many people had taken to hiding luxuries instead of torn upholstery and empty pantries.

The first time I went shopping for rations I wore my least becoming garment, a hand-me-down tweed coat outgrown by a friend's kid brother. Though cut for a man and rather short, it still looked fairly new and I dreaded affronting my wretchedly dressed neighbors.

I need not have worried. The news that an American had moved in spread quickly, and Americans stood on a pedestal too high for envy. We were simply unreal. Instead of being resented for wantonly smashing up the good with the bad in Germany, we were admired as winners stuffed with money. Ordinary G.I.s seemed to have access to a bottomless supply of chocolate bars which they handed out with charming political impartiality.

Even I, handing out nothing, was kowtowed to. As long as I was a novelty the shopkeepers treated me like a good fairy whose wand and luminous wings brightened their unlit, empty dens for a few moments. They could not praise my broken German fulsomely enough. How different from the disdain that ostracized me in Paris!

This stage soon passed. Instead of disappearing as befitted supernatural ephemera, I always seemed to be around like Nante on the Streetcorner, a Berlin folk character. At the start of each *Dekade* I would be back, holding out Max's ration card like a beggar's tin cup for whatever dribs and drabs happened to be available. They began to wonder. Wasn't it time to end my slumcrawl and return to happy America? I couldn't be meaning to stay?

Cautiously they probed, and I took it for well-meaning interest. The baker mentioned the name of an uncle in Milwaukee, did I know him? A niece of the butcher's wife was engaged to an American serviceman from Galveston, had I been there? From such preliminaries they proceeded gradually to the real question, and I told them I had married a German. That was no use; they knew Max by sight and were as persistently and shamelessly inquisitive as little children.

"Why didn't the *Herr Doktor* wish to stay in America?" pursued the middle-aged couple in the avocado grocery.

Max was not a doctor or a professor, having despised academic distinctions in his youth, but he finally gave up denying it. Most Germans set so much store by titles that they felt slapped when the honor was disclaimed; they themselves basked in it by association.

The couple had taken advantage of a moment to pump me when no one else was in the store. They converged from both ends of the counter into one double figure with eyes that sucked at me as if to extract at least a drop of the good fortune I was squandering.

"Patriot," I explained in one word, and they backed away in different directions. I had offended them. Lacking the parts of speech to form complete thoughts, I spoke so succinctly that people flinched. But what was wrong with pott-ree-ote? It seemed to hit them over the head like a board.

"We too are pott-ree-oten," the woman hazarded from farther off, and the man put in, "We were always *Deutsch National.*"

This term, often heard, originally referred to a defunct pre-Hitler party, but now meant only that one had not been a Nazi, one had been a staid conservative and backed that fine old gentleman Hindenburg with his mustachio and spiked helmet.

Converging again they inquired in unison with ingratiating smiles, "And how do you like Berlin?"

They had no idea of the stunning incongruity of this question. Almost everyone asked it.

The gulf between their bullying Thousand Year Reich and its complete annihilation was so appalling that they simply looked the other way. A kind of mass hallucination replaced the mass support of Hitler. As on a television screen before the aerial is mounted, pale shadows of picture-postcard idylls moved behind the one horrible channel they could receive. They saw themselves in a form of Eden, boating on the Wannsee, seated in a beer garden under rustling trees, dinner-dancing at Haus Vaterland on Potsdamer Platz, but everything had overlapping doubles like the vision of a drunk.

"Of course Berlin was *more* beautiful before the war," the grocer conceded, noticing my embarrassment.

"*Viel*, viel *schöner*," the wife obliged.

"Before the war" and "in the old days" were further popular euphemisms to veil the twelve-year hiatus during which nothing had happened in Germany.

Neither the man nor his wife produced scissors to cut off Max's coupons. I proffered the ration card once more.

"And the card of the *gnädige Frau*?" asked the woman.

I could hardly tell her that Max couldn't be bothered going after it. "I have no," I said.

"Ah." She smiled insinuatingly. "*Yet*." It was a question, the key question.

"Yet," I affirmed.

This closed the discussion as far as the husband was concerned. An American demeaning herself to the level of ration-eaters! He returned to his usual position at the back of the store, where he stood all day like a watchman and looked embittered. It was beneath his dignity to wait on anyone when he had a wife.

"And the paper bags?" she demanded, all business now. "I told the *Herr Doktor* to tell you" — she enounced each word distinctly — "that we give paper bags only one time. You must bring them for the new rations."

Did Max tell me? Very likely. He was always warning me about some contingency or other. Had I gone and used those flimsy, cone-shaped *Tüten* to start a fire? I stood like a schoolgirl called before the principal, and mumbled, "*Kaputt.*"

They could not be kaputt, she corrected. Where would we be if everyone made *Tüten kaputt?*

From the rear of the store the husband joined in, "You think someone give us *Tüten?*"

They lectured me at length with stern faces. No doubt the repetitious indignation they always had on tap served as therapy for the grudge they bore the world. One met with reproaches everywhere, even when one had demonstrably done no wrong; it was enough to present oneself. Reproaches were a reflex like the involuntary moaning that helps the sick cope with continuous pain.

In the end the woman took a couple of thin paper cones out of a hiding place and grudgingly measured Max's dry rations into them, flour, noodles, farina, whatever it happened to be. It varied. For the fat I had brought a cup; I knew that much. It was a kitchen cup the color of yellowed ivory, thick, clumsy and durable, a contribution from the Victims of Fascism organization.

"We do this only for you," she claimed. "This one time!"

Once I noticed a little boy ahead of me at the bakery who was unable to reach the saleswoman. In itself that was not unusual. Housewives of the master race simply had to be first, and it was easier to shunt a child out of the way than each other. But this child was Ule Kuckhoff.

The words for "my turn," "your turn" were among the first I picked up. "His turn," I said, taking Ule by the shoulders and steering him, and the saleswoman waited on him while I pretended to observe with an eagle eye her business with the ration card, as if I knew which coupon was which.

Ordinarily it was hopeless to argue about whose turn it was, it only led to a general squawking and ruffling of feathers which meant, "Why didn't you watch out, booby?" My rescue of Ule worked only because of the shock effect. I had stepped out of line. The only way to get ahead in a store was to keep your toes no more than a quarter of an inch from the heels in front of you. As in some depressing rite of communal buggery, the whole queue shuffled along as close as possible to strangers' behinds in order to prevent anyone else getting in illegitimately. Quick as a flash an old woman with hardly three hairs left on her head could wedge herself in with aggrieved whines of "I was here before! I was here the whole time! I was right here!"

Only if a man came into a store was he permitted to go straight to the front of the line. No one dreamed of contesting male privilege. Though he wasted everyone's time by stopping to banter with the rough women who presided like Fates over scale and scissors, the female customers bathed him in concupiscent smiles.

How I detested them and their sly looks! I hated even obviously suffering passersby in the street. Pity them? Had they pitied anyone? Playing harmless now, are you, playing put-upon; what did *you* do under Hitler, I would wonder angrily, how many Jews did *you* push into a gas chamber (a procedure of which, at that time and for a long time, I had only the vaguest conception). For my part the whole unappetizing kit and caboodle could be laid out in one vast morgue awaiting autopsies. Brain damage. Paralysis of the soul. Inborn vileness of a nation.

Back in the apartment my spirits were surprisingly unaffected by these impressions. My home was in Max. When I heard his key in the lock I was overjoyed and rushed to the door. In his arms I would answer the question "How did you make out today?" with light-hearted twaddle such as "There was nothing at the butcher's, just those beautifully tended plants they keep in the window and a few scraps of God knows what, appendixes, gall of goat," to which he might murmur, "The plants are carnivorous, they also have their rights." Who can recall twaddle exchanged so long ago; all the same there are incidents and words that stand out forever, as when I reported, "Everybody asks me how I like *Berlin!*" and burst out laughing. He broke from my embrace, turned away and hung up his coat, saying, "Poor devils."

However awful, however unreconstructible Germany appeared, Max ached for the whole dismal caravan of his compatriots dragging their loads or just themselves, heaviest burden of all, to one joyless destination or another. In the street or the train he could pick out at a glance a gray face that still expressed undefeated decency. The weary eyes might reflect nothing now but the drifting dust of *Götterdämmerung*, but he recognized them from better days.

"He is not the worst," Max would say after one of my intolerant remarks. "With him we can make a new start in our poor old Germany."

*   *   *

After his first shock at the sight of Berlin's moonscape Max had come to feel quite at ease in it. He regarded with grim companionability the bent girders projecting from collapsed bricks. The miles of ruins he saw downtown every day were the truth under which his mother's saccharine lies lay buried. Here was the deserved end of our dear Kaiser and his dear predecessors and successors whose fault it was that the German nation had finally foamed at the mouth and run amok.

At the *U-Bahn* (subway) station nearest us a huge rectangle of rubble was all that remained after a blockbuster struck. Unskilled women were constantly at work there searching out bricks that could be used again and chipping the old mortar off them. Six days a week in all weather they slipped and slid over hills of building material, sorting and passing the finished bricks from hand to hand downhill to the foreman, the only man on the site, who loaded them into small, trough-shaped cars on a narrow-gauge track.

The women looked decrepit and moved slowly, bundled up against the cold in layers of torn sweaters and shapeless skirts over men's trousers. Some added a wraparound apron. All wore battered shoes. Now and then one left the team to take a swallow of chicory, known as *muckefuck*, from the tin can heating over a brazier. The fire was tended by the foreman.

When Max and I passed the scene we both avoided staring, but always took a quick glance at the site itself to ascertain progress. The rubble seemed scarcely to diminish.

One day Max thoughtlessly tried to light a cigarette in front of the station entrance. It was windy. "Got one for me, Perfesser?" raucously yelled a crone who had been drinking out of the tin can.

He extended the pack, and as she came over in surprise I saw that she was no crone. Although red-nosed from the cold, with features distorted by aggressive self-pity, she might have been younger than I was. She took two cigarettes in her swollen fingers and at once the other women, perhaps twenty, surged down the hill toward us. Max hurried me into the station.

He wasn't sure how much they were paid, he said. Maybe seven, maybe eight marks an hour, the price of his rations for a *Dekade*; he himself volunteered for a three-hour shift without pay when he had a chance.

I was astounded. "*You*, working with *Nazis?*"

- 79 -

"Who else is there to work with?" he asked.

"It's their mess, let them pick it up," I said.

He did not argue. In the train we found seats and he lost himself in a manuscript. By the time we reached midtown the penny had dropped or at any rate unwillingly worked its way down. The good Germans were going to have to lump the bad Germans. There weren't that many good Germans. They only appeared numerous at assembly points like the Kulturbund Club, our first stop before the theater.

The Club was one of the few building still standing near Friedrich Straße after the war. Until 1932 it had been the "Club von Berlin," its members predominantly industrialists and bankers, including Jews. Its last membership record in 1931 featured such Semitic notables as Dr. Julius Flechtheim on the executive committee, Paul von Mendelssohn, banker, Albert Katzenellenbogen, doctor of law and judiciary councilor, along with the Aryans Hjalmar Schacht, future banker of the Nazis, a von Siemens, a von Borsig, sundry board members of IG Farben, and a scattering of petty country nobility.

When the Nazis got control of it and the Jews were expelled, it became known as the Herrenclub. Franz von Papen spun his intrigues there, persuading conservative tycoons to push Hindenburg into the Hitler camp and at the same time promoting himself as a credible short-term chancellor to pave the way. Titled gentlemen with large land holdings were particularly welcome in the Herrenclub because they could embellish the ration-free meals, one of its main attractions, with fish and venison from their own estates.

The Kulturbund's ration-free meals were not as stylish, but they kept body and soul together at a time when artists and key professionals would otherwise have been too faint to function. The club on Jäger Straße was a magnet for more "good Germans," or at least well-intentioned ones, than could have been found in such concentration anywhere else on earth.

It was an adventure to get there. A narrow footpath having been cleared through the wreckage of Friedrich Straße, one clambered rather than walked into a side street, teetering across unsteady boards from one pile of debris to the next. Dead weeds waved in the wind from cracks in the remains of buildings.

After minimal repairs, the Club presented as suave and exclusive an appearance as in former days. Up a marble stair with a portrait of Goethe on the landing were the dining halls, their decor unchanged since Von Papen's time — walnut panels in one, burgundy satin brocade lining the walls of the other. Only the flooring had been replaced. The same old attentive waiters in tailcoats who had worked in the Herrenclub still darted across the room with extended lighter the moment they spied a cigarette being drawn from a pack. Considering their age it was an athletic feat.

Once they had been confidential servants as well as waiters, expected to know at a glance who belonged at the long table for insiders and who should be ushered to a safe distance from their indiscretions. If, still earlier, they had served in the Club von Berlin, Max and his colleagues would have been the third elite to receive their courtly ministrations, but they gave no sign of noting a change. All who make it to the top impress the German philistine, especially if they consort with patricians. The Kulturbund had quite a few.

The rooms buzzed with stimulating political talk. Returned exiles mixed with kindred spirits who had remained in Germany, all of them excited to be meeting, eagerly visiting from table to table, weighing projects, retailing news and anecdotes. The old literary cafés that expired in 1933 seemed to have been revived under this roof. Only bohemia was missing, except in the memory of people like Max. Charred earth was not the soil for it.

All the same it was a time of exuberant hope, elation that one had survived to experience it, and a robust faith that the future was theirs to make. The atmosphere of those days in the Club was nostalgically remembered after the Cold War put an end to freedom. That it had ever existed came to seem incredible.

During the intermission of Sartre's *The Flies* we ran into our cherished Hans Meyer of Manhattan days, now in American army regalia. He was a first lieutenant. Joy at seeing him at first blinded me to his extreme discomfiture. And my own. His attire was not wholly unexpected—he had visited Max before I came; I knew he was stationed in Frankfurt doing propaganda or intelligence work. Still, the uniform gave me a turn. It was wrong on him and he knew it.

"I d-d-didn't know you were in Berlin," he charged defensively.

"Did *you* tell your plans?"

"How c-could I?" He was suggesting that all his moves were classified now, but admitted with a pooh-poohing grin that he lived in a Dahlem villa with German housekeeper thrown in. The cushy side of army life, but not his alone; "I sh-sh-share with another guy."

"Come and see us, old boy," Max said as the bell rang for the last act. He had not reproached Hans for staying away so long. I saw that the men's affection for one another was unchanged. The only disturbing factor, though not for Max, was me.

What could he bring me from the PX, Hans asked with phony heartiness. "Poor girl, you must be so homesick for ice c-c-cream!"

I said I was homesick for Ivory Flakes. The laundry soap we got on ration was like a stone.

"Ivory Flakes," he repeated smartly, "f-f-fine!" and he dropped in after supper a fortnight later in civvies, under his arm a box containing a tremendous block of chocolate, vanilla, and strawberry ice cream.

We regarded it with alarm. Our supper had been more than usually filling. "Eat it up before it turns to soup," Hans commanded. Max laughed. "Putting it on the stove in the atelier will keep it refrigerated for days," he said, but Hans, unlike his old self, pestered nervously. It would melt. It had been in his car. His car was heated.

Our starkly contrasting living conditions were only the visible aspect of the trouble. Somewhere deeper down we seemed to have got sorted into different chutes and come out on either side of a gulf.

Through no design of his own, Max landed in the United States as a destitute political exile, while Hans had organized affidavits from well-fixed relatives there, his own and his wife's. Max once corrected my impression that exiles and refugees were synonymous. He felt his honor impugned by the term refugee. Exiles were committed, they were on their way home by any trail that served.

Although disappointed to find Hans on a different course, he was not without sympathy for his friend's new allegiance. Hadn't he himself in a sense *married* America? And Hans was a Jew. A Jew had a right to another country. But this did not solve the problem for Hans.

Ill at ease in our primitive digs, he grabbed for one mask after another, played Dutch uncle, Santa Claus, Peck's bad boy. Perhaps he had always acted a bit, but he had done it gaily. This nervous bluster about first-name intimacy with the brass made me feel like a drunk who has stumbled into the wrong apartment. Twenty minutes after we had all forced down thick sloppy slabs of his incongruous treat, Hans made an excuse and hurried away.

By not discussing the hurt, I think we both hoped it might clear up in retrospect like a bout of inclement weather. I felt diminished by Hans' visit. The rooms he had passed through looked plundered.

I wrote to Christina:

> How utterly at ease I've become in these unlikely surround-
> ings with Max, away from everyone who reminded me of
> my former life, struck me forcibly last night. Hans was one
> of the people who knew me when I was mixed up and con-
> stantly tense. In Berlin I very nearly stopped smoking, but as
> soon as he walked in I began to chain-smoke and even show
> off in a dreadful way I used to do in America at my most
> neurotic. Max didn't seem to notice, but Hans did. He no-
> tices everything. I was glad when he left.

Loyally she tried to bolster me: "Bill sometimes discussed Hans with those who knew him quite well, and the general opinion was that he likes comfort too much."

The wound was not a mere scratch, and it did not heal. I didn't know then, but now I know that for me the process called Cold War had begun. Hans drew his own conclusion from the visit and never again showed up at a Berlin first night.

A few times a week I canvassed the neighborhood for off-ration goods. The take might be only a few dried apple rings, but these were not to be despised.

After our own block came an endlessly long street of flat-fronted ten-ements, mostly undamaged, yet desolate as if they had amnesia. No one seemed to inhabit them, no vehicles used the four-lane roadway, most of the shops appeared shut.

Of course they were inhabited. There wasn't an unoccupied room, niche, or recess in Berlin. I did once see a woman come out and walk de-fiantly down the street in a bright green brand-new felt hat made to look like a German general's, its crown rising at the same angle as an arm heiling Hitler, but this must have been after the black market budded. Some trader got hold of a job lot of that garish green, and general's hats for ladies broke out like chicken pox all over town.

Another sign of habitation was tobacco leaves on washlines stretched across ex-parlors, though these also dated from a later period; it was too early in the year for leaves on that particular day. The wintry rooms behind those impromptu balconies with their blanched wallpaper must have concealed tenants so vitiated by hunger, cold, and despair that they struggled down to the street and up again only when it could not be avoided. The front wall of their house still lay in a heap on the sidewalk.

Under the sign "Tropical Fruits" I saw nothing in the show window but dust. Under "Colonial Wares" a pyramid of rusty coffee cans with a defunct brand name stood on a block backed by haze. The sole display in a padlocked store was a square of cardboard hanging crooked, which urged BRING YOUR RAGS HERE FOR TEXTILE CREDITS! Who still had material to tear up, I wondered, until the meaning of the padlock sank in.

But opposite the *U-Bahn* station there were two shops crammed with goods. One was wedge-shaped, fitting the skinny corner it stood on. It was a former tobacconist's, consisting of scarcely more than a clean pane of glass, a door, and a counter at which three people could wait their turn. Behind the shopkeeper was a shelf on which lead-colored cigarette lighters in various unappealing designs were placed side by side. Naturally he had no tobacco, cigarette paper, or matches, nobody did, but under the counter were ampules of lighter fluid.

Across the road, grand in comparison, was a place the size of a furniture showroom and it did indeed contain a species of furniture: outsized coffee tables with curved, too-high wrought iron legs and brightly patterned mosaic tops, no two alike. I could imagine such a table standing in splendid isolation at the side of a Washington Heights apartment-house lobby not bothering anybody. The super could put newspapers and fourth-class mail on it, children could stick chewing gum to the legs. In a home it would stare everything else out of countenance. These mutations must have been recycled from twisted girders and smashed tiles, which should have reduced the proprietor's overhead, but they cost a fortune. Apart from an occasional American army officer dawdling away his boredom over the different models, no customers ventured in there.

Every neighborhood featured one cigarette-lighter and one useless coffee-table shop, and I never failed to gaze in. Starved eyes will light hopefully on anything.

Back home at the top of the stairs I heard peculiar sounds issuing from the apartment. The moment I inserted the key in the lock there was dead silence.

Terrified, I pushed the door open wide and took my bearings. From the threshold I could see an irregular trail of small objects on the kitchen floor that led from the table to the balcony. They seemed to begin at the bowl in which split peas were soaking. Not a sound, not a breath could be heard. Leaving the door open behind me for quick escape from an attacker I walked in one step at a time, listening for the telltale creak of a floorboard elsewhere in the apartment.

The objects straggled across a tomato box to the top of the balcony wall. Bending down I recognized little grayish-green skins that no longer enclosed anything.

Sitting pertly side by side on Greta's roof the culprits looked me straight in the eye, chirped loud challenges, and brazenly cleaned their wing feathers. One flipped its tail like an urchin showing a backside.

There were only seven peas left in the bowl. This was not funny. Wrathfully I went back to shut the door when another harbinger of frustration came panting over the doorstep, a wizened old man with a wizened briefcase.

"I was here before, but no one was home," he accused in the usual tone of insulted righteousness. "Electric company. Not even a nameplate on the door. Not even a scrap of paper. May I make so free as to look at the meter."

What he really said was "*Ich bin so frei,*" a rude declaration of intention unless obviously meant as a joke, as when a friend takes candy from a bowl already offered. The old man unlocked the meter as if reclaiming his own personal property. It was in fact the property of the electric company, but this was not my worry; I was still afraid of being assaulted and remained in the doorway with the stairs behind me. True, the little old character hardly looked like a rapist. He must have been a pensioner reemployed because so many able-bodied men were lost on the eastern front.

"So. I knew it," he scolded. "You have used too much current," and he unscrewed the fuse-holder from its socket. He dropped it into his briefcase and like W.C. Fields giving back the glass eye importantly handed me the fuse, which was the tenant's property. Into the empty socket he screwed a dummy, wound wire around it that ended in a printed metal tag, and sealed the whole thing with wax.

"*Auf Wiedersehen,*" he said coldly. Wanton malefactors had thought they could spit on his dignity and get away with it. Well, it was rehabilitated now!

Oh no, I thought, this isn't happening, I'm going to wake up in a minute. I plugged in the electric stove and waited for the comforting little crackle of current and the gradual reddening of the single coil. It remained gray and lifeless. I put down the fuse and moaned.

At this our bewildered, workworn Frau Gafert overcame her timidity and entered the open door with that almost transparent rag, a pail, and her precious *Schrubber,* a German cleaning implement consisting of a long handle that ends in a scrub brush. The once stiff bristles were reduced to stubble. Frau Gafert gazed at me in fearful supplication with great bloodshot eyes like those of a poor man's dog.

"*Gnä' Frau,* are you sick? I come in, excuse me, *gnä' Frau.* First I ring bell, bell no ring, bell *kaputt!*"

She spoke broken German under the impression that it would be easier for me, and I automatically answered in broken German even when I knew better.

"No *kaputt,*" I said, and pointed to the meter. "Man come."

Horror crept over her wrinkled, swarthy face. She set down the pail with a bang, as always, and stood the *Schrubber* against the wall in such a way that it immediately crashed to the floor. To the rag she clung as to life itself, and as her helpless eyes wandered about the kitchen she took in the other disaster. "*Gnä' Frau!* You let sparrows take peas! Why you let sparrows take peas? *Gnä' Frau* must put cover on bowl!"

Et tu Brute, even Gafert joined the queue of reproachers and accusers who were always lining up to make a heavy heart heavier, but hers at least was in the right place.

"Hitler!" she exclaimed ferociously, meaning that he had even corrupted honest little sparrows. "A Hitler we needed. A bloody STINKING HITLER!" In deep gloom she filled the pail with water and set about her work.

Frau Gafert was the janitress of two houses on our block and had a rent-free ground-floor flat in one of them. She was past sixty-five and should have been doing less work, not more, but she came to us for the bread coupons and the bonus from each CARE package. The money was just a tip, though as money went we paid fairly.

She was one of the few Germans who offered no personal alibi for the period between 1933 and 1945. It never entered her head that a person as lowly as herself could have influenced anything. As the cyclone mounted she had flattened herself and rehearsed Christian principles as best she could. Every time she woke up and saw again the havoc of her former world, she raged. Max had a deep affection for her.

All the same, he left precipitately if he happened to be still at home when she arrived. She was not so much a cleaning woman as a dust centrifuge. The dust she was most intent on redistributing took refuge between other people's feet. She would aim her rag straight at the spot where Max or I was poised and take a sharp crack. In vain one fled that scourge of the furies. Dirt was equivalent to Hitler in Gafert's mind, and whack! crack! The punished fibers no longer picked up dust or absorbed water. She darned her rag like a sock, but new holes grew around the darns.

We had so little to clean that I could easily have done the job myself, if only I had had anything to do it with. Neither Max nor I had thought to bring cleaning implements to Germany. That was why we kept her on. Or rather, it was why I, if I had a vote, would have kept her on. Max would never have let her go. She was helping me to be free, he thought, and enabling him to compensate her just a little for her hard life and indestructible rectitude.

Before leaving she held up dark gray tatters to show me the daylight between warp and woof. Her face was solemn. "*Gnä' Frau*, this my only rag. It is rag I clean home, it is rag I clean stair, it is rag I wash many many time, it is no more rag, *gnä' Frau. Gnä' Frau* must get rag!"

"But Frau Gafert, where I get rag?"

"Must buy," said Frau Gafert for the tenth time. "You go soap store. Go soap store and say 'I want rag!'"

"I go soap store. Soap store say 'No rag!'"

"Ask rag from America."

"Rag from America?"

This was a new move in Frau Gafert's indefatigable campaign. The kindly, understanding faces of dear friends, parents and beloved younger brother rose to my mind's eye, all going blank at the request for a rag. If a ruined country had nothing else, Americans would imagine, it must have rags. And it was true, many German households were so rich in discarded hangings and the like that these were refashioned into

the frightful turbans and sack skirts so many woman wore. Our last resort, the Victims of Fascism, had not thought of floor rags either. I was
checkmated.

The filmed eyes that bespoke so many years of unrewarded toil and
dumbly borne injustice hung on me with fresh hope. Frau Gafert surely
wondered why she, or at least I, had never thought of such an obvious solution before.

"Next week rag," I mumbled, and she recognized this as the craven
formula with which I ended all these discussions.

"*Gnä' Frau* got cigarette butts?" she asked resignedly.

Max saved them in an empty pack for Frau Gafert's son.

"Yes! Yes! I get!"

The punishment for wasting current was thirty days without current
and a fine one hundred times your normal bill. Max calculated that it
would take him three mornings at the very least to get the electricity restored and the fine canceled. He didn't have three mornings and I didn't
have the German to cope with a crisis of such complexity.

The first morning would be wasted running to one wrong authority
after another. Who knew which authority was responsible for what? They
kept changing the rules. The second morning the right people would
send him after various certificates and credentials from Aufbau, from his
newspaper, from the Victims of Fascism, a notary, a doctor, God alone
knew what wild goose chase they would think up next. Experience
taught only one thing: each new misfortune led into a maze with turn-
ings totally different from the last.

The third morning, clutching papers stamped with purple ink that
smeared and made their validity questionable, he would return to the
correct office and cool his heels at the end of a long line. If he was lucky.
If not, the door of the building would be locked and a passerby would be-
rate him, "What's wrong with *you*? They're only open on Tuesday." Or
Wednesday, or Doomsday. He would have to lose another morning.

"Don't you see," he reasoned, trying not to shout, "that we couldn't
possibly have used too much electricity? When, using what, could we
have done it? With three twenty-five-watt bulbs? We hardly cook! How
much do you iron? You shouldn't have let him touch the meter. Poor
thing," he relented, "it's not your fault." He walked about, distractedly
considering. "Look. If one more bastard tries to get in here for whatever
purpose you must say I STAND UPON THE RIGHT OF MY DOMICILE." He

repeated the magic German formula several times: *Ich bestehe auf meinem Hausrecht*.

"I stand upon the right of my domicile," I echoed.

Naturally I never had occasion to use it. To each calamity its own combination. But as the bard of "Deor's Lament" cheered himself centuries before Shakespeare: That passed. This will pass also.

On returning late and lighting the candle stub that now squatted on the electric meter, it was I who first noticed the shadowy mess on the floor. Max held the flickering candle over it and we both peered, he astigmatically, I myopically. The door of the low cabinet from Kreuznacher Straße was slightly ajar and there were little heaps and swirls of farina, flour, cornmeal and sugar in front of it. In the flour was a neat bird footprint. I opened the door wider, cautiously but not cautiously enough, and the paper bag of cornmeal pitched out, dumping the rest of its contents.

I groaned. There went our fried grits for Sunday breakfast! Each of the bags had been efficiently perforated by a bird beak just once, making a wee hole through which the contents could slip out. It was mortifying. I always kept the cabinet closed, but I should have locked it.

"I didn't think their bills were so strong," I lamented, but Max laughed. He was proud of such smart little brothers.

After that I always turned the iron key in the lock. Not even Max reckoned with the new collective bird brain our sparrows were evolving. They knew more about us than we did about them. We were their chief preoccupation.

Theater began in the late afternoon because of the hazards of getting there. For getting back after dark the Red Army provided orientation and a prop for terrified minds by attaching loudspeakers to the bulbless lampposts along Friedrich Straße and blaring Russian folk choruses all night. I was still terrified. It was eerie in that waste of skeletons moldering under ruins on either side to hear "Kalinika" roared or kolkhoz coloraturas keening of lost love and white hydrangeas. When the moon squinted through some gap one might at least see one's own feet groping, but then there was the danger of being attacked from behind. I went rigid at the crunch of a stranger's shoes.

Nothing would have kept me from going to theater though. It was marvelous in those days, even for someone who understood hardly a word. I don't mean only myself.

"Wasn't it fine?" I overheard one old woman from a factory theater party say to another after a gloomy piece by Ferdinand Bruckner played in semi-darkness while the whole audience had coughed; the other replied in heartfelt tones, "Oh yes, so warm and cozy!"

The coziness was new. When Max first arrived the critics down front wore one sweater over another, kept their coats on, and felt ice blow in their faces when the curtain rose. The winter of 1946–47 had been one of the coldest on record. Yet if the role required it, actresses with bare shoulders pretended to be perfectly comfortable.

Now the administrators of Berlin spared no expense in heating those temples of the senses and spirit and promoting their salutary illusions. The plush seats into which one sank were better than one's hard chairs at home. Long before footlights brought out the red glow of velvet hems and the curtains parted, one had been caressed and flattered by the auditorium itself. Gilded cherubs tickled the ceiling with plump fingertips while below them a thousand crystal droplets multiplied the glitter of the chandelier.

Theater again exercised a function akin to religion, restoring the wholeness of the world in enhanced form and making people forget the desolation outside. The weary and heavy-laden opened their lips to receive an exquisite wafer — blossoming parks whose existence one had forgotten, rosy silk-shaded boudoirs, a fire blazing in an Irish kitchen hearth, double glass doors opening on a blue lake, a throne room, bejeweled robes, sparkling repartee, but also lofty soliloquies that placed one's own troubles in perspective.

If the play was a German classic, Max explained the plot in advance and I filled in the details for myself, often stifling hilarity not intended by the authors. While he typed his review I sat opposite and dashed off a lampoon such as "Ham and Eggmont." He was taken aback the first time. "Clown," he said sadly after reading my spoof of a Lessing play. "You don't know how much of Minna there is in you."

"I hope not, imagine falling for a dope like Tellheim!" I hooted. "Feudal feminism!"

By the time I realized I was actually hurting him, pinching his sensitive literature nerve, he laughed himself. He even sacrificed time he didn't have to translate my silliness into elegant German.

A vicious north wind was blowing the day we went to see *Liliom* performed by a French troupe. It whipped through the cracks on either side of the warped gable window. It wrenched the heat up the stovepipe into the street. The little brown stove had no damper.

Before we left the house Max put a few more chunks of oaken heirloom and four briquettes into the grate, and we heard the flames race hysterically up the flue to join the storm. The room quickly became snug and the flames settled down to lick their wounds. When I opened the grate to look, a glowing lump turned over sleepily and jostled its neighbor, which wheezed and fell silent. The embers exhaled a powerful, peaceful heat full of false promise, and Max banked them with ashes.

Liliom being a play I knew backward and forward, it provided none of the comedy of misunderstanding. So while Max wrote his piece bundled up in two sweaters I crept into bed with a book on the reproductive vagaries of other animals, shedding on them all my surplus affection. I seemed to contain an affection generator that hummed day and night, except where Nazis were concerned. The embryo swam peacefully inside me while I lay afloat in the protective amnion of Max. I was a sea containing an island, an island in a sea.

"Wasn't *Liliom* lovely," I murmured in the morning.

It was not yet clear to me why we formed a two-headed mummy. For fear of dislodging the covers tucked tightly around us we were motionless as paralytics.

Nevertheless Max replied like a guest at a faculty cocktail party, descanting on the virtues of the French players in a rather muffled voice until, after a pause, he uncovered his mouth and said plainly, "We used up our last coal yesterday."

The temperature of the garret was in fact sinking with a rapidity new to a tenderfoot like me. The fresh coolness that washed over my face when I awoke had become an icy plastercast. Max leaped out of bed with an animal cry and I followed, clutching the covers around me. The queer sniveling I heard was my own. Max was flinging his clothes on. I tried to emulate him, dropping the covers and standing on them to protect my feet from the glacial floor, but in a moment my fingers were stiff.

"I can't fasten my brassiere," I howled.

"Don't wear it."

He rushed out to chop hunks off the buffet and make what he called a third coffee, boiling water poured for the third time on the same grounds. Dressed in several layers of clothes we clumped down the stairs after breakfast on feet like blocks and made for the heated saloon across the street.

While Max paid the entrance fee, a glass of tepid ersatz beer at the bar, the only drink they had, I spread-eagled myself against a huge white-tiled stove in the rear to heat every cell of me. After a while Max came over to tell me I was attracting leers. Did I now consider myself warm enough to stand upright? I came to attention.

"Let's go," he said.

"Go? Where can we go?"

"To Peter Huchel, to borrow coal."

Peter was a poet who lived nearby, Max told me, a very fine poet, though I might not care for his predominantly bucolic subjects.

"How will we get it home?" I asked.

Max pulled a soiled shopping bag out of his coat pocket.

"That won't hold much," I said.

"It will hold all we're going to get," said Max.

He was wrong. Peter and his new wife Monika not only insisted on our taking more coal than the shopping bag held, they presented us with a divan on which Monika's parents used to take their afternoon nap. "No use being sentimental," she said, "it's only in the way," and merry in the solidarity of need the four of us lugged all this booty down the Huchels' stairs, through streets covered with crusted snow, and up our five flights.

The cold had lost its menace and I had forgotten — a landmark! — to wonder whether our kind acquaintances, he so genial, she so sisterly, were "good Germans."

The irony of this turning point in my adjustment to Germany was that Huchel, an old friend of Kantorowicz from a time predating the Nazis, and temperamentally no Nazi himself, had found favor in the Third Reich as the apolitical poet of a bygone (if it ever existed) rural idyll. They included him in their racially aseptic Reich Chamber of Letters and he coped with the moral dilemma by confining his personal contacts to other nature poets. ("Burn me!" protested, in contrast, Oskar Maria Graf when the Nazis spared his books, but unlike Huchel he was outside Germany by then.)

Did Max know that Peter had written ten radio plays produced by the Nazis? The Soviet occupants knew. Nevertheless — in fact, precisely because of Peter's presumed radio expertise and because he got good marks in a Communist reeducation course — they took him out of their prisoner-of-war camp in the eastern outskirts of Berlin. About the time we ran out of coal he had been moved into the more appropriate post of artistic director. The Russians were hard up for able personnel. Huchel was not a war criminal. If he didn't work out he could be removed.

As it happened he did work out. A Marxist euphoria seemed to lighten the introverted aesthete's careful, brooding heart and to transform him for a time into a warm and outgoing human being.

Meanwhile we owed him coal, a more urgent matter than money, and this catapulted the question of my ration card to the top of our agenda. Managing without a housewife's meager food ration had been so easy that Max forgot how much coal I might be using. Even his extra coal from the Victims of Fascism had gone up the flue.

The nearest office that issued identity and ration cards, the latter being unobtainable without the former, was installed in an unused shop down the street and operated in a vaguely civilian capacity. Later its functions would be returned to the police. Defeated Germany was not, as yet, allowed a police force of its own.

Business was done there at the snail's pace that had prevented Max going after my ration card earlier. Of twenty-odd people waiting for attention, perhaps half a dozen had seats. The rest leaned against a wall and now and then vouchsafed the more fortunate applicants a hateful glare. The clerks sat behind a counter hunched over shabby desks and scratched away with old-fashioned school pens that needed re-dipping every few seconds. They acted as if nobody was present but themselves.

All of them were disabled, as became evident when they went to the counter or consulted at another desk, and all were as preoccupied by the gnawing in their stomachs as everyone else. The desk drawers in which they kept their hard slices of bread no longer slid smoothly in the grooves, which meant that one or another clerk was always pushing, pulling and jerking to get his bread out and close the drawer again. After one nibble or two the bread would be carefully rewrapped and put back, which entailed more pushes and jerks. German civil servants apparently have it dinned into them that if you perform more than one operation at a time you make fatal mistakes. Only after all possible nibbling, scribbling and related activities had been executed one by one with moody deliberation did the clerks summon the next applicant and come resentfully limping to the counter. The public ruined their whole day.

Max could not employ the time usefully by reading a manuscript and risk losing his turn. He kept one eye on his cheating countrymen and the other on his watch until the only female clerk, a puffy blonde of about forty, called us out of turn. Supposing that such odd fish must have strayed in by mistake she meant to get rid of us, but became excited when she heard Max's story and repeated loudly, "*American?*"

The indignant murmurs behind us ceased. The pens in front of us stopped scratching. She handled my passport like a newborn crown prince.

The public were considered too stupid to fill out their own applications; the clerks did it for them, calling out questions from their desks. Max answered for me hurriedly, coughing a little as he always did when pressed. He had answered these questions time and again to get me into Germany, but there was either no central file or no means to consult it. The blonde wrote with infuriating meticulousness, constantly dipping her pen and applying a blotter.

"Religion?" she sang out mechanically, and just as mechanically Max answered with a glance at his watch, "Jewish."

"What are you saying?" I gasped.

He flushed.

She searched my un-Jewish features for evidence that the incredible reply might be true.

Finally she demanded, goggling, "And you want to live *here?*"

"It's none of her damn business what I want," I said in English.

She lowered her eyes, dipped her pen and wrote.

"Make her tear that up," I said.

"It's completely meaningless," Max told me in a low voice which was a hint to lower mine. "The whole procedure is empty routine."

"The hell it is. We know their routines!"

I was close to vomiting. Was I religious? Did he tell them he was a Protestant? An Aryan? Jewish was a people minus six million. I was too upset to put this into words. I churned helplessly. To be thrown to slavering hyenas by Max!

In the street he pleaded for forgiveness, but only because he pitied my distress. He had been an idiot, he admitted, but fortunately it made no difference. "Such information can never be used again," he said, hurrying in the direction of the *U-Bahn*.

"We have to go back," I said. "She has to destroy that form and write a new one."

"That would only be making an issue of it. Come sweetheart."

"It should be made an issue of!"

I had stopped walking.

"Come," he repeated, and I took one step. "We are not ashamed of —"

I shouted, "It's the duty of a Communist to go to the highest authorities and protest at such questions being asked!"

He kept walking and I kept dragging behind like a furious infant who dares not lose its parent. At our house door he said, "I must leave you now. People are waiting for me."

"Is that all you have to say?"

"What else can I say? I can't undo it now."

"Who's in charge in this country anyway?" I bawled after his receding back.

Everyone, no one was in charge, the Americans, the Russians, the British, the French, and in the last analysis those Germans who were not evil or not yet (or never to be) proved so. Shorn of civil rights, with all the speed and initiative of poisoned earthworms, they were running the bureaucracy in their own traditional way because the victors could not be bothered. And the "good Germans," the great, the heroic Germans had less time than anyone else to iron out wrinkles in the fabric.

Upstairs I discovered that my ration tickets had been slipped into a folding card that said on the front MAKESHIFT IDENTITY BOOK (*behelfsmäßiger Personalausweis*). I tossed it into a drawer, never suspecting what endless complications, sorrow, and expense would result from a makeshift document issued by ersatz authorities in an ex-nation.

Max knocked at the Profts' door and asked Walburga's unemployed older sister to escort me to the coal yard. He would have preferred to leave the recruitment of Welta to Walburga, but she was away in the Soviet Zone taking a three-week crash course in Marxism.

I could have found my way to the coal yard alone. Not easily, but the real problem was that coal and wood were not delivered, they had to be fetched in a handwagon. People who couldn't even get hold of a rag or a *Schrubber* were hardly likely to possess a pre-war treasure that priceless. The Profts crammed theirs, gigantic as it was, into an apartment already choked with the furniture of two families — double-decker cupboards, mausoleal wardrobes, octagonal tables, carved armchairs, and sofas like walled cities. When the door was ever so slightly opened the pieces stored in the foyer loomed toward it like the prisoners in *Fidelio* starved for fresh air. In the cellar a handwagon would have been pinched immediately.

Welta and I managed to wrestle the handwagon down the three flights of stairs without dropping it or stumbling and breaking a leg. Outside it was still pretty cold, but I had wrapped a woolen scarf around my head and was wearing Max's pants for dirty work under my friend's brother's coat. Welta was dressed like a lady, even to mended leather gloves, thin stockings, and a German pot hat.

"I will pull the wagon," she offered dutifully.

I grasped the long handle, gave an initial powerful jerk to get the weight in motion, and was already under way down the middle of the road. Having once taken a course in body mechanics I was bent forward like a team of serfs towing a barge up the Volga from the shore.

Welta tripped along beside me, announcing the direction at each street corner and prattling about some sort of civilian government of the Western sectors. Oh yes indeed, she assured me, of course they had such a thing and she was trying to get a job in it. Her friend *Frau Doktor* So-and-so, a liberal councilor, had held out hope for Welta as a "fellow liberal."

"How far is this place?" I asked.

"How far? Oh! Not far." Her mind was on higher things.

It was at least a mile before I could yank the wagon through the open gates of that coal yard and stretch my stiff arm. Too bad the damn thing only had one handle, I thought. When it was full we would need two — and two oxen.

The coal man was my first Berlin wag, a famous breed beloved of local-color sentimentalists like Max.

"What's this for?" he asked, slyly indicating the handwagon. One of his sooty eyelids drooped and the other fluttered.

"Coal," said Simple Simon, and proffered ration tickets.

The waggery now squirted me in the face like a trick buttonhole: "There isn't a briquette in the yard!"

Welta asked in a respectful tone when there would be.

He shrugged, spread his black hands and smirked, implying that the coal deities didn't take mugs like him into their confidence.

I pulled the cart around to face the gateway and tugged it into the road, saying, "It takes so little to make some people happy."

"Beg pardon? Oh, I understand. Yes. So little," she agreed, and laughed several high-pitched separate ha's. "Yes. Americans have so much humor. That is a pity that he has no coal. And so then came the surprise for the Communists. The Social Democrats won the election with a big majority."

In New York I wouldn't have been caught dead in that getup with a wagon bumping along behind me, but hunched all the way forward as I was, grim with worry and not trying to hide it, I attracted no notice. A human pack mule was part of the Berlin street scene.

Welta prattled on in high good humor, a five-year-old on an outing. "It was a big shock for my poor sister. She did not want to realize Berlin was always Social Democrat. How will it suddenly vote for the Communists? Even rich people, even former National Socialists vote now for the Social Democrats!" National Socialist was the refined term for Nazi.

Out of the corner of an eye on a level with the wagon rim I noticed Welta's legs flitting along in those thin, laddered stockings. "Aren't you freezing?" I asked.

"Freezing? Oh yes. Yes," she agreed, always objective.

"The wind is worse," I said. "It's even colder than when we started out. Don't you feel it?"

"I have bored you," she granted, pleased as Punch. "My mother says I should be myself a candidate. Ha ha ha ha ha!"

"Is there another coal yard we could try?"

"Oh no. No. Unfortunately. We must go back to this bad coal yard. It is the coal yard for our district. I think he lies. I think he would give the coal for money. Or cigarettes."

"Why didn't you tell me this before?"

"I think of it now. You know? One cannot prove it. One *saw* no coal."

"Only on his face and hands," I said, and stopped in my tracks. We were almost home. My coat was spattered with black mud from the yard. Which of us was more asinine, Welta or I?

"Maybe he cannot wash it off," Welta suggested. "The soap is very bad."

How would I explain to Max that with my eyes wide open I had let another bastard put one over on me?

Pregnancy does not sharpen the wits.

"Don't wash dishes in the kitchen sink, the dregs will come up in the bathtub," Max had cautioned, so I absentmindedly washed some in the kitchen sink and found that it was not amusing to get rid of bathtub dregs without a rag. The thing to do was use a basin that sat on the cupboard. When the dishes were put away one trudged through the atelier with the dirty water, trying not to spill any, and emptied it into the john.

Walburga had given Max three flowered plates when he first moved in, and I broke one. He was grieved, but when I broke the second one he was angry and said I held Walburga in low esteem. I pointed out that I had also broken the lid of our precious Paris sugar bowl and one of the matching saucers. In the course of time I broke the entire set, though the hideous kitchen cup the color of yellowed ivory survives to this day.

Only after reaching the front of an endless queue did I learn that we were entitled to an unbelievable *six pounds* of fresh carrots. My shopping net held only two pounds, so the vegetable woman dumped our remaining four into the next customer's receptacle, a superannuated overnight bag.

"No! I come back!" I protested, but the coupons were already snipped off and gone through the slit in the cashier's cigar box. "I go home, I come back," I pleaded in despair, and the women behind me exchanged jeering looks. I didn't know that the quantity of rationed goods per customer was announced in the newspapers.

To me newspapers were something to make fires with. I crumpled half-pages into balls, as Max had shown me, and held a cigarette lighter to them before laying on the kindling. It didn't help much. By what arcane arts he made the stove in the garret respond — and so quickly! — I never found out. I knelt before it like a penitent, begging the wee flamelets not to flee the tinder before the coal caught on, but my briquettes only smoldered, sweated, stank, and became unusable.

Desperate to rate as an Eagle Scout I rushed at the bath boiler and made my first really roaring fire under it. The only trouble was that I had forgotten to fill it with water first. The pale blue cylinder still gleamed as good as new, but its inner wall was sucked together in the middle, never more to be pulled apart.

My long-suffering mate cared for me even after that. We would go to the public baths in Wall Straße, he said. They weren't what I imagined, but nice and clean, with huge tubs. His tenderness toward the contents of my belly knew no bounds. He seemed to realize that for reasons beyond my control my brain had curled up in its covering like a kitten in a chimney corner, while the unpiloted body went through alien chores and botched one effort after another. He was tactful enough never to ask how the novel was coming along.

Who finally fetched my coal ration I no longer know. It wasn't I. It had to have been Max.

Unnoticed by me the Huchels moved to the country near Potsdam, and I forgot their existence. In another era, after the Club's walnut panels and satin brocade had been ripped away and replaced by calcimine in pudding shades of banana and strawberry, Peter sat down at our table and I remembered having seen him only once before. He gave me a withdrawn and absent look and leaned toward Max to talk editorial business. By that time he held one of the most prestigious positions in the German literary community East or West, editor-in-chief of an intellectual bimonthly called *Sinn und Form*. Indeed he was its first editor. The magazine's highbrow standards were his standards. It was in that job that he eventually came to grief.

At the Club we met a funny, jolly Dutchman named Jan Böntjes van Beek, a potter who directed the industrial arts school. He picked up his briefcase from the floor under the table and asked me what this object was called in English. I told him and he broke up in uncontrollable hilarity. "It's not true! Briefcase! *Briefcase!* This is the craziest thing I ever heard!" Then he went on to recommend his wife's obstetrician, "a capacity" whose specialty was cesareans. All five of Jan's children had been delivered that way, and in my thirty-third year I too might be glad of such a doctor.

Dr. Leixl's bearing, though not immodest, suggested that here was a man at the peak of his powers. He was about fifty, with firm features, still-black hair, and capable hands. Leaning back in his office chair he studied me with a benevolent beam and assured me heartily that pregnancy was not an illness and I needn't come in again until labor started. This amazed me, but after all it was better than climbing onto one of those horrible gynecologist's chairs every couple of months and being embarrassed for no good reason. Later Max's secretary told me I would be attended by a midwife. Oh no, I cried. Silly, she said, midwives are an institution in Germany, no reputable hospital would do without them; don't worry, the doctor comes in for the last stage.

He certainly didn't do much for his fee, I thought, but Max was willing to pay it. I hoped he could afford it. I had no idea what he earned, it seemed indelicate to ask; still, I supposed that the editor-in-chief of the biggest publishing venture in Germany, as Aufbau was then, must have been receiving a commensurate salary for his part in making it so.

"I'd type I WENT TO LEIPZIG in red if I had a red half to my typewriter ribbon," I wrote to Chris.

> It was the first German city I've seen. Berlin doesn't count, it's gone. The return of the exiles to this waste makes no more sense to me than lemmings instinctively drowning themselves.
>
> Leipzig thrilled me. On the first mild and gentle day of the year it was opening its spring trade fair, the second since the war. The streets were so gay! My God, automobiles! People! Stands selling wurst sandwiches and beer! Honestly, it was as good as a holiday in Paris, better in a way. The old Rathaus is whole and so is Bach's Thomas Church where we got an incredible surprise, a boys' choir beautifully rehearsing a motet as we walked in. Max almost swooned. He had just explained to me that Leipzig "used to have" a superb choir of boys chosen from all over Germany and given a free education. And they were still superb. It

was a dreamlike experience. As we left trumpeters came out on a platform girdling a steeple nearby and played a slow fanfare. It was like a Germany minus Nazism, like its former self, alive, busy, almost hinting at prosperity if only to show off for the fair.

Sidewalk booths were selling crude and cheap but charming wooden toys and we bought some for our friends' kids in America, but really for ourselves. The one I most hated to part with was a little village with a pink wooden church, a pink town hall, a pink dairy, a white inn, a town gate and a few cottages with blue and orange roofs and window-box flowers painted on.

The industrial products we saw in ten buildings won't do us much good, they were for export and reparations, but they gave the town and us such a feeling of hope . . .

It amazes me, looking back, that we had "done" Leipzig all in one day that year. We left by rail from Berlin's Zoo Station before dawn, returned after midnight too late for the last *U-Bahn*, and tramped another five miles to Friedenau. "It's just a little bit further," Max cheered me on, "We're almost there." We were walking like robots by then, but instead of falling into bed when we got to it, we first unpacked our wooden toys, arrayed them on the table and played with them for at least an hour.

Often after Max blew out the candle we lay side by side for some time in meditative silence. The waning fire soughed its modest farewells with an occasional weak crack. Outside a steady spring rain would be falling. An irregular drip, drip-drip, plop could be heard from the atelier, where a row of pots were set on the floor to catch the leaks.

Max would take my right hand with him when he turned his back and would press it to his bony chest. It helped his asthma. I would massage the source of the trouble with a gentle rotary motion, gradually slow down, and at last leave my palm against it. The thin whistle from the bronchia did not appear to disturb his sleep.

Later he would find himself shut out and chilly. I had rolled myself into the covers. Inch by inch he tugged them free, distributed them fairly, turned to my back and laid his left hand on the slightly swollen abdomen with the tadpole inside. Tranquillity entered him from the tadpole. "My new world," he whispered. "Ol' world," I responded in a dream.

It was always he who fell asleep first, leaving me alone with the puzzle of our two identities. If I wakened him he would say, "Sweetheart, why must you philosophize when it's time to sleep?" When else could I philosophize? It was the only time when my mind could stretch out and consider.

What do the halves of a couple hold in their arms (haves, have-nots) when they hold each other and are imperceptibly changing roles and seeming precedence? Two conglomerations of accidental and peripatetic molecules, restless, willful, impatient of an interfering hand. Autonomous personages, regal, Queen of Sheba and King Solomon on their camels riding to meet in the desert, each followed by the whole train of a life's experiences, only the facts communicable.

The meaning, a will o' the wisp, escapes calculation. A Hansa patrician, poet, Communist, friend, and adviser to many of his country's most distinguished artists, his motto: Who knows God's home? An East Bronx plebeian, working girl, irreverent democrat, ignoramus, and truth-seeker, her motto: A cat may look at a king.

Why, I wondered, had he chosen a yokel like me instead of someone who understood his world? Useless to ask him, he never betrayed the privacy of his heart. Rosl was his wife, not I. In France they had become one. Only by a bitter fluke did she have someone else now, while Max had me. Didn't he write me when he got back to Germany that he had seen her and been "very much attracted"?

"Why did you bother about her husband?" I asked once.

"It wasn't him. It was you."

"Just because we were married?"

"I need you," he said, "it's you I need, your reactions to here and now. I need you like a reference work."

If I was his chart of the immediate, he was past and future to me. He gave me a prism through which centuries and their content were projected on time to come. I held it up to the light and revolved it, but it was not a child's kaleidoscope. As so often happens with priceless gifts (and sensing this made my heart ache) I did not find the key to its use until much later.

Only in our sleeping embrace could we contain one another.

Tiny green leaves appearing on the trees in front of our house cheered us with the thought of entertaining friends at last. The atelier had become temperate. As soon as we received our monthly hunk of beef from the Russians, Max began issuing invitations, usually to artists who had no privileges, and we blew the whole *payok* the following Sunday. Without refrigeration the only possible economy was to cast one's bread upon the waters, and it did return a thousandfold. Those one-course parties were delicious in every sense, hilarious and stimulating.

Once we had the honor of feeding Mary Wigman part of a T-bone steak. How I gazed worshipfully at that idol of my girlhood! In my seventeenth year I saw her perform *Dance of the Earth* in New York. At sixty she was a good sport, though no longer a dancer, and still a magnificent figure of a woman with reddish hair and a wide, laughing mouth. Having infuriated Goebbels and been blacklisted after she and her group did a dance that could be construed as subversive, she easily got permission from the Russians to reopen her school. She told roguish anecdotes about her contacts with them, stepping lightly — great dancer, great woman that she was — to avoid any sensitive Communist toes that might have been under our table.

For people who had their own *payok*, Max prepared a Sunday dinner more humble as to meat but exotic enough by the standards of the time, for example a risotto made interesting with Spam and — if we valued the guests very highly — a rare onion.

Two such guests, though I cannot swear we had an onion that day (if we got three in 1948 it was a lot), were Max's boss at Aufbau, the impressive Erich Wendt, and his sweet wife Lotte. We ate cozily in the gable room, where the tight fit promoted jollity.

Before they arrived Max cautioned me not to let Erich know I had heard his shocking secret, but Erich himself referred to it with a mischievous smile when I complimented him on his English. He said he had learned it in a Soviet prison from the only two sourcebooks his jailer could unearth in the prison library, Thackeray's *Vanity Fair* and an English-Russian dictionary. This explained why his English was almost too good, incongruously high-flown, convoluted, and moldy.

His exile in the Soviet Union started years before the Nazis came to power. As a boy he learned the printing trade, became a Communist in his teens, and published Party tracts that got the police of the Weimar

Republic after him. The Party recommended flight until the hunt was forgotten, but Erich proved so useful at the Soviet publishing house for foreign languages that they kept him on.

His thinking forehead, lean cheeks, strong aquiline nose, and firm chin reminded me of great nineteenth-century Americans like Oliver Wendell Holmes or William Lloyd Garrison. The entire attention of his deep-set, penetrating eyes was engrossed by the person speaking to him. Despite a natural austerity he seemed to me profoundly charitable. For a long time, Erich was the German whose moral excellence I trusted most.

He and Lotte were newlyweds in a honeymoon phase that never seemed to alter. His prematurely white hair and her happy young face made them look a generation apart, but the difference was six years at most. He called her Lotteken. The innocent fringed-gentian eyes and tiptilted dainty nose (every so often one sees a typically Irish face like hers in Germany) gave no hint of the risks she had run. In the underground she had been a courier, outwitted the Gestapo time and again, and finally escaped across the Swiss border by the skin of her teeth.

After they went home Max confided a still more horrifying secret: Erich had not been the only German Communist jailed through a misunderstanding in the Soviet Union. There were tales of worse fates than his, though one never heard them from the survivors themselves — insofar as they had survived. It was a tragedy. Some died before the misunderstanding could be cleared up. How, no one knew.

It stood to reason that more was going on in Erich's jail than a sympathetic turnkey promoting a prisoner's peaceful study of English. Honorable suppression of dishonorable truth was the Communist ethic in those years. An example I came to know well was Noel Field, innocent fulcrum of the Rajk and Slansky trials. Most kept silent to the grave.

As editor-in-chief of the Party mouthpiece *Neues Deutschland*, the paper in which Max's theater reviews appeared, Lex Ende was only technically Max's superior. If Lex had wanted a reviewer who needed supervision he would have picked someone else. The two men knew each other's strengths as only people can who have been together in concentration camp.

It was in New York by cigarette glow that Max first told me about Lex, his "best friend." In Paris before the Nazi invasion Lex had been editor of the German Party organ in exile.

The camps set up for Germans by the French collaborators were not death factories like Auschwitz, but a subtler kind of Gehenna. Inmates unsustained by any hope or faith died not only from the total lack of hygiene, the filth, exposure, hunger, and persecution, but in the last analysis from demoralization. Communists and Jews had to work alongside Nazis who were constantly plotting to waylay, beat up, or actually kill them. Pretending that one German was as bad as another, the French guards deliberately looked the other way.

On a logging work detail in the forest of Montargis, as Max was dreamily hacking off the smaller branches of a tree he had just felled, he heard a roar of warning from Lex and looked round to see another giant tree falling his way. He raced through the cleared aisle, and the crown just missed his head, but got him on the shoulder and bounced up once. In that split second Lex reached him and dragged him aside, saving his life.

Max was one of those for whom Lex wangled exit permits before the advancing Wehrmacht could close in on Marseilles. Readers of Anna Seghers' novel *Transit* will recall what an intricate proceeding this was, and sown with legalistic booby traps. It required not only money, smuggled by courier, but strong nerves and the cunning to find and cultivate contacts in the various consulates. When the last of Lex's flock was on a ship headed through submarine-infested waters for the Americas (not necessarily to arrive, but he had done his best) he slipped quietly back into the Maquis.

I was especially keen to meet this intrepid friend, but he was always too busy for a purely domestic meeting at our place, far from his usual haunts. We compromised. Lex and his wife invited us to a Sunday meal at their apartment in the Russian Sector.

The house where Lex and Trude lived was part of a dingy five-story row facing a dirt rectangle, formerly a small park, where children played and a few trees and sparse weeds still managed to hold their own. The other three sides were bounded by similar houses, part of a thickly populated area that by some fluke had escaped the bombing.

Lex was a dark, balding man in shirtsleeves, his eyes glinting with mischief. An electric, masculine dynamo inside him dwindled the living room as he strode restlessly about. Trude was a resolute brunette, as collected as he was mercurial. She was holding their little son on her lap when we arrived, and feeding him mush. She was not one of those compulsive Germans who, with both hands tied up, anxiously nod in the direction of their elbow, meaning you should grasp that or at least pat it in lieu of a handshake. With a composed smile she promised to attend to us as soon as the child was back in his crib. What she then served, such an absorbing question in those days, passed from my memory; I only know it was homely and generous and as good a German dinner as old Luchow's on Fourteenth Street might have cooked if similarly handicapped.

"Ah, you should have seen *her* when she was in your condition," Lex boasted. "She looked like a locomotive!"

"It was all in front and I carried it *this* high," she confirmed, basking in her husband's admiration.

And this is all I ever saw of Trude. When I try to remember more, all I can picture is something I never glimpsed myself, that belly preceding her in triumph from room to room. Once, fleetingly, about a year later, I saw Lex leaving the Club as I was arriving. He gave me a hurried nod of recognition. I didn't know it was to be my last view of him.

His drop from grace was not as precipitous as that of an elevator cut from its cables. It was more like the descent in slow, slow motion of one of those glass hotel lifts that slide down an open shaft in full view of the public on the ground floor. By the time it vanishes imperceptibly into the basement the cocktail drinkers in the foyer have forgotten there was a lone man going down in it. He had not banged against the glass. He had not shouted for help. From a distance he had looked perfectly well and relaxed.

Even to poisoned Germany June came, overwhelming me with homesickness. Suppressing a lump in my throat that spread to the heart I darned Max's socks and made a garbage-can lining out of *Neues Deustchland*, then seated myself at the typewriter. The novel begun in Paris was picking up.

An electronic noise downstairs drew me to the window. A small truck was moving slowly away as a loudspeaker mounted on the back kept repeating some message. It was June 24, 1948, a watershed in German history.

The truck could be heard weaving up and down other streets, the loudspeaker growing ever fainter; then it approached again. This time women and old men tumbled out of doors and tagged after it. Near the corner it stopped for a few minutes before crawling on its way. It was a radio substitute. We didn't even own a broken one.

After a while Walburga's Tante Agnes knocked. She was a retired schoolteacher with a characterful nose and erect bearing, who in her youth had fought for women's right to equal education. She courteously refused to impose by coming in, but between threshold and stair explained in her lovely Received English, doubtless polished on trips to the British Isles long ago, that sixty new marks backed by the dollar would be issued to every adult who handed in sixty old ones. It was the same currency they were already using in West Germany.

"I was afraid you wouldn't understand through all that crackling and blaring," Tante Agnes said tactfully. "Don't worry if you've no money in the house. The offer is good for two more days."

I thanked her and went back to the typewriter.

Max burst into the apartment that evening to exclaim, "I hope you didn't exchange any money!"

I had to laugh. The most money I ever saw at a time was ten marks. I didn't mind. In a place with no goods, what would I want money for? Berlin in its weird way was like the forest primeval.

He seemed greatly relieved that I hadn't soiled my hands, and we went out on the balcony to inspect his hard little green tomatoes. He knelt down and touched individual plants like an old country doctor visiting patients. Here and there he moved up the string that tied one to a stick. The string had been thriftily unknotted from CARE packages, the sticks hatcheted off our rationed kindling wood.

"Inside of a month you'll see how red and juicy they get," Max promised. "They'll be luscious."

He may well have been thinking that in a month we and our tomatoes could be blown to Hiroshima. He read the papers of all sectors and followed appalling altercations in the Allied Control Council whose details I learned only years later from brittle, yellow pages in an archive. He didn't want to worry me.

As it happened, things were worse than the most avid reader of German newspapers could have discovered. An independent Australian journalist covering the inter-Allied row revealed in a book published two years later (Wilfred Burchett, *Cold War in Germany*) that the new marks could have bought out the Soviet Zone's entire production in 1948; but it was neither in the Soviet nor the American interest to divulge this.

The word "American" here is my shorthand for "Trizonian." It was the Americans, after all, who called the shots in Western occupation policy. Britain was heavily indebted to the one ally which had been spared war on its own soil. France, a non-victor, was included as a gesture of calculated magnanimity.

A large vermilion and black proclamation signed by Marshal Vassily Sokolovsky, Commandant of Greater Berlin, appeared early next morning on the cylindrical billboard in front of our house. The new currency was illegal, it said. Anybody found with it on his person would be punished.

My neighbors barely glanced at the ukase, elaborately manifesting boredom as they passed. I noticed a couple of sneers at me for standing there and laboring to understand the German. A Soviet Zonal counter-reform had just wiped out nine-tenths of those people's savings, but good American money (i.e., marks based on it) was already being paid out across the street in the beer parlor, our neighborhood's exchange bureau for the three-day operation. People were emerging with crisp bluish bills that they waved complacently at the queue still waiting on the sidewalk.

What they could do with the money was still unclear. Berlin lay cut off from supplies one hundred and ten miles inside the Soviet Zone. All road, rail, and river transport leading to it from the West was now block-aded by the Red Army. Shopkeepers had let down their shutters, it looked like a national holiday. All you could buy was a newspaper for twenty old pfennigs on the street corner. A block farther on it cost two old marks. People grabbed them at any price, but the information was confusing.

Customers could pay "in whatever currency they preferred to offer," the scribblers suggested. They reassured people who worked in the East (the majority of jobs were there) that no one urgently *needed* the new money; it was only for extras. Rationed food, rent, fares, postage, phone calls, taxes, gas, and electricity would be payable as before in "East marks," a designation just invented. Those who worked in the West would soon be receiving a percentage of their wages in "West marks."

Sokolovsky chastised West Berlin by cutting off its electricity, and General Lucius D. Clay in a silly pet had the gas line to the marshal's own stove blocked; Sokolovsky was housed in a suburb adjacent to the American Sector and supplied by its gas works. But then Clay came up with a counterblow more appropriate to his rank and his country's resources: the famed air lift. It started with a hundred planes a day, a drop in the bucket. Coal for two million people and the "extras" promised had to be supplied, not just food rations. The operation was going to cost.

The Russians changed their tactics. They restored two hours of electricity out of twenty-four and offered to honor Western ration cards in their own sector. Yet most of West Berlin scorned the red bounty, despite the tasteless dehydrated airlift potatoes (they saved space in the holds) that stayed unchewable after three days of soaking; and not because the West Berlin municipality threatened to penalize those who accepted it. There was no need for such a threat. When Max came home to the American Sector cheerily swinging a shopping net full of real potatoes and the women in our street ran after him begging to know where to buy them, the answer made them draw back as if from a leper.

By whatever light filtered in from the street the storekeepers nearest us reopened their dusky premises. Most had little or nothing to offer. Herr Griesbach put a sign on the door of his minuscule beauty parlor, hopefully stating that he would "accept" either currency; and not only took my greasy notes with his usual politeness but thanked me for bringing the usual towel, briquettes, and soap from a Macy's sale (twelve cakes for a dollar).

The haberdasher, or was it lingerie or notions (how could a newcomer tell, when even the sign was gone) removed his padlock, cleaned the window, and placed in it an enticing pair of nylon stockings from heaven knows where, probably the American PX, a notorious blackmarket source. Nevertheless the soiled legend about rags for textile credits still dangled tipsily: who knew which authority would come out on top in the end? Beside the stockings was a tentatively penciled price so pale I could hardly read the word "West." Tropical Fruits displayed seven measly oranges on a plate, likewise accompanied by a timorous, almost illegible West-mark tag.

The pilots now zoomed so low over our balcony that I had to sunbathe in a swimsuit. It was a wonder any sunrays at all found their way through so many fuselages. The squadrons increased by geometric progressions, it seemed, and flew day and night. Still, no space was allotted in the holds for nourishment as bulky as garden fruit. Fresh milk for babies and expectant mothers was out of the question; instead imported undies and shiny hardware beckoned from some shop windows. Prices in the new currency were now marked on them brazenly.

Squinting up from my sun cot at the metallic dazzle I tried to count how many planes thundered over in an hour. The roughly one hundred and twenty-five I clocked were only the ones immediately above me. Planes were not only stretched across the whole sky but were flying in phalanxes one above the other in perilous proximity. Fortunately I didn't know this at the time, I couldn't see the upper layers. The unmated mourning dove that frequented our balcony eaves and sounded like a rumbling stomach now moved its beak unheard against the continuous roar. Was it edible, I wondered. Could a blowgun be made from a rolled-up sheet of typing paper?

Our faithful nomads Bill Blake and Christina Stead kept our accounts in one European country after another and mailed staples which nearly always reached us, but we hadn't thought of candles. Tante Agnes once helped from her own hoard after the meter was sealed, but how could I borrow now that the *Drogerie* (the "soap store," as Gafert called it for my illiterate benefit) was selling splendid tall white candles for only one-fifty West?

The woman behind the counter eyed me strangely when I explained that I had no such money. As one points a beggar to the back door she showed me an alternative for East pfennigs, a cardboard jam-jar cover filled with something congealed. In its center was a white knot that grew into a tiny end of string if coaxed with a fingernail.

It became one of my jobs, while Max wrote at night, to tend the fitful burning of this excuse for a candle. It guttered, it hissed, it waved its wick until it collapsed and snuffled in its sauce of adulterated tallow. To prevent the flame drowning itself I would sit on the bed and repeatedly lean forward to flick up the failing wick with a vegetable knife. As occupations went, this one was peaceful and mindless enough for a woman six months gone.

At that period I was wearing a preposterously glamorous long-sleeved bluish frock from the thirties, possibly even the twenties, lent me by Pagy's wife "Puma" (the artist Lotte Pritzel). She could no longer use it, diminished as she was by age, hunger, mental anguish under the Nazis, and the morphine she was still taking to deaden it.

A not-quite-serious party dress, once very expensive, its jabot cascaded from throat to hem while almost invisible paisley arabesques understated themselves in its weave; and I wore it day in and day out like a Hoover apron because there was nothing else to accommodate my girth. Besides being far too heavy for the season, these indestructible trappings were now so tight that the arrival from New York of a simple beige cotton wraparound that would expand indefinitely sent me into raptures. A present from Gina, it was my first, last, and only real maternity garment. I longed to go somewhere in it, looking normal in a normal scene.

But where? By next morning Max had an inspiration. He had seen a jumble shop ("Remember the one we used to pass on the way to antipasto in the San Remo? Wasn't it McDougal Street near Bleecker?") that might just amuse me. It was next to the Petri Church, two *U-Bahn* stops from his office. He told me how to find it, dumped some messy bank notes and discolored coins onto the table, and rushed to work.

Sun shone, leaves twinkled, I bagged my first Berlin pork chop. Budgeting every minute of electricity, which that week began at noon in our district, I first heated water to wash underwear. By one-thirty I had to be under the drier, the chop inside me and the dress ironed. It was crushed from its eight-week imprisonment in a box.

Our iron heated quite slowly, so to save time I started the chop. It smelled delectable as it fried. Returning to the atelier to check the iron I cleverly remembered to take the sun cot along lest laundry drip on it, and opened the door to the dark passage where it belonged. Mechanically I pressed the light switch, and pop! I had blown the fuse. Hadn't Max told me never to turn on a light if more than one electric appliance was plugged in? He had.

No time for despair, I ate the half-fried chop with a cold potato, standing up, put on Puma's dress and raced downstairs. Frau Hasse the house agent, a hard-looking young widow related to the landlord, lived on the ground floor in the right-hand ell of the court. She had grown prettier and more relaxed since the West mark, but also cooler to tenants who got their income in the Russian Sector. Maliciously she looked me up and down. "Where would I get a fuse?" she sneered.

"We pay rent, landlord gives fuse," I reasoned, glancing at my watch. She told me to buy a fuse from the electrician around the corner. It would cost only a few West pfennigs.

"Rent East mark, electricity East mark, fuse East mark!" I maintained hotly. "Fuse from house!"

"But your husband can get a fuse in the Russian Sector," she mocked, meaning she too had seen him swinging his bag of potatoes, or been told about it. The system of Nazi tattlers in every house still functioned.

I ran to look for Gafert and felt lucky to find her at once. She was cleaning the vestibule next door with a substantial new floor rag. The stick of her *Schrubber* was the same, but it had a new business end screwed on. She was just pressing its stiff bristles into the wet rag and giving the floor hell when I announced tragically, "Fuse *kaputt!*" She let go the *Schrubber* to clap her hands together once, resoundingly, at chin level, to demonstrate — as the stick banged the floor — how well she understood the dimension of the calamity. She cast up her rusty eyeballs and shook her head over the poor pregnant *gnädige Frau* and the poor *gnädiger Herr* whose principles made them so unrealistic.

"I only one fuse too," Gafert mourned. "Everybody one fuse."

Herr Griesbach spread his hands helplessly as I arrived breathless and perspiring to discover a usurper in my place at the basin. She had seized it in the time it took me to get back upstairs, fetch my towel, soap and briquette, and tear back down and around the corner. Frau Professor was ten minutes late, Griesbach pointed out. He apologized, but it wouldn't work out with the electricity.

Frau Griesbach was administering a henna rinse at the other basin, a fact whose meaning only sank is as I walked to the *U-Bahn*. A henna rinse! What world was this!? So that was why when she cried *"Guten Tag!"* her flashing smile instantly vanished. They wished I would instantly vanish. I wasn't ten minutes late, only five. A customer without West marks was like a Jew right after the Nuremberg laws were passed. I smoldered.

Getting out at Spittelmarkt station all I saw was a vast, completely annihilated space, silent as the Milky Way. It was not in the path of the airlift. Not a single landmark remained to suggest where the hospital or the market had once stood or where Spittelmarkt ended and its former surroundings began. The sun beat down, there was no shade.

As an elderly couple picked their way over the detritus they raised small drifts of ashy sand. Following them I finally made out a landmark, the badly marred Gertrauden Bridge and the weathered figure of Saint Gertraude herself overlooking an arm of the Spree River. To my left was the burned-out Petri Church minus its steeple and beside it a sort of cave under a splayed hood of rubble.

There is something infinitely reassuring about limits, walls, a low ceiling in the midst of emptiness. Down two steps, refreshing coolness came to meet me through the open door. An old woman sat huddled in semidarkness on a sagging armchair of figured plush. Around her shoulders was a three-cornered shawl with long, thinned-out fringes.

"*Guten Tag*," I said.

"*Guten Tag*," scraped the worn voice. She had little use for it any more. Her swollen legs were the same thickness from knees to soles in backless felt slippers. She made no effort to get up, only followed me about the cubicle with her eyes.

Surely not this immovable invalid, but someone, some relative, must have scavenged long among the ruins for every geegaw that could still be identified and dusted off. There were discolored beads, buttons that looked bitten on, a small, torn pre-Hitler flag, a doll with disheveled hair and one foot, a cracked graniteware frying pan lacking a handle, a chromo of a police dog with noble, attentive eyes, a bronze picture frame that was coming apart. I found bolts of different sizes, some not even rusted, but no screws for our balcony door; a disagreeably yellowish dish whose center shimmered like oil on water around the portrait of a Greek Orthodox priest; a covered tureen that wasn't bad, and much, much more, all so crammed together on battered furniture that at first sight it made an intriguing impression.

Circling around and about to rediscover the same faults in the same discards, I kept returning to the tureen. It seemed to have nothing wrong with it. No cracks, no chips, how was this possible? I lifted the cover carefully, conscious of the somber, steady gaze of the old woman. It was in perfect condition. So was the rim, over which I slowly ran my finger. It was oval, white. If only it had been plain white! It had an undistinguished border design in light green that resembled cross-stitch.

In New York Max often halted in the street and stooped, unselfconscious as a child, to pick up some piece of trash and examine it judiciously. The habit came from years of deprivation and concentration camp, but it embarrassed me. And now look at me! "How much this costs?" I asked.

"Twenty-five marks," the old voice scraped.

Max would have picked it up out of the gutter with a cry of delight. We owned no serving bowl of any kind, we dished food straight out of the pot. Eagerly I hurried to Aufbau Press with my tureen wrapped in newspaper.

The door to the editor-in-chief's graciously proportioned office inspired respect. It was really two doors, one backing the other, soundproofed with quilted leather on both outer sides and joined by smooth, noiseless brass fittings that made them move as one. The air between them as they opened or closed was displaced with a soft, luxurious whoosh. Bursting in was impossible.

Not that I dreamed of bursting in. The presence of Max's perfect secretary Fräulein Schmidt forbade that in any case, though she was no dragon. She had bright red cheeks and prominent blue eyes whose rolling she exaggerated to produce comic effects. Not much older than me, she praised amoral spinsterhood in quite good English, declaring it the most tolerable existence a woman could hope for. She would never love again anyway, she said, she had given her heart to that French slave laborer she hid from the Nazis; one couldn't love twice.

This story was the *carte d'identité* she showed whenever she met a foreigner, but I think it was true. I liked her without reservation and would have seen her with pleasure outside the office if Max hadn't forbidden it. That sort of "phony democracy," he said, was not understood in Germany.

What was phony about it, I objected. And I wasn't to call her Elli either. She couldn't call me by my first name. Why couldn't she? Whether I agreed or not we weren't going to mix business with private life.

"I'll tell your husband you're here," she said. Pushing the doors open just a little, not even showing her head, she called, "It's your charming wife!"

He came forward to greet me, cordial but wan and distracted.

"Look what I got," I said.

He pushed piles of books and manuscripts aside to make room on his handsome polished desk and I set the tureen before him, stepping back with the squashed newspaper in my hand.

He was somewhat at a loss.

"It's a tureen," I explained. "For serving beautiful soup so rich and green in. Or stew. To company."

Though well versed in Alice lore he missed the allusion, cleared his throat and said it seemed usable. "Where did you get it?" he asked, and "How much was it?"

The questions were asked out of politeness, just to say something, anything, lest I think he grudged me a minute or two. He didn't notice that I was still wearing Puma's dress instead of the new one. He lit a cigarette although his last one was burning in the tray. I realized that I was being one of those useless wives who sashay into the husband's place of employment and interrupt brain work out of sheer self-indulgence. The secretary doesn't even dare to peep in, has to call out "It's your charming wife," in her most ingratiating tone. I vowed to myself never to drop in like that again.

"Twenty-five marks," I replied.

"Twent—? No. *What* did you say?"

I repeated it.

"Twenty-five marks? For that?"

I lifted the lid. "Look, it's in perfect condition."

"I could understand such a price for Meissen ware," he said "Highway robbers. They took you for a sucker. What were you thinking of?"

Utterly dashed, I said I hadn't thought it was that awful. Oh, it wasn't *awful*. But twenty-five marks! He shook his head and walked away from the poor inoffensive monstrosity. "Good heavens," he said.

"Well, what's twenty-five lousy so-called marks," I demanded, beginning to feel aggrieved.

He had thought nothing of spending a *hundred* and twenty-five marks on a bottle of rotgut from a black-market man to celebrate Walburga's return from Marxist school. Rotgut was sacred, and above all it was *his* rotgut. Throwing away money on a binge, well! — *that* made sense!

I didn't say any of this. Probably both of us at that moment were hearing echoes from the time in New York when we were so poor and he drank so much and we nearly lost each other for good.

He came back from the window and said as gently as he could, "There's been a currency reform, don't you see? The money was revalued. Twenty-five marks today aren't as lousy and so-called as you think. The water's been taken out of them. They're all that's left of two hundred and fifty. Sweetheart, I explained to you about the stickers pasted on the bills. That's what they mean."

"You can't buy anything with them anyway, so what's the difference," I protested, but I was ashamed. Really, my head was like a sieve.

"They don't buy much, it's true," he said patiently, "but there's Party dues to be paid and union dues and Club dues and social security, all figured on a sliding scale, and it slides like hell."

"All right," I said, wrapping up the misfortune.

He walked after me to the door, apologizing, "I'd ask you to wait at the Club, but I've got a conference in ten minutes and don't know when it will end."

"I blew the fuse," I said.

"*Ach du lieber Gott. . . .*"

He said it with the utmost restraint, he even laughed and stroked my hair. "Never mind," he said.

In August we were granted a three-week respite at the Baltic Sea. We had looked forward to it intensely, for in Berlin we could neither write nor think. Laundry service was suspended. Without electricity or coal we were cooking over fires made with tomato sticks, when we had any to spare, or *Brennplatten* — brick-shaped inflammables that stank of tar and turned everything black. An airlift plane crashed on a roof just a few blocks from us, killing the crew and burning half the house down.

In the picturesque fishing village of Ahrenshoop there appeared to be no fish whatever, though we saw the men going out early in their boats and earnest Kulturbund artists sketching them as they repaired their nets on the beach. It wasn't just a charade. After dark the fishermen moored in a secret cove, smoked as much of their catch as they considered a just recompense for aggravation, and sold it on the black market.

The whole village, which had no say in the matter, had been contracted to the Kulturbund and felt put-upon. Our fishless meals were served in the *Kurhaus*, a white-painted hotel on the bluff, but as it had few guest rooms most of us slept in fishermen's cottages between the dunes and the road. They had thatched roofs and decorative carved figures on the rooftrees that enchanted us, but we had to share the bedsteads with fleas. Brought by the Red Army, our fisherman's wife told me acidly.

Survivors of Vernet or Les Milles joked that the hotel menu was no worse than the fare in any good French concentration camp. We were privileged, of course. No ration coupons were demanded for our small portions, and victims of fascism knew how to forage. It was Kantorowicz's portly nose that sniffed out a source of smoked fish. With his customary cavalier indifference to facts he glorified it into *Zander*, a highly prized river fish, which was like calling herring roe Beluga caviar, and he and Friedl invited us to their room to share it. Whatever its real name, we devoured it with shameless moans of pleasure and hysterical mirth (the landlady must have wondered what we were up to), using two hotel spoons to fillet it and hygienically licking them off like cats before passing them.

Once as Max and I walked along the wet sand, a wave swept in a shoal of sprats at our feet and swept them out again, leaving five behind which we grabbed. Ingenious Max grilled them in a deep hole with bush twigs from the dunes, and by God they were good! Another time, flushed with achievement, he brought two fresh eggs from somewhere which we ate as an after-swim snack he called yowza. It sounded like whoopee. (*Jause*: Austrian dialect for a late-afternoon bite.) Even the cheese at the hotel seemed to me "good though crude," as I wrote Chris, simply because it was my first cheese of any kind in Germany, but everyone else referred to it as Igelit, a linoleum ersatz. It came in rectangular lappets as tough as roofing shingles unless eaten within a day of manufacture.

But there was no ill nature in the guests' cracks, they were delighted with any excuse for hilarity. People who returned of their own free will to restore the country Brecht called "Germany, wan mother" expected nothing in those days but what they themselves put together. It was not the worst of times. As for the weather, they laughed that off too. The Baltic climate was seldom inviting, they assured me gleefully. My cotton maternity dress was useless, I had to wear a thick old raveling sweater of Max's over trousers donated to him in France by a fat Samaritan.

On their first day in Ahrenshoop guests immediately dug a *Burg* or castle in the sand, a capacious pit to keep them below wind level when lying down. Each castle was outlined by a circle of closely set stones, with initials in pebbles or shells at the entrance. To use a strange castle when its owners were out was bad form, nearly as uncouth as staring, oneself fully clothed, into the nudist castles farther up the beach. A castle cost upkeep like any abode; wind havoc made it necessary to reset and brush the sand off the stones regularly. Fanatics did it all the time. Distinguished writers, philosophers, and other luminaries strolled in bathrobes from castle to castle and chatted decorously across the dotted line of stones, their chuckles suggesting that bad weather was good for the soul.

A castle didn't help when it really rained. One had to rent a basket-chair of lacquered, closely woven wicker the minute one arrived (there weren't enough to go round) and turn its thick, reinforced back to the elements. Basket-chairs had lined, vaulted roofs, some adjustable to protect the eyes from sun glare, and straw seats for two covered with ticking. Unfortunately one's legs stuck out and the wind snaked up the inside of trousers. Couples with children needed a basket-chair *and* a castle, from which all fled together when it poured.

In the end I was relieved to be back in Berlin. Our tomatoes were red and firm, yet unattractive to sparrows, and the squash we had given up as hopeless was flowering. Even the water tasted good.

To Chris I wrote of having swum only twice, whereas Max, I bragged, plunged into icy breakers nearly every day. Of course we both rested and read aloud to each other from *Wuthering Heights* (without even noticing the Baltic aptness of the title).

When I first thought of writing this memoir and Christina sent back my letters, I was embarrassed to find one dated September 1, 1948, which credulously prophesied, "We understand the 'West mark' is to disappear from Berlin." It was a rumor floated by optimists after a conference in Moscow between Stalin, American ambassador Walter Bedell Smith, French representative Yves Chataigneau, and their British colleague Frank Roberts. It was the Western allies who requested the conference, as the *Moscow News* finally disclosed forty years later, or not quite: May 18, 1988. Smith, who did the talking for all three Western allies, offered to seek any acceptable currency solution on condition that the blockade be lifted.

To this Stalin replied (according to the bewhiskered release) that the introduction by the Western allies of a special currency for Berlin was calculated to disrupt the economy of the Soviet Zone and effectively split Germany into two states. Juristically speaking, he said, the three Western powers had themselves undermined their right to station troops in Berlin. The blockade would be lifted, however, if simultaneously the three Western powers annulled the special currency for Berlin and replaced it with the currency of the Soviet Zone.

Smith said he would bring this proposal to the attention of his government, but doubted it would be accepted. What else could he say.

With the baby due in November the search for a new home could no longer be put off. It was Max, sparing my heavy-footedness, who ran after the few leads he got, alerting me only when a place attracted him.

Every lead fell through. By mid-October Max was so exhausted and worried by the seemingly hopeless search that I felt like crying at the sight of him, so worn and old, as caved-in as the time his teeth were pulled.

Without telling him, I went to the American Military Housing Department. A poorly dressed, peaked and plain young girl was sitting at a typewriter in the outer office. Maybe there was no inner office. She was about nineteen and had a German accent. I showed my passport and explained our situation. "I'm expecting a child in four weeks," I said, and waited to be referred to the man in charge.

But the girl only asked in a businesslike way, "Is your husband a Victim of Fascism?"

Astonished, I said yes he was.

"Do you have his membership number?"

"No, but we can phone his office and ask."

She got right through, spoke to him in German, wrote down the information, and scribbled an address for me on a memo slip. The place was in the suburb Nikolassee, almost as far West as you could get in the American Sector. She gave me directions and wished me luck.

A slight, underfed German girl was running the American Military Housing Department as she saw fit!

We got the keys with a minimum of red tape. An army officer and his family had just vacated the apartment and gone back to the States. It was the lower floor of a two-family box-shaped white stucco house on the crest of a gentle rise, with woods behind it and neighbors in identical houses not too close together. It consisted of three and a half rooms plus kitchen, bath, terrace, and garden, and cost 150 East marks a month.

Love alone had kept Max from falling off the edge of his bachelor bed as my belly mounted and I had no idea which way to tip it any more. It had been a case of "Lie close to the wall, says Brian O'Lynn." On a piece of hoarding we tacked up a want ad for a second-hand double bed (still rare in Germany, salaciously known as a French bed) and two comfortable armchairs; and got them right away for East marks. Two weeks before labor began we moved in.

PART III

Autobiography would be better without its author, if this were possible. He would appear as a witness of the events and of his own person. That does no harm. A period is being viewed. The questions is: By whom? It obliges the author to introduce but not protrude himself. Parading the ego leads to contradictions. One's own moral muddle comes to light. . . . The period viewed is equally ignorant of itself.

— HEINRICH MANN
    A Period is Viewed

NIKOLASSEE, ACCORDING to Max, was one of Berlin's swankiest and most exclusive suburbs. Had been. For the moment it gave off no more atmosphere than a disused backdrop. Residents of rundown mansions without servants now, shamed by their shopping bags, looked neither right nor left in the street lest someone be inclined to greet them.

Even in our newish, relatively modest project where no fences or bushes separated the small rear gardens, neighbors refrained from overstepping. There were not even trespassing dogs; there were no dogs. The animal-loving Germans were not in a position to feed pets. The sparrows of Nikolassee had remained god-fearing, perhaps because few bombs had fallen there and the airlift bypassed it; they too kept a respectful distance.

An old photo snapped by my brother shows that on the terrace beneath our kitchen window the stucco was crumbling, but we never noticed it then. A fatigued Max just home from work sits sunk in contemplation of his ten-month baby's outdoor meal. I am invisible except for a bare arm and the hand extending the spoon as D. opens her little bill. How we acquired such a smart nursery table with built-in chair and colored rings along one side that she could twirl while eating I cannot imagine. It could even be converted into a high chair. Maybe Max was receiving his stingy minimum percentage of West marks by then, at first denied in reprisal for those potatoes he had bought in the Soviet Sector.

The day we moved in a young woman looked out of an upstairs window next door and gave me a kind smile in acknowledgment of my condition. From our window I noticed subsequently that she had small children, so when the time came I climbed her stairs to consult her about the pains coming at irregular intervals, and at once Max sped downhill to telephone. Four months later, a summer-hot Easter Sunday, she exclaimed, "*Goldig!*" from her window, ravished by the sight of D. lying naked on a blanket in the sun. In this way I learned the word for adorable, but we never got as far as asking each other's name. Too recently we had been enemies. I think we both feared some irrevocable gaffe if we fell into the habit of neighborliness.

The apartment above ours was unoccupied at first, which gave Max a chance to reconnoiter in the cellar and find an abandoned baby carriage. It waggled when pushed. A rear wheel had come off and been wired onto the axle, but it could be used in fair weather for parking an infant on the terrace. He also investigated the cellar of a bombed house down the slope, the only casualty in the project, and in two trips brought home a set of folding garden chairs with a matching table that needed only a paint job. No one noticed his salvaging, prudently undertaken after twilight. In early spring he bought a baby apple tree and transplanted it in the garden to grow up with D. She would get its first apple and lie some day under its branches to read the German classics.

D. stands for daughter, delight, dismay. It is not the initial of her real name. At eleven she forbade me to write about her ever again. It hadn't occurred to me that any of her classmates might read an adult magazine and make her feel like a fool.

On her first day out of the womb a hint of Max's bone structure in her face was alarming. The miracle awed him, but I feared for a girl with the armature of that extraordinary nose and so much space between the temples for brains. By the second day the threat vanished, at least outwardly. She was just another pink baby with a button nose, packaged in pink flannel for presentation by the smiling nuns of West Sanatorium. It was a merciful disguise. Through her I came to understand more about the mind of her father; and his vagaries in retrospect gave me a little insight into her.

I was hardly present at her birth. The labor had been so bad and prolonged that it was stopping, so Dr. Leixl made his first appearance and five masked attendants closed in. One gave me a whiff of gas and I presume it was Leixl who pulled her out with a high forceps. Despite all the *payoks* and CARE packages, so little milk was manufactured by my breasts that the desperate child bit the nipples bloody. One more time the doctor was summoned, sat back in a guest armchair as if he had all day and, smiling benignly, agreed to anything: "No more breast-feeding? No more breast-feeding!"

Leaving the hospital via wheelchair I was too enfeebled to notice that the main person was not with me. Max remembered at the last minute and hurried back to fetch her. He and a chauffeur from Aufbau carried us both into a BMW, out of it again and into the house, and the next day a combined nursemaid-housemaid moved into our extra bedroom.

Sister Margarete, as the nursemaid called herself, had neither a nursing certificate nor references, but swore that her last two alleged cases had been wives of American colonels who thought the world of her. Margarete's proudest boast, and this one we believed, was her employment in the household of Alfred Rosenberg, a pet of Hitler and editor of *Völkische Beobachter*, who was sentenced to death in the Nuremberg trials. With prurient relish she told me of the mornings when she used to bring breakfast in bed to him and his lady, both still naked and flushed from their sport.

She was a feudal relic whose self-respect was based solely on the master's might. Despising employers with secondhand furniture (easy chairs with the stuffings sticking out, and they're not even ashamed!) she soon began spoiling for a fight, brassily hectoring, not so much stealing as confiscating the baby's rationed milk powder for the benefit of a more deserving person, herself.

"They warned me at the hospital not to come here!" she flung at me. "You think you can treat me like a black Negro in America!"

"Black Negroes in America are a damn sight better than you," Max told her when she repeated this to him. He fired her on the spot and she went off squawking like a chicken, "And I so decent! I so decent!" In fact she was pleased as Punch, having deliberately provoked the firing the day before Christmas, which enabled her to collect the full month's pay.

Only then could we settle down in peace to study the exquisite little creature we had produced. She wasn't crying any more, now that her basket stood in the kitchen overnight. The bud of her serenity opened as soon as she was freed from the tobacco smoke and clacking typewriters of the one room we could afford to heat. Evening was her best time. Awakening thoughts like soft little breezes fluttered across her silken forehead and she regarded calmly the two skinny giants who gazed down at her through shining spectacles.

"One really has to love her," said Max.

The words came out like a confession wrung from him. He seemed bewildered by his emotion. All along he had wondered how and when love for one's offspring arose. Suppose it didn't arise?

One morning before I could stand on my feet without pain, a loud knocking compelled me to leave my chair. I was surprised to see at the front door the other American wife in our circle, a recent arrival in Germany. Her name was Alma. I had once met her at the theater. After I had squeezed my nine months immensity into and out of our row she asked in ladylike accents, but pointedly, "When are you — ah — expecting?" which meant, Do you want to give birth in the aisle?

Now she announced with mock bumptiousness, "I didn't come to visit you. It's your baby I want to see."

She led the way to the living room, from which wails were issuing, and I followed and resumed my seat. She leaned over the basket.

"But she's crying, and the mother just sits!" Alma crooned at the baby. She kept rallying it in a spirit of encouragement so engaging that the wails actually stopped.

"She's okay," I said. "She's been fed, diapered, and turned over a couple of times." Alma shot me a glance that meant, Is a baby a pancake? I could see she was fighting down an impulse to pick the baby up and tear around the room madly hugging and crushing her.

She was then thirty-six and still beautiful in an odd Spanish way that had nothing to do with her origins. Bright strands of differently colored wool were woven Mexican-fashion through dark, center-parted hair that framed a piquant face of almost decadent refinement. Beneath her small waist a pelvis designed for childbearing spread like a guitar's lower half. Physically she was a powerhouse. Perhaps this was why she failed to notice disability in others unless they were actually hobbling on crutches. Her insolent roving eyes sparkled as she took in the ludicrous details of each new setting.

She had carried both of her pregnancies easily, she told me. The elder son was fathered by James Agee. She ran away to Mexico when that baby was only a year old, and her second son was fathered by a German writer she met there.

The average young wife, no matter how neglected she feels, does not readily run off with a babe in arms unless the husband is a brute, which by all reports Jim was not. Alma with her arresting look, élan, and cash (sufficient for the time being) never doubted he would come after her. He did, but not instantly. By the time he got to Mexico she had fallen in love with Bodo Uhse, a dashing figure with a considerable past. Vying in mutual chivalry, the two men negotiated for her in a bar. She was present, savoring the romantic thrill of being fought for. Agee retired with a good grace, and out of personal and political sympathy later sent money to his rival. Bodo legally adopted the son.

For Alma, who had never known a day's poverty, their financial straits in Mexico were just another adventure in the picaresque novel of her life. After the war their return to Germany was delayed so long for want of the fare — they were a family of four by then — that when they did arrive they found themselves rich. Rich enough, at any rate, for that time and place. A mountain of royalties had piled up in Berlin, there was assurance of advances on new books, and by way of steady income Bodo was made editor of the Kulturbund monthly magazine.

"How did you find us?" I asked Alma.

"I came in the car," she said, as if this should have been self-evident. She never seriously considered public transport.

Cars could not be bought by private individuals, so I assume that theirs plus chauffeur was provided by the authorities. The chauffeur lived in their village and had nothing else to do but drive them, do their shopping, and tend to the car. Once when he had it jacked up and was underneath fiddling with the entrails the prop gave way and the car fell on him. At his shout Alma rushed out of the house, grasped the heavy machine under the front bumper and raised it high enough, long enough, for the young man to struggle painfully out from under. He wasn't badly hurt, but she — she told me with surprise — felt it in her back for a whole day.

Their house on a lake did not belong to them either. The horse did. Bodo bought it for Alma soon after they moved in, though it had to stay with its former owner until they had a stable built. Owning a horse seemed perfectly natural to Alma; she did not expect it to give anyone offense. Her family in upstate New York were well-to-do, and she had ridden all her life. Since she could not read German signs she galloped straight into a Russian munitions dump and was arrested and sternly questioned. Who are you? She told them. Nationality? Obvious in her case, but part of the routine. How did you get here? By way of *Leningrad*, she jested, literally true, but when I heard the story I could imagine how she tried, not very hard, to bite back the laughter quivering on her bee-stung lips. If the Russian freighter hadn't taken them aboard they might still have been in Mexico.

She didn't bother to carry identification, so no one believed she was the well-known writer's wife. In the evening he came to the jail in Potsdam and got her out. Russian soldiers returned the horse.

For people already intrigued by Alma this made a hilarious anecdote. Others did not find the incident funny, and thought Alma insensitive, Bodo weak.

She was taken aback when told of this. What did people want of her? Suppose she got rid of the horse, would that make the slightest difference to Germany's ruin? Born on the land himself, Bodo pooh-poohed the whole business. To him a horse about the home was normal. He wrote of Alma's in his sedulously kept diary as if it were a member of the family. "The days are full of festive beauty. Green grass, bright sky, and dark lake. At last the magnolia is blooming like white flames. Roland in his stable greets with a childishly eager and nervous whinny a horse whose step can be heard from the road."

The distance between their place and ours was easy enough to manage without a car, if one knew how. Max glanced at the sky and the position of the sun, and we set off. It was lovely weather for March. We each took a handle of the baby's basket and walked cross-country downhill through long grass, bearing west and passing the silly little pond overgrown with weeds that gave Nikolassee its name. At Wannsee, where a river bellied out to become a true, spacious lake, we took a ferry to the British Sector of Berlin on the opposite shore. A bus ride and a walk, not too far, brought us to the home of our friends in the Soviet Zone.

I say "friends" with reservations. It was the men who had something in common. They had been through Paris exile together, shared aesthetic insights and Marxist convictions, and were now working in closely related jobs under the same roof. Privately Max smiled a little at the peacock in Bodo that rubbed me the wrong way, but this did not lessen his basic liking for the younger man.

At first Max kept from me the fact that Bodo had been an ardent supporter of Hitler, though this was no secret to readers. In a transparently autobiographical novel he traced his own development from a Prussian traditionalist into a Nazi, and from a disillusioned Nazi into a Communist and a member of the International Brigades in Spain. I tried more than once to read an English translation, but it defeated me. I couldn't seem to find the people behind the names.

But what eyes Bodo had! Intensely light and deep set beneath shaggy brows, their characteristic expression was one of startled discovery. The light in them, the kind that shines through an overcast winter sky at the zenith, was a German color or want of color. At forty-five his rugged, sensitive face was already crisscrossed with lines. They became cruel furrows after tragedy struck.

Bodo did not suspect the extent of the pathetic drama in which he would soon be embroiled. He was incubating TB, the result of north Germany's dankness after the Mexican sun. He was also incubating a new love. This time it was his secretary, but she had scruples, she liked Alma, was frequently a guest in their home, and felt beholden. Danger was temporarily averted when he was sent to a sanatorium in the mountains.

In view of the events to come, which would materially affect our lives too, that carefree afternoon in their home stands out for me as a kind of holiday. I still see vividly the burnished, white-starred head of that horse poked into the open kitchen window to watch Alma cooking; Stefan, the two-year-old Uhse offspring, a plump little dervish rocking in drunken circles to a phonograph record; Alma grabbing him by his irresistible bottom, growling and pretending to bite it fiercely all over; Bodo flushing as he lifted the boy high in the air and exulted to Max, "Aren't children the best thing in life?"

After dinner Bodo lit a fire under logs in the fireplace, and Alma and I regaled the men with American folk songs. We ended with two dirty ones — one apiece, which constituted our entire repertory in that genre. Alma was so convulsed by the obscenities emerging from her own mouth that she kept breaking up as she sang. The men laughed indulgently. They could not reciprocate. Their language had no equivalent for the lighthearted bawdiness possible in English — only gutter filth incommensurate with their upbringing.

In our mothers' day Alma would have been called "artistic," in Jane Austen's "accomplished." She played the viola well, the piano quite passably, and altogether possessed flair. Among her atmospheric pastel impressions of Mexico one classical small self-portrait in oil stood out, just the head against a rich dark red background; the proud chin is raised, the eyes boldly meet the viewer's. To my knowledge she never achieved anything approaching its excellence again, but she was content with accidental triumphs. Having proved virtuosity in any line she would turn to another without regrets.

Villas like theirs had been precipitately deserted when the defeat of the Nazi army, never believed possible by the owners, took them by surprise overnight. Frantic to gain the safety of the West, they left everything behind but valuables they could carry in their pockets, enabling the Soviet administration to house a new German ruling class appropriately and at minimum expense. Most of the furnishings were still usable, but when Alma and Bodo showed us the upper floor I was surprised to see apparently brand-new blondwood furniture in the bedrooms.

"Gosh, where'd you get this?" I asked.

"In a store," Alma said with the same look of offended ennui as when she had replied, "in the car." She added curtly, "in Potsdam."

It was obvious she did not think much of my upbringing. She did not yet realize, perhaps she never realized, that among friends the question "Where did you get it?" was not considered uncouth in Germany at that time. Weren't we all in the same boat, seekers but seldom finders? Shouldn't we be happy to share a discovery? This at any rate was the reasoning of guileless souls like me and Max and his other friends.

A store that sold anything as improbable as new furniture did not exist in Berlin, so how would the sticks rate one? Whether Alma knew it or not, what she called a store could only have been a warehouse for supplying special people favored by the Russians — the so-called nomenclatura. Later such things became known even to us. Foreign diplomats shopped in stores closed to the public, in fact invisible from the street. Their East German counterparts, it turned out, were also admitted. Well, why not, we felt; they could hardly be sent abroad in threadbare pants and broken shoes, or entertain important visitors on their herring ration.

"Boy, that stuff must have cost them an arm and a leg," I meditated on the way back, or words to that effect.

"Thousands," Max agreed absently. His mind was focused on one of those manuscripts waiting for him at home, but he added in case my remark implied a criticism of Bodo, "He earned it, after all."

Alma and I only fitfully made contact during those years.

In the spring of 1949, seemingly disconnected events went off one after another like the firecrackers in Jacques Tati's shed, except that these were not so funny. To most of us the causality went unperceived for decades. Newspapers were not a source of information, they were smoke screens and cattle prods. We were like extras in a mob scene being shunted about a movie lot without even knowing what film we were in. Max believed that the confidences doled out to executives at special Party meetings were the whole story, and I believed in him.

So when at the end of April Lex Ende was fired from *Neues Deutschland*, Max was utterly unprepared and horrified. The entire staff, without exception, was thrown out with Lex, as if he must have contaminated the lowest clerk and night watchman. But how? What had he done? No explanations were offered. This was the more puzzling as ND had earlier in April published a eulogy for Lex's fiftieth birthday, calling him "a political journalist of stature, lucid, objective and keen-sighted, a propagandist of rare audacity and a rousing temperament admired by many."

At the Club, as if nothing had happened, Lex was the same old mettlesome optimist as ever. What could be more natural than personnel shifts, he seemed to be saying. Wasn't it an honor to function in any capacity at all if it helped hem in your antagonist's king?

If so, then which was Lex's new square on the chessboard? Where did he spend his hours? He skillfully eluded tête-à-têtes. When the company at table showed signs of breaking up he glanced at his watch and sped away.

Lesser staff members were assigned jobs in other enterprises. The theater critic was scooped up by an arts weekly called *Sonntag*, one of the Kulturbund's house organs. It reached far fewer people than the Party mouthpiece and was little more than a bulletin of approved events, but this was the least of Max's concerns. To his mind the Lex Ende affair must have borne a sinister resemblance to tip-of-the-iceberg stories like Erich Wendt's. Not that he said so to me. He could hardly have had the stomach to say it to anyone. There was a kind of superstition: if I express this it becomes true, if I express this I condemn us all. And everyone shared the superstition.

There had been other unpleasantnesses that hurt, the most unbearable of which, to Max, was the insulting treatment accorded Bertolt Brecht. At the beginning of January, shortly before the first night of his astounding play *Mother Courage*, Brecht had gone to the mayor of East Berlin to ask for a theater of his own. Two leading theater directors came along to back him, and the few middle-ranking Party functionaries present tried nervously to be helpful, but Mayor Ebert huffily ignored the bad boy Brecht, saying neither how do you do nor good-bye nor granting him so much as a look. To the others he dropped a brief, grudging explanation about "dubious projects that would only jeopardize those already established." Brecht's double offense was that he had just spent a successful year producing plays in a Zürich theater instead of rocketing direct from New York to Berlin, and that he was not (and was never going to be) a Party member.

He wrote in his diary that day, "For the first time I feel the stinking breath of the provinces here." Max felt bitterly ashamed that his party had behaved in such a manner to a genius — Max ranked Brecht with Shakespeare.

On May 12, three days after the paper appeared with a new masthead, the Russians abandoned their blockade of Berlin. Without fanfare, without audible hurrahs from the Trizone. As the airlift continued unabated, few people were aware that anything significant had occurred. I was no different. In his distress over Lex's uncertain fate my daily newsbringer must have forgotten to tell me. Perhaps he thought he had told me. Or he really had, and I was too preoccupied to take it in. That often happened.

When it got through to me I was bewildered. Hadn't this been an unthinkable reverse for the Soviet Union after taking Berlin at the expense of so much blood and the devastation of its own territory? What did the Party say? From Max I got the impression that it hadn't been a defeat but a necessary change of tactics.

He is sure to have explained this fully, he was an inveterate explainer; but some explanations seem to evaporate on contact with the air. What did stick in my mind was the horror he expressed of one Sepp Schwab, *ND*'s new overseer. I don't mean the new editor, Herrnstadt, a professional newspaperman from Weimar Republic days and an excellent editorial writer, who in Soviet exile had published a paper to reeducate Nazi prisoners of war. Schwab, a close associate of East Germany's future despot Walter Ulbricht, dismissed with a wordless glare mere gnats like Max, who had had the temerity to approach and try to speak with him as he stepped out of his official car at the ND building. Max had not been treated that way before by a person addressed as Comrade. Ignorant of the man's background — he had been an emissary of the Comintern — Max could only wonder why he was endowed with so much authority. It was deeply disturbing.

In Washington other explanations were heard, though not by the general public. John Foster Dulles told a selected group why the airlift continued despite the Russians having called off their blockade. The financial burden was a public relations necessity. The gratitude of West Berliners, he said, must not be allowed to flag before a West German government was in place. This would take a few more months.

On May 12 Noel Field, the unworldliest of Communists, vanished without a trace in Prague. Max was lucky he had never met Noel. Those known to have met him or any of his relatives, it made no difference how casually, were in trouble. The foundations of the Rajk and Slansky trials in Eastern Europe were being laid.

By coincidence, as it seemed, so were those of the McCarthy inquisition in the United States. Although the two sets of phenomena dovetailed remarkably, no one at the time seemed to be struck by the fact. It must have been the underdevelopment of television and the breadth of Atlantic separating yin from yang that kept the world so unconscious. (In the same way no one in Berlin seemed to notice that all the important replacements on *Neues Deutschland* had been exiles in the Soviet Union, from Sepp Schwab and Rudolf Herrnstadt to the orthodox theater reviewer whose hackles rose at the name Brecht.)

About the time I received permission to live with Max in Berlin a man named Lawrence Duggan died in a fall from a New York skyscraper after being questioned by the FBI in the Alger Hiss case. Duggan and Noel Field had become good friends while working together in the U.S. State Department. Whittaker Chambers, the agent who accused Hiss of spying for the Soviet Union, also put the finger on Field.

To avoid a subpoena, Noel decided to move from his home in Geneva to socialist Czechoslovakia, but was unable to get even a limited visa. While in Paris at a peace conference, he looked up an attaché in the Czech delegation whom he knew personally. Noel knew and had saved the lives of many refugees during the war through his Unitarian Service Committee, and at his own expense had later, in 1947, sent the Czech Artur London to Switzerland to cure the TB he had contracted in Mauthausen concentration camp. London seemed only too glad to be of service to a benefactor. It was no problem because, he told Noel, any delegate to the Partisans of Peace Congress who cared to visit Prague was automatically invited.

On arrival there Noel telephoned an American couple he considered his best friends. He had counted on staying with them while pursuing his quest for a residence permit. The husband, a refugee from the House Un-American Activities Committee, said his wife was out at the moment but had reserved a room for Noel at the Palace Hotel. Unfortunately they would be unable to meet him that evening. The next day Noel got the wife on the phone. Now it was the husband who was away, and couldn't Noel come to her office?

Troubled by this dodging he rang up the generous-hearted widow of Egon Erwin Kisch and found her the same good old Gisl she had always been, unsuspicious, unfrightened, and welcoming. She invited him to lunch in a restaurant and brought along her houseguest, Anna Seghers. Anna was warm too.

As he returned to the hotel he had a feeling that he was being followed. The same sensation had dogged him on the way to the restaurant. Another source of uneasiness was his large valise, which seemed to have gotten lost in the hotel. He asked the desk clerk whether it had turned up. The clerk apologized; some confused employee, thinking its owner had checked out, had sent it to a storage firm for safekeeping. He gave Noel the address and called a taxi for him.

The neighborhood looked strange, "a sort of Hooverville, only uninhabited," Noel told me years later. The taxi had gone. Searching among dilapidated buildings he found the house number, but no firm. A car drew up, a youngish man got out and asked if he was Noel Field. Thinking rescue had come, Noel thankfully assented and was at once hustled into the car and chloroformed. When he recovered consciousness he found himself handcuffed, his eyes tightly blindfolded, his head in a sack. His captors noticed that he was stirring and chloroformed him again.

★   ★   ★

On May 14 Max was jubilant over the headline "Gerhart Eisler on the High Seas." Two years after his closest friends in exile were repatriated, the government of the United States had continued holding Gerhart as a dangerous agitator. Neither his hunger strike in jail nor a coast-to-coast speaking tour by his fiery little wife had been any use. A last resort, his appeal to Trygvie Lie at the United Nations (wouldn't deportation be the logical way to get rid of an objectionable alien?) had likewise come to nothing.

While out on bail he slipped away from the agent assigned to him, bought a bunch of flowers, and went to see off non-Communist acquaintances on the Polish liner *Batory*. At the call "All ashore that's going ashore" he strolled the decks until the ship was too far out to turn back.

Max's joy was not only for Gerhart's sake. He felt sure his friend would be given an influential position when he reached Berlin and from that position would be able to right all wrongs. Why else would the U.S. Justice Department have taken such pains to construct an airtight case against him? They must have hoped to cheat the Russians of a particularly cunning operator.

Indeed, a week after the *Batory* sailed, Secretary of Defense James Forrestal ran through the streets of Washington screaming, "The Red Army has landed!" Although hurriedly confined to the Naval Hospital in nearby Bethesda, he managed to jump to his death through a *screened* window, so frantic was his delusion that now a Communist victory over the West was unstoppable. Within the month Attorney General Tom Clark resigned, telling the press he had been "the stupidest man in the country."

But after a melodramatic journey, Gerhart's arrest in Southampton by British police who had to tug him bodily from the ship, a trial in London picketed by pro-Eisler demonstrators, surprise dismissal of the case and tumultuous welcoming scenes at mass meetings in Berlin and Leipzig, he did not get the appointment Max and others had expected.

The decibels of those standing ovations undoubtedly made the wrong sort of noise in the ears of Walter Ulbricht, soon to become general secretary of the Party. He knew *he* would never be borne aloft on the shoulders of cheering youth. He not only totally lacked charisma, he abhorred what he lacked, regarding any form of grace or wit as upper-class tricks that could only undermine Party discipline. To a mind like his, the

— 135 —

whole Eisler family was tainted with a sickly intellectualism: the father a professor of bourgeois philosophy in Vienna, the once-Communist sister Ruth a renegade, brother Hanns a smart aleck who composed the music for Brecht's poem "Lob des Kommunismus" (In Praise of Communism) only to chuckle over the Party in asides like "Slogans have an important social function too, they take the place of thinking."

Gerhart's cardinal offense, however, was his opposition to Ernst Thälmann, head of the German Communist Party, hero of a workers' uprising in 1923 and stolid supporter of Comintern dogma. In 1928 and 1929 Gerhart had taken sides with Bukharin and Bykov against the Comintern and refused to keep his mouth shut when a close friend of Thälmann put his hand in the Party till.

All this had been so successfully hushed up and Thälmann so insistently canonized after the Eisler faction was quashed, that Max heard only vague rumors of some passing rift his friend had once had with Thälmann. "What was it about?" I asked. Max hadn't been in the Party then, he couldn't recall.

Ulbricht remembered, but graciously allowed Gerhart to make himself useful as head of a just created Office of Information. Its work was not spying, as might be inferred, but propaganda. The man in charge of spying had a ministry, not a mere office, and with that post not only the prestigious title but more power than most ministers. All the same Gerhart came home every night to the same guarded compound of private homes as the highest Party leaders. He continued to do so even after the Office of Information was abolished and he fell under suspicion in connection with the hapless Noel Field. The accusation was not made public, Gerhart was not jailed; but at no time was he in a position to right wrongs. He was up against an ironclad hierarchy in which Walter Ulbricht was only a viceroy of the real power.

Exiles who returned from the "West," an elastic location denoting any capitalist domain (even China), found that most jobs with any clout in Soviet-controlled eastern Germany were already occupied. Initially this seemed to them only natural, a first-come first-served proposition. Ulbricht and his team returned with the victorious Red Army; it was impossible to get home earlier or with sturdier backing than that. After all, the latecomers told themselves, the Russians had known their own

German exiles for years. Whatever their individual shortcomings, at least none of them was an enigma. None had vacillated in wartime conditions that were at best harsh, at worst unfathomable. There was urgent work to be done in the ruins of the Soviet Zone, and who else could be so confidently relied on to organize it?

The more tardily German Communists left the "West," the more mistrustfully they were regarded by the Party when they arrived home. Having been detained against their will or otherwise plausibly hindered was no excuse. The decisive question was whither they had fled and why. Who could testify to the probity of people who deliberately chose the comfortable West? Their closest comrades and sole witnesses had been exposed to capitalist enticements themselves.

Such imputations, not yet uttered, were the yeast that was going to foam up into uncontrolled hysteria. In what haven a European Communist fleeing the Wehrmacht had landed — that he landed in any, rather in the hands of the Gestapo — was determined by the wildest random spin of fortune's wheel.

Although it was Anna Seghers who so convincingly documented these perils in her seven-veiled tour de force *Transit*, she was one of the few Western exiles who seemed above suspicion in the eyes of the Party. For the sake of her other novels it tolerated the ambiguities of *Transit*, an international success if not a zealot's cup of tea, and idealized Anna as the delineator of an idealized working class, typecasting her (rosy image of virtuous womanhood that she appeared) as the unwavering Communist ingenue. The role became a cross. She was constantly pushed before the public eye, made to visit factory brigades and schools that bore her name, wrenched from her desk to speak at conferences in Germany and abroad. It was like being in the stocks, but she dared not refuse. The daughter of enlightened, art-loving parents, she learned to walk a tightrope between commitment and wary discretion from which there was little respite.

A former exile unique in straddling East and West was the poet-statesman Johannes R. Becher, scarcely known outside the German-speaking world. Not only the Communist literati respected him, or felt that they ought to. Thomas Mann himself could not withhold a gingerly esteem. Klaus Mann too, in one of his books, awarded Becher half a laurel wreath for his "relative tolerance."

Although the Soviet Union became his refuge as soon as the Nazis took power, he visited France for months at a time during his first two years outside Germany. He began his only novel in France and spent considerable time coaxing fellow exiles there to stop feuding and form themselves into a semblance of antifascist unity.

The novel *Abschied* (Leavetaking) was based on his own youth and his break with the values of a wealthy Munich family. In the 1920s he joined the Communist Party and learned to denounce his own early expressionist poetry. After World War II he was praised with clamorous monotony by the Party as the great poet of national unity. Irreverent young colleagues referred to him behind his back as Eggcup, a pun on his name (a *Becher* is a type of cup). To his face they kowtowed.

The Kulturbund was his brainchild and the Club his court. As soon as the imperial pate was sighted, space opened like the Red Sea and chatter hushed. Heavy of spirit, larger than life, he walked through the dining halls with lonely, measured step, and came to rest by preference on an elevated surface. Fortunately there was a dais at one end of the paneled room, but if Becher stopped for any reason on a humbler section of the floor the elevation seemed to have raced there and slipped beneath his feet just in time. For a long while I confused him with the portrait of Goethe on the Club staircase. Maybe this was because he confused himself with Goethe.

The chiseled lips and cleft chin were magnificent but forbidding; forbidding too the marble eyes that rolled off fellow humans to realms beyond their ken. I never saw him smile. He was a haunted man.

Soon after my arrival Max led me to the dais to be presented. Becher awarded him, if not me, a brief, condescending attention — Max had to edit his books after all, and it was Becher who had okayed him for the job. They exchanged a few civilities, during which the remote gray eyes in their higher orbit once passed noncommittally above me.

I felt mortified as Max steered me away. I had stammered that I was happy to meet Becher when I was not. I was transfixed, as by a basilisk, and turned to stone. I hated myself for being intimidated, I hated the way everyone else deferred to him, even Max, to whom — this was my firm opinion — Becher should have deferred. Why did I have to submit to this demeaning ritual? How dared that inflated bullfrog take universal homage as his due?

Oh, he wasn't that way at all, Max laughed. Becher was just shy.

It did create difficulties if one never found any equals to talk to, I said tartly, but Max maintained that as a poet and a man Becher did have greatness and I would recognize it one day.

His work is a grab bag. For every fine poem written in better moments he secreted a never-ending ooze of apostrophes to the Fatherland and other sacred abstractions. "Thou my," he would address them possessively, thou my this, thou my that. "Thou Myself" would have been an apt title for the autobiography he didn't write, probably for lack of time: the diary of a single year, his own personal thou my 1950, alone came to nearly 700 printed pages. He was up every morning of that year at 4 A.M. (he boasted of this as heroic self-discipline, but was probably just making the best of insomnia) to grind out nature news, rhapsodies over blue skies which he likened to the blue shirts of the youth organization, sententious observations about people he thought he knew, and even records of his outings and innings with pretty secretaries.

The latter passages were expunged by Erich Wendt out of consideration for his wife, Lilly. In the closing pages Becher preens himself on having been invited to Walter Ulbricht's New Year's party, "the best year's end I could have wished," that is, the most august society the frog pond afforded, and spews out an embarrassing effusion of love for spouse, homeland, socialism, and the future which culminates in a dream of Lilly dancing for joy on a table — only slightly more likely than if he himself did it. "Beloved thou art by all the people, in honor held by all," he rhapsodized in a eulogy of Ulbricht on the occasion of his awarding himself still another title. "Behold what life is his, one well worth living, / Whose strength he shares with everyone by giving / What makes them honor him and lovingly recall . . ."

Not long before he died he set down the truth about his knowledge of Stalin's crimes and stashed it away in a dark place.

> I not only guessed, oh I knew! . . . I felt that a moment would come when the questions that confounded me would be answered. And through no merit of my own the moment did come [the reference is to Krushchev's revelations at the Twentieth Party Congress]. I did not lift a finger to hasten the moment; that is the truth.

"One does not speak of these things" was the tacit etiquette we [the German Communist exiles in Moscow] observed, a rule that became our group's hypocrisy. At first we had discussed them with good friends, then only with a particular confidante, later with nobody but ourselves. Finally the monologue was broken off as unworthy and morbid. One worked still more intensely to sweat off in some degree that portion of the guilt one felt was one's own. . . .

Thirty years after his death the undated nine-page confession was published in *Sinn und Form*, one of the magazines he founded. It was the sensation of 1988 among East Germany's intellectuals.

This posthumous exposure of a large skeleton from the socialist closet, the skeleton of collusion in crime, revealed Becher in a light that dumfounded readers. Many old enough to have known him felt in retrospect a grudging pity for the man.

But as the shock sank in, more was shown up than Becher's seasick conscience. He had not been alone in keeping mum. Like invisible ink under a hot lamp the corollary soon stood out starkly. If he knew, they all knew. All who had survived Soviet exile, from Walter Ulbricht and Friedrich Wolf (author of "Professor Mamlock") on down, all of them without exception, even the seemingly amiable teddy bear Wilhelm Pieck, had been welded together in a conspiracy of silence.

A puzzle was solved. So this was why they had kept their distance from the "West" exiles! Apart from Erich Wendt, none of that crowd ever socialized with Max and me. They always exhibited heartiness and cordiality when one met them at impersonal places like the Club. I was quite moved when Lilly Becher, seeing me in the lobby near the end of my pregnancy, impulsively approached to reassure me, "We all come into the world the same way!" She very nearly took me in her arms.

Having said something pleasant, they drifted away. They had it down to a fine art.

I did not resent the repetitious, narcotizing tasks that fall to mothers of babies and isolate them from the world. I had ached and wept to have my baby too long to feel put-upon once I got her. The rapture of holding close that delicious, warm little being made me understand what a privilege such thralldom is. Caring for her was the greatest joy of my life. Nothing would surpass it. Nothing did.

I say "my" baby, but I knew before she came, and I never forgot, that she was not mine, not ours, and she amply confirmed the fact with her furious yells at poor service before she could even see; but also with the serene regard of a royal presence when her pure eyes opened at evening. We were hers.

My writing dwindled to a more or less neglected hobby, but it had never been much more and I thought myself young enough to catch up some day. Thirty-three was no age. At thirty-three Max went into exile and lost his best years, but with Dee I was living to the full. It was not her fault that all responsibilities connected with our hydra-headed household now devolved on me. The division of labor between me and Max, being traditional, seemed natural at first; I was tied down at home anyway. I put up with it, Max was evidently relieved, and at evening the kiss in the doorway repaid us both for petty aggravations during the day.

Sometimes I said lightly that I wasn't a real writer anyway. Or: "You only think so because you love me." Max turned on me. "What do you take me for?" To his mind it was just the other way round, I was insulting his judgment. He would not tolerate my copping out after he had tried so hard, and was still trying, to provide me with the peace of mind a writer needs. He must have wondered why I seemed to give up so easily. I wondered where my time went. The daily grind had gradually rendered me incapable of distinguishing the baby's needs from those of her nest, a Cold War household run like an obstacle race.

Starved for adult conversation, I could no longer initiate it myself. "Those damn diapers froze to boards on the washline! You could have hit someone over the head with them!" That was the level of my discourse. "I stood them on chairs in front of the stove, did you ever hear of such a thing? And then they were soaking wet all over again!"

Max listened with friendly sympathy for a minute or two, then wandered as if drawn by some physical force toward his ancient Remington. Unconscious that my mouth was still moving he began to hunt and peck. *Zhüüüüüüüt*, went the carriage, shooting all the way from left to right when he hit the "e," BAM it butted the other end.

Still, he remembered to bring me Aufbau's only precious staff copy of the *New Statesman* and *Nation* every week (it had to go back next morning) and once in a while a book in English he wanted my opinion on. Writing book reports was a zestful occupation that momentarily restored my sense of identity.

"Only nobody but you can read them," I pointed out sadly.

"I have more confidence in your opinion than anyone's," said Max.

But I wanted to be part of something, not just his pet opinion. I wondered what his staff thought of an outside reader reporting in a foreign language. I was getting paid for work they could understand only with difficulty, if at all. Wasn't it an imposition? And nepotism? Maybe he never even showed my reports to anyone. Did he at least mention my reasons for or against? Did he present them as his own? I dared not ask, I didn't want him to blow up. He quickly became irascible, which was new. He was working too hard. Often he got home so late that I was sleeping like the dead.

"They won't give me any more ration cards," I remembered to tell him at the last minute one morning. He was finishing his coffee standing up. "*Gott hilf,*" he responded quietly. God help. He saw at once what must have happened.

"Here," he said, turning crushed documents out of his wallet and various pockets. "Go back to Friedenau. . . ."

In his haste he jammed everything irrelevant to ration cards back into the most convenient receptacle, the wide-open briefcase — it was so stuffed it no longer closed — and rushed out of the house and down the hill.

It seems incredible that after so much experience with German red tape he could have overlooked the maddening intricacies of moving house. It was not enough that a dream apartment appeared complete with key, as if winged stagehands had lowered it from the flies of heaven. (Probably it was this miracle plus my imminent confinement that had addled him.) You had to go humbly to the police, into which our limping Friedenau clerks were already metamorphosing, beg to report that you wished to vacate apartment x in favor of apartment y, cajole from the grudging bureaucrats a transfer duly signed, stamped, and smudged, and present it, bowing and scraping, to their counterparts in the next neighborhood. This certified you as an obedient subject (of whom? of what?) entitled to calories, coal, inferior soap, and maybe a pound (sic) of textiles. Ration cards were issued only to obedient subjects — of whom or what you would learn in due course.

But because Max had forgotten to salute somebody's hat, a morning's formalities were dragged out to a fortnight of stern correction. Even if you had not been guilty of lèse majesté, such procedures took days. "If you haven't got it in your head you need it in your legs," Germans joked, having resigned themselves centuries ago.

The receipt of packages had become another nuisance now that I was the goat who had to fetch them. It was an hour's ride to the central post office downtown and another hour back. But while Dee's naps shortened, the elevated *S-Bahn* loitered as maddeningly as before. Trains came to inexplicable halts between stations, jerked forward, loitered again. Long queues at the package windows moved just as slowly. The worry gave me stomach gripes. Packages were never delivered, only notification by postcard. The very sight of such a card in the mailbox tweaked me under the rib cage. No time must be lost or precious gifts and coffee, coffee, coffee would be confiscated.

"Didn't little Hüppke show up?" Max would ask, a kindness to demonstrate that my day as a personality still interested him.

Little Hüppke was the only person in the Soviet Sector to answer our ad for household help. She was a short, round girl of twenty-one who looked like a quilted Russian teapot warmer with a red bead sewn on for a nose. I called her "Frau" Hüppke out of courtesy. She was engaged, as she called it, a common euphemism among the German poor. A respectable girl would say matter-of-factly, when it was over, that she was *un*-gaged. (**Verlobt, entlobt.**) "Oh, I do love babies, I'm mad about them!" she cried, clasping pudgy hands as she gazed down at Dee. She had lost her own baby. "It was in its carriage. I turned around for a minute and when I looked again it was dead."

My blood ran cold. It was not known then that "crib deaths" were not necessarily the mother's fault. But the problem of leaving Dee alone with her seldom materialized at first. She came at irregular intervals, pleading illness. It wasn't catching, she said. Sometimes she was moody and her mind so far away, due probably to boyfriend trouble, that in a closed, heated room she once piled covers on Dee, tucked them in tightly, and was taken aback when I removed half of them and freed the frustrated little arms.

Her happiest moments were when she could take Dee to the baby-care center for a sun-ray treatment, show her off in a lovely heaven-blue crocheted sweater from America, and undress her on the long partitioned shelf where a row of babies awaited the doctor or nurse. Dee had rickets contracted in my underfed womb. "All the other mothers were jealous," gloated little Hüppke.

Finally I let her babysit for a whole evening, so that Max could take me to an affair at the Club again. There I was shocked to discover that in the intervening months my status as a human being had sunk to nil. Men and career women who wanted to talk to Max asked me first with bright smiles how "the little one" was, only to turn back to him before I could construct a halfway grammatical answer. Formerly everyone had spoken a sort of basic German in my company; now nobody bothered. But another foreign wife, middle-aged and plump, with a smooth, eager face and a Swedish accent came over for the sole purpose of meeting me. Max introduced her as Mai Bredel.

"Oh, now I can practice my English!" she glowed, taking me aside. "But isn't it a shame Alma didn't come? I'm so disappointed, aren't you? How I admire that girl! Imagine," she burbled, "an American woman coming all the way to Germany, a ruined country, to share her husband's life! What courage!"

I was more than slightly nonplussed. If running after a husband all the way from America was such a heroic accomplishment, how about a little admiration for me? Actually Mai had been in the business long before Alma and I dreamed of it. A fashionable Stockholm girl, she had put up with exile and war in the Soviet Union for love of Willi, a proletarian writer from Hamburg, and still wasn't cured. But I knew nothing of this, I had never heard of Mai. Or Willi.

Perhaps it was not so much Alma's courage she admired as the lack of need for any, the adventurous chutzpah of a woman who marries a Communist without caring a pin for ideology herself; admired it artlessly and without petty female rivalry, for Mai was comfortable with herself as she was, an overweight but beloved homemaker whose candle went not out by night and whose husband sat among the elders of the land.

I was not comfortable with myself. That evening my already waning identity seemed to drop from me like panties whose tired elastic gives way on a crowded sidewalk. Smarting from Mai's well-meant tactlessness — she was only trying to establish common ground! — I returned to my refuge in Max's shadow. He, good chap, was making every possible effort to get me included in his conversations, but he couldn't constantly be shoving me ahead of him like a lawn mower and whispering hurried cues. He couldn't make me appear more than the domestic appendage I had objectively become, a Club member's wife taken along for the feed. I stood a step or two southeast of his parleys, most of them shop talk, and hoped no one was noticing that my hem was crooked.

But here, thank heaven, was Erich Wendt, all cordiality, fatherliness and antiquated English. What a relief! Max was relieved too, because now he could drift away for a bit; I would be all right with Erich. He asked about Dee, calling her by the tender nickname he himself had given her, and listened with the total concentration of mind and eyes that made him so endearing. He went on to inquire about my literary existence, and I was just diffidently answering when a strange man who mistook me for a potted palm shouldered between us.

Erich at first resisted uneasily, casting glances in my direction, but the man was highly excited about something. As he grew more vehement Erich had to laugh. "Oh come," he soothed the fellow, patted him on the shoulder, and began arguing persuasively. At this the other took his elbow and they walked away together, absorbed in their differences.

The abrupt desertion made my heart sink. Acres of empty floor seemed to spread about me and heave to eye level. Where was Max? Where should I go, what could I do with myself?

"It seems that to you a woman is air," I said with a lump in my throat to Erich when I finally discovered him with Max and Lotte at the buffet. They were sipping Alkolats, the only alcoholic drink the Club supplied. As it went down one smelled banana oil. "Would you dump another man like that?" I demanded.

"Oh no, no, no!" cried Lotte in the most acute distress. She was appalled to hear her husband maligned. "Erich isn't like that! You misunderstood him!"

She had never known a boorish Erich. Neither had Max, and he felt disgraced. Had I forgotten that this excellent man was his boss? Only Erich realized what had happened. "I thought we had concluded our talk," he fibbed, blushing.

On the way home in the train Max told me, "You cannot talk to Erich like that." He was not scolding, he was stating a fact.

"I thought it was best if we were to stay friends," I replied. "I don't want to be angry with a man like Erich."

"This is not America," Max said thoughtfully, to himself as much as to me.

At some point it must have dawned on him that I might not be transplantable to German soil. That may have been the point.

Max did not seem particularly German when I met him. He was leavened by years abroad. His love for me was the focus of an infatuation with America. There he never tired of hearing me sing "As I walked out in the streets of Laredo," and every week when I brought home the *New Yorker* he used to make me sit down beside him on the loveseat and explain all the cartoons from cover to cover. He would wait in suspense before each mystery, murmuring the oracular caption to himself until I gave him the clue. If it was very funny he could wave his legs like a schoolboy and chortle with glee. I also had to interpret some of the obscurer absurdities of S.J. Perelman, whose stories were the only *New Yorker* prose he took time for.

Naturally he was no less German than other Germans. Even his touching single-minded pursuit of American humor had something of earnest scholarship about it.

We both assumed that we understood one another on a supranational basis. Our tastes jibed almost perfectly. We believed that all peoples were fundamentally the same and that the brotherhood of man was near.

Now, however, Max's grim homeland was closing in on him and claiming him for its own. I can hardly believe that in his right mind he would have volunteered to take over Bodo's monthly magazine until the TB was cured. Who knew when that would be? The extra task was physically impossible on top of two other jobs. But once the Party decided he was the ideal substitute he went down on one knee, shouldered the burden, and stumbled to his feet again like all the other patriots floundering under triple loads.

Their history seems to have conditioned Germans to compulsive self-sacrifice, especially when locked in with their own kind. Paging through limp copies of the long defunct *Aufbau* magazine I wondered why these solemnly futile ponderings had been more important than a good man's health. But as a mutated species of selfish mankind, Germans don't weigh consequences in this way. They immolate themselves and their families for the work ethic because overwork turns out to be easier than struggling with their own hearts and souls. "How's life?" you ask an acquaintance on the street, and at once he presents his pitiful credentials.

"Much work, much work," he justifies himself virtuously, as if you had accused him of lolling in a hammock all day. "What's Helga up to?" you remember to inquire. Another resigned shake of the head: "She too. Much work, much work!"

Max never discussed the additional burden of Bodo's job with me. There seemed no time left to discuss anything.

Every day I prepared supper for two because Max just might arrive in time. The stabs in the stomach got worse from the uncertainty, the waiting when I was hungry, the postponement of cooking to a later and later hour, the disappointment of eating alone after everything was cold, the despair of finally throwing out Max's spoiled meal when food was so hard to get. We had neither a telephone nor a refrigerator.

I began waking up at the sound of his cough. It was no more than the light scraping of a throat cautiously cleared so as not to disturb, but it penetrated the paper-thin wall of my sleep. Relief would wash over me at the sound. A visitor to my queer prison without bars! The visit I most longed for!

Very quietly he opened the French doors that separated living room from bedroom. He only wanted to reassure himself that all was well with me.

He had already peeped into the tiny chamber where Dee then slept in an ornate white-enameled crib that had been rusting in his secretary's attic. It was a nightly ritual. He scarcely saw the child by day.

"Max!"

I was softly announcing myself lest he go right out again.

"Sleep!" he would whisper. "I have to do a few things." Whispering was a hint that my relief should be kept within bounds. It was late. Babies' mothers must rest.

If I stretched out a hand he stroked it hastily and withdrew. If I begged "Don't go," he gave a nervous cough of resistance to pressure and left the room.

On a Saturday afternoon when Dee was sleeping, I was ironing, and Max was typing, I said, "I must talk to you." This took some courage. Max didn't mind my working in the same room, I think he even liked it, but talking was taboo.

"Why just now?" he asked after awhile. The utterance seemed to come from behind a mountain range.

"When would be convenient?" I asked quite humbly.

Zhüüüüüüüt went the typewriter carriage on a mad spree from left to right. BAM. He pushed back the carriage and completed the sentence he was working on. Another sentence occurred to him and he attacked it with syncopated bangs.

"At least make a date with me," I said.

"Sweetheart, be reasonable," he muttered, not taking his eyes from the page, and I burst out, "We never make love any more!"

Shock flickered across his hollowed face.

I hurried on to prevent a shutter clattering down between us, "When we lived in Horatio Street you said too many couples forgot to make love, simply *forgot*, and that was why marriage went wrong!"

The subject faintly sickened him, I could see.

"You *always* have to work!" I talked back before he could express himself.

At length he said in a cool, measured way, repressing indignation as best he could, "Be thankful you have a chance to write."

I grabbed the nearest object and hurled it at him. I had never thrown anything at anyone in my life. It was a glass of water for sprinkling the laundry. I missed and the glass broke.

Surprisingly, his face lit up. Such a funny happening, it seemed to say. What did it mean? He made haste to fetch a dustpan, brush, and rag — yes, we had such amenities by then — and kept smiling as he restored order. Reflectively, uncertainly; shaken.

"But you do write? You write a lot," he ventured as he wiped up little puddles.

"I write letters! I have to talk to *someone!* I need friends!" I shouted. "I can't concentrate! I'm a squirrel on a wheel! I'm Alice running as fast as I can to stay in one place! Everything not directly connected with your goddamn work has fallen on me like a ton of bricks!"

"But who else is to do it?" he asked with a look of appeal, perplexity, and helpless contrition. Those words and that look sank into my consciousness ineradicably, summing up all that has gone wrong between man, including the finest, and his mate.

The saddest part of it was, I too was stumped. Should he do my work? Could I do his work? Could I undo an involuntary exile in which now he was entrapped as well? But when had I not been in exile? Why was I so moved by his thirteen years of exile? Exiles feel for one another, and there are many kinds. Richard Wright, the homeless black man, felt not only for me, but for all Jews and for all women. Women are exiles from human society, they live in a world apart which resembles that of men only in the furnishings, the chairs, the tables, the bed they share.

It would be twenty years before a few gallant women in the English-speaking West threw a lifeline to their stranded sisters. Their analyses and exhortations could not solve the classic insoluble problem Max and I had, but they could teach women to define themselves. What a difference that would make to me! It would not come too late. If a woman has learned before the last day of her life to cast off alien definitions and define herself, it is not too late.

Meanwhile, undefined, I wrote to Dick. I don't know what I wrote. I have only his reply dated July 29, 1949.

> Yes, words are hot and your letter was of just the right temperature to set me going — And you did it deliberately — ! Yes, I too miss you. Yes, I recall the long talks. I recall everything — your goodness and your "wickedness," that is, that time you attacked me so violently. One thing I must ask you — Really, you did not really mean all the hard and brutal things you said to me, did you? Please tell me. And look, dear, I shall not write to you if you, in your writing to me, feel you must write and tear up your letters. I want to know you, not the revised you, the corrected you. What good is that?

He said my letter had come at the worst time possible and that I should write him care of American Express in Geneva until the first of September. He was in the midst of a particularly agonizing crisis that did not bear talking about: "Enough to say that I'm so lonely that I wish I was a dog so I could go up to the top of a high hill at night and howl and howl at the moon."

If it were not for the fact that my own loneliness would soon be assuaged, I might have written him again, and again torn up draft after draft. The revised, corrected me was the only one I dared acknowledge even to myself. But in August Deborah interrupted her sojourn in Paris, she more bitterly lonely than I, and for a whole month we were cradled in the comfort of an old friendship dating from high school and the easy give and take of our own personal vernacular.

Dee was the perfect companion for our afternoon swims, at nine months a radiant enthusiast for new people. We pushed her recently acquired stroller down the long, long slope to Wannsee beach, where she was lifted out to make little sand messes. One of us would bolt into the water while the other played with her. She looked like Deborah then, except that she still hadn't a hair on her head and wore the comical sunhat that made us call her Drunken Charlie. The firstborn of Deborah's best friends all looked like her in their baby days. This was not only just, as Deborah never had one of her own, but suggests there may be other ways of influencing heredity than blunt procreation.

Max and Deborah, twin souls, perfectionist poets both (theirs, I often thought guiltily, would have been a marriage made in heaven if heaven hadn't blundered by putting me in his way first) went off to celebrate Goethe's two-hundredth birthday in Weimar and to see and hear Thomas Mann, who was making his first visit to Germany in sixteen years. He had already addressed an assemblage in Frankfurt, Goethe's birthplace, but would have considered it a disloyalty to the "Fatherland," he said, if his ceremonial trip had not included "the so-called East Zone." Particularly unpalatable to him was such a designation applied to Weimar, the united fatherland's last capital and the city where Goethe had spent his "colossal" life from young manhood on.

Staying at home I did not feel deprived. Deborah with her sensitivity to the German tongue would be getting more out of the occasion than I could. Besides, I had held a grudge against the guest of honor ever since one cold, nasty night during the war when I rushed from Penn Station in uniform to get at least a glimpse, before my next train, of the god who wrote *The Magic Mountain*. After that I never wanted to see him again.

The weather had been miserable, filling gutters with puddles, insinuating itself under overcoat collars, leaking into rubbers, blinding homegoers with its mean jets of windy rain. If Thomas Mann was anything like other people he must have been cursing himself for going out on a night like that just because of noblesse oblige.

Twenty minutes late he pushed through the revolving doors of the respectable restaurant where he was to read, and shouldered impatiently past some nuisance who tried to accost him in the entranceway. The pest was actually following on his heels, still nagging, when at the long table with the white cloth it came to him that this scarecrow in the ill-fitting suit was not a wino or autograph hunter but the person who was to introduce him.

The picture of chagrin, Thomas Mann turned his back on Max, handed his damp outdoor things to the nearest waiter, and hurriedly withdrew to greet, I assumed, one of the relatively prosperous exiles farther down the table who made these "Kultur" events possible. Two of them half rose from their seats with obsequious smiles, as if to remind him that they had met; I didn't wait to see more. For all I know, T.M. may simply have sought a men's room and a few minutes in which to collect himself, but I fled the sight of Max's hurt. He looked as if a whip had flicked his cavernous cheek and drawn blood.

Later it emerged that the god could snub his own brother and best friend Heinrich, a writer considered by many literate Germans to be the equal of Thomas and to tower over him as a human being. With his imperious sense of caste Thomas had felt positively poisoned by the odium of his brother's marriage to a demimondaine and had denied the couple financial assistance in California when Nelly was scrubbing hospital floors to keep them alive. Heinrich forgave; love was paramount in his existence. As for Max, he never let failings, however deplorable, dim his perception of genius.

I knew no one else whose physical aspect could change with his state of mind as totally as Max's. He could sparkle with an unselfconscious, irresistible gaiety, and he could contract at a rude touch like a snail. Lacking any instinct for self-promotion he was often passed over in the United States, simply not seen, not heard. It made him drink. At work or among the friends whose esteem helped him live and breathe he forgot he was in exile, but a slight from some dolt he had overrated could leave him defenseless, almost deformed.

Now he came home from Weimar erect, handsome, with a ruddy glow as if from a fortnight in the Canary Islands, and went straight to his typewriter. Thomas Mann had apparently risen above himself, lending his immeasurable prestige to a Soviet-sponsored festivity regardless of possible consequences. It would be unseemly, Max concluded the short piece, to thank him for the manifestation his visit seemed to imply, for it was not that. It was a celebration of "that gift not lightly granted," the gift of —

Did Max really intend to write "the gift of giving"?

What he thought was: *Donnerwetter!* At last Thomas Mann has put his whole self on the line, and God be thanked! But that would have called attention to the great man's former funking, so Max censored it and let facility run away with him. The blur was harmless enough, the whole piece a mere squib demanded by editors to introduce the real meat, in this case Thomas Mann's emotional but artfully corseted declaration of commitment to Germany. I mention it only because we were moving into a period where trifling evasions would almost unnoticcably pave the way to more basic ones. Soon it would be impossible to tackle the slightest truth or fact without a glove of specious apologetics. To make these convincing the writer would have to convince himself above all, or go under morally; and convincing oneself was going to require ever more elaborate, ingenious, and time-consuming constructions.

Armored by the security she had felt with us, Deborah went back to Paris determined to besiege it until her passion raised the portcullis. A hopeless enterprise in a city that resisted foreign wooers as if they carried cholera.

I was more fortunate at the moment. The pastoral interlude that began with her visit continued almost unbroken as my younger brother, the person to whom I was closest on earth, arrived at the beginning of September for a long, leisurely stay.

We were the only children of our parents, so alike in face and build that strangers immediately saw we were brother and sister. The age difference of six years was long since overcome. We were friends in ceaseless converse, for whom letters weren't good enough.

Since he was still scraping a living at the stupid tasks assigned to commercial artists by small-time advertising agencies, his effort to save up for this trip became a feat of devotion. He longed to hold in his arms the baby whose angelic photographic likeness he treasured, as well as to see me and Max as parents, our home, and, on the way over and back, a bit of Paris.

Another reason became important while he was saving. There was a girl he was tempted to marry, and he wanted a complete separation in order to weigh his feelings. It would be a second marriage. At twenty-seven he could afford no more disasters. His desire for a child, for children, was the more intense for having begun when he himself was small. He had thought me unbelievably obtuse when I explained that he would have to get a wife first. "Only *children*," he emphasized sternly, as if I might go out with a shopping list and bring back the wrong thing.

So there was much to talk about, not lastly our poor sad parents who, having lost me, now feared that John would never come back. They seemed to credit me with the powers of a Circe and John with none at all.

Max was relieved that I could bask in my brother's company for a while and give his conscience a rest. He got us tickets to *Mother Courage*, the play Brecht wrote for his wife Helene Weigel. The title figure, like the actress by then, is no longer young. As a camp follower in the Thirty Years' War she peddles provisions to soldiers along the shifting front, until her unthinking acceptance of war as a means of existence costs the lives of all her own children.

Max was of course too harassed by his multiple duties to go anywhere with us. For lighter fare he sent us to a nineteenth-century Austrian comedy with a song whose chorus lustily announces the end of the world. In high spirits we practiced *"Die Welt lebt auf kein Fall mehr lang, lang, lang, lang, lang, lang"* (the world can't last long-long-long-long) until we had it down pat, not suspecting how macabre the joke would become in our own time.

With the help of the Marshall Plan a capitalist Federal Republic was founded in the Western zones right after John arrived. This was answered a few weeks later by the proclamation of a not exactly socialist Democratic Republic in the east of Germany, with a fraction of Berlin as its capital and no financial help, only a gigantic war debt.

The date was October 7, significant to us for being Mother's birthday. It made us sad that in the continuing postwar mess it was impossible either to phone or cable to cheer her up. Bemusedly we gawked at the crowd milling about the former royal *Lustgarten* where a celebration had been called. The event's outstanding feature for us was the off-ration sale of delicious frankfurters, called *Bockwurst*, which we degustated on a seat provided by the gaping ground-floor window of a ruined palace on Unter den Linden. We didn't know it was a palace, as the rest of it lay in a heap behind us.

Although the new GDR was in no position financially to declare socialist intentions, both friends and enemies of socialism assumed that it would eventually. For Max one indication of this was the fact that Lex Ende had recently been taken out of limbo and given an editing job of sorts. *Die Friedenpost* (The Peace Post) was not a proper newspaper, only a bulletin of the German-Soviet Friendship Society. Hindsight would show that the appointment was just a cynical backhanded slap, but Max believed it must lead to a more fitting position as soon as one opened up. He may have received this impression from Lex himself, who true to form was behaving as if his new office was the ultimate in dignity.

God only knows what he really thought. The usual procedure of the Party in such cases was to present a nothing job as an opportunity for the culprit to "prove himself" after he had been persuaded through a series of interrogations that at some point he had made grave anti-Party errors which his own imperfect understanding had represented to him as correct. Almost any reinterpretation of an action or omission could be made momentarily plausible in this way.

A cat and mouse game was being played with Lex while the Party searched for something to hang on him. It finally seized on his very slight acquaintance with Noel Field in Marseilles, an irony because Noel (who hated to say anything even mildly unjust) told me in the '60s that he had considered Lex "rather a talker" and had discouraged his overtures. With a reticence unusual in the prosecuting branch of the Party, the charge was kept out of the press and buried in a file that did not come to light for forty years.

John and I tried hard to sympathize with Max's optimism and to suppress our own mistrust of a Germany in any form. On the *S-Bahn* as we returned from the *Lustgarten* we noticed what we considered a typical German, a middle-aged caricature out of George Grosz, who appeared to have emerged from the Third Reich entirely unscathed and oozing self-satisfaction. John remarked, against no opposition from me, that his mouth looked like an asshole. A little cigar stuck out of the pursed aperture, a little fedora sat on top of the head, and a newspaper called *Der Sozialdemokrat* was held close to thick eyeglasses.

But we were happy to discover untypical Germans in the same car, a bunch of surprisingly jolly, rosy-cheeked girls between five and fourteen with bowl haircuts who began singing pre-Nazi Social Democratic songs such as "Brothers, to Sunlight, to Freedom" and "Forward, Not Forgetting." A bigger girl in charge told me they were war orphans returning to their asylum in Potsdam, the station at the end of the line. They sang their considerable repertoire well and with a certain defiance, until the reader of the *Sozialdemokrat* could stand no more. He pinched the little cigar from its place and stretched the rubbery aperture to yell, "That's enough now!" A few other people looked as if they might agree with him, so I shouted, "It isn't enough, it's great!"

"Just like a German," I wrote to Christina, "he was immediately squelched."

I had overlooked a reason for the instant rout that should have been obvious to me. My accent was a dead giveaway, my Fifth Avenue suit still looked quite smart, John had American written all over him, and the train was passing through the American Sector. No German — except for a big threatening gorilla — could have squelched such a creature.

Bill Blake was extremely keen on visiting East Germany at this time, and Max despite his almost inhuman exhaustion had made one frustrating démarche after another to get him a visa. I assumed that Bill's motive was partly business, as Aufbau was translating his Civil War novel *The Copperheads*, and partly curiosity about a dichotomized Germany and how we and others were surviving in it. There was, however, a sadder reason behind Bill's eagerness which Max must have known but had forgotten to tell me.

The truth was that the banking job in Antwerp, on which Bill counted when he and Chris left New York for Europe, had fallen through. Financially Christina could not help much. Publishers feared that her extraordinary narratives would appeal only to a select, limited audience. This explained the couple's frequent moves about Europe. Bill now rated in the various consulates as a man of uncertain income, which meant that his visitor's visas could only rarely be extended. Although this did not apply in London, Christina being a British subject, her health suffered there from the damp cold and the inefficient heating.

By this time they were in such serious straits that Bill sought a teaching job at one of the East German universities. What a thing to want, I marveled (for out of delicacy Christina had not mentioned their troubles to me).

Max, however, considered it only natural that a man like Bill, fluent in German, of German descent, with incomparable intellectual treasures to share, would want to work in the native land of so many humanist giants despite its temporarily debased condition. Indeed, wasn't Germany a fascinating challenge for this very reason? Bill may have thought so too, but the deeper reason was surely his cherished Christina's tranquillity and well-being. It was an agony to him to see that woman of genius, who looked so strapping but became faint without red meat, forced to scrimp in second-rate lodgings.

I apologized in a letter to her that since the new government was installed no one seemed to know who was in charge of visas. Nobody knew to what extent the Russians would withdraw or what the new border regulations would be.

"People outside these wilds cannot imagine the obstacles to travel here," I wrote. "First Deborah, then John arrived exhausted and broke from having knocked around three days in German border towns where the local population makes a living on travelers' misfortunes. John paid thirteen West marks for bed and breakfast. You can get a pair of shoes for that. In the end they were both compelled to fly in."

The fleecing and the aggravation Deborah and John had endured to reach us were in fact a small enough price for safe arrival in Eastern Europe at that time.

Herta Field, as innocent as John, had like him set out in August, 1949. She traveled from Geneva to find her missing Noel in Prague, where she too was lured to a fake address and spirited away — to five years solitary confinement in Budapest. Neither Noel nor Herta knew of the other's fate.

A year after they disappeared their foster daughter Erica, searching for traces of them, was trapped in East Berlin. Prior to banishment in Vorkuta above the Arctic Circle she was subjected to mental torture by a two-man team, one Soviet, one East German, in a small cube of a prison that Max and I often passed on our way to theater. We thought it was a disused air-raid shelter. It had leering slits instead of windows and rusted metal doors that looked as if only dynamite could blast them open.

John quickly lost interest in Paris, where he had nothing real to do. A few days after his return to New York in November he wrote me, "Dear Würstchen [a synonym for *Bockwurst*], I've missed you very much. I didn't feel, though, that I was going back forever. I'm sure I'll be able to see you again before too long."

He was mistaken about that. This time the separation was to last twelve years. As if sensing it, I nearly died of coal gas poisoning. I had never become really proficient at burning low-grade brown coal, but while awake I at least smelled what was happening. It was Max's return home around midnight that saved me by a few minutes.

Little Hüppke's attendance record, exemplary during John's visit, deteriorated to normal, as did her powers of concentration after he left. Life began to imitate art. Like Klärchen's mother in my Goethe play "Ham and Eggmont" who, in her confusion over the great Count Eggmont's visit to her humble home, curtseys herself out of the way stammering, "I think I smell something burning — I left my mending on the stove —" Hüppke put her brand-new green socks on the coal stove in the kitchen to dry after they got drenched with snow. They did dry, but then the feet burned off. "It's my own fault," she said crossly, as if my innocence in the matter was the most annoying thing about it, and for weeks she did not return. But her absence had nothing to do with this or other resentments.

She arrived one day looking slightly less round and eased over the doorsill, of all things, a strange baby carriage out of which she proudly lifted an infant with a half-witted face and hardly any back to its head. She was so lost in admiration of her crown prince that she never noticed the horror and pity I was striving, probably none too successfully, to conceal. At her own suggestion, generous through happiness, she did the floors of two of our seven rooms and left again for an indefinite period.

My dreams became more vivid than my waking hours. In one dream I was walking along an abandoned railroad track that went through a wood. Underfoot it was sloppy and puddly from a rainstorm just past. I was heading for a party at the beach where there would be young married or soon-to-be-married couples, and where only I would be unmated and a stranger. But when I arrived and saw the house on the long beach between Oak Bluffs and Vineyard Haven I realized (although the house itself was a dream invention) that I had old friends there, Nelson and his older sister Eunice, and I said not very graciously to the hostess, "I could have come without an invitation!"

In the living room I saw only Eunice lounging in shadow on a sofa, with newspapers. Everyone else had vanished. I went directly upstairs to find Nelson, the boyfriend of my youth on Martha's Vineyard. We had met when I was eight and he was nine.

He was alone in a rather large bare attic reminiscent of his parents' crazy, uninsulated summer house of raw pine, in which one could see the boards of a high, sloping roof by simply looking up from the ground floor. Instead of filling the drafty space with an upper floor, Nelson's father had built only a gallery with two narrow cells as bedrooms for his children, but they gave onto a balcony where at night the three of us used to gaze up into the unmasked, dazzlingly bright firmament of the Northern Hemisphere as we could never observe it in electrically-lit New York whose glare blanked out the whole universe.

Nelson looked as he always looked in my dreams: friendly, shrewd, solitary. His eyes were as wise, his hair as curly, and his nose as snub as when he was thirteen, but otherwise there was nothing childlike about him. He was the slim young city man, the sophisticate who knows addresses. Yet there he stood waiting and was not married. And I was not married. My relief at the sight of him was tempered by only a little doubt and I asked timorously, though with a bold air, "Are you busy?"

"No," he said.

"Because I'm on the loose," I said.

I felt that he would understand what I meant by those ugly, wild words. He knew how hope always plunged from my heart in rough utterances when I was lost.

But in the dream there was no ugliness, as there had been in life when I limped back to him after a derailment. I was not suffocating from suppressed tears nor churlishly tossing him a cruel, blunted challenge: *Make* me love you. I was not dragging a broken wing (like the little wild duck we found dying by the shore of Lake Tashmoo, the first death either of us had seen, and knelt over, helpless, until the rattle stopped in its throat).

No, I was well and nothing was driving me, I was alone but not lonely. A little of the old uncertainty, but only a little, hovered near, but I was free, I could afford to say now, "Are you busy? Because I'm on the loose." And there was no wife and husband problem. Not only was neither of us married; neither was wondering anxiously every moment, *Shall* we be married?

He understood. He took out a torn-off piece of newspaper that had house addresses printed in a sort of classified ads column, and drew a circle around one of the addresses. I read it. I was to meet him there. He explained that it was an apartment which belonged to a friend who was away for the summer. I was slightly disconcerted that he had to borrow an apartment. I had forgotten those years when one had no place of one's own; but it did not matter and I quickly adjusted myself and looked forward to the borrowed apartment. I thought and thought about our appointment, about how it would be, and I was glad. I felt almost sure that this time it would turn out well and we would be happy.

Then I woke up and saw Max still asleep, tired-looking as always, not even at rest while unconscious. He was a night person whose day mind only started functioning around 11 A.M., a fact of whose legitimacy he had finally convinced his superiors; if he worked every evening, as he did, and was brilliantly creative, why insist that he be at his desk by 8:30 like clerical staff?

The room was still dusky, because the Venetian blinds were down. The American army family had left them behind. Some chinks were wider than others, one slanted, letting a faint sun ray waggle across the heaped underwear on a chair. I could hear Dee talking to herself in her little room off the hall, but she was not complaining, only uttering experimental syllables in a light, questing voice, so I could go on lying quietly and thinking about the dream. It held me strongly.

Its fascination was like that of the small landscape on my parents' dining-room wall that made me wish, as a child, that I might creep in through a corner of the frame and keep walking until I had seen the whole unexplored countryside it hid from me, and become one of its people. Just so did I wish I could follow the trail back to the life I never lived with Nelson.

But now there was a complaining note in my baby's syllables. They were turning into little yelps, still half playful. I sat up in a hurry and discovered my slippers near the foot of the bed where Max had inadvertently kicked them when he undressed in the dark. He lay trying to make himself sleep on, his eyelids twitching, his whole body concentrated on not breaking the charm. His wife was a day person, good for the baby, bad for him, for both of us.

The moment I opened the door to Dee's room she laughed out loudly and gave a yell of joyous welcome. Her head was round, her cheeks were rosy, my perfect baby, strong, straining against the halter to get up, to break loose into life. She smiled encouragingly for me to untie her and let her jump up out of the covers. "Oh, you darling, my little darling!" I cried. I was enraptured, kissing the downy silk crown of her head, my fingers fighting against the knots that tied the halter to the crib's white grille. She kept straining, eagerly babbling as I tore at the knots, until at last I could lift her high in the air, all joy on both sides, the dream dispelled.

An hour later I strode up the road to get her fresh milk from a farm about half a mile's walk through a sparse wood that started behind our house. It was a mean, cramped farm whose one miserable cow stood in the dark of its filthy stall all year round because there was no place to graze it. The owners, a couple with gnarled troll features, told me it didn't mind, meaning they didn't mind, but I boiled what the hag troll wrung from the unhappy udder and at least it was more nutritious than powdered milk.

Dee was more than a year old when my father forgave me sufficiently to start saving my letters and noting the date when each was received. Almost certainly Mother had urged him to do this. She could not even scrawl a date any more, her hands trembled too much. He may also have been influenced by John's reports and the photos of a grandchild and a lifestyle that at least outwardly made a reassuring impression.

I had always written home regularly from Berlin, but when I understood how yearningly my parents pored over Dee's photos, how appreciative they were of every bit of baby lore I shared with them, I began to write much more often, sometimes at intervals of only three days.

> I have to keep an eye on her now when she sits on the pot. She decides she is finished and rises as well as she can with the pot sticking to her behind and its contents dribbling all over the place. If I catch her in time and ask whether she's done anything — perhaps she doesn't even know — she murmurs "Laddle dilla?" or some such thing, putting her head shyly on the side.

For such details, over which — John wrote — our parents went on chuckling for hours, Dad touchingly rewarded me by deluging us with packages, now delivered to the door. It became his comfort and a way of life to send us everything conceivable, whether asked for or not: bed linen, corduroy, moccasins for Max, that indispensable halter to steady Dee's first steps outdoors — a thing I would never have thought of myself.

> She barks companionably at dogs. When we go out for a walk, she on her leash and the dogs on theirs strain toward

one another with cries of recognition and joy. Then she sits down on the grass, crawls, and finds things. She finds a chestnut; she finds a pine cone. Her boyfriends gather around and give me advice; said a three-year old, "She might swallow that chestnut. Many do." A nine-year old: "Isn't the ground too cold for her?" Sweet kids, eh? But at fourteen they get just like their parents . . .

After many years the rediscovered letters became a priceless bonus in enlightenment about the little strangeling deposited in my womb. The stories were not necessarily cute. Sometimes they were eerie. Loud noise in the night never alarmed her, but if I softly entered to make sure she was covered the faint rustle of my skirt was enough to make her cry. It was never darkness or being alone that disturbed her. In the middle of the night she could burst into peals of laughter. Once she laughed for half an hour, so loudly that I went in to soothe her, afraid she would wake the family upstairs. She whimpered with annoyance and after I left the room laughed again for a few minutes before falling asleep. It filled me with happy wonder that she laughed instead of crying in the night; I had never heard of such a thing, I thought only how lucky I was.

Under the tranquilizing influence of Dr. Spock I believed that apart from heredity and environment one baby was like another. Various kinds of screaming were explained and disposed of. Naughtiness was growth. At so and so many months infants did almost exactly what the kindly doctor had predicted. Any alarming change in Dee's behavior sent me in a hurry to the battered pocket edition, confident that it would set my fears to rest, and it did. What will I do, I used to wonder, when she reaches the age of four and Spock's manual ends.

I had forgotten in the welter of daily necessity those first weeks of her earthly existence, when we saw the Serene Highness in the new soul and fell to adoring as the three kings and the shepherds and the animals adored. Spock was right, the three kings were right, and the outcome of heredity and environment remained to be seen, but the letters have helped me as they once helped Dad and Mother, albeit for different reasons. All along there are character signposts that escape harassed parents, but with luck we may retrace them one day as glints in the dust.

In November, 1949, Max took me to the first night of Brecht's comedy *Puntila*, about a Finnish landowner who is genial and magnanimous in his cups but otherwise an unprincipled bastard. I was astonished during one scene when from backstage a baritone was heard singing to the tune of a Scottish ballad I knew well. He sang it in German, of course, and with totally different words written by Brecht. The program notes called it "The Ballad of the Forester and the Lovely Countess."

The only time I ever saw Brecht close up (I can hardly call it "meeting" Brecht) had been at a party the summer before in Gross Glienicke, where the Uhses lived. So many celebrities were invited that they overflowed the Uhse home into the house next door, which Kantorowicz and Friedl had rented for the summer. In the Kantorowicz living room Helene Weigel asked me if I happened to know the song "Henry Martyn"; she had been told that I knew a number of English folk songs. When I said I did she was delighted and asked if I would sing it to Brecht.

He was sitting in a wooden armchair whose straight back was higher than his close-clipped Roman head. He looked bored and rather crumpled from the heat in a blue Chinese cotton jacket buttoned to the chin. He wore only such jackets, never a shirt.

"She can sing 'Henry Martyn,'" Weigel informed him, and prompted me, "Go ahead!" Embarrassed by the honor, not daring to ask what it was for, I sang the first stanza in my keening country soprano. "Continue," she encouraged me, and I sang it to the end while Brecht, sunk motionless in the chair, regarded me through steel-rimmed glasses with something like a cryptic smile. Perhaps in repose his thin lips always looked that way.

Afterward I was momentarily bewildered when in the foyer I saw another man wearing a Chinese workaday jacket buttoned to the chin. In slavish idolatry he also wore his hair clipped close to the skull. He glanced at me with an indefinable expression, as if we might have been introduced and I ought to say something, but I was confused and proceeded to my destination, the john.

I assumed at first that it was Brecht who had so perfectly retained the tune that he could convey it next day without an error to the composer noted on the program of *Puntila*. He might well have, being musical himself, but during the performance of *Puntila* it dawned on me that the imitation-Brecht I had passed in Kantorowicz's foyer was Paul Dessau, the composer, who unnoticed in some corner had jotted the melody live on his mental staff paper.

"He has a nerve to claim he wrote that tune," I said to Max. Max shrugged; he saw nothing wrong with artistic swiping that injured no one and made humanity richer. Brecht swiped. Shakespeare swiped.

But we had both misread the program. It attributed only the "Puntila Song" to Dessau and not the Scottish ballad.

West marks had become the sole legal tender in West Berlin. From one day to the next the glamorous supermarket where I bought Dee's imported fruit and vegetables was out-of-bounds. If I paid the 150 marks rent out of Max's absurd 200 West exchange, I would have only fifty left for everything else, so I switched the reckoning, kept the 150 for everything else and handed the dumfounded renting agent fifty.

The electric company then had the gall to charge us retroactively in West marks for a bill incurred in Friedenau before Dee was born. "We never got that bill," I told the collector indignantly, but he instructed me that orderly people noticed when a regular bill failed to come and would notify the company of the error in time. I could not relieve Max of going to court, a maddening waste of time whoever won.

"We'll have to move, won't we?" I asked when our paths happened to cross.

"Oh no," said Max, "out of the question. The Party says that no matter how tough things get, comrades have to stick it out here."

To bore from within. This was fine for those who had time to bore from within. They did not include Max. Even Aufbau had realized this and awarded him a car to take him to and from work. The chauffeur lived a few blocks away from us and kept the car overnight, which saved gas. The fact was that life had become somewhat easier for Max as a result, not tougher, and with Bodo's return in March it would be easier still. So the idea of moving from his peaceful terrace and garden at that point was too grotesque to consider at the moment.

I have forgotten who won the court case over the electric bill. It hardly mattered. When for the third time the renting agent received only fifty marks, he handed me a notice of eviction. He was surprisingly polite about it. Almost obsequious.

Evidently it was not to be the sort of eviction we knew in the '30s when New York tenants and their belongings were heartlessly dumped into the street. The West Berlin landlords' best interests required as speedy and pleasant a parting as possible from tenants like us (there were quite a few), so that the premises could be rented to hard-currency earners. Why antagonize people unnecessarily? Who could predict the twists and turns of politics in Germany?

The agent, a young man of about thirty, lived in East Berlin, he told me, and knew plenty of people in a position to take our place. Not himself, no. He could not afford it, he said with a nice smile. All we had to do was advertise. Of course we would have to sign an agreement promising to pay back the withheld rent as soon as we had the money.

Drafting and placing an ad was Max's province, or his secretary's, but no answers came. Either the agent was wrong about potential bidders or Max was procrastinating. I didn't check, I had other fish to fry, I needed money right away, East money, as there was no likelihood of my getting the other kind.

With Max's fiftieth birthday approaching I was determined to reward that sterling man's fidelity to me *and* to his ideals, increasingly a tightrope act, with a gift that should demonstrate my reverence for him.

A year earlier he had taken me to the atelier of Paul Strecker, a painter and stage designer who lived in Nikolassee and whose work Max vastly admired. With my heart in my mouth I went back there and asked Strecker if he could spare some very minor thing that a housewife might afford. Not a gallery piece, just any little sketch, because whatever he did would be good to look at and deeply satisfying to own.

Strecker was a fine-looking man whose age I guessed at about forty-two, though he was ten years older than that. A bit bemused, he walked me slowly about the atelier considering this, rejecting that, until on an impulse he went straight for a huge oil. "The house next door was the model," he said. "I remember now that your husband said he liked this painting especially." It was stunning. What did I think I could pay, he asked. The amount I mentioned, blushing with shame, was hardly to be taken seriously, but he said five hundred East marks was enough and he would rather a man who knew art like Max had it than "some stupid banker from Kansas City."

I didn't even have the money, I had to earn it with an article on E.M. Forster's *Aspects of the Novel* for Bodo's magazine, but Strecker didn't care, he wanted to wrap up the painting for me right away. "It's too soon, I have no place to hide it," I explained. I would call for it at the end of March and still have two weeks in which to get it framed. That would do, said Strecker. He gave me the address of his own frame maker and my heart sang all the way home and whenever I remembered the delicious secret.

Inspired, I not only did the article faster than my usual writing pace but also completed the novel begun in Paris, so that Bill Blake could take it along after a whirlwind visit and submit it to his agent in London. He had rocked the town with his jokes and made a number of important contacts, at any rate contacts that would have been important in normal circumstances, so that we all three felt that things were looking up, and I saw my life immeasurably enriched by the nearness of Christina.

Three weeks before March ended Paul Strecker died suddenly in the night of a brain inflammation. When Max, quite broken, came home with this terrible news I burst into tears. First I cried for the painting, and after I told Max about it I began to cry for beautiful, magnanimous Strecker.

PART IV

*There is much that I cannot understand in this late-summer night of 1952.
I have given up trying. Time has accustomed me to my present state. But
there are moments, especially between waking and sleeping, when despair
seizes me by the throat. Why had it come to this? Will Time ever give me
the answer? There is something wrong, dreadfully wrong, somewhere. Oh
my dear wife, my closest associate, could I but talk to you! How often in the
past did you help me to see things straight! Here, in this primitive cell, I
"celebrated" our silver wedding more than two years ago. Where were you
then? Where are you now? Shall we ever meet again?*

— NOEL FIELD
"Hitching a Wagon to a Star,"
Mainstream January, 1961

*A totalitarian dictatorship, by its very nature, works in great secrecy and
knows how to preserve that secrecy from the prying eyes of outsiders.*

— WILLIAM L SHIRER,
The Rise and Fall of the Third Reich

THERE WERE BETTER PLACES than East Berlin to start a new life in the grim year 1950. Max wanted a house, even if we had to buy it with a loan, but the only one we saw was a disconsolate Charles Addams habitation in a muddy plain with half its roof burned off. The view was of factory chimneys and in the near distance a siding forgotten after freight tracks had been removed.

Our own ad for an apartment brought in a flood of offers, but Max was too fed up to help me investigate them. I was on my own.

The only way to get into East Berlin was by swapping, because much of its own population was waiting for a roof over its head. West Berlin, on the other hand, refused anyone presumed to want a pension in West marks. I settled for a three-way exchange. The occupant of the apartment I coveted, a white-haired old widower who could not possibly have afforded our place in Nikolassee, agreed to move into a dark, cramped dump I had seen behind an *S-Bahn* station. The villainous-looking tenant of the dump, a regular masher out of an early silent film, snapped up our apartment after barely glancing at it. Me, however, he treated to a prolonged sardonic up-and-down leer which meant among other things, "And you, my good woman, an American forsooth, give *this* up?"

For my part I wondered how the old widower could bear to leave the pleasant flat in Grünau, a water-sports paradise, for such a depressing slum. If it was only to save money, why did he depart with such cheerful alacrity? Was he fleeing from something?

But this possibility only occurred to me after I got acquainted with our honey-tongued, shifty-eyed landlady with the aristocratic, assumed name of von Lovtzow. He was just the right age for her, and she was not one to let human material under her own roof go to waste.

"She's an ex-madam," Max announced with the same absolute certainty as when in the Rembrandt section of the Metropolitan Museum in New York he pointed out some fakes, a discovery corroborated years later by better-known experts and published in the *International Herald Tribune*.

And sure enough, Frau von Lovtzow, who allegedly stemmed from the austere and refined officers' caste, ran about like a little yelping mongrel spreading calumnies suggested by the scum of her own younger days. She maligned our upstairs neighbor Frau Braun as "a common whore" and her old mother, Frau Sauerzeit, as a "panderer" because the still youthful war widow Frau Braun, a dressmaker with two little girls, had stubbornly refused a few hours of long-missed pleasure with a Russian officer who *in addition* promised bacon and cigarettes. Of which Frau von L. had expected only half.

She kept in her own apartment an enfeebled consort she called "the brother-in-law." According to Frau Braun she whacked him with a rug-beater when he didn't jump instantly to do her bidding. She must have known something very ugly about him which she could report if she chose.

Her figure by then was a bulging, ruptured mattress and her hair degraded to tufts like absorbent cotton glued to the pink scalp, but in her prime Frau von L. had made a good thing of her profession. Besides the house in which she occupied the garden flat, we the one above it, and the Braun-Sauerzeits a small converted attic, our landlady owned a nearby second villa as well as apartment houses in West Berlin.

She liked to hang over the fence and waylay passersby with embroidered gossip, often pure inventions, in the hope of a quid pro quo even from little children; but these were wary, knowing how quickly her phony sweetness could turn sour. "Cannon fodder is all you're good for!" I heard her screech at some youngsters playing "too near" the gate.

She dared not address Max, who froze her as he passed by, but on me she tried every saccharine blandishment in her repertoire. Before I could stop her she had given Dee a little bag of cherries from one of her trees, and couldn't she sew my curtains for me? It would be no trouble at all! The brother-in-law would be so happy to put up curtain rods! Do let me give you some lilacs, I have so many!

Blinking her eyes continually in a mask of love, she wheedled, "I like you so much! Don't you like me a *little*?" *Everyone*, she gushed, considered me so pee*konnt* and mo*dairn* (daring and up-to-date). When she caught me just inside the gate she asked dozens of question while detaining my sleeve. Why had I come to Germany, why did we move from the West, could I afford a steady maid, would I feed her if I had one, didn't I think one mark an hour a bit much for a maid, wouldn't I like to buy fresh eggs for West marks (illegal in the East and much dearer than in the West). She was by no means well-off, she complained; would she keep chickens otherwise? — and I only made my family ill by patronizing those off-ration state shops whose eggs had no lecithin "any more," as if cunning Commies knew how to extract it through the shells.

I stood with a noncommittal expression and let her nag until at last she let go of my sleeve and after a baffled pause turned and went into the house.

But oh, the apartment, so near the shops and the station and yet so quiet! Never mind that one room had no coal stove, only a radiator from defunct central heating, we still had a bed-sitter for ourselves and a bedroom for Dee, and I was thrilled with the gas boiler in the bathroom whose pilot light never went out, the large livable kitchen, the green radiance from southern, eastern, and western exposures, and the *pièce de résistance*, that square wooden balcony overlooking, beyond the garden, a huge expanse of May meadow with woodland at the back of it. Even Max, still grieving for his apple tree, could not help being pleased.

The balcony had a sturdy railing that kept Dee from harm, but what she most enjoyed at this stage were the spaces between the rails through which she could poke things that landed in the grass below. As long as it was only a plastic soap dish, the bathroom cup, an old rattle, the garden's mistress graciously handed them back on request as very special favors; but when it came to my mother's second-best silver-plated spoons Frau von L. only expressed great grief and could not imagine where they had gone. "A magpie, perhaps? They're very quick, you know, when they see anything shiny!"

In compensation she pressed on me thin gray spoons she called sterling silver. They bore curlicued Gothic initials, but no 800 on the back, and were so consumptive that my thumb and forefinger might have met through the necks if I pinched hard. She called these eyesores, a cheap German alloy, "family treasures" she didn't need as badly as we young people just starting out in life with a baby. The dear soul, and such tact, not noticing that Max was as old as the century.

The day of our arrival all the children from our block crowded about Dee, an irresistible doll in the raspberry-colored baby coat and matching bonnet my parents had sent, and ran her around on kiddie-cars and tricycles, becoming her faithful guardians and enabling me, for a start, to go straight upstairs with the moving men and show them where to put the furniture.

One of the pieces was a yellow wardrobe with its Cupid's-bow cornice outlined in crimson. It was so exceptionally wide that if you grasped the crimson knob and opened the single door all the way from left to right it would hit something. I had first encountered it, a relic of Friedl's first marriage, in the atelier of our count and countess.

With Dee's little friends as a regular audience, and using any available medium from house paint to nail polish, I transformed the monstrosity into a blue-green Garden of Eden, leaving the knob crimson to match the apple on the Tree of Knowledge. Standing under its great spreading branches, still innocent, an Adam with Max's bony body and an Eve with approximately mine, their heads somewhat too large and their eyes Assyrian, but — as I came to realize in long retrospect — a perfect expression of our true inner state at the time, held in raised, cupped hands a pear in one of hers and a cluster of grapes in one of his. A bird was perched on her other hand, a butterfly on his, and a dear white lamb copied from a dictionary illustration sat at Eve's right while at Adam's left a lion from another page meditated wisely.

In the panel below them an eyeless snake lay in decorative waves, not dreaming of evil; its soul was yet unformed. The bottom panel was devoted to a plant whose delicate branches bore tiny five-pointed rose-tinted white flowers. Just below the cornice two frivolous cherubs proffered pink and yellow daisies and floated in air, their pale blue draperies on the verge of slipping off. I muffed the stars. In the two scallops of the cornice sky, smears betrayed clumsily hidden mistakes.

The children sitting on the hallway floor gave shrieks of happy shock as I painted Eve's nipples, giggling when fig leaves took the place of both characters' private parts. Doubtless these touches were the source of my reputation as pee*konnt* and mo*dairn*, for while the children probably reported nothing to our gorgon of a landlady, they must have told their mothers.

The distinguished sculptor Gustav Seitz, my wishbone, liked best the flowering plant at the base and the two beetles, one on either side of it, but he wanted the whole closet and offered me six hundred marks for it. The compliment bowled me over. "But where would we keep our clothes?" I temporized. Seitz looked puzzled. Crude as the job was, I wouldn't have sold it for any money.

"Is it Early Christian?" hesitantly asked Wolfgang Harich, Aufbau's reader in charge of philosophy and Marxism.

There were surprising gaps in the erudition of that flippant, spoiled and effeminately handsome, later notorious youth. An overspecialized child prodigy of academia, he was at twenty-three a university professor and editor-in-chief of the philosophy journal, though more child than prodigy. He made easy conquests of a succession of magazine-cover beauties, never seeming to notice what kind of people they might be, as I pointed out to Max; but Max only smiled bemusedly. He had been delighted to get Harich for his editorial staff.

Max could be taken in by scintillation in a field where he felt himself insufficiently conversant. He expected an integrity in outstanding people that matched their brilliance. In this case even I, so ignorant compared to Max, but not so easily deceived as to character, was dumbstruck when that intellectual fop nimbly turned state's evidence after his arrest and without a qualm implicated a number of his Aufbau colleagues and betters in a high-treason trial.

But I am getting ahead of my story, in which the paint has scarcely dried on the Adam and Eve closet; the Harich case would explode long after Stalin's death, two years after Noel Field's discharge from prison, and a few months after Khrushchev's revelations at the Twentieth Party Congress — a time when one believed persecution in the courts of the socialist camp to be a thing of the past.

At first sight of the apparently peaceful tree-lined streets in our neighborhood, anyone might have supposed the house-owners at least had the run of their own property, but this was no longer the case. The more commodious the villa, the more roomers had been inflicted on them by the housing authority. These were mostly bombed-out Berliners and resettled Polish-born Germans. Landlords and unwelcome tenants alike felt put-upon. Tempers were short.

By the time we moved to Grünau half the children were fatherless, even though their fathers may have returned from the war intact. A lot of them had been "hauled off" again, including men already discharged from Allied prisoner-of-war camps. I often overheard that expression "hauled off" among housewives talking in murmurs, but audibly enough, while we waited in line with our ration cards. They avoided the eye of an inexplicable American who had no business being in such a line, a woman who would never understand the peculiar suffering of the Germans. They were fiercely embittered against the Soviet occupants who nabbed their men as Nazis, some of these only small fry, to be either summarily executed or thrown into supposedly closed-down concentration camps; while just over the border in West Berlin "de-Nazified" families were getting a fresh and privileged start.

We, on the other hand, so disgusted with Germans who claimed they never knew of the Nazi atrocities, were ourselves unaware that at least eleven "former" concentration camps and prisons were not former at all. They had continued operating under Soviet control since the end of the war.

Among those interned were antifascists arrested by the Red Army on the basis of never-investigated denunciations. The conditions of their internment were scarcely better than in the death factories devised by Heinrich Himmler. Regardless of their politics, tens of thousands of inmates died of hunger and dystrophy, untreated fevers, pneumonia, TB, and dysentery, especially in the winter of 1946–47. It had been Germany's coldest in living memory, when Max wrote to me with frozen, swollen fingers "like fat red frankfurters with open skin," saying he envied the members of the Byrd expedition then in Antarctica "who probably had the means to protect themselves."

Church leaders, who had known of the conditions for at least two years, prodded President Pieck and his formerly Social Democratic Prime Minister Grotewohl into demanding clarification from Moscow. Talks were then initiated which dragged on until the camps were at last closed in 1950. But it took another forty years and the collapse of the GDR before antifascist survivors or relatives of the dead conquered their fears and/or scruples sufficiently to tell the facts to an investigating committee.

So in 1950 I listened with a poker face to the stories of hauled-off husbands, and I doubted there were as many rapes by brutish Russians as the

German housewives suggested. Obviously none of those who prated about it with such lubricious gratification were the ones it had happened to.

"Frau come" and "Uri uri" were the two repeatedly heard code phrases, accompanied by harsh laughter, that summed up East Germany's resentment of a victor despised as barbarian. According to the women I overheard, these savages always announced their intentions by saying "Frau come," as if they had learned it in a crash course for military tourists. The chivalrous, self-denying Wehrmacht, one would have supposed, only touched their caps and absently said "Good day" if they happened to notice any females on their sweep through Poland and the western Soviet Union.

I did believe the "Uri uri" story without reservation, having been told it by a cheerful friend of Puma who gave me German lessons.

On the last day of the war Libussa had been crouching in a Berlin cellar to avoid the machine-gun fire. When the shooting seemed to have ceased and the only sound she heard was a regular pounding of boots she peeped out cautiously, then on an impulse rushed over to the nearest savior to thank and embrace him. "Uri uri," he replied, pointing to her wristwatch. Thinking he wanted to know the time, she held up her wrist to show him, but in hurried sign language he demanded she take the watch off. Bewildered, she did so. He pocketed it and ran to catch up with his company. It seemed, said Libussa, that there were vast areas of the Soviet Union where nobody had ever seen a wristwatch, let alone owned one. She laughed ruefully. Another illusion gone! From then on she saved her enthusiasm for the G.I.s.

Hundreds of Red Army men were stationed in Grünau. As they were forbidden to fraternize, they passed us in the street looking as frigid as the guards at Buckingham Palace. Seldom did we see more than a pair at a time, individuals never. There was a wood, however, where detachments performed odd jobs at some distance from the unpaved path which many people used as a shortcut. They variously dug, pruned, or did surveying, to what purpose I had no idea, but once when I stopped with Dee in her go-cart to get a better look they burst into jeers of such unmistakable sexual hostility that I never used the shortcut again.

Walburga, who was then working as a reporter for East Berlin radio, came to interview me about being an American in the German Democratic

Republic. She was particularly interested in my opinion of the McCarthy witch-hunts in the United States. I answered cautiously.

As a woman railroader during the war I had once given an interview to *PM*, a daily I considered left-liberal, only to find it had scurrilously turned to ridicule the campaign we were waging for the same hours and pay the men got. My fellow trainwomen were ready to lynch me for having made fools of us all; they could not believe a young woman from a newspaper, instead of trying to help us, would have had herself a cynical laugh at our expense.

Still, I answered Walburga as honestly and correctly as I could, considering the holes in my knowledge of the latest developments. At the same time I expressed doubts that German radio, East or West, had a right to put such one-sided questions about the American scene. I had noticed, I told Walburga, that the GDR's media were eager to forget German war guilt and the massacre of at least eleven million people; they preferred to fill the papers and the airwaves with virtuous finger-pointing at other countries' misdeeds.

Walburga was nodding emphatically in agreement as she scribbled all this on her pad. A rookie's interview with an unknown woman didn't rate a tape recorder. (Maybe they had no tape recorders.)

When I received a postal money order in payment for the interview I protested to Max, "This is ridiculous, I don't want to be paid for talking to somebody for a few minutes."

"What's the difference?" he asked.

"I was only doing Walburga a favor and getting in a few licks of my own," I said. "Maybe it will help!"

"Spend it and forget it," Max said.

"I want to send it back. Do you know the address?"

"Good lord, you'll mess up their bookkeeping for the entire fiscal year," he said, and turned to more urgent matters.

I switched on the radio when my interview was scheduled and listened eagerly for the licks I got in, but they had been taken out. Again I protested to the only authority I could reach.

"*Tya*," he said. "Walburga can get the interview, but she can't influence the editing."

"That's not editing, it's distortion," I cried. "They have a nerve to do that!"

Max hated to waste words over spilled milk.

But several outbursts later he explained to me that ultimately it was the Party who determined down to the last detail what the government and the whole society had to do. Nonmembers could have their say in mass organizations, ministries could make proposals, the four other parties (used as window-dressing) could offer opinions in the People's Chamber, but in a pinch a single SED member could carry more weight than all the subsidiary parties put together.

I began to consider joining the SED as a way of getting in my licks, but decided against it after a whole family of Grünau Party members agreed I would have to renounce my American citizenship. They all well-meaningly worked on me as we sat around their dining table.

"Why not? You came so far to share your husband's life. A person who says 'A' must say 'B'!" a gray-haired woman told me.

"Surely you consider yourself an internationalist, don't you?" a young man argued with a persuasive smile. He was chairman of the local branch.

Of course I considered myself an internationalist.

"Then what difference does it make whether you're American or German?" he pounced, as if this vast question was the clincher in some high school debating society.

Rather than say something tactless I asked why, if *they* were internationalists, they couldn't welcome a foreigner at their meetings.

After a moment one of the women said, "Why not come back after you've given the matter more thought?" It was left at that.

When the People's Police summoned me to appear downtown with a passport picture and my West Berlin "makeshift" identity card I also quickly flashed the glamorous green passport I was issued in New York, telling the officer in charge that I had no intention of giving up my American citizenship. He was perfectly unruffled, said it was no problem; I would be carried in the records as a person of double nationality. I was relieved that such a civilized possibility existed; I did not think to ask what disadvantages might be involved. In all likelihood he could not have told me anyway. No one there could have told me; law in the GDR was as unpredictable as the weather.

A period of indistinct doldrums set in. I don't know when it started. Homesickness ebbed and flowed, as regular a part of my existence as the menses. My life in Germany came to resemble the deadly boredom of elementary school when home had been a so much nicer place to be. I was afflicted by that hopeless feeling of the fourth-grader. Must I go on being a child until I'm ninety? Except that I dared not frame the immediate question: will nothing release me from this ghastly country? And suppose the release is worse than the country?

I stood on the bank of a sad, flat canal faintly gladdened by the sight of water, but feeling hemmed in by it too. It was as if this trafficless canal were the boundary of my whole life. I told myself: The barbed wire around a concentration camp is a lot worse, chum. But the poor inoffensive little canal was only a metaphor. I walked back slowly through the pine wood with my eyes on the carpet of last year's faded needles, so as not to miss the odd mushroom hidden among them. I wrote to Christina Stead:

> There isn't even a bar where a couple of women can go and have a drink. Remember, Chris, that nice bar on Gramercy Square? Nothing like that here. Oh, plenty of those ugly saloons they call *Kneipen*, but no place where women friends can sit and chat without being thought prostitutes or comic.

At the Club the Kulturbund posted floor plans of five different house types, some in Grünau, and Max put his name down. Pushing Dee in her stroller I walked over to the site. Nothing as tangible as a foundation could be seen as yet, only wild grasses bending with the breeze and in their midst a large sign whose post had been hammered deep into the ground. It said in heavy black letters

27 HOUSES FOR THE CREATIVE INTELLIGENTSIA
WILL GO UP HERE.

I was aghast and went home in great agitation. I shouted at Max, "Creative intelligentsia! How do you think this will make ordinary people feel? Do you want your child beaten up?"

He had learned to take my protests with outward equanimity. He barely reacted. "You once said you too dreamed of a house and garden," he pointed out.

"But that sign!" I cried. "Can't houses be built without such an overweening affront to the whole neighborhood?"

He saw no affront and nothing overweening about the sign. What, he asked, was offensive in being a creative person or a member of the intelligentsia? Such people were badly needed by all of society; or was it better for them to live in conditions that impeded their contribution? My notions were sheer egalitarianism, he said.

He, in any case, wanted to get out of our landlady's vicinity. Two usable rooms were not enough for the money we were paying; in our haste we had both overlooked the single glazing in that unfortunate living room where no one could live, the crumbling mortar that opened holes beneath windows, the shuddering of the windows at the slightest provocation. There was a broken pane in the sliding door that admitted drafts to our studio; all the ceilings were grayish, and here and there the discolored wallpaper hung in furtive tatters.

When at last Frau von Lovtzow sent a workman, he only tested the radiators for possible leaks. The workman was about fifteen years old, an apprentice plumber she could get cheap. He arrived so early in his smeared, baggy work pants that Max was still gratefully sleeping; it was the GDR's first birthday, a national holiday.

"That's all right," the boy said, "I'll come back to this room at the end." Only he forgot and I forgot and it happened to be the one room whose radiator had an open pipe.

Water was creeping out from under the soaked rug when Max got up, three pails full. Barefoot we bailed and swabbed while Dee watched from her highchair shrieking with joy. She adored catastrophes, loved it when a dish smashed, yelled gleefully, "*Kaputt, kaputt!*" when with panache I swatted several flies in succession.

"Bring Mommy a towel," I said when Max had delivered her from the high chair. I wondered if she knew what a towel was or where to find it. To my amazement she returned with a very shy look, head hanging, looking up at me from under her eyebrows and holding out a washrag. I was inexpressibly moved. It was her first errand.

"My heart and soul reside in that little girl. Just what I intended to avoid," I wrote to my parents. "I hope she never notices." But Dad wrote back that he could read between the lines of my letters. He saw that I was not coming home for a visit. The rueful words *"Tempus fugit!"* brought tears to my eyes. They meant: we are old.

One world indeed! "I never dreamed when I came here that it would be split in half and that the money in one half would be useless in the other," I replied. Private hopes and wishes were crushed under the wheels of some horrible juggernaut. Supposing Dad paid for the ticket, how could I risk taking Dee for even a short visit? We might be separated from Max by some other unforeseen horror — a real war like the one in Korea. Maybe forever! "Of course you'll see Dee, but not in her baby years." I wrote. A fine consolation. I prayed they would live that long, I hoped John and Gay would hurry up and produce a grandchild they could fuss over.

Max was again beginning to come home later each day. He seldom explained why, nor did I ask. As he often spoke warmly of a West German writer name Irma Loos, then visiting Berlin, I once kidded him, "Been out with that Loose woman again, eh?" He disgustedly rebuked a vulgarity which was "beneath my level."

At other times he came home early, rosy, genial, and in a faint aura of *schnapps*, to announce buoyantly after the doorway kiss, "Laxness [or some other courteous noted author] sends you regards!" If they had confided any fascinating information, Max passed it on to me. Halldor Laxness, for example, thanks to Iceland's geysers of various but always reliable temperatures, had in his home five different pipes for cold, not so cold, lukewarm, hot, and very hot water.

It was diverting to be told the latest from Utopia, but being a squirrel on the wheel of a household, I was unlikely ever to hear such stories first-hand. Little Hüppke did not return. A Frau Kristan had to be fired because of the incessant, senseless jabber that streamed from her mouth, driving us all to dementia. I so intensely hated the peonage of housework that I sometimes heard in my mind an unuttered scream.

At this time Gerda and Arnulf Lefcourt, close friends of John, wrote asking me how they could get visas to enter the GDR. Travel agencies in the U.S. could offer no suggestions.

The young couple had been something like mascots in the exiled German community in New York, which was predominantly middle-aged and elderly. Gerda often helped out as a volunteer in the office of Max's paper, where Gerhart Eisler also got acquainted with her. It was pure coincidence that I had already met this couple through John. I was especially fond of Gerda, a big blonde, forthright and very funny when she shouted in her good-natured, bossy way. Arnulf was a good foil for her, quiet and prudent.

They had long dreamed of returning to Germany. Both had been taken to America as children, Gerda before Hitler at the age of eight, Arnulf at fifteen as a Jewish refugee. She was as Aryan as she looked, but disdained that — on the contrary, she had always been attracted by Jews. They would have returned to Germany earlier if earnest, responsible Arnulf had not so strongly felt he must complete the college education interrupted when he was drafted. He thought that this would make him more helpful to his sick native land, besides being a sensible step in any circumstances.

Gerda was a commercial artist with a special gift for fancy lettering, and Arnulf was a persuasive agent for her work. As a team they had prospered, furnished an apartment with a studio for Gerda, and confidently brought a baby boy into the world, so that there seemed no earthly reason to sacrifice their modest success and go off into the blue.

They were romantic. Rosy childhood memories were strengthened by Red convictions. Despite East Germany's straitened circumstances they were sure the baby would be better off there than in an America under thought control. By June, 1950, the prospect of socialism in Germany looked especially bright against the McCarthy gloom, now even more frightening since the invasion of Korea. Friends in New York envied them for having such an honorable way out of the nightmare.

Unfortunately the government of the GDR did not bother about visas, a fact we and they still had to learn. It scarcely had a legal code it could call its own. Brand-new problems were settled on the spur of the moment by someone in high office whose initials were enough, and no precedents were established. This was the recourse most convenient for a masked dictatorship. Instead of providing democracy it continuously cited high-minded Marxist principles and mounted the profiles of Marx, Engels, Lenin, and Stalin one behind the other on public buildings as if they were a sort of Supreme Court.

"See Gerhart," Max said, and I went downtown to the Office of Information.

Gerhart was as cordial and jolly as when I first met him. "People come here all the time without visas," he told me with his disarming chuckle, "so why shouldn't Gerda and Arnulf? Tell them not to worry, just get to West Berlin and take the *S-Bahn* to our side."

Maybe he was thinking of John Peet, a brilliant young British journalist who had only just quit as head of Reuters in West Berlin to do that very thing, except that Peet probably used his own car and not the *S-Bahn*. It was a coup that Gerhart himself had secretly helped to mastermind, as Peet's autobiography *The Long Engagement* broadly hints. I have no concrete proof, but everything points to it, not least Gerhart's ebullient mood when he received me that day; and the location of the press conference in his own building, where Peet arose from his seat among the other newspapermen (what staging!) to announce his defection.

Gerhart had invited Max and me to this press conference, promising a sensation, but when I heard the young man's statement — he and I were about the same age — I was filled with anxious pity for him. Whatever nasty surprises might have been in store for Gerda and Arnulf, they were Germans, this was their country. As for myself, there was no reason to believe I would never see home again. Gerda, Arnulf, and I had made our beds for good reason, but how would John Peet console himself when he woke up to loss and loneliness on the hard mattress of the GDR? He was blithely burning his bridges, saying he simply could not take part any longer in the warmongering that not only threatened the Soviet Union and the "People's Democracies," but was also well on the way to converting his motherland Britain into a powerless American colony.

Meanwhile Gerhart and Hilde Eisler invited us to a small dinner party at their home. We hadn't been there before. Although the two-story house was located in a government compound (we had to wait at a barrier while Russian soldiers made inquiries) it was the most spartanly furnished dwelling I had yet seen among our circle of friends. Gerhart was certainly no accumulator of frills.

The other two couples who, until that evening, had always spoken fluent English with me and obviously enjoyed doing so, now responded strictly in German when I said something in my own language. So did Gerhart and Hilde. I felt chastened. They seemed to be hinting that in Rome one did as Romans did, and it was time I learned at least this much elementary etiquette. They had evidently heard rumblings that unnerved them.

Indeed we had all been horrified by the suicide early in June of Lex Ende's right-hand man on ND, a nice fellow with no airs. Rudi was another of those suspect "West exiles," although his byline still appeared occasionally. Suddenly he took poison.

Had he reason to expect a far worse blow than being fired from ND, which after all had affected the whole staff? It wasn't like him. His wife was so frightened by the quaking ground under their feet that she had left him and gone back to Mexico with their children months before. Was this what started his despondency or was it only a contributing cause?

The explanation, which came out only decades later, was much simpler. Rudi had slightly known Noel Field.

"This is the only decent thing that ever came out of the United States," Gerhart joked as Hilde poured the beverage into our cups. "Coffee. And that's from Brazil." The two other couples laughed obligingly.

Gerhart's embitterment over the persecution he had suffered in the United States at an ugly moment of its history was understandable, but a cheap witticism like this, it seemed to me, was an affront to an American at his table. He realized I would take it that way the moment the words were out. "Well, it's true, isn't it?" he blustered, trying to laugh.

When the Lefcourts reached Berlin they came straight to us on the S-*Bahn.* I moved my typewriter back into the bedsitter so that they could have the quite large unheatable room where, since summer, I had been working on a chronicle of the railroad women during the war. Sharing with another family did not cause too much disruption, rather the contrary. Gerda helped with the household chores and shopped, and when the babies had a scrap that led to tears and howls she calmed them. It was a pleasure to have her with me.

The only real problem was that foreign guests needed a permit from the police to live anywhere. If they had none it was a misdemeanor to harbor them, so from his desk downtown Max hastened to phone various authorities and try to straighten out their status. The frustration of being constantly redirected reminded him of his struggle in 1947 to import a wife, except that now there was a sinister difference. This runaround was not caused by the paralysis of a listless civil service answerable to so many bosses that none counted. Now Max was up against an impenetrable Party fortress at whose gate sat a Central Committee Cerberus named Joos. "Joos" rhymes with verbose, which he was not; he came straight to the point.

"So it seems you are now regularly arranging trips for Western foreigners," snarled Joos.

Max went white inside. The allusion was to Bill Blake. A description of the man whose very name struck terror into former exiles has been found in the Johannes R. Becher archive, written by the poet's twenty-one-year-old son, offspring of a former marriage. The boy lived in London. Long desirous of meeting his father he came to Berlin in 1951, but the chronically terrified Becher refused to receive him without the Party's permission.

> They gave me a long questionnaire. It demanded information about you, my father, and about my mother. Why from me? I sweated blood filling it out. Who is this Anton Joos they sent me to? A little gray-haired man with hard, cold eyes in a face that never produced a smile in all the long hours of my interrogation. This little man, this flea compared with you, dictated to you — you, a leader of the new Germany — how you were to deal with your son. And you obeyed without a murmur. Reading your work I think I understand what seeds you meant to plant, but when I see what has come of it all I am glad our ways parted.

Max was no Becher. His honor fought the fright and his pride concealed the struggle, driving it into his vital organs.

In Grünau there was still one astounding loophole in the housing bureaucracy, a two-story frame hotel with dilapidated porch and turret. It was called *Jägerheim*, or Hunters Lodge, and may have been pleasant at one time. Gerda and Arnulf were only too thankful to get out from underfoot and move into a room there. Unlike our haphazard accommodations it at least had real beds, probably hard ones, but our friends were not the complaining kind. As it offered no dining facilities Gerda and son Hans ate lunch and supper with us.

Arnulf spent his days differently. As if going downtown to a regular job, he took the *S-Bahn* early in the morning to the Office of Information and sat doggedly for hours in Gerhart Eisler's anteroom. Gerhart seemed never to be in, but Arnulf stuck to his purpose. The secretary finally snapped, "I tell you he's out of town. He's not expected."

I began to hate Gerhart.

It never occurred to us that the walls of Jägerheim might be bugged. A useful loophole. Why could the Lefcourts stay *there* without a permit? We simply put it down to the inefficiency of the system under which we were living, insofar as it was a system at all. We also believed that socialism was basically benevolent and that this flaw in the bureaucracy

would eventually become the rule. It was the middle-echelon functionaries who were always so narrow and obstructive, Max contended.
Where could cleverer ones have come from? The best leadership material had become bonemeal in the concentration camps. This diagnosis
sounded credible and I accepted it.

Day in and day out a barrage of insistent peace propaganda poured
from Gerhart's Office of Information. Since no one could possibly object
to peace, especially in ravaged East Germany still staggering under reparations (from which West Germany was exempt), the constantly bela-
bored theme aroused a vague resentment that made people feel guilty.
Another spur to guilty self-examination was the continuous lauding of
heroic antifascists who had been murdered by the Nazis. Their anniver-
saries were unfailingly observed with lengthy encomiums that all
somehow sounded the same. The fact that those antifascists had never
been involved in factional disputes with Communist Party leaders could
only have been noticed by a few ex-dissidents like Gerhart, who had
learned to tread more cautiously. For all that, if those colorfast comrades
had lived, they too might have become candidates for a kick in the pants
— as so many of the faithful did. The browbeating effect of all that sanc-
timonious verbiage depressed the survivors.

"If you can imagine peace jingoism, that's what is going on here
now," I wrote to Chris and Bill.

In the despairing letters I so often wrote to them I was doing something for which Max once reproved me in his restrained and pithy way,
"My best friend is not my psychoanalyst." He added not another word,
and this impressed me, but I continued unburdening myself to
Christina. "My marriage is a shell," I wrote at one point, but then:

> The clouds of suicide (which could never really threaten
> me and I am a pig to use the word at all) lifted very simply.
> I acquired a maid after months of drudgery.

The boon of Hedwig came to me shortly after the Lefcourts had
moved to Jägerheim. She was old and plain and placid. On being hired
she asked for permission to take her shoes off. She also removed her
stockings, revealing feet so discolored and misshapen by immense warts
that they looked like outgrowths on an old tree stump. Born into serfdom
on a Polish estate near Danzig, she had never worn shoes in her life, only

wooden sabots when she entered the back door from the muck outside. Like hooves her feet were an adaptation to the natural environment. Forcing them into shoes must have been agony.

As a serf she had never noticed political upheavals. Hitler was a name she had heard, but it meant nothing to her. She didn't even know she was a serf or that unpaid servitude was illegal. Rumors of some tremendous cataclysm in 1945 failed to penetrate until her masters, their children, and the other servants fled before the Red Army in a truck. Left behind in the road, stumbling after them, the old woman begged and cried to be taken along until at last the dust of their departure hid them from view. Theirs was the only home she had known. She wept again as she told the story.

The problem of where to go was soon solved. As a German national she was swept along in the trek of the other Silesians and walked barefoot all the way to Berlin. There the authorities forced her on her sister and brother-in-law, the only relatives she knew of. The sister barely remembered her. Hedwig never mentioned either of them again and showed no eagerness to go home at night.

Unfortunately her departed owners were replaced in her feudal affection by us. The pay she received, although not ungenerous, bore no relation to what she gave. No money could have reimbursed that absolute devotion, that tender, patient adoration of the child, or the ceaseless labor Hedwig did. She told me that while she was out of work she got sick, all her bones ached and she thought she was dying. Work was the only solace she knew.

And this enabled me to work at my own solace. I shuttled back with my typewriter into the vacated living room and resumed the railroad book Max had so long urged me to write. He never quite understood what stopped me from writing before Hedwig came into our lives.

It was bliss. At noon she brought me my lunch without saying a word. Having been unseen and undisturbed by Dee all day, I emerged at 4 P.M. a human being delighted to see my beautiful little girl, and took her for another airing, often with Gerda and Hans, until suppertime. I bubbled over with friendliness to Max. Dee also throve on Hedwig. At bedtime she said from under her covers in utter contentment, "Goo-gine, so-sol" (good-night, so long). Then followed the daily amicable argument with Hedwig about going home. "I just have to finish this one little piece of ironing," she would say.

I felt secure with Hedwig around, exactly as if I too were a child. I knew there would always be a clean, but a *very* clean and creamily ironed blouse, the pile of diapers would never dwindle to one, Dee would be put on the potty at just the right moment and not be yakked at until her nerves gave way. It was like the life of the rich. Was it really happening? Could it last?

In the fourth week of August and the sixth of Arnulf's anteroom campaign, the Central Committee of the SED completed its paranoid resolution "The Connections of Former German Political Emigrants with the Head of the Unitarian Service Committee Noel H. Field." The date on it was August 24, 1950.

Erica Wallach, née Glaser, in search of clues to the disappearance of her foster parents Noel and Herta Field, arrived in West Berlin's Tempelhof Airport on August 26 and walked into the trap that a trusted friend had helped to prepare. As she entered the offices of the SED Central Committee in East Berlin she felt a heavy hand on her shoulder.

She might have been saved at the last minute if ND, instead of waiting a week, had published the resolution the day after it was signed. A headline in an airport kiosk could have alerted her to fly back to safety on the next plane. As it was, her husband and two babies had to do without her for seven years.

Did Arnulf and Gerda read ND on September 1? Possibly Arnulf bought one. Would they have known what conclusions to draw? Probably not. I was too busy to wade through the thick mud of German newsprint ("Tasks of the Trade Unions in the 5-Year Plan," "Greetings to Romania on National Holiday," "Storms of Enthusiasm for Wilhelm Pieck," "Why a Unity Slate in the People's Elections?" "The Road to Peace," "Fifteen Years of the Stakhanov Movement") and I probably used that ND to line the garbage can. Max said not a word about the Noel Field resolution, which he had of course read. He kept inside himself the horror he must have felt when he saw in bold type at the top of the page that Lex among others had been expelled from the SED. He must have searched feverishly through the document for the wild charges against his friend and known they were unfounded because he had been with Lex in the French concentration camp throughout the time of the invented misdeeds.

Five days later we went to the Baltic, leaving Dee with the Lefcourts, who moved back into our apartment to look after her. Hedwig was taking care of them all, so my mind was easy. I was only concerned about Max's.

From the fishing village of Ahrenshoop I wrote Christina of a "vacation delayed nearly two years," during which I did not touch my manuscript,

> or do anything else but concentrate on Max. He was practi-
> cally mad from fatigue. There was no resemblance between
> that crazy ghost and the Max I came all this way to live with.
> Now he is all right again, but I hate to go home. He really
> ought to stay two months. Max continues to swim in the
> cold sea, but yesterday I gave up. I rushed in — one must
> rush, same state of mind as a soldier going over the top —
> but only to the knees, & then rushed out again. I can't
> imagine how Max stands it. His resistance is amazing.

Thus despite everything, it would appear that Max was still managing to be sanguine, convinced that between Marxian political economy and Lenin's efficiently honed "new type of Party" all must come right in the end. With this faith the old fighter in him knew how to husband his physical resources and take advantage of any opportunity to restore himself. Part of this self-control was not telling his excitable wife too much. For the space of that holiday, having locked away all political conundrums in a strongbox at the back of his mind, he was a delightful companion. It was as if he had reverted to the schoolboy figuratively turning handsprings at the prospect of summer recess, his sole duty to beat back the ocean waves and develop his skinny chest.

Seeing this I too revived, like a trapped butterfly when the window is opened. After Max's second plunge in the afternoon, we had a Nescafé and a nosh in exceptionally charming quarters we had acquired by some fluke, but decided to keep (though to Max the expense meant waiting one more year for a good camera). There, with an occasional glance out at the waves we read aloud to one another from Christina's novel A Little Tea, a Little Chat, savoring every masterly word. It was an escape into a world we had never known, nor ever would know; not a pretty world, but a curious, sleazily voluptuous antidote to the enforced rectitude of our surroundings.

"Why can't Aufbau publish her?" I asked again, and Max sighed, "In ten years. . . . They won't understand her now." I did not feel qualified to argue. The content of German heads was a mystery to me.

When it was time for our no-choice meager supper, we walked up to the *Kurhaus* on its hilltop, where the company at our table made up for the shortcomings of the meal. It was so congenial that the Arnold Zweigs usually joined us after the inevitable dessert of five stewed plums.

On Gustl's farewell evening he treated us all to a great platter of chicken. Still more thrillingly, he then produced a fistful of smoked eels, thrust them straight at me, and said, "Gorge yourself, darling," as unconsciously phallic a mild declaration as I ever dared dream, though the eels were of course for everyone. Mrs. Zweig, a fine, slender little wilted lady with manners that predated World War I, archly told Hanns Eisler, a Schönberg rather than a Glenn Miller man, "We'll dance to your new hits at our house in Berlin, a very big affair, we'll open up all the glass doors and turn the place into a grand ballroom!"

For her there had always been and always would be a social elite, so she simply adopted our crowd as such and sat up late with us after Arnold had gone to bed and Tete Busch, a warm and amusing ex-actress, started telling her off-color dialect jokes. Mrs. Zweig, excited by her own temerity, would take as many as two drinks. (Surely not that ghastly "Alkolat"? Was wine to be had by then?) At *Kurhaus* dances she made her nearly blind husband fox-trot with her, she made every man dance with her, and did not retire until the last guest had risen to go. In a general conversation at table she seemed lost and could only listen to the initiated with the expression of a frazzled, puzzled bird. All the same she had to be kidding Hanns about turning her house, which I have seen, into a grand ballroom. It would have involved knocking down walls.

Years afterward, at her one and only exhibition in the GDR, actually a belated retrospective, I was abashed to discover that this seeming leftover from a past era was a painter of considerable distinction and no more out of date than Arnold, who introduced the opening with a learned, respectful speech that made us take notice. I longed to own one delicate, joyous canvas of an apple tree in blossom. Small as it was, I hardly dared ask the price; but it had none. She would not sell a single picture, she would have missed it too painfully.

The Zweigs had spent much of their exile in Haifa. She was happy enough in the bare, wild Holy Land to remain there forever, but her husband, the world citizen and friend of the Soviet Union (if not quite a socialist himself), had his mind set on the unholy land from which he had fled, and he chose the part of it under Russian occupation, where he expected to find basically humanist policies.

To Beatrice Zweig any part of Germany was now loathsome. Unwillingly returning in 1948, she had recoiled from the remnants of Nazi benightedness and mediocrity she observed everywhere, had sunk into melancholy, and often seemed to lose the power of speech.

Arnold, a friend and correspondent of Freud, piloted her in loving therapy to every kind of social event, where she shrank into a corner; and he frequently visited the corner, bringing someone to be introduced or just standing or sitting close by the shocked, disoriented woman who, it was generally assumed, must have been rather an embarrassment to an internationally famous author. His loyalty was considered the more touching as he was notoriously susceptible to pretty young ladies and, because of his weak eyes, always had one read to him in the afternoon. He sees *them* all right, wisecracked the flip.

For Beatrice the hiatus in Ahrenshoop may have represented a kind of coming-out party. At table with kindred spirits, the painter and former belle seemed to be sensing how at least her own limited sphere might recover its iridescence.

Joos had meanwhile assembled a complete dossier on the Lefcourts. It pictured Arnulf as a gilded youth, scion of a banking family. He need not imagine, Joos berated him, that anyone in the GDR would believe his absurd fairy tale of coming to live there in hardship with no ulterior motive when he could be raking in the shekels, and was doubtless already doing so with extras from the U.S. State Department. Joos seemed to relish drawing out his inquisition, summoned Arnulf back again and again, and listened contemptuously to his Jewish victim's protestations. Tiring of the game, or in obedience to a higher-up, he abruptly ordered the Lefcourts to leave the GDR within a week.

"We will go to jail first," Arnulf said, and meant it. He and Gerda had decided on this course weeks before.

"We are not here to feed and shelter you," snapped Joos, "You will be taken across the border in a truck and dumped in no-man's-land."

They waited up for us the night of our return, told us the bad news, and carried the sleeping Hans back to Jägerheim. Dee too was fast asleep and unaware.

Homeless, cast out, down to their last reserves, the Lefcourts had to live in a dank basement in Hamburg that made them all ill. For a long time the young parents sought work, and no uncle with a bank held out a helping hand. If there had ever been such an uncle, the Nazis would have expropriated and gassed him long before.

A month after their expulsion Lex Ende was also placed beyond the pale, but differently. He was banished in imitation of the Russo-Soviet policy of sending nuisances to Siberia. It was not necessary to send him all the way, however, or even to slightly nearer Vorkuta. Small as the GDR was, it contained an ideal site for the banishment of a local boy: "the Wismut," as it was known, a region in the Ore Mountains under Soviet military control where uranium was mined for the benefit of the Soviet Union in Soviet labor-camp conditions.

The ideal part of it was that Lex's suffering could be narrowly observed and gloated over by those who had sent him there; although, by the same token, bits of information about his fate could leak to friends in Berlin, which would have been impossible from, say, Lake Baikal. The information was vague, of course, and could not be confirmed.

Thus at first we thought Lex had been sent to "prove himself" again, this time in some humble job in a small town. Then it came to Max's ears that Lex was in fact in the Wismut but had been moved from the grueling conditions underground, which were killing him, into a menial desk post at the mine entrance. Nevertheless he died within two months of his banishment. Of cardiac infarction, Max heard. A former sweetheart of Lex said in a magazine interview in 1990 that it was suicide, but she could not prove it. My own feeling is that a healthy heart which might have beaten without a flutter for another twenty-five years had simply broken.

When we ran into Gerhart Eisler at the Club I ignored his greeting. This upset Hilde, who took me aside and pleaded, "What happened to Gerda and Arnulf wasn't his fault! If you knew what he was put through!"

Max, I noticed, did not judge Gerhart. He forbore to pronounce judgment on anyone, least of all a beloved friend.

Sometimes I wondered at his patience with a gloomy Eeyore-woman who used to haunt the Club. She would go from table to table and make people uncomfortable, never sitting down with them on a vacant seat (he sensed she was not wanted), but forcing conversation on them and hovering with her donkey muzzle so close to their lifted forks that they could have fed her. "Why do you encourage her?" I asked Max. "She's part of the furnishings," he said lightly; but then he told me her story. In Holland she had broken under Gestapo torture and spilled names in a kind of hemorrhage.

"None of us can imagine what he would do under torture," said Max, as if mentally crossing himself.

But he knew too that there were subtler forms of pressure that could make a man like Gerhart drop a comrade or a promise like so much ballast over the side of a balloon's gondola. One had only to be a German Communist in the GDR to know this. On the other hand, weren't the Lefcourts lucky to have been kicked out of it? While we agonized over them and Lex and others, the man at the root of it all — Noel Field — was enduring a physical and mental martyrdom he had never anticipated.

Noel had lived the privileged, seemingly charmed life of a well-bred Superman flying through the air to rescue people in distress, not dreaming that his own gentle self could be seized, manacled, and subjected to a course of refined tortures. When these things did actually happen he was confounded, shocked, grieved beyond expression that "comrades" could so maltreat a comrade — but he was one of those who do not break.

Another was the handsome, gifted young German matinee idol Wolfgang Langhoff. At the very beginning of Hitler's reign he found himself being viciously battered by the clubs and fists of half a dozen SS-men in the cell where they had flung him. Reeling, whirling from the barrage of blows, fallen on his knees, trying to shield his head, bleeding from nose and mouth, he kept thinking in astonishment, "So that's how it is! This is what they do! . . ." All his upper teeth were knocked out. "I felt no more fear. It was as if I were someone else looking at my body on the floor."

Langhoff had been arrested because he was Communist Party secretary in a Düsseldorf theater. A son of the liberal Weimar Republic, he had considered his political activity perfectly legitimate. It was he who, as a director in East Germany after the war, risked his Party standing by demonstrating solidarity with the officially snubbed Brecht and lending him the facilities of his own theater.

He had another distinction, one that made his name known outside Germany. It was he who wrote the earliest concentration camp book *Moorsoldaten* (The Peat Bog Soldiers), published in Zürich, 1935. He had composed the song of that title to give courage to his fellow slave-laborers in Börgermoor. It was sung in many parts of the world and after the war taught to the SED's youth organization. Perhaps this was why, in the Noel Field affair, the Central Committee hesitated to expel Langhoff along with Lex Ende. It only "stripped him of his Party function," secretary of another theater's Party group; but it came as a severe shock to Langhoff. Max was as anguished over it as if it had happened to himself.

"Did Langhoff really know Noel Field?" I asked.

"Met him at a party, I think," Max replied. He told me it was even dangerous to have brushed shoulders with Noel's brother Herman.

We both pictured a casual introduction in someone's home in Berlin, an exchange of pleasantries, an absolutely meaningless mischance.

It was dangerous to *be* Herman. An architect who lived in London and happened to be a firm antifascist, although no Communist, had been jailed in socialist Warsaw simply for trying to locate his brother there.

Langhoff had not met Noel *at* a party, but *through the* German Communist Party in exile in Switzerland. He had fled there after Börgermoor, and everyone else in his group was now under suspicion with him. It was one of them who, in a vain effort to mollify the Soviet-dominated SED, had advised the Fields' foster daughter to visit its headquarters in East Berlin.

With age Langhoff's inner qualities further spiritualized the fine face he had been born with. He was one of the most beautiful men I ever had the privilege to see; perhaps because a component of that beauty was sublimated pain.

Those fortunate enough never to have lived in an atmosphere that causes otherwise rational human beings to stand up with the crowd and sing an absurd minor hymn like "the Party, the Party, it is always right" may have little patience with the suffering of an idealist deprived of his Party function. What may sound like a mild slap on the wrist was far more ominous; worse than the realization that the beady eye of socialist power was now permanently fixed on him, such a punishment made the culprit question his own understanding of right and wrong.

Was Joos a double agent? For years he methodically ruined the lives of as many honest and useful "West exiles" as he could catch. It was a grievous loss to a society half capsized from the uneven balance of forces between unregenerate Nazis, a few earnest Communists, and a majority of scared onlookers and opportunists. One day, much too late to help those he had harmed, the word went round: "Guess who took a powder! Joos!" For whatever reason, he himself had to cross no-man's-land in haste, never more to be heard from.

The Noel Field resolution as Max read it was not identical with the bound record dated two years later, 1952, and finally resurrected in 1990. While the newspaper version angrily castigated a few German Party members as downright inexcusable traitors, its allegations against Noel were couched in surprisingly dry, thin, and unconvincing language. This weakness was corrected in the bound version with a lurid tale of "moral depravity" which portrayed Noel and Herta as sly mealymouths secretly wallowing in a "repellent sex threesome" with Erica, their "alleged" foster-daughter who "was in reality a hireling of the Americans."

Innocents abroad, inveterate do-gooders all their lives, the Fields found the sixteen-year-old Erica in Spain half dead of typhoid fever and adopted her because her own German father and mother, who had run a Loyalist hospital until the debacle in 1939, were fleeing for their lives from Franco's forces. The parents could neither leave the helpless girl nor take her along, but Noel as secretary of a League of Nations commission could move about freely, and by saving Erica also help Dr. and Mrs. Glaser to save themselves.

Noel was the son of an American scholar who imbued the boy with his own Quaker ethic, love for one's fellow man and a sense of personal responsibility for peace. When he was nine and German-born Herta eight they met at elementary school in Switzerland and fell in love. Neither ever glanced about for another partner. Perhaps because of their time-consuming penchant for rushing in where angels feared to tread, they never stopped to produce a child of their own. Each became the other's child. Their relationship when I knew them in the early sixties reminded me of Hansel and Gretel walking blue-eyed through a wood that had become a jungle. She called him "Laddie," as his mother used to.

"Have you been true?" each asked the other in 1954 when they were released from solitary confinement after five years. They meant *true to the Party* despite all the sadistic falsehoods with which their tormentors tried to make them despair. ("Don't tell us the Party soiled its hands on swine like you. You'll never be freed if you don't confess. The world has forgotten you. Your friends have given you up for dead.")

They wept for Stalin in each other's arms when their ex-jailers told them he had died the year before. In 1960 they still believed. For *Mainstream*, a soft-pedal Communist publication in New York, Noel wrote an article about his faith called "Hitching Our Wagon to a Star."

When I met him in 1961 Noel was editor of the understaffed *New Hungarian Quarterly*, an intellectual advertisement for Magyar culture. I became one of the assistants who came to Budapest at different times — whichever one of us could make it — when an issue neared the printer's deadline. Our job was to correct the English written by Hungarians. A hilarious headache.

Noel was too modest and too conscious of what other people had suffered, through him, to complain of what he himself had undergone in that Hungarian dungeon. In the first year of our acquaintance he admitted only to having been beaten on the soles of the feet, a method of extracting confessions which is said to be particularly excruciating; but Noel did not admit this. In a lowered voice (out of embarrassment for the Hungarian Party) he told me he had quite recently seen the man who administered those blows window-shopping on Petőfi Sándor Street. That was where we at that moment were heading for our favorite café, Vörösmarty, a glamorous relic of the Austro-Hungarian Empire. We used to spend our mid-morning break at one of its little round marble-topped tables over a brioche, because Noel fancied brioches, and a sweet red vermouth or one of those powerful espressos called a double, though it looked like a sample portion at the bottom of its short tumbler. There we talked cabbages, kings, and shop while celebrities of the arts and society pointed one another out to contacts from abroad ("and that gentleman with the snow-white hair who looks like an English lord is Noel Field; went white in solitary, you know, so did the wife; no, that woman's not her . . .").

Jokingly Noel told me that his worst ordeal in prison had been the night he was forced to sit up until dawn manufacturing an elaborate history of his sex life, a virtually unknown quantity even to himself at that time, while the imbecile on duty kept shouting at that chastest of men, "Is that all? You take us for fools? Get on with it!"

After their release from jail Noel and Herta refused to be a sideshow for Western reporters. There was no way in which they could distinguish decent ones from the more shameless members of the pack slavering for a scoop. These accosted them whenever they left or returned to the rose-colored stone bungalow in the Buda hills given them in partial compensation for their sufferings. It was dread of just such harassment, to say nothing of another jail term, that prevented their return to the United States. Seldom has circumstantial evidence contributed so fatefully to persecution and the morbid pursuit of hot copy.

Noel had indeed known Allen Dulles, a classmate at Harvard, who later became head of the Office of Special Services during the war. Soon after Harvard they had met again as employees of the State Department where Noel, however, was assigned only to the innocuous League of Nations desk, a lost cause. An influential relative had maneuvered him into this position, thinking it — however dull — a good start for a young gentleman's career. Although a diplomatic career was not Noel's choice (he had not yet felt mature enough to choose) the assignment pleased him at first. Later he saw the futility of the nearly defunct League's paper operations and started looking about for more effective ways of working for peace. Trustingly, in letter after letter from prison, he recounted to a fatherly fairy-tale Stalin with pipe, mustachio, and understanding eyes the history of his gradual approach to Marxist theory and the Communist Party, in which he saw the only hope of ending man's inhumanity to man.

Obviously Noel could not make copies of those letters in a prison cell, so I can do no more than approximate their content based on what he and Herta told me in the only interview they ever granted. It took place in their tiny bedchamber at Héviz, a Hungarian spa they frequented for the orthopedic and other ailments they had contracted in prison. I promised them not to use the material until after their deaths.

Those who ordered the kidnapping and jailing of Herta must have realized that in all things she only followed Noel's intellectual lead (which is not to say that once involved she lacked enthusiasm). So she was not subjected to the physical tortures Noel endured. Instead she was kept for a whole year in one of those foul, pitch-dark, vermin-ridden isolation cells where only the toughest, most committed fighters hang onto their reason. Plucky Herta (who had driven alone in her car from France to crushed Spain, where Erica and her mother were hiding in a pigpen, and smuggled them under rags past Franco's border guards to the safety of Perpignan), now slowly went mad. She murmured incoherently to herself and the Noel of her memories, never hearing another human voice. The period was stored in her mind as a jumbled nightmare in which time, dates, seasons, daylight, humanity, and all reality had ceased to exist.

Noel, apart from having nothing to confess, could not be persuaded as other victims of Stalin's justice were, that he would be helping the Party he honored if he signed preposterous falsehoods. So after about a year he was simply left to his own devices, which proved extraordinarily rich and varied. At no time was he ever brought into court to testify, either in Budapest or a year later in Prague — he, the ostensible source of so much ostensible guilt in the Rajk and Slansky trials, he who became a transatlantic symbol of the Cold War. He would only have been an embarrassment to the prosecution. The daily and nightly "interrogations" of Noel Field ceased; he did not know why.

Sitting on his cot he would concentrate his mind on great works of art he had seen, read, heard, and try to recall them vividly in detail. He succeeded in remembering poems he thought he had forgotten. From the measureless depths of his subconscious he dredged up German lieder, selections from operas, entire movements of symphonies.

Or he relived decisive scenes from his life, such as the time he got Ann Burlak, leader of a famous strike in Passaic, N.J., to pack with striking workers a Communist meeting which the Party had feared no one would attend but intellectuals attracted by the name of Henri Barbusse. The Party would be disgraced before Barbusse! "We'll feed them," Noel promised Ann Burlak, thereby thoroughly cleaning himself out, but reaping the praise of H.W.L. Dana as they all marched singing through the center aisle up to the platform. "Now I know you're a real Communist!" said Dana, a descendant of Henry Wadsworth Longfellow. To Noel this compliment meant more than a Nobel Prize.

And interminably in that cell he discussed politics with an absent Herta of whose fate he knew nothing, but whose cheery, youthful voice still rang encouragingly in his ears.

By then she was returning to semi-sanity in a moderately clean, daylit cell. For company she invented a large family of the children she never had. Every day she saved a little of her bread to moisten with spittle and to shape, when she had enough for one small doll, into a son or daughter to whom she gave a name. She carefully moved them about, scolded them when they were naughty, praised and kissed them when they were good, and invented a farm setting for their home and their harmless little adventures. These resembled the ones in the girls' serial novels she had read as a child and continued in endless installments like a radio soap opera.

One day, she could not say in which year, she heard a sneeze from the corridor outside her cell that brought her to her feet. It sounded just like Noel's sneeze. A column of male prisoners was apparently being marched past — "To the barber," Noel interrupted, "they did march us to the barber!" — and both of them beamed at me, joyous at recalling that first ray of hope in Herta's five-year eternity. The sneeze repeated itself over and over again in her mind that day and every day, telling her she could not possibly have been mistaken. He must be nearby, he is not dead! And she began asking the jailer for books. Once she had to wait two months for Shakespeare's complete works because another prisoner had them. Noel, of course; but the jailer would have been fired for telling her.

And why? Why, when the authorities realized that they were stealing the lives of two innocent people, could Noel and Herta not have been let go? Because think of the scandal! The Soviet Union had accused Noel of being an American spy, the American government had considered him a Soviet spy, the impression had got around that he must be a double agent, but above all: the Party, the Party, it is always right!

At last new jailers with happy, secretive eyes took away their prison garments. Each was bathed in a proper tub and all but perfumed. Then in fresh clothing tailored to their new, diminished measure they were led separately through long corridors, like one of those bridal pairs in some ancient culture who are never permitted to set eyes on each other until the wedding day. Each was ushered into a different waiting room to receive a full apology from the prison director, not the one who had presided over their incarceration. Then two doors were opened into his office and two freed prisoners, aged fifty and forty-nine, scarcely believing the miracle and with inexpressible emotion, walked into each other's arms.

Their property was returned to them, including all of Herta's bread dolls, individually wrapped and placed in a shoe box, after which they were driven slowly through the beautiful avenues of a capital they had never seen and across the Danube to their new home. A maid-gardener couple housed below stairs had made everything ready and were waiting at the door to welcome and serve them at state expense forever and a day . . .

I used to urge them to visit me in Berlin, where theater was probably the best in Europe, and they longed to see Brecht, the German classics, and in fact any play in a language they could understand: for despite conscientious application even Noel found literary Hungarian beyond him. But they would not go to the GDR until its rigid Party rehabilitated them. This did not happen, either in their lifetimes or that of the GDR.

Herta took to reading and rereading Louisa May Alcott's *Little Women*, the book she had loved best as a young girl. She seemed never to tire of it. After Noel's death she gradually lost her memory, then her mind, and when at long last Erica could visit Budapest, Herta was raving and recognized no one.

Sometimes when I told Max details of his daughter's day he would gaze sentimentally into space and say, "Remember when she was just *so* little and we carried her to friends in a basket?" No one knew better than himself how famished he was for those priceless hours that I had and he was cheated of.

But whose fault was that, I thought. No sooner was he relieved of Bodo's magazine than other responsibilities rushed into the vacuum, and he let them. Were we no more to him than the last couple of sacks he had stowed aboard his covered wagon? Would he never look round from the driver's seat to see how the bumps were jouncing the riders in back?

He dared not look round, dared not heed misgivings, dared not weaken his own resolve, and I could not guess what he did not communicate. My notion of dealing with the inequalities in marriage was for both sides to put their cards on the table and then sort them out. It was easy for me to do this. My cards were on the surface and ever ready and willing to leap into view. His were not. If he could be said to have cards. The mere mention of such stuff turned him off.

"Girls are funny," he used to say in a dialect that sounded ruefully comic, as if to neutralize any possible impression of reproach. Now he was simply stumped. He had never before been exposed to a continuous day-in-day-out (with the prospect of year-in-year-out) life under one roof with a creature whose problems were so different from his own. On top of political puzzles cheerless domestic surprises made him more and more evasive. He had brought me to this place, he was responsible for me; it went against the grain to confide his shocks and fears, to hint at mysteries beyond his grasp or his power to solve; could I not at least *sense* this? Did I think he was superhuman?

I wrote to Christina

> Max is getting into that vicious exhaustion again that knocked him flat just before our vacation. It worries me to see it and there's nothing I can do about it. This time I'm trying to keep calm and not aggravate him by making objections. It means I live alone in every way and that makes it all the more important for me to get into the life here and have other connections.

A conflict between writing and living had plagued me chronically since my twenties. Inspirations flashed on me precisely when I was too absorbed in the world outside to write them down. It was maddening. I was driven by an urge, irrepressible as lava, to be out there, just as at college I had been driven from my studies by wild surmises of love. This was equally distressing. Full of turmoil as a sophomore I wrote in my diary at the time, "I must marry quickly and free my brain for knowledge." The swaddling of a new-wrapped mummy could not have been more airtight than the chrysalis of my illusions.

At thirty-five something told me I was at the height of my writing powers. The something was a sort of physical pressure between the throat and the diaphragm which a valve in my mind relieved the moment I sat down at the typewriter. As long as Dee had needed me constantly, the conflict between writing and living had been held in abeyance, but now my own need to get on with the railroad chronicle grew strong in me. I knew that while Hedwig remained reliable, this was my chance.

I had to grasp it. I had no right to be champing at the bit, looking back across the Atlantic to what was irrecoverable; or forward, bursting with impatience, to getting the book done and out of the way. (Barely begun, each became an incubus.) I had no right to be periodically crying for home, old friends, more love, love as Nirvana, love as Lethe, love as Lord High Everything Else.

Meanwhile long red streamers fastened across public buildings and factories were constantly advising everybody that "To learn from the Soviet

Union is to learn victory." Shorter and punchier in German, the slogan could have been interpreted to mean "Remember Stalingrad? Well, shape up, slobs! Build socialism or else!" It certainly had that impact on a great many Germans.

In smaller format the message also hung framed ad infinitum in corridors, offices, schoolrooms, machine shops, labs, libraries, orphan asylums, tram terminals, and interiors in the public sphere. Near it, inevitably, were enlarged photo portraits of (not all at once) Stalin or Lenin and their humbler representatives Wilhelm Pieck, Otto Grotewohl, and/or East Berlin's extremely unprepossessing mayor, Friedrich Ebert Junior.

Art was not meant. A product so irrelevant to production quotas, so slippery to the grasp of literal minds, art would have been the last thing to occur to slogan grinders. What, after all, had Marx said about it? They kept saving it for later, until time ran out and art ended up for Communist Parties of the twentieth century as a weapon in the class struggle — if only one knew how to sharpen it without losing either the art or one's head.

All the same, thanks to that persistent exhortation, the Christmas season brought a special treat to the GDR. Sergei Obraszov, an innovator in puppetry, arrived with a mere sixty of his enormous company; in Moscow he had a highly sophisticated, partially subsidized theater that employed three hundred. With ever more skillfully constructed figures he developed the art of his performers to a perfection comparable with the Russian ballet and Moscow circus; yet no news of him ever penetrated the cotton wool of GDR insularity until his troupe reached East Berlin.

Even then it was a wonder we learned of the performances in time to fight our way into the theater.

Satisfied with its propaganda mill, the government of the GDR had no interest whatever in the other uses of newspapers and never in all its forty years acquired any, despite the example of John Peet's entertaining miniature paper for readers of English abroad. It made the GDR look good and was indispensable to foreign correspondents in Berlin who relied on its succinctness for the main points of eight-to-sixteen-page government reports. The Party, it seemed to me, should have gone down on its knees to John Peet and begged him to train proper newspapermen (they wouldn't have had to beg) but the apparatchiks were too inflated with their own brand of German megalomania to believe a non-Soviet foreigner could teach them anything. In the end they decided his so-cialist idealism had gone too far, and they closed his paper down.

So reporters unconscious of the first ground rule of journalism, "what, when, where," were now hastily sent to rehearsals in the only venue that could be requisitioned for Obraszov at the last minute. Inco-herent with enthusiasm, they could neither explain what sort of jacks-in-the-box they had seen nor how these miniature beings so brilliantly mimed or caricatured real people with no sign of human intervention. They were not hand puppets like the jolly loudmouth Kasperle (the German Punch) familiar to German schoolchildren, but no one could detect strings either. In any case, "Don't miss it!" they urged, predicting a new role for Kasperle in the reconstruction of Germany, but neglecting to mention the theater, the dates, or how to procure tickets.

Puppets were a passion I shared with Christina, except that — rare case! — I probably knew a bit more about them than she did, at least from the practical side. As a going-away-forever present when she de-parted from New York after the war, I gave her my most recently made marionette, the only one I had left, tearing it out of my heart.

Once I had meant to make a career of puppets. I tried to get myself apprenticed to noted practitioners, first Tony Sarg, then Bil Baird, who played primarily to adults. They gave me short shrift, Sarg absentmind-edly, barely listening, amidst milling admirers and brightly costumed marionettes that hung from hooks on a rack; Baird and his wife Cora in their great yawning loft, incredulously and with celerity steering me, a pesky fly, out the door into which I had just buzzed.

What should they have done with me? Puppeteering was expensive self-impoverishment, a luxury, not a living. On the tombstone of a great Czech puppeteer of the nineteenth century was engraved, after his name Matêj Kopecky, the word VAGRANT, and things were not much better in the New York area a hundred years later. A puppeteer still needed in-come from some other source, or donors, not apprentices who picked up his secrets and became competitors. A rank beginner required at the very least one equally fanatical partner with a contrasting voice who was happy to labor from dawn to dark, and some minimum spare capital for a small truck, a modest workshop, and materials.

I couldn't even find a partner. No one I knew cared that much about being the soul of a puppet while invisible himself, and no one I knew had a cent. The depression had dragged on for eight years. So all I ended up with was a splendid, too too solid stage that my still-loyal boyfriend Nelson had built for me, virtually untransportable, gathering dust in my parents' cellar.

Yet here was Obraszov offering, we heard, to share his secrets with the GDR's puppeteers! A congress had been called where the curtain hiding the mechanics of his miracles would be drawn aside. Anyone could ask anything, could handle the puppets and see how they were made. I was dazed with a desire to be among those lucky people. I could write for marionettes part-time, there would be contracts in the wilderness. *Somewhere* I would be an insider again.

As a critic Max automatically received two passes for every first night, but this time none came. The agency responsible for ticket distribution had apparently been passed over.

Probably through some important acquaintance who couldn't go himself, Max did snag two good seats for the "Puppet Concert," a sort of vaudeville show that charmed us, and during the intermission stood on line to buy tickets for the following evening's "Under Your Lashes' Fire-Flashes."

The second evening we were in row 27.

From our privileged places the night before we had not noticed that all the rows in this dusty dump were on the same level. It must have been a dance hall once. More recently it had been in use as a cinema where the lack of grading mattered less, as long as the screen was fixed high enough to be craned at by all alike. What we were missing was a full-length play, said to be a tragicomic satire on the film industry in Hollywood.

Applause signaled the intermission and Max grabbed my elbow. The first two rows were always left unsold in case some member of the top nomenclatura deigned to find time unexpectedly. Fast walkers, we slipped into vacant end seats in the second row just before the lights went on and were about to move farther in — there was plenty of room — when a lone head in the first row with a naked dome and folds of fat on the back of the neck turned around like that of an almighty school superintendent to see what presuming, obnoxious louts had had the gall to come so close.

The dome over the suspicious squint was so oversized that in retrospect I see it doubled, bulge above bulge, as if the upper cranium was one of those props that an actor thankfully removes in his dressing room.

Max whispered a warning: "Ebert . . . !"

The squint had become an outraged glare. "Those are not your seats," brayed the mayor of East Berlin. "Get out of them and go back to your own!"

This was the donkey who had denied Brecht a theater and would not even glance in his direction for a hello or good-bye. Art, artists, and their ilk inspired no respect in Friedrich Ebert Junior, a typical philistine ignoramus. Quite the contrary: he mistrusted them as born subversives.

It was the name of his father, Social Democratic president of the Weimar Republic from 1919 to 1925, that lent a vicarious luster to the ill-favored son, making of him the perfect figurehead, empty-head, and yes-man to be cast in the role of East Berlin's mayor by the SED. After all, it wasn't the son's fault that Friedrich Senior had helped smash the German revolution of 1918; in fact the relationship was a political advantage now, making the younger Ebert look more like someone from the center, a distinguished Mr. Average who might appeal to all.

By 1950 Friedrich Junior was more than his father's son and more than just a mayor of East Berlin. He was a Politburo member and as such — if only as a rubber stamp — a somebody in East Germany's dictatorship "of" the proletariat.

The tiny word "of" had become a deceptive misnomer. Innocent young Communists used to think "of" meant "by" — as indeed the young Karl Marx intended and expected — but in practice that "of" was soon subverted to "over," dictatorship *over* the proletariat and over everything else in the system, all the way down to such subsidiary matters as who should get which tickets to a puppet show.

For in still another hat Ebert was president of the German-Soviet Friendship Society and in that capacity not only publisher of its bulletin and obedient hirer, firer, and rabid calumniator of its first editor Lex Ende ("unmasked parasite of the peace front"), but also the official host of Sergei Obraszov.

Naturally the idea of inviting Obraszov was not Ebert's. None of Ebert's moves was his own idea. It was the science of hierarchy, one of the few things he understood, that prompted him to follow with servile alacrity any instruction (the mildest suggestion was an instruction) from the Soviet Military Administration. Nothing in East Germany was higher than the SMA, whose cultural attachés, sent directly after the war, were not only specialists in the defeated country's history, language, and culture, but turned out to be fair and sympathetic in their dealings with its grateful East German artistic community. It was not long before such human attachés were recalled without explanation, but at this point it might still have been Brecht's warm advocate Colonel Dymschitz who saw that Obraszov was invited.

Max's non-review ran, "The success of Obraszov's company seemed to come as something of a surprise to the promoter itself, the German-Soviet Friendship Society, for it had been quite incapable of reserving suitable places for representatives of the arts and the press whose duty it was to be there."

The result was that he promptly received front-row tickets for all succeeding performances. I at least — Max had no more time — saw most of them and was deliriously present, adoring the master, at all three days of a puppeteers' congress and subsequent workshop.

But Obraszov had more than a bag of tricks. He could fit two plain wooden balls over the forefingers of his right and left hands and make them perform a love scene. To do this in such a way that an audience laughed and cried he had to be a great human being as well as a consummate artist, and he proved this in other ways.

His kind heart must have sunk at most of the performances put on by those he magnanimously called "my German colleagues," at their mental desuetude, the repetitious display of outworn figures of Kasperle, the vulgarized versions of Faust whose meaning they had never wondered about. He understood, however, that even the two or three real craftsmen among them, older men who had been in a rut for years, were not only inspired by having seen his work but "simply slain," as one expressed it. But with what compassion and tact he stood them on their feet, gave hope, shared wisdom! He realized that their provinciality was no individual's fault but dated back to pre-Germany, that web of miniature states whose watchdogs kept out any new idea; and if it occurred to him that any or all of them had followed Hitler he did not show it.

It was a thrill to hear him warn his audience against letting puppets represent workers or peasants, for to glorify workers and peasants was a dull duty imposed on all art forms in East Germany. "A puppet can only play a type," he pointed out. "It cannot play individuals. But every worker and every peasant *is* an individual. To represent them with puppets diminishes them."

We hung on his words.

But I began to realize that in the confined world of East Germany's family-based puppet stages I would not find such contacts in the wilderness as I had imagined.

What I really wanted, I who had never managed to get my tongue around the rich dumpling of a Russian syllable, who groped like a dunce from one Cyrillic letter to the next, trying to make CAT out of kuh-aa-tuh — I wanted to be in Moscow among the master's lucky black-clad troupe who, bursting with rosy youth and pride, marched across the stage at the end of each performance holding up their puppets. And it dawned on me that I was neither rosy nor young any more.

One day two antiques arrived in a package.

Mother used to wear a seal coat which I had always regarded uncritically. No doubt it cost Dad a lot of money when it was new, and that was why she kept wearing it year after year. To me it was simply a part of Mother. She had also acquired at some point a fox fur piece worn rather like a scarf to dress up a plain coat or costume. It consisted of a fox's head and its long bushy tail, plus a daintier fur pendant on whose narrow top the teeth bit to clamp the whole thing together. The bite was effected by a spring in the hinge of the jaw; I liked making it bite my fingers when I was a little girl. Fox fur pieces were considered quite smart in their day by bourgeois ladies. Mother must have been afraid I was freezing in Germany, hence the seal coat; and knowing I was as mad about fashion as she had been in her younger days she made Dad pack the fur piece along with it.

The seal coat was impossible. Not only had it taken on the short barrel shape of Mother's non-figure in her sixties, but tufts of the fur were missing in many places. Her eyesight must have been failing badly, and Dad did not interfere: his not to reason why, he obediently wrapped what he was told to wrap and took it to the post office. I threw the poor old thing away.

But as Max and I were to meet downtown for dinner with friends and I felt really desperate for a touch of fashion, had in fact seen nothing smart since I got to Germany and had forgotten how it looked, I slung the fur piece over a suit I still liked, the rust-colored wool with black leather buttons that I had bought in a sale before leaving for Paris. The skirt may have bagged a bit, but the jacket concealed that, and I could not *always* wear the gray corduroy dress that had so smitten Gillian's husband on my last birthday.

In the lobby of the suave new Neva, an Intourist hotel, Max tried not to look askance — he tried not to look at all — but as we walked toward the dining room he saw the bushy tail drop to the carpet, leaving the head gritting its teeth on my shoulder (I grabbed it by the fur pendant and ducked to pick up the rest). He was beside himself with glee and said it served me right.

There were no other witnesses, but I noted with mortification that something had undermined Max's all-forgiving love for me. Marriage, what else. Being an appendage, dependent, fur pendant, pend pend, something that hangs, heavily hangs from a husband's consciousness, something always needing household money when money is used up, something that becomes nothing, a hausfrau, former working girl, who went downtown decked out like Mary Off The Pickle Boat.

There was the real life and the underlife. A frequent dream was that I had returned to New York and was looking for a job under the most humiliating circumstances, unable to find one, growing old, all alone, and with no memory of Max or Dee. Once I thought I was dreaming of my father. He was monitory and kind. On waking and realizing that the man in the dream had been Max, I was ashamed and angry. I did not want Max as a father substitute. But in the underlife our will does not count.

April 20, 1951

Dear Chris,

Girlish, eh? Yes, I'm girlish. I don't know how much longer I can get away with it. The ups and downs of my marriage with Max would give some epic poet material for a lifetime.

The creature had been neglecting me grossly for weeks. I became quite pitiful and pleaded for attention. On top of my other dolors I was reading *Jude the Obscure*. One day Max said some horrid things to me, the kind of things that make any self-respecting woman walk out of the house and stay out. I finished *Jude* and cried loudly in the bathroom, but as I could not walk out and stay out — where to? using what for money? — I removed myself "spiritually" from Max's existence. Spiritually means I did not expect him to come home for dinner, didn't care whether he came or not, and busied myself intensely about my own affairs, for example writing a puppet play in the manner of Obraszov about four intellectuals who talk so much that they don't know what the hell is going on around them. They take turns talking and the other three point their noses to the talker as if listening, but they are only waiting for their turn because each has a completely different obsession.

In the midst of all this Max had a birthday. He was too proud to ask for a party, so I asked him as a fellow mortal whether he wanted one and he said yes and specified a cake with raisins and which guests to ask. Among them was the sculptor I have the crush on, and I was delighted. I got the party ready but stopped saving up to buy a rug, decided to let Max buy his own damn rug for his future house. I would buy myself some clothes, and I did.

At the party Max was so drunk from toping while cooking that halfway through the meal his head hung down and he made crazy tyrannical pronouncements until he finally drooped off into the other room and lay down and fell asleep and stayed that way until after the guests had left. When I went to take his shoes off it was in the capacity of well-wisher on birthday, not wife.

He woke up, recovered, drank the half glass of wine that was left, ate a piece of birthday cake, and became quite lively. Naturally I did not reproach him, not being his wife or giving a hoot. The next day I put on my new clothes and was able to go downtown in the Aufbau car because it came for Max just as I was ready. To my surprise he climbed into the back seat with me. He hadn't sat next to me in a car or anywhere else for ever so long.

In the car I asked him as a person with a dispassionate opinion if he thought Gustl loved me a little. He did not know. That night he came home unusually early, although it was one of his famous and ever-increasing "late nights," and actually apologized for his behavior. Being proud, he was not quite specific as to what he was apologizing about. The next night, to my astonishment, he came home still earlier; true, it was not one of his "late nights," but his early nights had been working their way towards 11 P.M. in contrast to the late ones at 12:30 or 2. The next night he again came home early, although it was a late night. His behavior on all these occasions was sweet, friendly, almost loverly. He did not snap at me, he did not slap down my opinions with the one word "QUATSCH!" which usually concludes our discussions before they begin.

Last night, 4th in the row, we went to a housewarming at the sculptor's. All this social life with the sculptor is quite unusual. Max knew I was happy to be going. I spent the day very girlishly indeed, didn't write a line, only mooned and went to the beauty parlor and painted my fingernails a famous dark shade of Revlon called Chili Bean. At the party I sat beatifically in one spot for hours, eating and drinking everything that was handed me and gazing at Gustl as he went about his hostly duties.

We were shown the bedroom: white drapes made of sheeting from ceiling to floor and more white sheeting on the beds, so that it all looked hospital-antiseptic. They called it, he said, looking me straight in the face, their "unerotic" bedroom, and joked that only lazy people required erotic bedrooms. At one point he kissed me — casually? meaninglessly? — in the presence of his wife. Her expression of concerned commiseration told me, "All women are in love with my husband. It makes not the slightest difference to me or him."

I'll tell you something about Gustl. Although he is admired by brilliant, articulate men, cerebration is the last thing on his mind. I realized that it was precisely this that gives me so much pleasure. I always thought I could care only for brainy men, but my wishbone's talk is more like musk that he gives off. He tells a story, no one understands it: a friend of his asked a slightly moronic girl selling gum under the marquee of a movie what was playing inside, and she answered, "The blind are best at playing Bach." A physicist groping for the meaning asked, "Is that surrealism, or what?" and Gustl said, "No, just vulgar materialism," and he and everybody else, especially me, laughed uproariously, hardly knowing why. He talked for some eight minutes about a car he wanted. He had asked the government to get it for him (there's no normal way to acquire a car of any kind; and he is a special pet, has the National Prize — a lot of money and what else should he spend it on) — but they offered him a make he didn't want, so now he still has no car blah blah blah. I was astounded at so much inanity coming out of that handsome, rosy face, so Gallic in its muscular vitality, so full of infectious good humor even though he was complaining (he only looked a bit hurt) and then I saw how tickled I was by this quite dreary self-centered rubbish. Instead of being disillusioned and wanting to throw my wishbone away I am filled with an ever unholier delight in him. Max once said I was Faust. Maybe I begin to see what he meant, hellfires and all.

Max refers to Gustl's wife as a *Pastorentochter,* meaning not only that her father actually was a Lutheran pastor, but that her upbringing in a manse had made her virtuous above and beyond the call of duty. I have met the widowed mother, an old icon with consuming eyes that terrify people, scanning them for at least one saving grace she knows they haven't got. Luise is an extremely tall, lovely looking, fair-haired woman who moves like a young wild horse. She is sweet, gentle, sensitive, gracious, and wholesome. She's full of sympathy and understanding no matter what one says to her, but the sympathy always seems to overshoot the mark, while the understanding falls short.

And a wishbone, you think, is what keeps marriage pure? Maybe I'm missing your actual meaning. What I think keeps marriage pure is a husband who doesn't forget to make love to his wife, who in fact wants to very much. Toward the end of the evening I was sure Gustl loved Luise and would prove it to her as soon as we were gone.

But Max grows daily more attentive. And I didn't do it to spite him; not at all. I merely did it more or less openly (did *what,* for Christ's sake?) because I figured Max didn't care anyway and I might as well be foolish, if possible. But now the foolishness is over and I am only wondering if I shouldn't perhaps keep up a little pretense of it to ensure that he comes home to dinner. Other women have figured these things out by the age of 21 — or 6 — but it has taken me all this time.

I finished writing the puppet play. Elisabeth Hauptmann, one of Brecht's coworkers is generously smoothing out the German, and Max added a little verse for the song that comes at the end — part of his being nice. His verse is so good that it saddens me. The whole trouble with Max is that he is *all* poet, yet grants himself no time for poetry of his own. The play concludes with burglars stealing the room out from under the talking intellectuals' behinds, and they go on talking. The host's wife departs through the window with a lover, because it seems more fitting than going by way of the door, which she might as easily have done. She shouts at her husband, "I'm going away with a lover! You cannot keep me from it!" but he is not listening. It has a happy end with three puppets singing a march tune called "A woman isn't made of wood." Here is Max's verse, which follows mine:

Nicht aus Holz
Aber stolz
Springt sie über Tisch und Stühle
Niemand hört
Was sie stört,
Vernachlässigung der Gefühle.

(Possible translation: Proud, good / Not of wood, / Up she springs through floors and ceilings, / Would not show, / None should know, / How neglect could hurt her feelings.)

Under the circumstances, was it not very sweet and significant that he wrote that verse?

PART V

*My cogitations much troubled me,
and my countenance changed in me;
but I kept the matter in my heart.*

—DANIEL, 7:28

A dream between then and now.

Somewhere in the Grünau Colony of the Intelligentsia my parents were sleeping, each in a separate room. I was explaining to my grandson about life and manners. I had never seen him before. He looked about seven. I explained to him about waking up: a parent comes in and tells us it's morning.

There was a great crowd of birds up in the sky. I noticed that my heart was beating too strongly. It must have been from the cortisone Professor Conrad prescribed after nothing else stopped the pain in my arthritic fingers. I also noticed that I had to pee, so I got up and made a perfectly round puddle about two feet in diameter on the rug. It was that new long-haired white rug (llama?) that later ended so ignominiously in the jaws of a rubbish truck and nearly broke them. How Dee and I laughed at their frustrated gnashing! But what would my parents think when they got up and saw I had peed on it, and what kind of example was this to my grandson?

E VERY FEW DAYS DURING the spring and summer of 1951 I went to the building site with Dee to argue with the foreman and hasten progress, until at last someone at the Club hinted to Max that they would never bestir themselves until we moved in.

So he called the movers and they came as summer was waning. In preparation he got a case of beer for the men and packed a small bundle of his papers. Hedwig in a state of dithers and foreboding managed to pack only the kitchen things. Dee suddenly realized that she would never again dig in the sand pile by the meadow and composed a sort of Gregorian chant called, she said, "My Mommy Taken Away." I was surprised at this tragic confusion.

At the end of July after her first day in nursery school, she had composed such a jolly song called (she knew the title of her songs the moment anyone asked) "The Land Where the Boy Hopped." And had she not seen the new house inside and out, over and over again, had she not been shown her bedroom and our bedroom right next to it?

"Darling girl," I said, "there's nothing *but* sand piles around our new house." Not to mention a shipment of combined electric and coal stoves waiting in the road for various owners, cement mixers, paint pails in the foyer, ladders, bricks, and bits of lumber everywhere.

At the front door Hedwig balked. She would not even put her foot on the bottom step of the small stoop. She spent nearly all of moving day outside the house moaning, "I will never get used to it, never. Never. Never." But when through the open door she saw the mistress put on some old pants and start waxing the living-room floor, she could not bear the unseemliness and came in to say grudgingly, "When your knees begin to hurt I will take over." And Dee after her first night in the house sang a chant of contentment called "In the Bathtub," followed next day by part of a Mother Goose number I had taught her, "Upstairs and downstairs and in my lady's chamber" which her own busy expeditions through the mess apparently suggested.

There were, God knows, more than enough chambers in that house, and stairs down which to hurl impious old men by the left leg. I needed them like a hole in the head; but to Max, who had grown up in twenty rooms, our mere seven plus kitchen, upstairs bathroom, downstairs toilet, corridors, foyer, and cellar did not seem unduly large, immodest, or burdensome. Besides, there was no choice. Too much house was all the house we could get.

Max was especially enthusiastic about the living room's flower window, a glassed-in space to be filled with greenery through which we would gaze into the garden even when it was covered with snow. "And who's going to put the greenery into it?" I had carped mildly while we were still at the Lovtzow residence. House plants seemed to wilt at the sight of me. Rather than risk a reply he said I would be delighted with the wonderful modern laundry room in the cellar.

I soon made its acquaintance. Dirty laundry was piling up, and Hedwig was too shocked to come to work.

A round-bottomed porcelain vat was attached to a boiler under which a coal fire had to be made. By then I remembered to let water into the boiler first. After the laundry was washed, fished out, and placed for the moment in an old baby bathtub, I groped about in the dirty suds to take out the stopper, but couldn't find it. I panicked, there had to be a stopper, I must have put it in before, and I kept feeling all around the smooth sides and bottom of the vat, finding nothing but smoothness. How was I to rinse the laundry? My heart sank, I was exhausted, I blamed myself as usual, I was a nincompoop.

Between our house and the sunset lived the Grünberg family. Karl Grünberg was a bona fide proletarian writer best known for a novel called *Brennende Ruhr* (The Ruhr Aflame), about how German miners foiled a right-wing radical putsch in 1920 by calling a general strike. He looked older than his sixty years. He had been through the mill, was a charter member of the Party, risked his life in the anti-Nazi underground, somehow survived concentration camp, and was now treated with every honor by the East German government. To his wife and daughter he was the center of the universe; they literally worshiped him. With us he was polite but dour. We were not his sort.

All I knew of his work was a play entitled *Golden fliesst der Stah* (Golden Flows the Steel), whose first night we had attended in the fall of 1950. I was in stitches when Max explained to me what the title really meant — not, as I imagined, glamorization of the GDR's proud steel output, but actual gold detected in a foundry after the mysterious disappearance of the chief engineer. Western saboteurs had pushed him dentures and all into the molten steel. Max laughed too, but not so callously. Western sabotage was real enough and could be quite vicious. People got killed.

Brecht, however, had his own point of view on this. In a private letter he congratulated the director on having solved "one of the most difficult and important problems of our theater: portrayal of the worker." From then on Brecht tried vainly to emulate that example. "I cannot write a play about the GDR," he finally confessed to a mutual friend, the Dadaist and ex-publisher, Wieland Herzfelde, who told me Brecht's secret "in strictest confidence."

I knocked at the Grünbergs' door. Frau Grünberg had been a pioneer, one of the first to move her family into the project. Her house was neat and clean inside, if rather gloomy, and her lot cleared of builders' leavings. Without neglecting her household, she nevertheless found time to observe from an upper window the comings and goings of the other colonists.

So the door was opened the moment I knocked. Tall, erect, gray, Frau Grünberg tended to peer suspiciously, though she felt it behooved her to mean well. At first she failed to understand how the laundry apparatus could present any problem. "Ours works," she offered.

I was ashamed to put my stupid question into words. "How does one let the water out?" I stammered.

"I dip it out with a pot," she said.

Did she and Karl, I wondered, laugh over this afterward, repeating between hoots and guffaws the incredible joke "Didn't know enough to dip it out with a pot!"? Probably not. It was hard to imagine anyone in that family helplessly laughing, or laughing much at all. The bony, shy, and nervous daughter had not recovered from the anxieties of a straitened, Nazi-haunted, father-deprived childhood. Once she told me how terrified she still was when fireworks celebrated some GDR holiday. They reminded her too vividly of the sky over Berlin in 1945 when bursting bombs had also looked so pretty.

I went home and rigged up a siphon with a length of old garden hose Max had found in Nikolassee. Good thing I went to high school. We learned siphons the first year in General Science. I did not use the laundry room again, but Hedwig must have been enthralled with the siphon, for she began doing more laundry than ever.

Just before dawn there was an immense sweep of dark blue cloud over the wood and at its edge the twenty-seven houses of the presumably creative alleged intelligentsia. Crows in vast numbers left their trees every single morning around 2 A.M., cawing me out of my shallow sleep. I wanted to machine-gun them. Their population had increased in geometric progressions since the war because Germans were not allowed lethal weapons, not even a BB-gun, and the foresters who were supposed to safeguard the balance of nature took no notice, as yet, of a local suburban problem.

Max never heard the raucous horde. He was so tired that once he achieved sleep, increasingly aided by alcohol, he slept through anything.

After midnight when I lay awake frantic at the thought of the accidents that might have befallen him, the first reassuring sound I heard was

Edith Anderson, eighteen-years-old.

Max Schroeder and his sister Thea, ages five and nine.

The twenty-room mansion in Lübeck where Max was raised.

Edith Anderson's Father.

Max, his older sister
Thea, and their
mother, circa 1920.

Johannes Becher, 1920.

Anna Seghers and Thomas Mann,
1955. © Sovfoto/Eastfoto/PNI.

Richard Wright. © Archive Photos/PNI.

Max, Herbert Ihering, Unidentified, and Brecht at the Kulturbund Club.

Georg Lukács and Max.

Berlin, 1945. © Culver Pictures/PNI.

Max, Edith, and Ilse Langher, 1948.

Max and his four-month old daughter, 1950.

Max painted in 1931 by Albrecht Schiestl-Arding.

Noel and Herta Field,
1949. Courtesy of
Werner Schweizer.

Hans Eisler, 1950.
Courtesy of Gerda
Goedhart/Akademie
Der Kunste, Berlin.

the familiar cigarette cough that resembled no one else's (like Noel's sneeze) as he came along the path leading from Stefan Heym's house and across the scuffed dirt that was our street. The second sound of cheer was the piss he aimed through the bushes that lined the fence on the street side of the house. It became one of his homecoming rites, the late-night one when there were no witnesses and he could assert his owner-ship of that dream come true, a house and garden, like a dog marking its precinct.

"Couldn't you wait until you came inside?" I asked the first time, just out of curiosity, there being nothing wrong with his kidneys. He ex-plained. After that I fell asleep as soon as I heard the long whish in the leaves. I was barely aware when he lay down beside me.

As it happened we did not own the house. The government changed its mind after a few months and informed all twenty-seven households that it was rent we were paying, not installments. It was the typical un-fathomable socialist muddle, but our reaction was typical too. What dif-ference did it make? The house was as good as ours, they'd never put us out! A socialist government was like extended family. And goody for us: it, not we, would be liable for necessary repairs.

We felt so ridiculously secure that before we heard the house wasn't ours Max had ordered a magnificent ceramic stove for the living room, just in case we did not receive enough coal for the central heating. (Nor did we.) He told me proudly that the maker was famous and venerable; he was thrilled that the firm was operating again. And to make life that much more exquisite he also had a brick fireplace built in his library, and I wrote home for a corn-popper.

A couple of years later the extended family sent us a thumping bill. Max was incensed. "They're crazy," he said, "I'm not paying that bill! Don't they realize that such a stove and such a fireplace increase the value of this property?" They neither paused to realize anything nor did they give a damn. They sent a bailiff who pasted stickers all over the movable furnishings, but not on the stove or fireplace, which could not be uprooted, were part of the house, and would be lost if we moved.

The German slang word for such stickers, a badge of shame to the non-bohemian, is *cuckoos*. If we were indeed in Cloud-Cuckoo Land, the cuckoos were ourselves. Not that we were alone in this. We were legion.

The reader may wonder how we could have been so gullible after the cruel expulsion of the Lefcourts and the unmerited bitter punishment of Lex, Langhoff and so many others, more and more of them. The newest misfortune, the one closest to Max, was Rosl's attempted suicide. It was prompted by the abrupt recall of her husband from a Party assignment in West Germany. As a West exile he was no longer trusted, and she panicked: where could they go now?

I can only say we had all begun to exist on different levels of consciousness, automatically slithering from level to level depending on whom we were with — friend, foe, nut, or question mark. This applied equally to Rosl after she was saved and her slit wrists healed. The severed nerves could not be mended, she could never again do fine needlework, but she labored all the more sedulously to spread the socialist word in the East Berlin neighborhood where they eventually settled. Their circumstances were humbler, but not dire.

In any case this sort of subconscious scene-shifting in the absence of hard fact is a function of self-preservation. We learn in childhood what not to blurt out. Later we learn what not even to think. Blessed are those who perceive this and resist. Or at least know they are doing it. Though the truth may hasten their ruin.

There was a further hitch. If anyone apart from God had whispered the truth to us then, we would not have believed it. Partly because it was still in the making and might yet prove reversible. But there are moments in history and in a lifetime when shocking facts are rejected out of hand because they oppose an all-engulfing need.

Such a moment came for me when I was twenty and a chance guest in the Martha's Vineyard summer home of Max Eastman and his Russian wife. I was stunned to hear from this charming woman with the white ringlets and lively blue eyes that her brother was doing forced labor in a Soviet mine. They had moved heaven and earth to rescue him, but nothing had worked. What stunned me was not the story, to which I gave absolutely no credence, but that a delightful woman like Ilyena could make up anything so preposterous. She didn't *look* mad. She was a perfect love, and a fantastic cook. I had read a book by Max Eastman about laughter, and admired him. He taught me to play horse shoes that day on their lawn. We talked about art — how to mix the base for an oil painting according to the methods of different old masters. We played with the kittens, Dimka and Willimantic. We all — even Eastman's paid tennis partner Danforth, who had brought me there and didn't seem the type — took a nude bathe in the waters opposite Chappaquiddick. (Was I the type?) I tried to hide my shame at seeing and being seen by strange men, especially Eastman, who was quite unconcerned about his pendulous old flesh. After dinner his stomach talked unselfconsciously as he rested on the living-room sofa. Ilyena and I did the dishes and were merry.

In the fall she invited me to a party at their home in Mt. Vernon, near New York. I was actually terrified when I heard her sweet voice on the phone. I made an excuse.

For years I had been shopping around in a welter of leftist organizations to find the true Communists, but in a metropolis like New York the choice was hopelessly confusing. Communists, Socialists, Socialist Workers Party, anarchists, Lovestonites, Trotskyists, they all professed similar ideals, yet each of those organizations or splinter groups fiercely and inexplicably hated all the others. Although in my opinion this did not bode well for any of them, I kept trying to learn more because I wanted a world in which I would never again, as in 1930 and 1931, pass homeless men purple with cold who had frozen to death in doorways during the night, or little children selling newspapers in the subway after they should have been asleep in warm beds.

I wrote in my diary:

> Max Eastman and his wife were kind to me, human and warm. They swore that Bolshevism had been betrayed by "Stalinists" — that Russia is a horrible, tyrannical prison — that the trials were a frame-up. They could prove it. Ilyena knew the instigators personally. She called the British intellectual John Strachey [at that moment highly regarded by the Communists] a paid agent of Soviet betrayal. And many other fine people call Eastman an enemy of the working class, a Trotskyist; and swear that Russia is truly happy in its planned economy and we should all become Communists. Arguments, facts, pamphlets, proofs rain down from all sides.

At about that time I met Norman again. A former classmate in high school, he was bluff, open, direct, no hater, not petty, and he patiently answered all my objections to the Communist Party until I was brought round to saying to myself, He's right, no one and nothing is perfect, I will go in without exaggerated expectations and just be a soldier among the rest. He even talked me into marrying him, though I was against marriage. What particularly impressed me was his persuasion that Marxism was an actual science. We studied *Das Kapital*, part I, together, and for the time being I could doubt no longer.

During Gorbachev's reign a deputy editor of *Izvestia* enlightened a radio interviewer from BBC on the meaning of the word intelligentsia. In your country, he was explaining to the Englishman, "it simply means intellectuals. In our country it has always meant those people who take a conscientious interest in the welfare of society."

My old abridged Oxford dictionary (a curiosity published in socialist Poland) gives a definition distantly related to the Russian one, "The part of a nation that aspires to independent thinking," but this was hardly the idea of the functionaries who planned three colonies for the "creative intelligentsia" in different parts of East Berlin. To judge by ours it seemed to mean anyone at all who was not absolutely stupid, yet for one reason or another was accorded domicile privileges.

The only genuine intellectual I saw in the Grünau colony, apart from Max, was Gillian's husband Harry. Max and Harry were the real heavies of the place, sorters of ideas, yet full of natural poetry and deeply concerned for the welfare of society. Harry was a learned all-round musician, whose high Jewish brow hoarded galaxies of sonority in which error was minimal and in any case correctable. He rather awed me. It amazed me that Gillian could so lightly refer to him as "the old man" (nothing to do with age, he was only three years her senior) or, when she got suddenly fed up, "that sssssod," a prolonged hiss before she released the *od*. I had been shy with him from the first, but since hearing how "smitten" he was with a dress of mine I had avoided looking directly at his hooded, too curious eyes.

From our bedroom window I could see their house diagonally across the road. They could see ours from the south window of Harry's L-shaped study, their most generously proportioned room with the Steinway and all the scholarly books.

It was the two husbands who had planned this proximity, thinking we girls would be pleased, and we were pleased. So were they of course, not having discovered as yet that Wagner moved Max to tears and Harry to tirades.

Tommy was a good little chap a year and a half older than Dee, and did not blubber constantly as I expected at first sight of his fat, pouting mouth. He did cry with rage when she knocked down one of his block towers just for the pleasure of seeing it tumble, but he did not hit her. As if he had read Spock he treated her with grandfatherly consideration, teaching her all the wonders of the world as soon as he learned them; and she was a wide-eyed, receptive pupil.

Each needed a sibling, but as Gillian and I were unwilling to sacrifice the rest of our youth for pregnancies, labor, diapers, and teeth rotting from the calcium loss, we were doubly grateful for such a providential arrangement. Our infants became a brother and sister so close and peaceful that Tommy exogamously selected a little Nettie from down the road to play doctor with. Gillian's suspicions being aroused when she saw from the garden that the curtains of his room were drawn, she walked in and said briskly, "Pants on, out in the garden, you two!"

"I do think education is so important with small children, don't you?" she said the day we met, at a party swirling with people. She was only making conversation, a gift she had and I lacked, but she meant what she said and probably expected more of education than it could accomplish. She feared that I didn't take it seriously enough. "You make too many jokes with Dee," she reproved me once. "How is she to learn what really matters?"

My first view of her was from the back. She was extremely enticing from the back. Arm in arm with Harry she had a lilting walk that made her honey-colored curls bounce on the nape of her neck.

"That's the music fellow I told you about," Max said. "The girl must be his wife." He spoke with a certain excitement and strode faster, not to catch up with the couple who themselves were moving along at quite a clip, but in expression of his gladness that here at last might be the right friend for me. We were all just a bit late to Hanns Eisler's cocktail housewarming, hence the race. Hanns and his wife Lou had shopped around Central European capitals all year for the best composing environment and had at last, holding their noses, taken the risky plunge into the GDR where his brother Gerhart was, and Brecht, and guaranteed privileges. The swirl of people as we entered was very distinguished indeed.

(Alma Mahler, wife of composer Gustav and others, relates in her autobiography that when she asked Lion Feuchtwanger in California why he, a Communist sympathizer, did not also go back and settle in East Germany he replied, "Am I crazy?")

No doubt it was Lou who had delayed the final decision, but now she was making the best of it in royal receiving posture, not moving an inch, on glossy new parquet just inside their immense music room. Short but commanding, she resembled a floor vase with a burst of dark peonies for a head, and dispensed that Viennese charm interlarded with Viennese contempt which is democratic in that it leaves no one out. No Hapsburg after all, only the daughter of a rich confectioner, she did not care for causes if they involved hardship. I remember her jubilation when she finally made up her mind to quit Hanns and return to Austria, telling everyone, "Thank God, a Marshall Plan country!"

From the front Gillian was as lovely as her back had promised, with bright and clever blue eyes that missed nothing. The interesting nose was like a ski slope that stopped upbeat and just escaped being too long — an investigative, adventurous nose. She had no shyness, involved new people at once in some banal but conversation-producing topic. Her confidential asides suggested that intimacy was just around the corner; she would glance quickly round as if to make sure no one was eavesdropping, and thoughtfully demur if your opinion slightly differed from hers: "Ah, but you see, cock —"

Across the room, within the curve of the grand piano, her husband stood in deep converse with some other egghead. Harry's narrow shoulders were slightly stooped with scholarship, his long face pale as chalk. He was homely. Black hair receded from a high forehead, the nose was as big as a Mussulman's, the lips heavy. He looked so intimidatingly brilliant that in my ignorance of most classical music, to say nothing of theory, I wondered how Gillian managed to keep up with him. Would her merely liking the stuff satisfy him? *Did* she like it?

"Gillian and I are having a wonderful time," I wrote to my parents. "For both of us it's like a new game, an everlasting hen party. One of us is always trotting across the way to borrow something or ask advice, but it's all more or less an excuse to gossip. It's the first time in Germany that either of us had such a feeling of being at home among friends. I can hang out the window and scream, 'Gi-i-i-illie!' and she can appear in her window with a dustcloth and red dusting bandanna she ties around her head and yell back, 'Wha-a-a-at?' I love that!"

We seemed to say the same things every day, but they always had some slight variation, as in Gertrude Stein's *Melanctha*. That story's continuous repetitions do not madden the reader like "a rose is a rose is a rose," but draw him in their wake from one surprise to another. It was like aging, which proceeds so invisibly that from bloom to weariness to withering we always think we see the same face in the mirror and ultimately discover our true reflection only in other people's pleasure, compassion, or total blindness to our being. Yet the very repetitions between two people, the necessity of these repetitions, as between Melanctha and Rose Johnson, has a meaning that eventually reveals itself.

One evening when Max and I had invited Harry and Gillian for a fireside visit and Harry rhetorically asked Max after the first half hour, "What goes on between these two?" Gillian at once looked very mysterious and teasing, and I laughed, although to her knowledge and mine nothing went on between us at all, we did nothing but jabber; she merely enjoyed seeing the master of her fate nettled by an intimacy he could not penetrate, and in which he was neither needed nor welcome.

Max was so embarrassed by this sort of talk that he rushed out of the room, pretending he had to do something in the kitchen, and made no haste to come back.

"I had five brothers," Gillian often told me, spacing the words out meaningfully and with the same emphasis each time, "so don't tell me about men!" I did not dream of instructing her about men, whose unexpected failings still mystified me; that was just an expression she used. "Sssssods, all of them. They way those sssssods treated their girlfriends! The way they jeered behind the backs of those poor cows!"

She would amend these generalizations.

"Oh I don't mean *Harry* is a sod"; but at once she held up a forefinger and said, "He *can* be!" A laugh, another moment's reflection. "He's a gorgeous person. . . . The mothers ruin them. Then it's up to the wives to show them they're not the center of the universe. Not — so — simple, ducky!" she said, spacing out the words.

"I *manage* my marriage," she declared. "You don't. You let Max do as he pleases. If I don't like Harry's shenanigans I withhold myself."

I had to laugh. "Max wouldn't notice if I did."

She sobered. "Poor poppet. . . . No wonder you look so drawn."

"I look drawn?"

"I don't mean you're not attractive," she said quickly. "I just mean —"

I looked in the mirror afterward, but apparently people make a special mirror face which is unenlightening. Certainly I was never quite well in those years.

Christina's analysis was that I was going hungry. It was quite common, she wrote, for housewives to deny themselves while making sure everyone else got enough to eat. I thought this extraordinarily perceptive. I hadn't even known I was going hungry, only that my appetite had slackened.

Our expenses had mounted since we moved into the Colony. The garden side of the living room being nearly all glass, Max had bought, heaven knows where, yards and yards of a superb reddish-brown textile that matched the ceramic stove and expressed the idea of Aufbau, that is, reconstruction, through a raised pattern of little Breughel men doing every kind of skilled and unskilled labor. A professional decorator was needed to cut and hang the material, which Dee adored as an endless picture book. It was pleasant and luxurious at night to be able to draw these handsome drapes in their thick folds all the way across the room, but as the Colony of the Intelligentsia — its official designation — was a local attraction, we also needed glass curtains to defeat gogglers during the day; another job for the decorator.

Then — incredible windfall — Max found on some obscure street downtown a little carpentry shop that had enough desperately needed matching bookcases, tasteful ones, to line his library, a room that extended all the way from back to front of the house. He bought out the shop. One had to seize the moment when something so important appeared, never mind the cost, go into debt, because — and this was everybody's experience in East Germany — nothing comparable would ever again appear. And it never did, any of it.

I did not ask Max what he paid. I was not curious, and I considered his taste impeccable. I only asked (hating to do it) for household money. I suggested that he give me a fixed sum every month when he got paid, and I would manage with it, but he said no, that wouldn't work, so I was compelled too often to ask and ask. Looking troubled he would say something like "I could give you two hundred marks next Wednesday," which reminded me of his own favorite remark from Wimpy, the referee in Popeye (in New York he had found this hilarious): "I would gladly pay you Tuesday for a hamburger today," and while waiting for Wednesday or whenever I would run so low that he had to give me ten marks, twenty marks, five marks with which to skimp, so that when Wednesday came it seemed to him a fresh imposition on his limited resources.

Once I mentioned this difficulty to Alma, who was dumbstruck. She said, as if it were any use to me, "*Bodo* leaves money on the night table every morning before he goes to town. It's *always* there when I wake up." A glimpse into the seraglio? I didn't know whether to laugh or cry.

But things were not that cut-and-dried with Alma and Bodo after all. Early one Sunday afternoon a car was heard pulling up outside, and presently Alma with a furious face and Bodo looking unbelievably hangdog marched into our living room. That is, she marched and he *was* marched, not quite by the scruff of the neck, but that was the dramatic impression their entrance made.

"I want to talk to Max," Alma announced, the tears already starting from her eyes. "Bodo, you stay here."

She opened the library door, Max followed her in, and the door was closed.

Bodo slumped into an armchair, defeated.

"What's wrong?" I asked.

She had caught Bodo and his secretary Wilhelmine *in flagrante*. Bodo did his writing in a little closed pavilion between their house and the lake, where no one was allowed to disturb him. I was astonished at the way he sat like a bad boy in the principal's office, humbly telling me what was none of my business. He could have said he was sorry, it was not a thing he cared to talk about, but if Alma wanted to pour her heart out to Max, and if this helped her, it was probably his duty to come along. Then I could have asked him if he preferred coffee, tea, or schnapps. On the other hand, what would we have talked about? We were virtual strangers, and his domestic trouble was working in him like a meat-grinder.

I have already said I understood little about men. "How could you do such a thing to Alma?" I demanded fatheadedly, as backward as he was foolish.

"I've always been a gambler," he muttered.

"I'm not talking about leaving the door unlocked," I said like some amateur prosecuting attorney.

Leaning forward in the witness stand he threw at me with a desperate look, "You really want to know why I did it?"

He's going to tell me Alma's no good in bed, I thought, so out of feminine solidarity I said no, I didn't want to know.

Bodo never forgave me for that afternoon. I was a ball-breaker. I had been a ball-breaker from the first moment, when my entire response to his flirtatious sallies had been a deadpan skeptical gaze.

Before next payday Wilhelmine was fired. Not by Bodo. He hid.

"If they're so goddamn moral why don't they fire him too?" I raged.

Bodo was an investment. A girl with no protector could be replaced. I smoldered for Wilhelmine of the handsome dark eyes and the apt surname that meant "free-gait." In the man vacuum of her unlucky age-group she had held out long and nobly for Alma's sake.

Alma meanwhile embarked on a course of unrewarding promiscuity which Bodo took fatalistically with guilt-bowed head. Too fastidious for adventures without romance, he aimed at a gradual reconciliation with Alma. She was not only the mother of the son he doted on, but an original and sparkling hostess at parties where foreign authors could mingle with congenial German counterparts. All of them delighted in Alma.

She had no idea that these international parties, which were pure fun and glory for her, coincidentally served the GDR 's diplomatic interests. Bodo, in growing despair over the decline of his own literary productivity, realized all too clearly what such occasions were worth to him in prestige and government favor.

But he also earnestly rejoiced that in his own unique way (for he too was a charmer of men) he was helping to put the GDR on the map. Literally on the map. West German cartographers were instructed to show a blank space where the GDR was; the Adenauer government boycotted any foreign state that recognized the blank space as a legitimate nation, and arrested West German kids for attending a youth festival there; West German radio newsreaders were trained never to mention the disreputable initials (DDR in German) without drawling them sarcastically: "Uh Day, uh Day, uh Air . . ."

All the same it was possible in the GDR for a man too, even a man who commanded great respect, to lose his job over a sex embroilment. It was extremely unusual; but it had happened the year before to someone Max would soon know well.

I have two vivid and very different memories of Walter Janka. The first time I saw him was at an informal Aufbau dance held in its canteen off the entrance court, apparently to celebrate the existence of the canteen itself. I was not introduced to him and had no idea that this brand-new canteen had been his creation. Up to that time the employees used to bring a sandwich lunch from home and eat it at their desks, or stand between rain puddles in the war-damaged, leaky shipping department shed in order to have company as they ate.

Dark as a gypsy, with an almost unnoticeable scar on his upper lip, Janka was dancing every dance with the same lovely young woman, one of the editors, while most of the dancers changed partners after each set. No one could have failed to recognize the budding understanding between this stranger and the fair-haired girl as rapt in his arms as if born to them, fated to them, flying in them. Each was loath to let go of the other. It was hard not to stare. I hoped for her sake that he was not married; but what striking man of thirty-five would not have been married? It didn't occur to me then, but in long retrospect Janka embodies for me the quintessence of Heathcliff.

I was never again to experience this resolute man in a mood so young, so carefree, so tender. I don't know how things developed between him and his dancing partner. One day in the nudist section of the Ahrenshoop beach she shared a "castle" with me and Dee and didn't mind my photographing her gorgeousness; but she was not one to share secrets. If she confided in anyone it was her mother, with whom she lived until the mother grew very old and died.

Born into a proletarian family, all of them Communists, Janka was not a man to be pushed around. Tough, bold, almost forbidding, he had been decorated for heroism by the Loyalists in the Spanish Civil War and promoted to major at only twenty-three, which made him the youngest commissioned officer in the International Brigades. Although lacking a higher academic education, he had in Mexico successfully published the works of German writers in exile there, and himself used words with skill and discretion.

Such a history and awesome reputation would in normal circumstances have saved any man from being fired over a silly, shallow affair, but Janka the rugged individualist made alarmed and vengeful enemies. Fearless, he did not obey orders automatically just because they came from a Party superior. He was uncompromisingly and intimidatingly upright, even told off the wife of the dread Walter Ulbricht for shamelessly cheating, claiming a whole liter of milk with her *payok*, and he forbade the slightest hint of a patronizing attitude toward himself. He took literally the claim that the GDR was a workers' state, hence by birthright and commitment his own.

When he first returned from exile in 1946 the Party recognized his value, but handled him guardedly. It was displeased when he quit his first assignment with no by-your-leave; he had felt he was wasting his time in Party headquarters. Nevertheless, whether to discipline or flatter him, the personnel chief tried to place him in a post where a hard man was required, head of state security in an industrial town; but found that the formally well-mannered comrade could be choosy and bristly and say no and stick to it when he smelled a rat. Experience in Spain with a German bully paid by the NKVD had made any secret-service henchman odious to him. He would not make himself cheap; he wanted a publishing job.

Now piqued and determined to capture him by hook or by crook, the security branch sent him a silken emissary, director of a publishing house that specialized in German-translated foreign literature. Well-spoken, with silvery hair and fine features, this publisher had made Janka an extraordinary offer: he could start tomorrow as assistant director, with the prospect of becoming director in a short time. The publisher himself wanted to go back to film-writing, he said. Janka would receive substantially more pay than he had been getting, as well as a villa in Babelsberg (Germany's little Hollywood) surrounded by "Soviet friends" with whom the publisher had cultivated excellent relations. Janka would get the benefit of these. He had almost said yes, and gladly, but the piling up of superfluous inducements made him leery. "I will never work with that man," Janka told his wife. "Too bad."

So the Party presented him with an Augean stable to clean out, the already corrupt film studio DEFA whose board members were paying themselves a bonus for attending their own board meetings. The business manager had a habit of elaborately ignoring visitors admitted by his secretary: he would play with mechanical tin mice at his desk until he was good and ready to raise his eyes and acknowledge that someone had come in. The last chairman of the board had just been fired for signing a contract with "our Soviet friends" — this expression was solemnly repeated in the most incongruous circumstances — which denied DEFA any right to make films of its own choosing. "We need someone," Janka was told by Party representatives, "whom the friends will respect on the basis of his political past."

"I have to be made boss," Janka prompted them. They agreed and he took the job, arranged a revised contract with the Soviets, and subjected the studio to a rough and thorough cleansing from top to bottom that made him still more enemies.

The business manager, to whom he had given a tongue-lashing for his arrogant tricks, ran off to Hamburg with sensitive DEFA papers. Sent by the Party to recover them, Janka was visited in his hotel bedroom by an attractive lady, the mistress of DEFA's most treasured film director. "If he plays around, why shouldn't I?" she said frankly, and Janka could not resist. The director, under special contract from a West German studio, raised a terrible row, and Janka was told he was compromising the Party with an American agent. He had had enough of the light adventure anyway, but this charge was simply too stale and preposterous. He demanded proof that the lady was an agent, and was told, "The Party is not obliged to cite proofs." Words flew, he felt his character and intelligence impugned, and handed in his resignation.

Busy Sepp Schwab, one of the Party's highest-ranking peripatetic firemen, was for the moment Janka's successor. After thanking him for the orderly handover of records and West-mark accounts, Schwab added innocently, "Except that exactly a thousand marks are missing from the safe. . . ."

Outraged, Janka demanded to know who had opened it. "No idea. Not I." Schwab was in his mean element. "I'll sue DEFA for burglary and libel," said Janka. "You won't sue. All we need is one more scandal. You won't find a lawyer who would touch the case," Schwab sneered.

But this was just a gentle love tap from the Party. It was not about to let a cadre like Janka go to waste.

Erich Wendt had been made general secretary of the Kulturbund, which needed a firmer hand. Everything seemed to need a firmer hand. Although the post was represented as a kind of promotion, Erich was not too happy about it. Johannes R. Becher, as president of the organization, was apparently too grand in his own estimation to soil his hands on practical matters, but Erich suffered at being parted from the publishing house he and Max had built up from scratch.

When on top of that the Party sent a young fellow with a slightly stained escutcheon to be his stand-in, straitlaced Erich received him with barely concealed aversion. He warned Janka that the literary side of Aufbau would remain under his own supervision for an indefinite period. The Kulturbund offices were, after all, only three blocks away.

The terms accepted, Janka at once started eliminating humble messes whose existence his employers, shuttling between their polished desks and the white tablecloths of the Club, had registered only as minor evils, unpleasant, but not top priority.

My second vivid memory of Janka dates from a period long after Erich had handed him the reins of Aufbau. Janka, his wife, Max, and I were lunching with the West German author Leonhard Frank and his wife Charlott at the Hotel Neva. When wives graced a lunch at which a GDR publisher entertained an author it was no idle gesture on the part of either. It was a declaration of mutual trust beside which business paled.

Leonhard Frank, then an old man who had just completed his last book, nevertheless looked fit and was tall and straight, with a lean, thoughtful face. As my mother had read and recommended *Karl and Anna*, (although I never got around to reading it) I at least had some slight clue to his international reputation.

He had been a poor boy, never forgot it, and considered himself a socialist. But like Lion Feuchtwanger he was not "crazy enough" after exile in the United States to throw in his lot with a Soviet protectorate. He had chosen the vantage point of Munich in West Germany from which to cheer on socialism.

He was not the less sincere for being prudent. He truly believed in the title *Man Is Good* that he chose for his volume of short stories. When another writer remarked, "The title is good. I doubt that *man* is," Frank replied, "He is when he gets the chance," and went on to entitle his next and final work *Left, Where the Heart Is*. He meant that too, but he loved to tease his Communist hosts by pointing out discrepancies between theory and practice in the GDR. The day of that lunch in the Neva he went at them hammer and tongs.

But with ease, brilliance, and wonderfully good humor Walter Janka delighted the equally good-humored Frank by upsetting all his ninepins, from the sly twits to far more earnest jabs.

Janka was a well-versed Marxist as well as a pragmatic believer, and Leonhard Frank enjoyed the fireworks of a good knockdown argument between friends. The rest of us sat back astounded, enthralled, and very proud of Walter's performance; Charlott too, for she never cared how a debate came out as long as fun was involved. She herself was a great teller of amusing anecdotes, to which Frank listened as avidly as if he had never heard them before, nor had he quite, because each time the details were different. Full of admiration he once cried out, "All lies, makes up every word!" and she basked in the compliment.

Janka and Frank quickly became close when Walter went down to Munich to meet, woo, and win the popular author for Aufbau — and get him for East marks. Class brotherhood was the basis of their instinctive response to one another, and this also partly explains why, before that, Frank had been completely turned off by Johannes R. Becher, the spoiled, marble-eyed son of a wealthy judge. Becher had very nearly put Leonhard Frank off the GDR for good. In contrast Frank started saying "*Du*" to Janka at their very first meeting, no light thing in Germany, and insisted that Janka, who could hardly believe his ears, drop the "*Sie*" to which he had cautiously continued to cling.

Later Janka became a cherished guest of the Thomas Manns in their patrician home Kilchberg, near Zürich. (After exile they had never returned to Germany to live.) There was obviously no exchange of "*Du's*, although Janka soon called Erika Mann by her first name (plus *Sie*). She called him "dear Janka."

Dinner at Kilchberg reminded him of *Lotte in Weimar*, where Thomas Mann describes how Goethe lived. It must have made Janka feel like the bard of the Twenty-third Psalm: "Thou preparest a table before me in the presence of mine enemies. . . . My cup runneth over." He related in his own book, *Traces of a Life*, how Frau Katja Mann drove him back to his hotel "in her big Fiat. I was content with God and the world."

The relationship culminated in Aufbau's gold-ornamented ivory parchment-back edition of the complete works in time for Thomas Mann's eightieth birthday — again for East marks, probably the greatest single publishing coup in the short history of the socialist world. And it was Janka unaided who brought it off despite nearly insuperable difficulties from the West German publisher who held the rights, and from Johannes R. Becher as Minister of Culture who thought the expense of twelve such volumes unjustified ("Why not one book at a time? Who reads the four volumes of *Joseph and His Brothers*?"). Goaded as he was by a roiling ambition, an unappeased hunger for vindication before the Party, Janka had to bring it off.

When only a year and a half later at the height of his career he was seized in his office and hustled to prison, he simply could not grasp that this was happening to him in a socialist country. The other times it had been the class enemy who thought prison would break him. That had been a grim honor.

When Walter first came to Aufbau Max had little contact with him, which is probably the reason we were not introduced at that dance in the canteen. All the same the efficiency of Erich's taciturn new business manager impressed Max, he told me so; and I remember his laughing over the silly fuss that led to DEFA's firing the man.

If either the editor-in-chief or the business manager was particularly conscious of any class difference, it would have been Walter, in whom burned the awakened proletarian's ambition to show he is every bit as good, if not better than those born to privilege. Max only began to concern himself about the reality of this person with the faint suggestion of a chip on his shoulder when told by Erich that Janka would now be director in Erich's place. Erich himself would move into the building next door to the Club, ending a brief but decisive era in Max's life.

He confided to me that he was uneasy. He and Erich had worked so beautifully as a team, each respecting the other's unique merits. How would Max and this formidably self-possessed new boss get along?

Walter saw to it that they did. So, of course, did Max. But it was only by virtue of having attained the pinnacle of his ambition, director of a large, distinguished German publishing house, higher if only by a technicality than the editor-in-chief, that Walter was able to relax at last and make it agreeable for anyone, of any class, to be in his company.

I wondered more and more about class in the Marxist sense, class as in "class struggle," "classless society," dictatorship of the proletariat. Repeatedly invoked, these terms demanded genuflection, which was an exercise that stretched the skin uncomfortably. Society in the GDR was not classless. The class at the top of it was not the proletariat, for there had been no revolution, but it needed and flattered the proletariat.

It plastered posters onto house walls featuring a man whose hands and crude, uneven features were black from mixed sweat and coal and who in large, aggressive letters was saying, I'M A MINER — WHO IS MORE?

The class that ran the GDR, an amalgam not foreseen by Marx, used the proletariat as a propaganda monstrance and a stick with which to intimidate those most credulous citizens, the artists and intellectuals. During the formalism debate started by the Party in 1951, the year the Brecht-Dessau opera *The Trial of Lukullus* was banned from the boards because "nobody" understood the music (Max did, and I was riveted by the magnificent production), obviously faked letters to the papers expressed the indignation of industrial workers over formalism and decadence in the arts, as if anyone toiling in a mine or mill had time to juggle with such foggy concepts.

The cream at the top of the GDR's blue milk awarded National Prizes and Fatherland Orders of Merit to the most productive workers and to entire exemplary "brigades" in various plants; but who was that cream? How would Karl Marx have explained its rise to the top?

"Why," I kept pestering people on my level, none of us having personal contact with any leader in the government, "doesn't some brilliant mind come up with an analysis of the new class relationships that develop in socialist society?" The people I pestered would look slightly surprised, muse for a bit, and say yes, it would be quite interesting. But they didn't seem to care much, or it may be that some realized indistinctly (or all too clearly) that nobody would risk his hands putting such a naive homemade bomb together.

Max believed that the government earnestly desired a classless society, but that all movement toward it was retarded by the Cold War, forcing the socialist countries to waste their resources on a self-defense that included, alas, inept propaganda and what came to be called "heartless bureaucracy." And it was true that the Cold War retarded a healthy development of socialism. That was the West's purpose, and no expense was spared to ridicule and undermine socialist efforts. Which is why many good people agreed with Max, among them the man to whom Lex's job on *Neues Deutschland* had passed.

Whether Max at that time regarded Rudolf Herrnstadt as a *good* person is doubtful. Only a saint could have thought so generously of a person whose promotion involved the ruin of a friend. On the other hand, who could say how Herrnstadt himself had felt about inheriting Lex's job? He might simply, like Lex himself, have bowed to the collective judgment of the Party — as every true comrade was supposed to do.

But Max did very soon see that Herrnstadt was a journalist of unusual stature. His editorials had, as the Germans say, "hand and foot."

Herrnstadt had not sprung from nowhere. Before he took on ND he had edited a mass circulation paper with the same prescribed viewpoint, but with features that were easier for the man in the street to read. Although his exile had been spent in the Soviet Union, he had got his newspaper training under one of the most influential liberal editors of the Weimar Republic.

One day Max came home greatly excited over a Herrnstadt essay called "Colleague Zschau and Colleague Brumme." *Colleague* was the term of address at one's workplace which indicated that the person addressed was not necessarily a comrade. A title suggesting human interest, rather than a Party exhortation, was unique in ND. The essay read like a detective story, one couldn't put it down — and it was long, two whole large-format pages. Zschau, a mentally indolent trade union official, and Brumme, a factory manager with an uncontrollable temper, cripple an important plant by losing the confidence of the workers. The story was true, Herrnstadt had researched it himself; only the suggestive names were invented.

In it he attacked the high-handed proceedings of Party and trade-union functionaries whose "thimblerigging with the interests of the workers, playing fast and loose with their good will" had led to a justifiable bitterness and indignation in the working class, for which the SED bore most of the blame. In fact, he wrote, the whole social concept of the GDR would be seriously endangered if, within a short time, it were not made attractive to people throughout Germany. Otherwise, he concluded, "We will lose our shirts and our heads."

This was mind-boggling stuff. Yet nothing seemed to happen to Herrnstadt. What inevitably had to happen was still a glint in Ulbricht's eye. For the General Secretary of the SED was not a hasty man. He prowled round and round a problem before raising his hatchet. The whole constellation of relationships — domestic, inner-Party, East-West German, and international — had to be auspicious, and Ulbricht had to be sure the unpredictable Soviet Party would back his move.

So the impression arose that if Herrnstadt could so boldly blame the Party for bitterness among the workers, and get away with it, then there must be grounds for general optimism. Somebody high up must have wanted these things said in the Party's mouthpiece.

What Nadja Herrnstadt wrote about her father in *Das Herrnstadt Dokument* applied equally to Max:

> The "maturity and wisdom of the working class," that fond illusion of bourgeois intellectuals who become Communists purely out of human sympathy, remained an undeviating principle to which he clung throughout his life.

Max the cultivated aristocrat, who saw through the pretensions of his own class and feared he would never quite rid his own character of its blemishes, felt humble before a proletariat he imagined, but never knew. Yet traditional class distinctions and irritations have a way of betraying themselves. Whether conscious or not, class superiority like race prejudice is ineradicable, the difference being only that class is colorless; but how it stains!

For a time Max had a likable, possibly proletarian, possibly only lower middle-class young chauffeur named Herr Lehmann, who reminded me of the fellows I used to know in my East Bronx high school. When occasionally I went downtown in the Aufbau car, a tolerated passenger in the back seat who was not supposed to interrupt thoughts, Max sat as usual beside Herr Lehmann. Since he could not exist without smoking he took out the pack the minute the car started, poked a couple of his terrible cigarettes into position — all one could get was terrible cigarettes — and tipped them toward the chauffeur. Lehmann said thank you and placed one between his lips. Max extended the lighter to him before lighting his own.

This seemed to be the extent of his relationship with all chauffeurs, a fact which visibly discomfited him. I think he would dearly have loved to demonstrate fraternity in other ways, but which? None occurring to his already overloaded brain, he quickly addressed his attention to ND or some manuscript, and Lehmann and I kept quiet. If Max had to say anything to the chauffeur on the way downtown, such as "Please stop at the post office in Fransöische Straße," embarrassment made him clear his throat first, which did not happen with equals.

As soon as he got out at the post office, or wherever it was, I would start chatting with Herr Lehmann. I knew he was already married and the father of a small child, and we would jest about life's puzzling vicissitudes. We felt at ease with one another, being class equals or equivalents: he in a lowly job and I a woman, besides being an American bored by the stringencies of German etiquette. But as Max was so strict about it, I tried to use the pronoun of formal address to Herr Lehmann and probably succeeded most of the time.

One chilly evening, fall or winter, Herr Lehmann had to drive us to a party at Bodo and Alma's. It must have been a particularly significant occasion, because quite a few official cars were parked outside. The chauffeurs were sitting in their various cars, and Herr Lehmann didn't drive away either.

"He's not going to *wait* for us?" I asked.

Max said he was.

At this time Bodo and Alma were no longer living in the Potsdam region. They had moved to an intelligentsia colony at the opposite end of Berlin from ours, a neighborhood from which we could have returned home by public transport; true, not without changing from streetcar to *U-Bahn* to *S-Bahn* to streetcar, and not if it got so late that everything stopped running. Seeing what was in my head, Max assured me that the chauffeurs would not be forgotten, they would be asked into the kitchen in the course of the evening.

All I remember of the guest list is the French writer and filmmaker Claude Chabrol and the venerable Cuban poet Nicolás Guillén, as well as Stefan Hermlin, an impressive young man just my age whose self-assurance was years older. A respected German poet and a close friend of both Bodo and Alma, separately and together, he was almost always to be found at their international parties as a sort of assistant host; but there were many interesting faces that evening and foreign voices dotting with bits of English the Romance languages in which Bodo, Alma, Hermlin or Max could more or less tolerably pinch-hit.

Like Max, Hermlin had been born to wealth and cultivation, except that his family was Jewish and forced to flee when the Nazis came to power. He neither "looked Jewish" nor did his real surname suggest a non-Aryan background, so there would have been no temptation to change it on that account, had he been so inclined. The name Hermlin, which suggests ermine and started as a pseudonym in Swiss exile, must have related to the kind of self-image he chose to project. In his handsome, noble profile a jutting pipe lent more force to features that were still vulnerably youthful. The pipe, however, might just happen to be resting with quiet refinement in the palm of his hand. He did not gesture with it. His manner was that of a crown prince.

Yet despite this persona and the unobtrusive lordliness with which he entered a room or merely sat in a chair, he had been a Communist since adolescence, and out of noblesse oblige stuck to the Party no matter how bafflingly its leaders behaved. With the better Western writers his standing was high; while regretting his politics they respected the show of unruffled constancy and the tenacity that could not have come cheap. He fought against the Party's Jesuitical literary dogmas and lost, hiding his distress from public view while his own well of poetry inexorably dried up.

Something about him always suggested an official presence, as if he had the backing of a government. He did for some years have the ear of Erich Honecker, whom he knew well from youth-movement days. Honecker took pride in the prestige his poet-friend lent their poor, struggling little country, and this enabled Hermlin to get a fellow writer out of trouble now and then. But after Honecker supplanted Ulbricht as dictator, he told his protégé that these intercessions would have to stop; they were becoming an embarrassment he could not afford.

Hermlin had never been a government representative. If he made that impression it was because he was predestined to bring the best writers of East and West together for the sake of an ideal eventual unification. It was simple, he was their born peer; and this consoled him to some extent for the attrition of his own muse.

He may not originally have meant to be a snob, but I think in the end he accepted being one as his prerogative. He shared that Olympian blindness of the élite to anyone who plays no recognizable role in its preserves. His preserves were above all literary; crude manners would not blind him to a man's talent, and Hermlin's encouragement would elevate it to a higher plane.

It was women who presented difficulties. Because he could never quite place me he might vouchsafe me an awkward nod, much as Max offered Herr Lehmann a cigarette. It was the only awkwardness I noticed about him. Two or three times married, Hermlin went to parties as untrammeled as a bachelor. He had known I "belonged to" Max, whom he venerated, but he tended to forget, and a woman in public had to have a husband who counted before she herself came briefly into focus, then faded from it. Unless of course she was a great luminary in her own right.

When the food was served at the Uhses' party that evening I remembered all at once how ridiculously cramped the intelligentsia kitchens were ("Not big enough to swing a cat in," Gillian remarked with the bright, cool English laugh that meant "Mustn't grumble!"). As Alma's kitchen had exactly the dimensions of mine, the only place for her still new but already unsightly fridge, latest triumph of GDR manufacture, was the foyer, where its indelibly stained front was the first thing that greeted company. Where would the chauffeurs sit?

All the rest of the space on the ground floor was designed for entertainment, one unusually spacious apartment with Mexican decorations, a choice of inviting conversation areas, a grand piano, and the stair to the bedroom gallery which Alma like using for self-satirizing grand entrances that embarrassed Bodo. Once she came down in a crazy skirt with a jagged hem that she had sewn to her slip half an hour before. "Notice anything?" she demanded another time, going from guest to guest and fluttering extra-long pasted-on eyelashes in their faces. Only Bodo minded, everyone else was delighted, it was such a relief after German stuffiness.

But would the chauffeurs have to stand in a sort of breadline between the fridge and the kitchen door? There was no room for chairs in the small foyer.

After the party was over, we found them pacing in the cold to keep their blood circulating, and when we got into the car, I burst out to Herr Lehmann, "I hope they at least gave you something decent to eat?"

"Of course," he said, "very nice, and good coffee too," and turned the key in the ignition.

Sitting beside me in the back Max was silently seething. I had accidentally called Herr Lehmann "*Du*" instead of "*Sie.*" Worse, I had used the word *fressen* for "eat," to make my question jokier, but the dictionary says *fressen* means devour. Human beings *essen*, only animals are said to *fress*. Among friends Max also used the word *fressen* jokingly. And Herr Lehmann knew I didn't picture him on his hands and knees gobbling out of a dog bowl.

At home Max tried to explain to me how impossible I had made myself in the car. My face burned.

"Herr Lehmann didn't care, he's used to my German."

"He cared," said Max. "You embarrassed him in my presence. Apart from intimates, only children, pets, and social inferiors—" I put my hands over my ears. "He had to think," Max went on, "that you were talking down to him. And '*fressen*' . . . !"

His deepest sensibilities were outraged. In an analogous situation (which I didn't recognize at the moment) mine would have been equally outraged. Suppose in America Max had called a grown man "Bub" or a black man "boy" or a stranger by his first name — only he never would have. (Early in our relationship he said, not quite jokingly, "If only you could give me a brown child you'd be perfect!")

Once he tormented himself inordinately when he caught himself telling me in German — it could only be expressed in German — that someone had "carried on like ten naked savages." I saw nothing offensive in it. The German for savages is *Wilde*, wild ones, which could mean anything. Besides he always laughed when he said it, just as his parents used to laugh. He begged me to stop him if he started saying it again, but he never did. *Wilde*, to him, was as bad as "natives."

Nonetheless the leveling of traditional social barriers was now making Max uncomfortable. He had shown no sign of such feelings in America, but on his own soil they had insidiously crept back. They caused conflicts in him, to be sure. But there they were.

I had agreed to work two mornings a week for an international women's organization that had recently been banished from Paris. As French remained its official language the administrators had been seeking someone in East Berlin who could translate into English.

I admired Hettie, the girl who recruited me. I had been corresponding with her for two years, ever since someone sent me her trenchant and spirited little pamphlet on equal rights. It excited me as the first sign of life in the American women's movement since we had won the vote. It went a few steps further than the founding mothers, who could not have had access to Engels's *Origin of the Family* (maybe he hadn't written it yet) and further than the daughters and granddaughters who thought the vote all-important.

I knew a bit about the movement, having pored over its history while on the railroad. I had a regular run to New Brunswick for a time, and could spend my daily four-hour layover there in Rutgers University library.

"My French is pretty bad," I told Hettie, remembering the hilarity of Mme. Vidonne.

"Anyone with a year of high school French could do it," she said, which turned out to be true, if not for the reason I thought. It was the

French version of Party Chinese, a vocabulary so limited that in a few days I had it down pat and could concentrate on giving the translations a slick veneer.

So there were three inducements to work at the Women's International Democratic Federation: Hettie; women's rights, which I assumed were represented by the WIDF (otherwise Hettie wouldn't have agreed to be American Secretary); and money. I was in debt. I had passionately wanted two Windsor chairs that reminded me of my Colonial rocker in New York. Max refused to finance them at four hundred marks apiece, so Gillian said, "Don't tell the old man," meaning Harry, and slipped me the eight hundred.

Max asked no questions when he saw the chairs, though he understood at once why I had craved them. But I also needed a sewing machine, corduroy for a slack suit, soap that didn't smell like disinfectant, and enough electric bulbs. Despite their short life they cost a fortune.

The immediate problem was the loss of Hedwig, without whom I couldn't go to work for even half a day. Between homesickness and maidlessness my spirits fell so low that I got a feverish cold that kept me in bed. Gillian, who had no help either, took both children to and from kindergarten. One day, returning in a downpour, she found two bedraggled young girls knocking at her front door. They wanted work! She rushed them to my bedside. They were both fifteen, had no references except each other, knew nothing, and wanted to live in because there was no room for them at home. The talking one said they were fond of little children, the other only cried. I grabbed the crying one, whose name was Edeltraut. Gillian had already taken to Dagmar, who seemed more self-reliant.

Now that someone was helping, however ineptly, to keep my household running and Dee tranquil — Dee loved her — I too found myself adopting "little helper" euphemisms to describe her job.

Edeltraut had the anxious, almost pathological hunger of children who have scrambled for every crumb they ever got, whether of food or affection, and she was still growing. I fed her the same amounts of the same dishes we ate, plus as much bread between meals as she liked, but this did not staunch the appetite that must have nagged at her mind and body without respite.

Feeling ambitious one evening, Max brought home some expensive off-ration meat from a state shop. It looked so alluring that he went straight into the kitchen, which seldom happened any more, and in his Escoffier mode conjured a ragout for the next day, when it would be even more delicious after the wedding-night of the ingredients. In the morning, as we had no fridge, I briefly boiled up the creation to keep it from spoiling, and explained this procedure to Edeltraut. Again the heavenly aroma floated through the house and must have driven her mad. While I went shopping and picked up Dee and Tommy from kindergarten, Edeltraut took a taste and simply could not stop.

Perhaps she thought, or hoped, she had only taken her share, since she would not be with us at suppertime; yet as she herself strongly doubted this, she tried to restore the ragout's original appearance by pouring water into the pot up to the gravy line.

She was just leaving as Dee and I got home. "You said I could go to the movies with Dagmar," she reminded me. "I know," I said. "Have fun." It was Wednesday, their evening off.

The pot of stew looked odd to Max when he lifted the lid, but he flew into a passion when he tasted it. Poor Escoffier; poor little helper. He looked so formidable when Edeltraut crept in out of the night in her torn brown sweater that she denied everything, rushed upstairs to gather her few belongings, and fled from the house. I ran after her down the dark road pleading, "You haven't even got your pay!"

"I don't want it," the girl sobbed.

She left behind in her haste a well-preserved cookbook published about 1910 for the households of Junkers, with recipes that called for eighteen eggs and pails of heavy cream. I could send neither the book nor a money order because she had not given me an address. She had sworn she would never go back to her mother, who beat her, actually threw her down the stairs once and took every penny she earned.

"She'll come back for her pay," Dagmar suggested uncertainly. She claimed not to know where Edeltraut might have gone. Perhaps this was true.

Despondent, I told Gillian, "The whole relationship is fundamentally wrong."

"Well what's the answer, cock? Either they're the servants or we are," said Gillian. "Or do you see our two getting down on their hands and knees to scrub floors?"

Edeltraut was followed by Fräulein Ida, an almost stone-deaf spinster in her fifties. She brought her hearing aid to work because I insisted, but did not stick it in her ear. "You must yell as loud as you can when you have to pee," I instructed my daughter, and returned to the office on Unter den Linden.

But there was no more red-haired Hettie at the other desk in our room. "She went back to America," someone told me. "She only helped out temporarily. We have a permanent American Secretary now."

My heart hit the floor. Why would Hettie go back without saying anything? She'll write me, I thought. She'll tell me what happened. She never did.

I was too hurt to recognize one obvious explanation. Why, after all, were my letters to my parents full of sunny descriptions of our life, whereas to Christina I at least told a fraction of the truth? Who wanted truck with secret services? Sealed envelopes might as well have been cellophane. Had Hettie discovered something about the WIDF that disturbed her too much to be told even to the oldest, closest friend, which I was not? Or did her replacement have a greater claim on the consideration of Moscow?

Easy enough for me to suggest such possibilities now. I didn't dream of them then. I had no idea how centralized the management of such international organizations was.

Gillian and Harry had been married for seven years. So, for that matter, had Max and I, but the famous seven-year limit after which the most uxorious husband is supposed to grow restive was not my problem.

"Harry is faithful," Gillian said. "I could tell if he weren't. But these seven years are the first time in his life that he tried to be. He and Lilo had a theory about living honestly. They reported to each other every time they were unfaithful, even went into details. I *ask* you! It was she who introduced us. A beautiful woman, but by then they'd made such a mess of their marriage that they were just good friends. *As it's called.* But seriously: she really wanted to see us happy together.

"I didn't love him in the beginning," Gillian admitted. She had still been mourning Nigel, her great love and first husband, killed on a bombing mission over Germany. She could not forget Tom either, an American officer stationed in London during the Blitz who taught her Marxism. He was her second-greatest love; Tommy was named after him.

"In fact" — she laughed, with that instinctive wary glance over her shoulder — "even while I was pregnant I was unfaithful to the old man."

She didn't realize she had told me all this before, or the next part that went, "But I love him now. I love him very deeply. . . ."

Her voice always seemed to sink into a pool in a dark cave when she repeated this, and the spot where it sank seemed to send out concentric ripples. For a moment or two she would be so moved that she had to pause before finding her voice again. Then with an expression of astonished revelation she would say softly, "I do, you know . . . deeply love him."

I think the reason she was unconscious of repeating this performance so often was that she had confided in too many women over the years to keep track of who had heard what. Not that I doubted the essential truth of what she told me. Nor was I bored by hearing it over and over again. I'm sure I too repeated myself, unhappy as I was over Max's mysterious absences when he was present. I had to unburden myself to someone, but not knowing the sound of my own voice (does anyone?) which might have acted as a prompter, I was not reminded of my own repetitions, whereas I hear the inflections of Gillian's to this day.

Our confessions were the fabric of our relationship, which existed in limbo. That the tapestry we were weaving kept showing the same figures, like a machine-made pattern, wasn't so important: we were each other's bridge across daily alienation. At neither end, alas, did the bridge have supports on solid ground. We were extraneous. Our men lived and were needed in a world where we played no part.

We did have one organic and meaningful bond, which was literature. It was Gillian who introduced me to the mature Colette; she had a precious English paperback of *Chéri* and *The End of Chéri* published as a single novel (as they should be). I read it enraptured. And enlightened, which is more than I can say of Marie Stopes' *Married Love*, a standard sex manual of our generation. Gillian, who could barely write a letter because of the infernal bother of it, was the ideal reader.

"Why don't you show me a bit of *your* writing?" she asked long before we moved into the Colony, and I read her the first chapter of the railroad book. She kept pestering for more, an incalculable help to me. I was forced to hurry and not sit stewing too long over doubtful places. Since she lived just across the way I could leave a new chapter with her overnight instead of reading it aloud.

Gillian was an eminently practical woman who never lost count of the minutes. Far better organized than I, it was she who stopwatched our colloquies. "Well, there we are, ducks!" she would say in a tone of broad, bland finality related to her experience as personnel chief of a large London firm. This did not mean that the subject was forever closed, like the prevaricating "We'll call you!" to some unfortunate job seeker. It meant that we weren't likely to find the philosopher's stone that day but would surely continue searching tomorrow or whenever our mates, children, floors, meals, laundry, shopping, washing up, and furnace-tending gave us a moment's peace.

"We're slaves," I said.

"Let's face it, cock, we're whores," Gillian replied. "Well, we are! All women are whores. What else can we be! Don't tell me about men, ducky, I had five brothers," round and round in the same groove, one scratched oldie talking to another scratched oldie.

But with the intelligence behind that extraordinary nose she sniffed out in short order anyone's background, traits, daily life. She could ask a well-placed question casually, as if accidentally, then seem to forget all about it; but these were the things she did not forget. Did she do it on purpose, or couldn't she help it?

No matter how curious I was, I never found out private things if the information didn't drop into my lap. That was why I had no clue to Hettie, why she came, why she left, why she sometimes studied me with a wry, quizzical look, and changed the subject — whatever subject it happened to be. I was too ladylike or clumsy, apprehended people in retrospect, mulled over oddnesses, and took a lot on trust. Too late I discovered that while Gillian had an instant feel for anyone else's topography she had no map of herself.

She habitually used sardonic pronouns such as "our two" when she meant our husbands, or a dismissive "mine" when she meant only Harry. But she had one trait completely at odds with her English assumed coolness, a morbid and superstitious anxiety exaggerated to the point of masochism. It was as if, by conjuring up dangers such as the seven-year itch, she was insanely beckoning to them.

I first noticed this when a horse got loose from its wagon and raced down our road. The commotion of the stampeding hooves brought everyone out of the houses, including herself and me. Our children were safe in kindergarten, but she cried, "Oh Christ, suppose Tommy had been crossing the road! If anything ever happened to Tommy I would *kill myself!*" She very often said that sort of thing, reminding me of the White Queen in *Through the Looking Glass* who screamed because she was going to cut her finger.

"Don't you worry about Dee at all?" she demanded.

I worried when she had a painful ear inflammation and the first two shots of penicillin hadn't worked. But that was real and present.

Perhaps, I thought, Gillian's anxieties came from living through the war in London. I only trembled at the air-raid sirens in New York and frequently woke up from a bomb nightmare, but drills were all we had. Gillian experienced the life-and-death Blitz, lay alone with diphtheria under the v-bombs when no doctor could be reached (it left her with a weak heart) and lost not only Nigel but two sisters who had died of TB, so that TB was a natural and persistent worry. I had never lost anyone close to me. Sometimes I felt ashamed of having been so lucky.

During the day my ears did not pick up slight sounds, but Gillian's were as vigilant as an animal's; she could not be taken unawares. I would be standing about in their living room sipping cognac out of a shot glass when she leaped up from her mending or knitting and exclaimed, "Mine's here! Must see what my casserole is doing!" Only then did I register the car door slamming outside, and set down my glass. "Why are you running off? Harry doesn't bite," she would say, disappearing into the kitchen. I dashed out the French doors onto the terrace, reaching the garden gate just as "hers" scraped the mud off his shoes, opened the front door, and greeted "his."

I hated being caught in their house when Harry returned from the university. He and Gillian would take their places on the three-seater sofa with one upholstered cushion between them. I, pressed by both of them to stay a bit longer, would sit in an armchair, embarrassed by the incredibly dull rites that attended Harry's homecoming. Without the slightest interest (or so it appeared) Gillian would ask him prompting questions about his day, at the same time keeping her eyes on her knitting needles, although every so often she would glance in his direction with a sprightly smile. If a natural disaster or a political setback had just occurred, one of them would be sure to deplore it and the other chime in, "Oh, dreadful," "Disgraceful," "Impossible." It was like the drone of catechism from the open windows of a Catholic school.

Surely, I thought, they didn't talk that way when no one else was about? So much propriety was simply depressing. This was not the

Gillian I knew, or thought I knew. What the real Harry was like I had no idea. I concluded that the element of humor, glee, sheer silliness, must be missing between them. I was sure Harry would never, like Max, refer to a certain Politburo member as a behind with ears (there was really no other way to describe him) or to a dishearteningly mediocre writer with a bald pate from which hung long hair, as Greta Garbo. "He's his own uncle," Max explained the poor fellow's joyous delusion that he was a favorite of the young and that this endowed him, too, with eternal youth.

Apparently Harry complained about my abrupt departures. The shot glass, perhaps not quite empty, was the giveaway. They didn't drink, they kept liquor only for guests, but efficient Gillian usually whisked the shot glass into the kitchen since I was leaving anyway. The next time I made for the French doors she said, "Why do you always rush away? Harry thinks you don't like him." "That's silly," I said, and flew.

Inevitably a crimson thread was introduced into the faded pastels of our tapestry.

"I don't think Harry can stand this faithfulness much longer," Gillian was ruminating. "I wouldn't be angry with him if he gave way. It's the kind of man he is, he's not like Max, he's champing at the bit. I'm just afraid for our marriage."

She was talking half to herself, turning over possibilities, trying combinations that would benefit all concerned.

She liked to benefit people. She brought home sad-looking, manless women as others take in stray cats, treating them to tea and sympathy and at least a few minutes of Harry, to whom — in their presence — she would talk in the clipped tones of a department head giving sales staff their order of the day. Perhaps this was meant to demonstrate what a paltry thing marriage was after all, to stave off their inevitable envy and make the poor cows thankful they were free and had the privacy of their four walls.

Now, however, she was seeing a chance not only to benefit a poor cow, but to kill two of another species with one stone. "If he had an affair with someone I can trust, like you, I wouldn't mind," she mused.

My heedless ears suddenly picked this up.

"You wouldn't take him from me, I know. Neither would Pam." Pam was a friend of hers from England doing something or other at East Berlin's university for a few months. "I know he finds you both attractive," Gillian said. She was looking at me anxiously. "I would ask only one thing, whether it was you or Pam. *Just don't let me know it's happening!*"

"It won't *be* happening!" I exploded. "Are you going crazy? Do you want to ruin our friendship?"

I went straight home and was still too agitated in the next few days to look in on her. Neither did she come over.

Once, laughing, she told me about Aggie, an upstairs neighbor in London years ago, whose husband was so continuously horny that she begged Gillian to take him off her hands every other night. Gillian obliged, it being an exceptional moment in her gay young life when this was convenient. I laughed too — it was like a joke out of Boccaccio.

Another incident she related concerned her best friend Fanny and Fanny's utterly beautiful husband Roland. The three had once lain together in such complete rapport that it only deepened the friendship between herself and Fanny. This was something I could imagine, if not for me. I wanted the total embrace of just one other. But I could empathize, just as I did with Colette's courtesan Léa and the idle, selfish boy she only meant to teach and fatally fell in love with; and he with her.

After a few days Gillian and I inevitably met again, probably in the road, one of us shouting for Dee or Tommy to come home to supper, the other running out to reassure: "He's coming!" "She's coming!" Gillian was the one skilled at smoothing things over as if there had never been a hiatus, and this gradually seemed to be the case.

I had almost forgotten the incident, the non-incident, when one evening as I sat alone darning Max's socks Harry phoned and said Tommy had fever, his throat hurt, he wouldn't swallow his aspirin, and did I know how to make him do it? I stuffed the sock and the darning egg into one of my apron pockets and dashed across the road without a jacket. "Where's Gillian?" I asked. It seemed she was in Leipzig for some reason. "Give me the aspirin," I said, and went into the kitchen and crushed it and mixed it with a teaspoon of jam, which Tommy unsuspiciously swallowed, after which he was content and ready to sleep. I started for the door.

"Don't go," said Harry.

I saw no reason why not, except that it might appear stupidly impolite. Only after we entered the living room and Harry took his usual place on the couch and I mine on the edge of the upholstered armchair did I notice that he was wearing a good dark suit, as if for a state funeral or one of those ceremonies held in the opera house where, for example, medals attached to ribands were handed out by some muckamuck to a few — or in fact several masters in various fields, more decorations each year; for it was becoming increasingly imperative to reward merit publicly and avoid brain drains to the wealthy, wheedling West.

Harry looked so bewilderingly stiff in his formal disguise that I became conscious of the smeared apron I had on, and remembered I hadn't even glanced into a mirror before hurrying across the road. I don't think he knew what I was wearing. His normally rich, deep, resonant voice stuck in his throat and all that came out was a stifled emission of the words ". . . falling in love with you."

"Don't be ridiculous," I said, getting right up and making for the door to the foyer.

He got right up too, blocked my way, and tried to put his arms around me, but I pushed him violently, slapped his face, and tore out the front door.

I have forgotten where Max was going that evening, probably to a first night; but Harry must have noticed the date and calculated approximately how much time he had before Max came home.

There is a song in *The Threepenny Opera* where Polly Peachum tells how careful she always was not to lose her head. She explains the policy dinned into her throughout her girlhood: "And though he has money and though he is nice, and his collar is clean even on workdays, and he knows how to act with a lady, I tell him No. . . . The moon may shine all night long and the boat be loosed from its moorings, but that's the end of it. No, one cannot simply lie down; no, one must be cold and heartless, no, too much could happen: All one can say is no." But then:

> *One day, and the day was blue*
> *there came one who didn't ask.*
> *He hung his hat on a nail in my room*
> *and I didn't know what I was doing.*
> *And because he had no money*
> *and because he wasn't nice*
> *and his collar wasn't even clean on Sunday*
> *and he didn't know how to act with a lady,*
> *to him I did not say no.*

I understood very well about Mac the Knife. At eighteen I lost my virginity to just such a one. Gillian's husband in no way resembled him and

I felt only anger as I ran from the house. Nevertheless that night I had a wild sex dream about Harry.

Surprisingly, in April, 1952, Dick wrote me from London where he was alone and had for two months been setting down the first draft of a novel. Now he was playing with the idea of coming to Germany to complete the work. "What zone do you live in?" he asked.

> How is it? I'd not like to get mixed up in any politics what-soever. I've enough to do to get my book finished. In fact, I'd like not to meet any folks of a political nature who would make it known that I'd be around. I don't mind meeting personal friends, but I do want to avoid arguments from both sides until I'm through with what I'm doing.
>
> You know, as much as we have talked in the past, you never did even glimpse my point of view. Some day I'd like to make it known to you. You may not like it, but at least you ought to know it. I miss you, and you know that.
>
> But I'll wait before saying any more until I hear from you; and you must realize that I want to live very cheaply if I come up that way. What are the chances?

Max was keen to help Richard Wright in any way he could, although this would not be easy. Dick was obviously confused about the two Germanys and what benefits might be expected of either. He admitted he was "a little skittish" about the divided country. People had told him there was no food and that prices were high. I knew how spoiled he was when it came to creature comforts. But if someone like Johannes R. Becher were willing to promote an invitation, wouldn't it redound to the credit of socialism to have the author of *Native Son* housed and fed at nominal rates in the GDR? There was a Kulturbund lodge in Bad Saarow about fifty miles from Berlin, where Stefan Heym and his wife had been put up at first. They had hated the isolation, but it was just what Dick said he wanted.

The first problem was his desire to remain incognito and avoid any sort of political discussion. In a French village no one would have asked pushy questions of a foreigner, no matter what color, as long as he paid the bills, but Dick's incognito would not be safe among the provincials of the GDR. They gawked at strangers like mountaineers in the Great Smokies. A fellow guest might be tempted to ask questions, and then blab.

Even the average Berliner, native of a big city, was no more cosmopolitan than hayseeds I used to see leaning against storefronts in Canton, North Carolina. Despite the World Youth Festival the year before, which had been colorful in every sense, Berliners still goggled at an unaccompanied individual with brown skin. Hope Foye, a very pretty young singer from Harlem invited to do some recording after the festival, was terrified when she went out alone and Germans gathered around her and touched her cheeks to see if the color came off.

The second problem was just as knotty. Somebody would want to know where Wright stood politically *today*. The poet Johannes R. Becher was known to be broadminded, but the political Becher would have to give the government some sort of guarantee. After intense cogitation Max had an idea: if Dick would only let the World Peace Council use his name, that would clinch it. Brilliant, I thought, and framed a letter to Dick. Max approved the finished draft and I sent it off.

The World Peace Council was then only a year and a half old. It had its headquarters in Helsinki, which afforded a neutral veneer, and was supported by quite a few international headliners innocent of Communist affiliation. Its president was the radium physicist Frédéric Jolio-Curie, son-in-law of Marie Curie. Its vice president was the Italian socialist Pietro Nenni, former foreign minister, still an MP, never a Communist, though for a time he favored cooperation with Italy's Communist Party. When the World Peace Council held its first congress in East Berlin I wandered in from the street, and with excitement saw in the otherwise deserted circular lobby shy Shostakovich in his tin-rimmed spectacles walking in slow, meditative laps around some architectural centerpiece (a statue? a fountain?) to breathe something more like air than the stuffy atmosphere of the meeting hall, and to relieve his exquisite hearing apparatus of the translation drone.

ND did not mention the presence of a composer proscribed by Soviet officialdom, but it did note with pride the grandfatherly maverick Hewlett Johnson, dean of Canterbury, at that time a darling of the socialist "Peoples' Democracies"; and Pablo Neruda, Chile's diplomatic representative in various countries until he became a Communist.

Surely Dick would not be so narrow as to regard Neruda, who everyone said was Latin America's most distinguished poet, as the sort of Communist dear to the American Party?

Brecht was there too. Arnold Zweig was there, and the snowy-haired patriarch Martin Andersen-Nexö, whose novel *Ditte* about a servant girl had made me sob, and Jorge Amado, and Joris Ivens. Paul Robeson, his passport denied, had to sign the final appeal in absentia. Dick could be in *their* company, and what did it matter if there were a few slogan-mouthers among them?

Besides, regardless of which power was the probable initiator of the World Peace Council, Dick could certainly subscribe — so Max and I thought — to the organization's aims: peaceful coexistence, disarmament, abolition of atomic weapons, anti-imperialist solidarity. . . .

I had no idea how hounded Dick felt, or what sort of novel he was then writing. The Rajk trials were being continued in the Slansky trials, and Dick of all people would have been most sensitive to the way these witch-hunts formed the yin to the McCarthy Committee's yang.

When he first decided in 1946 to try out Paris as a home, he had his own difficulties getting a passport. He was not simply a famous black writer. In *Native Son* he had "performed an act of leadership that affected race relations as much as any act of any protest leader," wrote Lerone Bennett, editor of *Ebony* magazine. In the end, however, the U.S. State Department thought of a more effectual stratagem than locking him in. He had, in fact, threatened to make the matter public. So the document was issued and two big black embassy cars were awaiting him at Orly airport as if to honor him, in reality to display powerful and inescapable presence.

From the time Dick arrived in Paris, he was regularly importuned by embassy aides to give lectures there. He refused every time, which does not mean he endured these confrontations without turmoil in his heart. A biography by Constance Webb quotes him as swearing he would "die first" before he worked for the U.S. government or, for that matter, "anybody's government," by which he probably meant that of the Soviet Union.

At one point late in 1947, if Webb's information is correct, he and his close friend Sartre actually believed that the Soviet Union might invade France *and execute him*. Wild as this may sound, have we not in the last few years seen horrors beyond anyone's wildest imaginings? From my own experience of so-called neurotic fear, which may have a perfectly rational base, I know how fear can multiply itself to the point of immobilizing both mind and body; and it was at this very period that I last saw Dick, lying listless in the American Hospital and evading any explanation of his infirmity.

According to Webb he had just bought three tickets to the United States for himself, Ellen, and Julia, just in case. There must have been times when he felt himself caught between two walls of steel, a collaboration on some level between CIA and Soviet agents closing in to crush him. Not for nothing did Martin Luther King, Jr. visit him in Paris in 1959, the year before Dick's unexplained early death, and urge him to write on and never give up the fight. The two are said to have talked for twenty-four hours.

The novel on which Richard Wright was working when he asked me about Germany was *The Outsider*, which damned the American Communist Party and by implication all Communist Parties. It elicited a "strange kind of indifference or even outright denigration" when it appeared, one scholar wrote regretfully, admitting that it was indeed "a very imperfect work," even a "lurid potboiler"; but he felt that second to *Black Boy* it was Wright's finest achievement.

In what amounts to another lifetime I finally read the "lurid potboiler" myself. The characters *in their relations to one another* were so grotesquely improbable that the recoil of critics was not surprising. All the same, much of what Dick wrote in *The Outsider* struck a deep, resonating chord in me.

> It was something [the Communist movement] had and did not know it had that was seducing [Cross Damon, the black hero]. It was its believing that it *knew* life; its *conviction* that it had mastered the art of living; its *will* that it could define the ends of existence that fascinated him against his volition. Nowhere else save in these realms had he encountered that brand of organized audacity directed toward secular goals. He loathed their knowledge, their manners, their ends; but he was almost persuaded that they had in a wrong manner moved in a right direction for revealing the content of human life on earth.

Cross Damon is "not a little shocked" at the "colossal self-conceit" of a certain member of the American CP's National Committee. He thinks to himself: "he acts like a God who is about to create man. He had no conception of the privacy of other people's lives."

As far as I could see, colossal self-conceit not only characterized the National Committee, it infected the Party hierarchy all the way down to ordinary Joes like my first husband who (charity begins at home), thought it his prerogative to create *me*, to tell me what to do with five dollars I was saving for a hat (give it to the Fund Drive), and lecture me for writing unsolicited poetry instead of going out and organizing. Having appointed himself a professional revolutionary, *nebbich*, which also exempted him from getting a paying job, he considered my privacy his backyard.

Naturally Dick did not answer my letter suggesting support for the World Peace Council. I never heard from him again. But I would remember much later, and always oftener, that apt phrase "organized audacity."

I had contrived during World War II to meet and talk with one of the people who best exemplified that organized audacity, Elizabeth Gurley Flynn, then in her midfifties and the only female on the Party's all-important National Committee. Her reaction to my errand gave me a jolt second only to the one I got when the *Daily Worker* fired me.

Before the Russian Revolution this woman, as a beautiful young girl of sixteen, was already a rousing public speaker for the IWW, a labor organization founded in Chicago. The Communist Party as I knew it never tired of citing the onetime "rebel girl," by then a veteran of every American working-class campaign of our time, as a great example of militant womanhood.

She herself in her memoir *I Speak My Own Piece* — required reading in the Party — praised the two books that first launched her into socialist activity: the amazing *Vindication of the Rights of Women* by Mary Wollstonecraft, in the eighteenth century the first literate explosion of British radical feminism; and August Bebel's *Die Frau und der Sozialismus* (Women and Socialism) a century later in Germany, which in a sense is even more amazing because a man wrote it, and did so in a country with no women's movement at all and scarcely a male advocate so informed, so exercised about the exploitation of women and so perceptive of their needs, including sexual needs — *and sexual rights* — as Bebel.

Yet these inspirations of the young Elizabeth Gurley were never reflected in the Communist Party of the United States, which viewed women primarily as auxiliaries. The *Daily Worker* loved to describe wives bringing soup, coffee, and self-effacing sympathy to striking husbands, joining their marches, distributing leaflets at factory gates. At home, male Party organizers automatically treated their own wives as auxiliaries, and some admitted it with a twinkle of pretended contrition.

Flynn was the grand exception, the token heroine, and the Party intended her to remain just that, to be looked up to, but not emulated by us ordinary hens. Her regular column in the *Daily Worker*, with a dignified, motherly-looking photo of her at the top, gradually deteriorated into a bulletin of her home life, whose purpose was to illustrate the human side of the Party. I found it wearisome to read about her adoring sister Kathy, a regular body servant who seemed to anticipate her every wish. Kathy was Elizabeth's auxiliary, and the Party was Elizabeth's meal ticket. She had apparently never thought of emancipating herself within the Party by insisting that it honor Wollstonecraft and Bebel as she did, or used to do, but had let herself be so misled by its fulsome flattery that she could now take pride in being the grand exception who could look smugly down on the rest of us.

Hadn't I perceived that before I made my way to her office in the Party building? Yes and no. The problem was: to whom else could we working women turn? Something had to be done about an urgently needed women's trade union federation to ensure that we kept our so-called war jobs after the war was over. "War jobs" meant the kind traditionally reserved for men, but the term spread like peanut butter to jobs that had not been a man's before the war.

"Well, what am *I* supposed to do?" snapped the erstwhile rebel, whose femininity had long since sunk into folds of fat. "Why don't you go to someone like Eugene Dennis?"

"But you're the woman on the National Committee," I protested. "You're known to have contact with prominent trade union women. Maybe you could influence them to get together across craft lines —"

"Do you think because I'm a woman I have to be interested in *women's* matters?" she interrupted indignantly. As if I had come about fashions or monthly deodorants; as if anyone could see that women's matters were garbage. She thought she could secede at will from the female sex. (I have met many women who thought this, but they were not leaders of a Communist Party.)

"My special interest is the miners," Flynn growled.

"Don't you see that we have to fight for our jobs while we have them? We've proved we can do them. We're in the trade unions. We'll lose every gain we've made if we don't start a national *women's* union immediately," I persisted. "Soon it will be too late."

Cornered, resentful, obviously wondering who the hell I thought I was, she said she had no more time. I should write her an outline of my proposals and bring it back to the ninth floor, from which eyrie Party eagles saw farther than sparrows pecking at manure in the gutter.

Between runs I wrote three pages, delivered them, and heard no more. Elizabeth Gurley Flynn had caught from Party males the contagion of their arrogance toward women and their entire "wrong manner of moving in a right direction," as Dick would later express it in the words of Cross Damon.

In those days it never occurred to me that other Communist Parties could be as self-annihilating as ours. Ours had to be the feeblest, I assumed, because the world's most powerful capitalist system could squash such a tiny organization like a bug. There was a rumor long before I left for Germany that half the members were FBI agents. Keeping a secret from the FBI was impossible.

During a period when we still hoped World War II could be prevented, I was present at a supposed "surprise" demonstration to be staged in Times Square at 10 P.M. Mingling with the crowd always there at that hour, we watched the clock on the Times Building and at ten sharp unrolled our rolled-up posters calling for peace, and silently held them high. Instantly mounted troops with brutal, hate-distorted red faces burst out of side streets to ride us down, and several people were crushed by horses against the locked doors of shops.

If we rank-and-filers suspected we were infiltrated, what sort of fool's paradise did the big-shots inhabit? Or did they think it salutary to the development of "political maturity" to send the Jimmy Higginses into such a trap? Were they stupid, crazy, or what?

I knew Mildred Olsen, another of those big shots, quite well in the part of her life that had ceased to be a life. A high official of the American CP just below National Committee rank, her entire existence had been botched up by the Party in 1950.

Although her head was loaded with brains she had taken a piece of idiotic advice that amounted to an order, with the result that she became permanent American Secretary of the Women's International Democratic Federation without the slightest inclination to do so. There was simply no place left on earth where she could go.

The advice was to apply without delay for American citizenship. Otherwise, under the just-passed McCarran-Walter Act, she could be deported as an undesirable alien to the country of her birth, which happened to be Poland.

Mildred knew that her parents had brought her to the United States when she was a baby, but never until the Party told her to check up did she discover they had applied for citizenship only in their own names. No doubt they imagined that a baby required no papers. Too shocked to think coherently, Mildred did as her comrades told her and soon found herself thousands of miles from her true occupations in a country whose language full of tsishing sibilances she saw no good reason to learn.

Yiddish had been the language spoken in her home. As it was derived in great part from Middle High German she assumed it would help her in Berlin, where an agreement among Parties had placed her. It did help somewhat, and as a temporary expedient the Federation was better than being cast adrift in a country of virulent Jew-haters. But under the circumstances, what did "temporary" mean?

Conscious that there were far worse fates, and that she was not the only exiled and homesick National Secretary, she held her head up and threw herself into campaigns she would normally never have chosen. Her school French and Spanish and a smattering of Russian grew impressively fluent amid the Federation babel, but she took no more interest in the specific problems of women than did Elizabeth Gurley Flynn. She too thought herself a grand exception. When she once described herself to me as "a very hot-blooded woman" she was making the point that most women deprived of men would hardly know what they were missing.

She was divorced, between forty-five and fifty, a strongly built woman more like a broad-bosomed Russian than a Pole, but with dainty ankles. When she walked into a room she carried herself like a government minister, and deployed great charm when she cared to.

She was extremely pleasant when she found me in the office that had been Hettie's, but as soon as we had exchanged a few items of basic information about ourselves she took her seat at the window desk facing mine and said without a question mark, "Would you take a letter."

Surprised, I put aside the translation I was doing and jotted in my almost forgotten shorthand, amplified by scribbles, a letter to a writer in New York whom I knew slightly. When almost finished with the typing I asked, "May I add my regards?"

After a moment she said coolly, "Why don't you write to him yourself." There was no arguing with that. Certainly it was improper for a secretary to butt in with regards. I was not her secretary. Was that what I had meant to convey? I was not aware of having meant anything, but words always mean something and she caught the unintended message.

Not knowing one's place in a given situation may be a congenital defect. Mildred had the opposite defect. She assumed a position of command by divine right as naturally as I resisted the assumption. In this case I grasped that someone had given her a false impression of my duties. No one had even troubled to introduce us.

Misunderstandings, we were both to learn, flourished in the Federation like green algae on a stagnant pool. Some people hired from abroad never found out what they were hired for, although they thought they knew when they packed their bags. The place swarmed with bosses and deputies whose orders didn't jibe, a fact that became clear to me only gradually. The sole boss of whom I was then aware was Käthe, a Romanian-born German who ran the whole shebang on behalf of the East German women's organization, together with her factotum Irene, the ever-beaming, bumbling office manager.

I was deeply sorry for Mildred as a victim of the McCarran Act, and there was no point in making an issue of her few letters. I was a fast enough translator and typist to make up the time easily.

We had one thing in common, the passionate attachment to homeland that makes exile an almost unremitting anguish. For moments, longer or shorter ones, you forget it, but all at once it comes back in a rush of tears. I at least had a husband, a child, a refuge, and could dream of the day when I would show my still adorable little girl to her grandparents; but short of a miracle Mildred would never go home again.

"Wouldn't you like to come out to my place for dinner?" I asked her one day. She looked at me incredulously.

No one had told her it was customary for local non-German employees to invite foreign staff to their homes. It was against Federation rules, but Commonwealth subjects and a few others with a cavalier attitude toward prohibitions were delighted to escape the cloister for a few hours. Their weekends were empty. On workdays they were ferried back from the office in Federation cars to their Federation villa far from central Berlin, where they roomed with, talked, ate, and shared a kitchen and bathroom with the same people they saw all day, month after month ad infinitum, until they had all so thoroughly got on one another's nerves that only heroic natures could control the impulse to run shrieking through the nondescript streets of Hohenschönhausen.

True, most of them had heroic natures, or they would not have come to East Berlin for such long and sexually self-denying stints. Men friends, a security risk, were out of the question. Soviet staff shared the social life of their own military community, over which the WIDF had no control (just as Käthe had no control over the Soviet Secretary), but the other inmates could look forward only to the occasional reception for members of the diplomatic corps or, once in a blue moon, a concert or opera to which Käthe or Irene would chaperone them.

The law-abiding French technical staff and a few others refused our invitations (the French sternly and without thanks, implying that we were some sort of criminals), so we had to give them up. On Bastille Day one year the obedient ones all joined hands and with rising hysteria in the mid-July stuffiness danced and skipped and leaped through the office corridor, wildly belting out *"Dansons la Carmagnole"* until they were hoarse and sagged against the walls, and Betty Reilly, the Australian Secretary, pointed to her head and grinned, "Three-year cases . . ."

Mildred decided not to pull her punches this time. "If I took off, with all the work I have here, it would be for something important," she told me, "something I could learn from. At least a movie."

Years later she would compliment me, "When I first met you, you were *nothing*. I must say you've improved."

But as I seemed hopelessly far from betterment in those days, somebody else had to tell her she was missing out. Apparently I kept quite an interesting and distinguished husband under my roof. And without turning a hair, not the least bit embarrassed, Mildred passed this report to me in the congratulatory tone she reserved for lesser beings who had hit some jackpot, and granted me the opportunity to re-invite her.

She was not disappointed. Max impressed her, and she opened wide the floodgates of her charm. Occasionally after that, having spent a

Sunday afternoon with the Heyms, she might stroll around the corner to look in on me and Dee for a few minutes. And Max, of course, if he emerged voluntarily from his study.

But she was not expecting to see him, and it was not what she came for. Perhaps she was not too clear about her purpose, which I believe was twofold. Like a child compulsively running its hand across each rail of a railing, she needed to make contact with every American home base within reach. On touching it, however, she was also covertly observant, taking note of things she would store in her memory file for good or ill. It was part of her Communist Party training.

Norman and I and our friends often discussed the difficult question of Party versus personal loyalty. Despite some hedging, the general conclusion was that friends, however much it hurt, must be sacrificed if they went against Party principles. A few of us backed away from this dictum, but most high functionaries lived by it. Friendship with them was risky, they blew hot and cold, and my relationship with Mildred remained at best a cagey truce, each of us watchful of the other's hidden intentions.

Mildred's real friends could only have been other American Party leaders. She never spoke of them or of her ex-husband to me. Once she mentioned Gomulka, a Polish Party chief not yet fallen into disgrace when she met him, I assume in Warsaw. "*That's* my man," she said with the deep satisfaction best described by the Yiddish word *kvell*: to swell with pride in someone else.

Was it also in Warsaw that she first met Gertrude Heym? The Heyms had been waiting there for permission to live in the GDR. Or she may have met Gertrude before that in Prague, another of their common way stations. I never thought to ask, but in his autobiography Stefan sarcastically mentions having come across the "Grande Dame" as early as his student days in Chicago; so any initial sympathy must have sprung up between the two women.

Ever suspicious of Germans who hadn't rushed home as soon as the war was over, the East German Party let the Heyms cool their heels in Poland for quite a while. Even after Stefan made the dramatic political gesture of returning his World War II decorations to President Eisenhower with a letter condemning American aggression in Korea, the SED Central Committee mistrusted his motives. No other repatriated German had applied for American citizenship. And what best-selling American author would give up the prestige and the material prospects he had amassed with a first novel, *Hostages*, for the hard life of a devastated half-country pulling itself up by its bootstraps? Wasn't his real concern that as a reserve officer he was in imminent danger of being called up for service in Korea? If he had at least been in the Party! His wife was. How convenient!

Erich Wendt decidedly disagreed with this view. He saw in Heym a man who could be an international asset to the GDR. As General Secretary of the Kulturbund Erich pulled every wire in his power to persuade the government, and was also instrumental in getting the couple into a just-vacated house in Grünau.

It was not the best location, which may have been the reason the first tenants left. It was the house at the outermost limit of the Colony, exposed to the most stares, easy surveillance by spies, and perhaps even violence from angry ex-Nazis. Still, it was as good a house as any in the Colony, and eventually Stefan bought a fierce watchdog that had been trained to terrify and attack.

Our relations with the Heyms got off on the wrong foot immediately. It was sad and bad, and everything that could possibly go wrong did go wrong. We had absolutely no comprehension of one another's ways; it was a kind of culture shock. I suppose all of us were at fault, if fault is the word. And at the very moment when things were at last taking a turn for the better Mildred threw the fatal monkey wrench.

It was Gertrude I met first. They had just arrived in Berlin, either during or just after the World Youth Festival, and Hope Foye, the enchanting young singer sent me by Deborah, told me she had a sick friend who very much wanted to make my acquaintance. We went up to a room in the Party's guest house where the Heyms were staying until more permanent accommodation could be found.

Stefan was out. Perhaps Gertrude had chosen the hour for that reason. Sitting up in bed with pillows propped behind her, she shone with a smile that could have broken up the ice at the North Pole. "I'm *so* happy to meet you!" she cried, leaning toward me with arms outstretched and the brilliant smile continuing unabated. It became alarming, more like an attack than a welcome; *I* wasn't anybody, for God's sake. Had Hope praised me beyond all reason just because I introduced her to susceptible Harry? Impulsively he had arranged a little house recital for her, himself accompanying her on the piano (which he regretted, especially after she answered one of his teacherish questions with "I don't *need* to practice.")

In any case that was not the explanation. Weeks passed before the slowly soaking negative developed into a picture.

The rights to *Hostages* and *The Crusaders* had been sold in West Germany to a house called List. List had a branch in Leipzig, East Germany, also private of course, which meant that once Stefan Heym settled into socialism he would be tied to List's Leipzig branch and at a considerable disadvantage. Paper in the GDR, a precious commodity, was strictly rationed. The lion's share went to government-sponsored publishing houses, with Aufbau in the lead. On the wrong side of the Atlantic Stefan could not have known this, but now he was determined to get into Aufbau at the first opportunity.

How to make one? Aufbau had already rejected a weaker novel of his, *The Eyes of Reason*. To my knowledge the book had done quite well in the United States, where Stefan had written it for the understanding of American readers. The East German rejection was a blow. Not only because small editions mean small royalties, but because Aufbau itself was a veritable Olympus of renowned German writers, among whom — Stefan and Gertrude felt — he rightfully belonged.

While Gertrude did indeed single-mindedly and obsessively do battle for her husband, she was not of those absurd wives who tell you that "we" are working on "our" last chapter. A successful career woman in her own right, an editor for Metro-Goldwyn-Mayer, Gertrude ably and lovingly went over the entire manuscript of *Hostages* with Stefan, smoothed out awkwardnesses due to still-faulty English, and with a few expert touches — as Stefan himself relates in his autobiography — "made dull passages gleam."

At a party he was first attracted by her legs and a youthful vivacity that belied the gray shadows in her hair; but he became bound to her through this deed of selfless partnership which blazoned his name worldwide. Although his agent had interested a respectable publisher, it was thanks to Gertrude's editing that the book was actually sold and flown to Hollywood on a magic carpet of rave reviews.

Orville Prescott, dean of American book critics at the time, was so impressed that he declared *Hostages* not merely comparable with Anna Seghers' *The Seventh Cross*, which had a similar message, but (I quote again from the autobiography) "far superior" to it.

The young author's head swam. Writing of himself in the third person, he described his feelings when he and Gertrude read the reviews: "All at once the sacred halls of great art lie open before him, with a single coup he is accepted among the ranks of the immortals; and he grasps the hands of the woman who was the first to recognize in the still rough, unfinished version what he was trying to shape, and kisses her."

One weekend afternoon not long after they moved into the Colony, the Heyms judged it time to beard the editor who lived so comfortably close by and might be so important to his future. The two men had never met in the United States, which on the face of it seems odd, both of them having edited anti-Nazi newspapers there; but they did it at different periods. Stefan's fiery little one-man paper (he was only twenty-four when he started it) had already gone under when Max was still in Paris, never dreaming that he might land in America some day.

Gertrude was an experienced negotiator. She knew better than to come to the point during a first visit. The idea was just to drop in, Lafayette we are here: folksy, American-brand neighbors, potential chums. It never crossed their minds that turning up unannounced might inconvenience anybody. Why stand on ceremony; they had Gertrude's overflowing warmth and humor to offer and the boisterous Big-Wind-Blew-In-From-Winnetka jauntiness that Stefan (not by nature a boisterous man) must have acquired on finding himself an immortal in the sacred halls of great art.

As we stood on the stoop wondering how to suggest a more favorable occasion without giving offense, Stefan was already making his ungainly way through the foyer into the living room, where he threw himself into one of our two secondhand overstuffed armchairs and looked about with expansive approval. Making himself twice as long and large by spreading his own arms over the chair's, and spraddling his legs across the hairy white rug, he exclaimed with jovial intimacy, "Max, you've just got to turn this place into a club for intellectuals!"

The words struck ice into our hearts. We didn't quite believe the awful vision was to be taken literally, but who could tell. Were they going to burst in here every time they were bored?

Gertrude enthused over everything, touched the drapes appreciatively, loved the stove that radiated maximum warmth from receding circles in each tile, and its right-angled mantelpiece that just begged for ornaments; and expressed a wish to see the rest of the house.

In our bedroom under the low, sloping ceiling there was a scarcely damaged café chair which Max, the indefatigable scavenger, had found abandoned in Aufbau's attic along with other old lumber. It was a nice enough little chair on which to toss one's underthings while undressing. Gertrude turned it thoughtfully to one side, saying she loved a chair in profile, and didn't I? I made some sort of helpless joke. "Do you know what this chair is *worth?*" she reproached me, and offered to buy it.

There were twelve years between Gertrude and Stefan, a difference which can become tragic when the woman is the elder. She had known this all along and even run away from him once, but the bachelor of twenty-nine saw in the vivid, youthful widow of forty-one an asset too good to relinquish. She was fifty by the time we met her, but it was still she who despite heartaches looked the younger and he who had aged beyond his years.

Primarily he was a political man with a well-organized, fertile, industrious mind, a sense of justice ripened in early youth, and a prolific pen. Critical newspaper journalism was his true forte, as we saw in later years when he wrote a weekly column for the *Berliner Zeitung* called "Frankly Speaking" that didn't mince words and was eventually suppressed by the Party. When in the end he could publish novels only in West Germany, he added television appearances to his forum — not, needless to say, GDR television.

Unfortunately, the private persona he showed us was in no way appealing. At a party his cold eyes would pause upon each nubile woman in the room and assess her with bland obviousness as an assortment of sexual conveniences. This look and his persistent innuendoes sickened me and Gillian; we detested him, and were baffled when Gertrude always cooperatively laughed, as if bad taste were just fun and irrelevant to their own ideal love. Painful to witness, she would actually vie with him in coarseness, playing the good sport. Couldn't she, we wondered, see that she was being grossly humiliated? She could and did, but there was no returning. She had plucked up her roots, and already her grown son was on his way to join them.

Looked at one way, Stefan owed Gertrude, his wife, his mother, his editor, his flag bearer, everything but the brains he was born with. This burdened and increasingly irked him as his debt to her grew and her gallantly concealed aches and pains became more apparent and disabling. Lacking sensitivity to others, he was always putting his foot in it and having to be saved by the one person who watched Argus-eyed over his welfare.

I happened to be present at the first or second meeting of the writers' union that Stefan attended. Gertrude, not being a writer herself, would have required a special invitation, so there was no one to restrain him.

Fed up with the sloppy arbitrariness with which the meeting was conducted (he didn't realize — hardly anyone did — that there was method in it, namely to make sure the status quo was preserved) he strolled up front when it was almost over and unceremoniously took the floor. With indulgent complacence, as if talking to children, he instructed his fellow members that in America "we" ran union meetings democratically on the basis of parliamentary procedure. Offhand he didn't remember the German for this expression, so he used the English, explained it, and was of course perfectly right; except that his tactlessness came across as intolerable arrogance.

I was just as ignorant as Stefan of the fact that we were all deliberately kept in the dark about the true function of the writers' union. I had still not grasped that it was neither a trade union as Americans understood it, that is, a fighter for its members' security, nor a guild like the League of American Writers, which considered literary readings and discussions an essential feature of its work. Nor did the younger East German writers, disillusioned with fascism and still euphoric over socialist promise, yet suspect that like all other officially approved organizations theirs was simply a corral. None represented the group it professed to represent — women, miners, white collars, blue collars, anybody. All represented the Party line, and their role was that of a sheepdog driving the membership in a prescribed direction.

Alma once took a job at the radio for a while, just for fun. She, of course, could not be driven in any direction. When her immediate superior suggested that she join the GDGB (Free German Trade Union Federation), she asked what for, thereby sending the poor fellow into a panic. There seemed so many obvious good reasons, but they all flew out of his head and he stammered, "If you're not in the union, who will organize your vacations?" "My husband," Alma replied truthfully, meaning no harm.

Not that she was impervious to socialist doctrine, provided it *was* socialist doctrine, and crossed her path at an opportune moment.

She and Bodo became infatuated with a Viennese couple, he a writer of science explanations for laymen, she a wife with time on her hands. The two women took to reading books together that they had neglected hitherto. "You know who's a marvelous writer?" Alma challenged me one day at the Club. "No, who?" "Lenin!" she cried, only partly to shock, amaze, and tease; she herself was astonished, and was laughing seriously.

After Max told me that it was the Party which ultimately decided everything, I should have borne it in mind, but I forgot. The fact is, we both kept forgetting because we *saw* the pie in the sky. Didn't the prices of necessities go down regularly? They did, every few months, sometimes twice within a fortnight. Weren't books and theater tickets dirt cheap, rents commensurate with income, health-care free, union members' two-week vacations provided for peanuts?

Aufbau being an FDGB shop (what else could it be) Max and I took union vacations two or three times, costing under 35 marks a head — not per day, mind you, but for thirteen days of not bad food and acceptable lodging. The drawback for us was the atmosphere of regimentation and mental fug, the dead air of a no longer admissible past. The standard greeting between trade-union vacationers seemed to be "Mahlzeit!" (Mealtime!) — short for "Blessed mealtime!" — which may have started as an avoidance of "Heil Hitler!" One had to reply "Mahlzeit!" or be the one who said it first. When I said "Guten Tag!" (Good day!) they would look surprised and say nothing.

It made no difference that the last meal was digested and the next one three hours off, they kept saying mealtime and thinking mealtime. They formed up punctually for guided walking tours. There were song evenings where everyone "shunkled," long rows of seated people linking arms and swaying to the rhythm from side to side, dragging you to right or left with a sadistic jerk so you got an elbow in the ribs or nearly fell off your seat.

In one holiday lodge in the Harz Mountains a union brother observing Max's cigarette ash lengthen and drop onto the stair carpet rebuked him, "Use the ashtray, Colleague!" Max couldn't stand being addressed as Colleague, particularly if correction was involved and the self-appointed monitor old enough to have been a Nazi. Seaside FDGB vacations were even worse because there was no escape from loudspeakers. Dozens of them posted along the beaches alternately broadcast corny singing, news headlines, and weather reports, drowning out the sounds of waves and seagulls and inducing mass catalepsy. "Once at the sea with FDGB" was enough for a lifetime.

As Stefan Heym's chances of publication in the United States had been blasted by his new allegiance, and Gertrude saw that Aufbau was not going to raid List, she made a shrewd move. She got backing (with Erich Wendt's help? I don't know; *somebody* had to help) to found a small English-language paperback company under the aegis of an established publisher. This would provide some compensation for the loss of larger editions in German. Stefan in any case preferred English for its brevity and cogency, Gertrude could edit it, and he could then write it over in German more easily.

The advertised purpose of Gertrude's Seven Seas was to bring out the works of blacklisted and otherwise unjustly neglected "progressive" authors in all parts of the world. Not surprisingly its very first two books were written by Stefan.

"By way of sheer routine," I wrote to Christina, "I shall offer them my railroad chronicle when it's finished, but I expect to be turned down with mouthings about how they can *only* use, dear Edith, works of high *literary* value."

Much worse was to come.

Why the writers' union did anything so frivolous as to run a dance I have no idea. It must have been the first and was probably the last dance it organized. A whole spacious restaurant built on the shore of Grünau's river had been hired, and Alma along with another adventurous beauty, Georgia Peet — Bulgarian wife of the ex-Reuters man — both at loose ends because their husbands were out of town, decided to attend and pick me up first.

We were just embarked on our first drink when Stefan Heym walked in alone. Gertrude may have been in Prague seeing her doctor, or she was simply indisposed; this was often the case. Not a dancing man, Stefan surveyed the room for a talking partner, noticed the curious, mocking eyes of my attractive tablemates, and came over.

The German Party's idea of decorous dance music (ND had attacked jazz as corrupt), the few colorless male writers who weren't dancing exclusively with their wives (interesting writers shunned the affair), and the heavy presence of Stefan and his attempts at light conversation were literally driving me to drink. Armenian cognac in any case was as good as Martell, so I kept ordering another and another, and when it was time to go I was drunk.

The other two women vanished in Alma's car. Stefan could not help walking by my side because we had the same way home, and I saw no escape either. After we had paced in oppressive silence a hundred yards or so I got an idea I thought uproarious.

"Hey Stefan," I said, "I've just been reading your novel *Goldsborough*, and I don't understand why on page one if you've got to have a working-class hero we find him sitting on the can. Is that a suitable place to introduce a working-class hero?"

"Your style of criticism is not unfamiliar to me," he replied. "I happen to know it was you who wrote that report on *The Eyes of Reason*."

The venom behind those words and the shocking disclosure sobered me in an instant.

This was a bad happening. It was not going to sink away like water in sand, I knew. Someone at Aufbau had meanly violated the secrecy rule on book reports.

On the other hand, was there something intrinsically illegitimate about writing a negative book report? When I wrote that one, I had never met Heym nor read anything else of his, so that personal aversion or a previous disappointment with his work were out of the question.

One problem with *Eyes* was that Stefan had never intended it for a German audience and its specific concerns. The novel was inspired by the 1948 coup in Czechoslovakia that brought a Communist government to power, and was aimed at a comfortable book-buying American bourgeoisie alarmed by such a development. Still living in the United States, Stefan had hoped to raise the level of American political tolerance while making a few bucks at the same time. And why not?

But while the average reader in Germany was too obsessed with his own quite different national quandaries to worry much over a bloodless coup in another country, he might have been gripped if the novel had introduced at least a couple of recognizable human beings with whom they could identify. This was not the case.

In those days in East Germany antifascists were extremely earnest about reeducating the Nazi-brainwashed citizenry. Publishers' readers looked for material which served that end or at least did it no disservice — by boring people, for instance. One way of boring them, as in *The Eyes of Reason*, was by introducing protagonists who represented abstractions, such as a class viewpoint, instead of being personalities in their own right. It was difficult to care what happened to invented cardboard people pushed from situation to situation in an arbitrary plot, like strategy pins on some general's wall map.

A few years later I would know that Stefan's rejected novel had been no worse than many others which GDR publishers saw fit to accept. Did *they* reeducate anybody, and if so, to what? Had *they* provided medicine for sick Germany? Could anything? What price well-meaning instruction in the morass of the unforeseen?

As if things were not bad enough between us and the Heyms, Gertrude, who obviously had as much right to get drunk as anyone else, took it into her head at some party to vilify and sneer at our beloved Bill Blake, whom she barely knew by sight; and I blew up. Perhaps she was embittered because Aufbau published *him*. Knowing nothing of our friendship with Chris and Bill she must have been as shocked at my rage as I was at Stefan's after that accursed dance.

Things seemed to soften after the arrival of her son David, a sweet and civilized young man who soon fell in love with and married the daughter of a Colony resident. They were a touching couple, and their devotion to one another lasted. They would come by and pet Dee, whom Gertrude presented with doll dishes, and the three of them took pictures of one another beaming on our terrace steps with Dee sitting between them. Then Gertrude approached me and Gillian with petitions to save Ethel and Julius Rosenberg from the electric chair, assigning us eight Colony families apiece to canvass for signatures. Momentarily this relieved our sense of alienation, made us feel that home could be anywhere; we were helping, or trying to help, and we were doing it together.

Soon even Stefan would play a beneficent role.

June 17, 1953 happened to be my paid "household day," granted all women employees in the GDR once a month to get their chores done. Absurd, of course — how could we do a month of chores in a day — but the ruling was at least a step in the right direction for a poor country, better than the rich Germany next door where there was no recognition whatsoever that working women worked a double shift.

Having household help at the moment I hardly needed this, but it was one of our few freedoms. No one spied to discover whether or not we were really beating rugs and cleaning the silverware with ammonia. I slept until 10 A.M., then phoned Alma at John Peet's little newspaper office, her newest fun job, and asked, "How about lunch at the Club?"

"Don't you know what's going on here?" she said. "I can't talk now," and she hung up.

The day before, I had in fact seen something inexplicable on Unter den Linden, though not very clearly. A delegation of Korean women was being received in the Federation's large meeting room, and we had all been summoned from our desks to hear their reports of the war. One ancient with a broad, lined face as unmoving as a death mask had at one stroke lost her husband, all her children and grandchildren, her brothers, sisters, cousins, nieces and nephews. The entire village had been wiped out, and she alone had miraculously survived — for what? "I can never cry again," she said. "I have no more tears." As she spoke we became aware of some dim tumult outside the building. Out of consideration for these stricken women, no one stirred at first. Then Käthe apologized, and some of us followed her to look out of the one open window.

"It's nothing," she said, closing it and shooing us back to our seats. So that day we did not find out that what resembled a rather ragged, undisciplined May Day demonstration was a protest by the building workers of Stalin Allee, the ambitious "first socialist street in Germany," a housing project which had been under construction for two years. They were angry that their work quota had been increased, but not their pay, and with no prior consultation. They were carrying placards I couldn't quite read before Käthe closed the window, and were actually striking — they who had no experience of strikes, who purportedly needed no strikes. Their union was looking the other way, but soon other defenders joined their march, people from the other side of town asking sympathetic questions and full of good advice.

The opportunity for the West was too good to miss. Early next morning paid ruffians appeared all over the GDR. Brecht described those he himself witnessed in a letter to his West German publisher Peter Suhrkamp as "the sharp, brutal figures of the Nazi period who had not been seen in such numbers for years, but had been present, on this side too, all along." They streamed through Berlin's Brandenburg Gate at the sector border, overturning cars and newspaper kiosks and setting them ablaze, while cries from watchers on the sidewalks that started as "Down with the government" quickly became "Hang them!"

One column that turned into Friedrich Straße yelling imprecations would have ignored John Peet's building if he and Alma hadn't waved a red flag from their balcony and shouted their own opinions at the mob. As police were nowhere about, the nearest thugs rushed into their building. John and Alma hastily locked the office door and moved heavy furniture against it, which did not stop the invaders getting in, but doubtless out of respect for English and American accents they only grabbed the red flag and made a bonfire of it in the street. That was when I phoned.

Meanwhile Soviet tanks finally arrived in strength from their camp outside Berlin and ploughed unhurriedly through Unter den Linden, scattering people in all directions. A part-time WIDF employee, who believed she saw, claimed she saw, or really did see victims flattened by the tanks came upstairs crying and incoherent and remained hysterical for days, until Käthe fired her. To my knowledge, however, neither her story nor West Berlin radio reports of blood oozing from under caterpillar tracks were ever corroborated, not even in after years when "now it can be told" revelations made people's hair stand on end. In Berlin no violence was ordered against demonstrators, and the only armed police force was confined to barracks.

This was not true elsewhere. Blood was shed in Saxony, where heavy industry was concentrated. At least thirty strikers were shot down. In Halle long-endured grievances burst open like boils, just as Rudolf Herrnstadt had warned in his "Zschau and Brumme" article. With RIAS broadcasts urging them on, several thousand workers stormed past dazed policemen to the jail in order to release the innocent political prisoners they assumed were inside. A few guards shot at them, but by the sheer numbers and rage of the workers the police cordon was forced apart and over two hundred women were released, of whose records the avengers knew nothing. One happened to be Erna Dorn, a former Gestapo hand later employed in Ravensbrück concentration camp — not the "commandant" GDR papers made of her, just an average bestial Nazi still mindful of her duties, who rushed to Halle's marketplace and made inflammatory speeches.

I, knowing nothing as usual, thought I might as well go shopping on my household day, but I got a shock when I reached the nearest grocery store. It was jammed with housewives buying out goods no longer rationed, everything they could hoard to keep their families in staples for as long as the war lasted. If they knew nothing else, they knew how wars began and what to do before their neighbors got ahead of them. Their radios were always tuned to RIAS for the moment of deliverance. The grocer's shelves were already half empty.

I had thought the neighborhood was used to me, the crazy American who lived among them on purpose. There were even people who would nod to me in the street, rather distantly no doubt, but now as I entered the store lips whispered, heads turned, eyes flashed contempt and hatred, and I recognized this as the look that precedes stringing someone up on a lamppost. When I finally got to the counter, nothing was left that had been on my list. If it was, somebody had hidden it in the back for tardy insiders.

That night all the men in the Colony who had a place of work, an office building, a school, a theater, anything with walls and a roof on top, had to stay in it until morning to "guard" it with their bare hands. They came home briefly to tell their wives that although the border to the Western sectors was now sealed by Russian soldiers, the provocateurs unable to get out of East Berlin would be hiding wherever there was cover, and I actually saw a straggle of men as twilight darkened sneaking quietly into the woods on the other side of the Grünbergs' house. Max had handed me one of our empty beer bottles, the kind with a top that clamps on tight, to keep under the bed in case anybody broke in. "But with water in it," he warned. "Otherwise it's no weapon at all."

Since Stefan Heym had no place to work but his own home and was young enough to be considered able-bodied, he was chosen to protect the women and children, which he did by making the rounds of the Colony every so often with great dignity and solemnity to let us know he was watching out. He didn't even have his dangerous dog yet — this may have been the occasion that finally persuaded him to get one — and even with the dog he could no more have rescued us from real trouble than Max, Janka, and the others could have rescued Aufbau unarmed, but I appreciated his seriousness as a would-be protector and was surprised that he could be so concerned even for me.

All the same, when my chronicle of women on the Pennsylvania Railroad was finished and I took it to Gertrude, she said she had no time to read it, she was just so overwhelmed with letters to answer — here she dropped several names of famous writers — and surely I would understand; perhaps in a few months? I waited a few months and offered it again, but now she had even less time.

At some banquet that Max had to attend, Gertrude made a speech lauding her own achievement in Seven Seas, and Max rose to agree that it did indeed deserve respect; he only wondered, he said, why she was so choosy as to which manuscripts were worth her attention. Her face showed an eagerness to conciliate, Max told me — she was only waiting for him to finish — but Stefan forestalled her, leaping to his feet and snarling, "And how did *you* treat *my* book *The Eyes of Reason?*"

An eye for an eye of reason.

The Germans call this sort of happening "an éclat," not in our sense of brilliance (nor would we speak of *an* éclat) but in one of Larousse's preferred definitions, "something violently broken in two, as a length of wood" or "a sudden, violent noise like a thunderclap."

For a moment or two there was a stunned silence. Then, coffee being over, the guests got up and gathered in little groups for a final chat, avoiding the Heyms if they could. Not long afterward Gertrude telephoned to ask me for the manuscript, which I promptly delivered, but a few days later it was back on our little foyer table. Their maid had left it with our maid. Inside the envelope was a note, "You're very talented, Edith. Try again."

There's a game, "Happiness is . . ."

Happiness is sitting on the rim of the bathtub and watching Max shave at the mirror over the washbasin. I never thought of watching him shave in any of our previous five bathrooms, they were too cramped, but in Max's dream house the bathroom was bigger and brighter than the bedchambers, and I got a relaxed view of each grimace he pulled to make a taut surface for his razor. He enjoyed having me admire that secondary wonder only men can perform. Like a comedian sure of his act he made a quip or two, and was careful not to cut himself.

Great happiness was when Max took us to the Belgian circus one Sunday instead of working. Everyone was saying "Acrobat, *schön!*" even if they hadn't yet seen the three Rivel brothers who dragged out the word for beautiful, "*schö-ö-ö-ön,*" with a mounting, intoxicating rapture that sent people into helpless fits of laughter. We had ringside seats, never mind the expense, it was Dee's first circus. She laughed so hard that one Rivel turned around, walked straight over to her and whispered the word for her alone, then stepped backward fast, holding her thrilled eyes in his and fiercely beaming until he had reached his brothers in the middle of the ring.

Afterward Max took us to dinner at a new restaurant in the roof garden of one of Stalin Allee's four towers. In flattened Berlin, eleven floors was a tower, not only for small Dee but for her parents who had looked down over New York from the top of the Empire State Building.

Weeping together at Puccini's *Manon Lescaut* was happiness of another kind. Drenched and blinded at the end we went into the street clutching one another for support. Max knew the opera well from his youth, but I doubt he had sobbed over it then. Nor, despite having read the synopsis in the program notes beforehand, was I prepared to be so shattered when Manon, deported for debt and followed by her faithful Des Grieux, tries to cross an endless desert in America and dies of exhaustion in his arms. Max's exile and mine had run together like the confluence of two streams, and become a moment of catharsis.

Yet when he brought home our first phonograph and the armful of *Lohengrin* LPs and wept over Lohengrin's farewell to his swan I became embarrassed, then irritated.

Elsa, for heaven's sake, was a big fat stupid woman who asked personal questions after promising not to. What had Lohengrin seen in her in the first place? What possessed him to rush off and do battle for *her* of all people? I could bathe in the music (this was precisely what Harry had against Wagner, that he wrote baths which drowned the brain) but wasn't it sheer sentimental histrionics to make Lohengrin dismiss his lovely swan, the last taxi back from the boondocks, before he took one good look at his blind date? I had always wanted to do a Lohengrin travesty for marionettes, and here was Max taking it all as seriously as if it were happening to himself.

But perhaps it was. Didn't I make demands he could not meet because he would not? How profoundly he would not, how intensely he suffered from the permanent dilemma of his own needs as against mine, was demonstrated by those tears I viewed as self-indulgent. Whatever symbolism Wagner may have had in mind, the swan for Max must have been his freedom to do unhindered what came first for his own soul.

To every thing
Turn, turn, turn
There is a season,

Turn, turn, turn
And a time
To every purpose under heaven.

In the language of Pete Seeger's song from Ecclesiastes 3, Max's time for casting away stones was when he left Germany. Now was the time for gathering stones together, our house, Germany's house. The time to embrace was past for Max. The time to refrain from embracing had come.

Why? There could have been one cause or many. It is likely that Max himself didn't know. I think of Mordechai in *The Last of the Just,** who obeys an inner compulsion he cannot put into words. At bedtime he clasps his beloved, still beautiful fifty-year-old Judith to himself as always, then unaccountably puts her from him, turns to the wall of the alcove and says, "Good night to thee, my wife." She lies still, disconcerted. On reflection she realizes that this ending of an era has not come entirely unheralded. Mordechai's embraces as he grew older had sometimes bespoken a dim resistance, as if the act were no longer appropriate and the call of her womanhood a levy on his spirit. Afterward she sees that in their daily life he is more a friend, more considerate, kinder, and that when his eyes rest on her from a greater distance only love for her remains in them.

But Max and I were not an aging couple long together like Mordechai and Judith. Our lives were not, like theirs, molded by a stable, ancient culture, one in which answers to the greater questions were found in the Talmud and the Torah, in the judgments of sage rabbis and according to a legend dating back to Isaiah's time, in the righteousness of thirty-six just men upon whom the world rested. Our certainties were not much older than ourselves, and our world was cleft by unjust, unseen powers whose doings behind locked doors we were too ignorant and hopeful to imagine.

* André Schwarz-Bart. New York, Atheneum, 1960

PART VI

It breaks one's heart to witness the birth pains of a new social order.
How much courage, talent, discipline, heroism, how much grueling
labor, how much intelligence, and how much stupidity . . .

— HANS EISLER
1953 Diary entry

W RITING WAS SELDOM AS EASY as when, in my thirties, short stories used to fly to me like steel filings to a giant magnet. Three days after starting one without a plan, without a clue as to what was driving me, I had said it all, felt good, and put the thing away in my desk. A couple of years later I would come across it by accident, examine it dispassionately, switch paragraphs around, change a few words, and store it for the future.

A book was different, an ordeal. Books were for the present, but the present is a fast swimmer and I found myself struggling after it as one walks through thigh-high water. I was lucky when I became ill only at the end of the long, lonely stretch. The part-time job downtown that tempted me away from writing meant not only money of my own but an illusion that I still belonged to the world and might even be helping to improve it. Best of all, Mildred had been granted a secretary from New York, a fat little lickspittle on whom she doted, and I was moved into a congenial translation pool.

At congresses abroad we toiled in humble back rooms day and night for up to two weeks, cheerfully indifferent to personal glory. None of us could have qualified as a cabin star, but we wholeheartedly admired the sleight of ear-brain-tongue which enables some people to take in one language while simultaneously spewing out the sense in another — or the nonsense, as the case may be, either because the original is a mess anyway or because such virtuosos barely know in their happy trance what they are saying or how they look. Ann, a Dutch girl who in Berlin managed the sober shipping department, shone at congresses and never knew how beatifically she beamed through the glass pane of her cabin.

In capitalist countries we saved our food allowances to splurge on luxuries for husbands and children in the straitened GDR, seldom buying anything for ourselves apart from local bread to go with the East Berlin salamis and Baltic tinned fish we had brought along. Like giggling sophomores in a dorm we spread out and shared our contributions of mustard, homemade cookies and the like in somebody's room and swapped the latest simultaneous translation jokes, such as "stalwart men holding up the fronts of women" uttered by a cabin Russian. This clanger gave us particular satisfaction because the Russians always brought their own congress translators from Moscow, not trusting mere us to do justice to their gobbledygook.

In those days, of course, we referred to them as Soviets, not Russians, because that was the politically correct form. We never even noticed that the Soviet women who came and went in Federation headquarters were always and only Russian. We did notice their snootiness, however, and as normal human beings chortled among ourselves when one of them slipped on a banana peel.

Obviously they had been instructed not to fraternize, but just as obviously they liked not fraternizing. What was wrong with them? Weren't we in principle of one mind, sisters in the fight for women's rights, members of the greater family of nations beyond the USSR that would include the whole world some day, perhaps even within the lifetime of our children? Not that we actually discussed these ticklish matters with one another. We moved with instinctive care through the unacknowledged fog, knowing only that we as a group were good friends.

An illustration of our one-minded doublethink in the '50s was the delight we took in a shaggy-dog story told by Lilly, a biologist and cabin whiz who freelanced at our congresses when she could. She was a German Communist who happened to be in the French Resistance when she was nabbed by the Gestapo, then actually escaped Auschwitz in fulfillment of a pledge to her husband. Technically she had been a Soviet citizen since the end of World War II, the husband having been born in swallowed Latvia, and she knew more jokes than anyone I ever met except Ann. (Some correlation between cabin talent and jokes? Both Ann and Lilly were certainly blessed with a long comic memory.)

The shaggy-dog story (I trim it somewhat) was about an international conference of Communist Parties called in Moscow. As the various national delegations filed into the great hall they noticed a thumbtack placed in the center of each seat with the pointy end up. The English delegation sat gingerly on the front edge of their chairs so as not to disturb the tacks. "This is sabotage," hissed the French, who stuck the tacks into chair legs, but honorably put them back in their former position after the conference. One group wrapped them in handkerchiefs and stowed them in jacket pockets without comment. Only the GDR delegates told each other stoutly, "The Soviet comrades must have had *something* in mind when they did this," and sat down on the tacks.

Bedroom picnics were unnecessary when a Federation congress was held in a presumptively socialist country. My first such congress was in Romania, where we were housed in Bucharest's most palatial hotel. In each of our single rooms we found fresh flowers, a bowl of fruit, a tall pitcher of iced orange juice, all regularly replenished, and a silk scarf. At meals we were stuffed so mercilessly (Take more! But you've hardly touched it!) that at a nineteen-course banquet (or so it felt) supposedly given in our honor by President Gheorghiu Dei, who was nowhere to be seen, my brand-new raspberry taffeta dress from the GDR's first elegant modiste split down the back alongside the zipper, which ended approximately at my coccyx.

After the last of the desserts, we had all been enjoined to take hands in an immense ring around the tables and were improvising a dance step to faster and faster folk music when I heard the rip go "Ach!" and was instantly surrounded by a cluster of Romanian girls hiding my shame and blocking every possible crevice through which Men might have peeked. As in a rehearsed choreography they gently nudged me back to my table, a corolla of black-eyed Susan petals with me as the black eye. One of them, despatched to get a needle and thread, was back in a minute and sewing me up at top speed. In the midst of the same impenetrable phalanx — the hasty baste might give way — I was discreetly ushered to my room. At about midnight, writhing with indigestion, I was attended by four different medical specialists and cured by morning. Nothing would cure the dress.

It was easy to be dazzled by Bucharest in those early hours before the July heat set in. The splendid white state buildings erected for kings glistened under the sun, each in its own space set off by greenery. Crowds of handsome, healthy-looking young people were hurrying to jobs, the men's shirts immaculate, the girls wearing crisply laundered summer dresses and on their heads spotless white scarves which I took for a relic of folk costume. They were that, but not only, and as usual I had to learn the hard way.

Not for nothing had each of us been presented with a scarf. I rushed out bareheaded during lunch hour on the last day and was soon rushing back without the artsy-craftsy presents I had meant to buy. My cranium was bursting from sunstroke, but it would have been too embarrassing to call a doctor again and get four more distinguished specialists, so I plunged my whole head, and damn the hairdo, in a basin of cold water until after ten or fifteen minutes it felt normal again. Wrong remedy? I've often had occasion to wonder when I do something especially idiotic.

But apart from the violent midsummer heat, Romania's variant of socialism seemed to exude a charming, triumphant prosperity very different from what we saw in the spare GDR. It gave us rather a pang until we noticed the cracks in the surface. When Marjorie, a spirited English girl married to an East German composer, invited our Romanian translation colleagues to join us in her room after work they looked frightened. "My husband wouldn't let me," said one. "*Let!*" cried Marjorie with a hoot of incredulous laughter. "I'll ask him," the girl corrected herself. No one else said anything, and the awkward subject was dropped.

On other subjects their responses were similarly discouraging.

We worried when we saw gypsy women, whose dark breasts had been pulled to rags by too many babies, sitting in entranceways to suckle the most recent ones, themselves obviously ill-fed and sheltered only by the shallow lintel of someone else's door. Passersby appeared not to see them, in effect really didn't see them, any more than a stray cat would have attracted their attention.

"They want to live that way," we were assured. "They only give our country a bad name." Equally disregarded were nattily uniformed little boys as young as eight, not gypsies, who worked all hours in our hotel carrying luggage for able-bodied adults.

From a bus taking us and our bathing suits out to some castle on a lake we saw with amazement the abrupt cessation of the capital's white glamor. It was as if we were in a film where someone had yelled "Cut!" and the next frame showed the backside of Turkey.

There had been nothing one might call outskirts. I saw no thinning suburbs or scattered light industry before the first farms and fields as was usual outside other capitals. Suddenly the paving was gone. As mud slowed the bus we got a view of unrelieved squalor, cracked cement hovels with chunks missing, and between the hovels great puddles, the kind that never sink into the ground. (In the week since we arrived it hadn't rained once.)

Small children dabbled in the mud. A couple of men wearing stiff suits sat in Sunday immobility where they could find shade. Women, shawled despite or against the heat, cooked over fires in the open. Dogs that looked and slunk like hyenas nosed furtively in rubbish, as if expecting a kick at any moment.

It was those hyena-dogs — hyenas were certainly their immediate ancestors — that shocked me most. I had never before seen canines that were neither pets nor watchdogs living in a human setting, their only relationship to it being that of bluebottles on excrement. No one would have given them names, no child would have called or stroked them, nobody would mourn when they died.

This was the sort of thing that in the eighteenth century Prince Potemkin, adviser to Catherine the Great, ordered concealed behind pasteboard village façades, lest along the route of the queen's planned journey to the Crimea she see the reality of rural Russia from her carriage windows. Admittedly every state residence from Versailles, Sans Souci, and Washington to cozy green toy-town Bonn (the latter destined to become a Potemkin Village par excellence) all served the function of a screen before stench and vileness. Young people now cover any official showpiece with the impotent contempt of graffiti, a form of protest not yet invented when we were in Romania. Neither were our reservations about that country very clear in our minds. Still, I don't think any of our translation team cared if we never saw the place again.

Someone indiscreetly told Max he had been recommended for the National Prize. He did his best to stave off belief, but did not wholly succeed. As I had ached to have a child, so his frail ego kept longing for the official recognition due him, and it did not come. Some dignitary suspicious of an aesthete who was both self-denying and West-tainted had probably whisked the recommendation, or recommendations, off his desk with a "Not *this* year." Another year might turn up a more acceptable solution to the vexing problem of Max and his respected well-wishers, and sure enough — the prize eventually went to the whole publishing house, the money into Aufbau's bank account and the felicity divided up so small, one imaginary segment for each employee, that only Aufbau's Party group could feel like patting itself on the back. At least there was no envy, a self-pitying national trait that poisons much of life in Germany.

Once a truly nice thing happened to Max, and as truly nice things were few and far between I was grateful, the more so as I myself had enjoyed a similar privilege without even earning it. A couple of months after the trip to Romania Max was included in a delegation to meet writers and publishers in Prague. It was his first respite from Germany since he had come back from America, and it transformed him for a while.

When I fetched him from the airport his face was a dreaming blur, his eyes like a sleepwalker's adrift on other scenes. He did take gentlemanly cognizance of me, got into the back seat of an Aufbau car with me, unwrapped a sample of ancient Prague's modern costume jewelry (very pretty) and asked about Dee's health and my own. He was like an amiable stranger of whom one thinks, "What a pity not to know this man." I sensed there had been a woman, and was glad for him.

For soon enough, as if the last lull had been too long, there would be another of those mysterious storms in the SED that arose like a long-tailed tornado seemingly out of nowhere (it wasn't nowhere, it was the Soviet Union) and blew many German members innocent of wrongdoing off their feet and into perdition.

On such occasions all Party documents (the membership book was known as a document) were called in and personal records reviewed, such as the curriculum vitae which might have to be written anew and checked against the ones written earlier. During the review, which might last for weeks, people lived under a pall of subdued anxiety and vague guilt until a sort of all-clear was sounded and most got their "documents" back, or new ones were printed and distributed. For some members none were reissued, and they could put away in a drawer forever the lapel pins showing the famous two clasped hands, those of Wilhelm Pieck, Communist, and Otto Grotewohl, Social Democrat, when they founded the Socialist Unity Party.

I could guess the relative severity of Party punishments from the tone of Max's voice when he mentioned them. True, his tone on this subject was carefully noncommittal, meaning it was not for him to comment without the necessary facts which had to be kept from a vigilant enemy, hence from everyone else; but there were nuances in Max's tone. Criticism in the press was not an actual punishment, just a frightening noise in the dark. A "stern reprimand" from the Party was the stage of disapproval just prior to expulsion, whereas a plain reprimand had been no worse than a boxed ear, a red face, or the beginning of an ulcer, depending on one's constitution.

Even expulsions could have stages. A person could be expelled from the lofty Politburo, yet remain in the warm, safe airlessness of Party life. Only if his danger to Walter Ulbricht became acute could he be excommunicated, as was Rudolf Herrnstadt after June 1953, banished — not despite his weak lungs but because of them — to the poisonous fumes of a chemical production center, and ostracized to his own bitterly brooding company for the thirteen years that remained of his life.

This sort of thing happened only to people so dangerously close to the top that they could witness and agonize over Ulbricht's intrigues. Herrnstadt went in desperation to the Soviet Party's High Commissioner in the GDR, an honorable man like Brutus, who sneered in his face and promptly reported him to the intriguer. Only the other people in the Politburo, shaking in their shoes, knew how Herrnstadt had met his fate.

As far back as 1949, however, ideological v-bombs signed A. Zhdanov had started dropping onto the socialist camp, each heralding a campaign of abstruse bullying directed at writers and artists. This troubled the Communists living under capitalism as well, who were better informed than we were, and eventually transformed them into ex- or anti-Communists.

In one of her increasingly rare letters, one of my most treasured friends in New York, clear-headed Helen, wrote me in 1951 out of the cellar of McCarthy's reign,

> The climates (individually and in conflict) of the two worlds you and I inhabit make easy intercourse hard. By now it is almost a reflex to hold back more than half one's real expression.

I tried to get through to her in cautiously worded communications, myself groping, often failing to notice an irritant because it seemed so trivial. For example the abbreviation of a name to "A." Zhdanov. It had become a Soviet custom to denote first names of leaders by a single capital letter. Off and on I wondered why. What had become of the good old

Russian patronymics made so familiar to us by Tolstoy and Turgenyev, Chekhov, Gogol, and Gorky? Only Josef Stalin, who wasn't even a Russian, still had his Vissarionovich, although abbreviated to a "V." Obviously (if not to me) the ploy was to rob us of any such homey familiarity with the Party and make already inaccessible leaders totally faceless, like those balaklava helmets later affected by criminals everywhere.

The Zhdanov campaigns, actually cobbled together by J.V. himself, began with "cosmopolitanism," a hitherto unknown deviation which meant wantoning with Western decadence. Mostly Jews like the "dangerous cosmopolitans Einstein and Freud" were held responsible, a notion doubtless acceptable in Russia, Poland, and other parts of eastern Europe where the pogrom mentality still throve, but a severe embarrassment to the SED so soon after the Holocaust. While an obedient faction on *Neues Deutschland* attacked as "Zionists" Party members cursed with Jewish names, a stronger faction gradually put an end to this indecency, after which ND published the dearest, sweetest photos of Einstein it could find, put smarmy captions underneath, restored Freud to his former oblivion (Germany had never taken much interest in psychoanalysis) and day in and day out raged against U.S. persecution of Ethel and Julius Rosenberg to demonstrate its disgust with anti-Semitism.

Nasty cosmopolitanism was followed by nice socialist realism with its "positive" literary heroes and "typical" supporting characters. Apart from the fact that no one except Zhdanov understood precisely what made a character typical, socialist realism seemed innocuous enough in the beginning. Hadn't Maxim Gorky, one of my darlings, plumped for it? We were told so. I did wonder how one realism could differ from another realism. It surprised me that intelligent people took precious time wrestling with the imaginary distinctions they claimed to perceive. Yet socialist realism by itself did only minimal harm. Only after it was raped by the bugbear "formalism" did it give birth to a mad monster.

Helen's letter went on:

> We get here repercussions of your stated problems with formalism and socialist realism. J. [her new husband], still writing for the paper now and then [she dared not say the *Daily Worker*] gets hit by it directly every once in a while [she meant cracked over the head]. It seems [when a thing only *seems*, one is tiptoeing with exceeding care] that though

we are in entire agreement with the literary aims of socialist realism, there are interpretations and interpretations, and often J. is interpreted as a formalist.

I don't know what the argument means to you there, but here for us it is a senseless deterrent, not only as I say in its theory but in the way in which it slams shut avenues of alliances. So many avenues are shut already, with new ones closing down every day. It becomes harder and harder here to count your friends — no less to count *on* them. We shouldn't at such a time be finding ways of driving away what friends we still have.

She thanked me for sending Aufbau's new art calendar. It had been conceived by Max, and the selections were influenced by his discernment. "In these formalist discussions," she wrote,

I am constantly showing it around and using it as the clinching argument about the breadth and depth of artistic taste it indicates. Will you tell Max?

Of course I did, and it made him briefly happy.

But Deborah, my beloved friend of longest standing, reacted quite differently to the difficulties of communication between our worlds. After a Brecht-Dessau opera was brutally damned, then banned, she concluded from a letter of mine that I had approved of such treatment, and sent me an infuriated dressing-down.

She knew Dessau well from her stay in California, where she had met the entire Brecht crowd. Apparently I was the one she didn't know. That broke my heart. Not all at once, because I was sure I could make her see reason; but her replies to my circumstantial explanations were cool and brief and finally ceased altogether.

The sad irony of the break with Deborah was that she had always been tone-deaf, a freak in the genes of such a fine poet. From Bach to Bartók, from Purcell to Prokofiev, all music was meaningless to her except certain songs whose words moved her; so what was the sense of my writing that to me twelve-tone music was just one long, incomprehensible noise? Not only had I forgotten her handicap, I had lacked the imagination to perceive that she might be ashamed of it, hence defensive. Maybe that was why she accused me of denying other people the right to their own music "theories," as if theory had anything to do with likes or dislikes in art. It was I who hadn't known *her*, I who had idealized the exquisitely beautiful girl as a figure on a stained-glass window, a pre-Raphaelite blessed damozel against a night sky in a shower of stars.

To Christina I wrote:

> My usual dream is that I am in New York looking for a job under the most humiliating circumstances, unable to find one, getting old, being alone, and with no memory of a life in Berlin. Last night I had a new dream: I had gone home to America and was full of hope. I had no fear of not getting a job, I was willing to take anything, a selling job in Macy's, anything, and I felt sure I would get it. I was received with enthusiasm by all my old friends. Suddenly I had a misgiving: "It was a terrible crime to desert Dee." When I woke up my first feeling was relief that I had not deserted her. My second feeling was disappointment that I was not in New York. Only it was worse than disappointment. It was a desperation so deadening that I couldn't raise myself from the bed.

In January 1951, as if in fulfillment of a New Year's resolution, the formalism rumblings had escalated to an all-out bombardment of the GDR art scene, with special attention to painters. The opening gun in a Soviet-controlled East German newspaper, whose line ND naturally copied, was an ignorant tirade so lengthy that two days were required to publish its full-page halves. It was signed N. Orloff, of whom no one had ever heard.

Formalism now held absolute sway over painting in the GDR, the mystery man accused. Art magazines promoted "a cult of ugliness and immorality." The newly founded Academy of Arts did nothing but encourage "more or less realistic" artists to tolerate in their midst "antidemocratic decadence hostile to the people."

As it happened, none of the artists abused by name was interested in art classified as abstract or nonobjective. All were earnestly devoted to realism, each in his own manner, which meant that they did not prettify the underprivileged third of Germany to whose socialist strivings they were committed. Now they were lamed by shock and fear.

Brecht and Dessau, however, kept calm. Brecht because he never let himself be distracted from the irons he had in the fire — always several in any one year — and Dessau because he felt safe in the lee of Brecht's resourcefulness. Both men were looking forward to the opening of their opera about Lucullus, a Roman conqueror in the first century B.C. Its clear antiwar theme could not possibly have been misconstrued, and supposing worst, did come to worst they had a friend at court in Paul Wandel, the Minister of Education, who had returned without a murmur the twelve-tone score Dessau sent for his approval.

What did the Minister of Education have to do with music? The cagey Politburo had installed an arts department in Wandel's ministry rather than set up an independent one for "culture" that might get big-headed and run wild. Wandel, a faithful Party man since his youth, son of a worker, member of the Soviet exile group, was considered totally reliable despite a leaning toward art and artists.

Max, always grasping at some straw of hope, praised Wandel to me as "a liberal." This was a widespread impression, not only Max's. The man did have a sensitive face just short of real distinction, diminished as it was by a weak chin, but he vastly admired Brecht — surely the acid test? — and also thought very highly indeed of Dessau, whose unforgettable songs contributed so much to the success of *Mother Courage*.

The Minister of Education cannot really have examined the score Dessau sent him. It is doubtful he could read notes at all; he simply believed in Dessau. But after he himself was attacked by "Orloff" for "incontinently squandering the people's money" on "quite absurd formalisitc paintings" for the GDR's museums, he must have felt sick and in grave danger. He may well have known who Orloff was, namely Vladimir Semyonov, adviser to the Soviet Control Commission in the GDR. (Two years later as High Commissioner it would be Semyonov who sent Rudolf Herrnstadt into exile.) Wandel was no hero, as he demonstrated in the case of another Orloff victim, Horst Strempel, one of the finest painters and unluckiest pitiable schlemiels ever to drift innocently, mothlike, into the Party flame.

Orloff had accused the relatively unknown professor at East Berlin's Art School of having a "destructive, abstractionist influence on his students," so at a word from the Party Wandel hastened to the phone to tell Strempel he should ask for suspension from his job on grounds of ill health.

The GDR had plenty of its own little Orloffs, who had been picking on Strempel for three years because of a mural in East Berlin's main railway station at Friedrich Straße. It had come there quite legitimately: the railway staged a painting competition to inspire people with the message "Away with the Ruins — Start Building," and Strempel won it soon after moving to East Berlin from the West.

Unfortunately, being just above large MEN and WOMEN signs identifying the public toilets, it may have inspired more rude jokes than heroic deeds. In any case I could hardly make out the details in that dim concourse. By the time Max pointed it out to me it was so dusty that after craning my neck and straining my eyes for a while I could only declare it a sad effort and was surprised when Max disagreed. He had probably seen in one-man shows the spontaneous, unsponsored, and starkly colored work by Strempel that sprang from his indignation at injustice and hypocrisy. What to me resembled just another WPA post-office mural Max saw as a detail in a distinguished career, a not unworthy detail that consciously harked back to the left-nurtured *Proletkult* of the 1920s.

Long afterward, in what amounted to another lifetime, I went to an exhibition in the Märkisches Museum to see the few Strempel canvases that could still be recovered, including the color sketch he had made before starting his maligned mural. It had been painted as a triptych, with horizontal rows of look-alike little workers facing alternately right and left on the side panels, but featuring in the center a determined superman who bursts out of the foreground across ruins, rubbish, twisted wire, and helmeted skulls, swinging powerful muscular arms with an oversized, rocklike right fist to defeat destruction and a big open left hand curved to grab up the nearest urgent task. His angular profile, like sawed pine, means business, his sleeves are rolled up, his trousers bag with his stride, and Picasso might have painted the bare feet with the short square toes of equal length.

As if *people* looked like that, the Party philistines had growled. An insult to the working class! Who could identify with a figure that had toes of equal length, a wood-carved profile? *Proletkult!* This was even worse than Expressionism! For in 1951 it suddenly emerged that *Proletkult*, so dear to Communists in the Weimar Republic, was now also proscribed. Since when? Why?

A month after the Orloff article the mural had disappeared overnight under a gray coating that matched the dirty concourse. Strempel's admirers became still more apprehensive. It was not clear which vandals had done it, at whose behest, and nobody suspected that Paul Wandel, the protector of Brecht and Dessau, would have chosen this moment to hound a hapless art professor.

A photo of Strempel in the Museum's catalogue shows a preternaturally modest little man seated on a coffin-sized crate in front of his mural sketch, messy palette in hand, beret set jauntily above sticking-out ears. Bright-eyed and radiant as a trustful child, his spectacles slipping down his long nose as Max's used to, he seems overjoyed at this chance to be useful to socialism.

But he confounded Wandel. After so many devastating losses since his flight from Nazi Germany in 1933, each frantic move entailing the abandonment of all his latest work, Strempel was no longer quite the blue-eyed schnook shown in the photo. The worm had turned. He declined to cooperate in his own and his family's ultimate calamity; he demanded a formal dismissal in writing.

Wandel backed away from his telephone and left it to dogs with stronger stomachs to finish off the quarry. These loosened Strempel's hold on the art school job through a grotesque accusation of spying, which made him realize that his next stop would be a Soviet labor camp or worse. In haste he took his wife and child to West Berlin, once again obliged to leave all his new work behind.

I had never seen the unfortunate man in the flesh — such as it was, for to judge by the 1948 photo he was spindly from years of privation. Nor did he and his family get much to eat in West Berlin on returning there. As a Communist he was denied refugee status, paid work, welfare, and a place to live.

Dessau was versatile enough to have composed an opera in any style. He had chosen twelve-tone music despite the risk because it best expressed the avenging character of the libretto, as well as his own reaction to war and to the just rage of "eighty thousand slaughtered, half-lived lives," the victims of Lucullus, who as jurors in limbo condemn the war criminal to eternal oblivion. Brecht supported the risk, although to be on the safe side the two agreed to present the first night in March as a tryout rather than a premiere.

But when Wandel, wakened to reality by the Orloff blast, asked for a second look at the score, Dessau suggested to Brecht that they postpone

the opening until fall. This would give him time to work in a few com-
promises.

Brecht would have none of such talk. For him a political drama's
hour of urgency was when he himself felt goaded to write and present it.
The anticommunist belligerence of the United States, from its hot war in
divided Korea to its cold war in divided Germany, together with the State
Department's ever greater leniency toward "denazified" upper-echelon
Nazis, demanded — Brecht strongly felt — a reminder of the Nuremberg Trials without a moment's delay.

Besides, why fear criticism? "We will meet it or turn it to account," he
said with the serenity of genius. But his wizardry in getting out of tight
corners was not a skill possessed by Dessau.

Another difference between the two which Brecht seemed to over-
look was his friend's fealty to a Party famously vindictive where its own
children were concerned. In the hysteria prevailing since the Orloff article his own most cunning maneuvers might just fall short of helping a
man with the Party pin on his lapel.

And indeed Walter Ulbricht, proud of having attended the Schiller-
Rossini opera *Wilhelm Tell* fourteen times (diddy dum, diddy dum, diddy
dum dum dum, diddy dum, diddy dum, diddy dum dum dum), felt personally insulted by *The Trial of Lucullus*. Its dissonances, he pronounced, were "aimed against the efforts of exemplary workers to learn
more about the beauty of the classics." Ulbricht "took art so seriously," as
Brecht's biographer Werner Mittenzwei remarks, "that artists and public
alike lost all pleasure in it."

True, there was no organized booing at the tryout, such as the Party
ordered for later offenses against its leader's mummified tastes. There was
no booing whatsoever. No one stirred after the finish, then hands were
clapped sore. What a spectacle it had been! I think we could all have sat
gazing the whole night at the sensational sets and costumes, the
pageantry of a larger than life-size Pompeian red and gold procession
through the streets of ancient Rome, and in gray contrast the weird but
riveting spectral trial where the conqueror's victims wail, "Into nothingness with him and into nothingness with all his kind!"

There were repeated curtain calls, cries of "Bravo!" and insistent demands for author and composer to appear. Brecht came out quietly for
a moment, but Dessau actually turned a handspring on the stage in his
elation. He must have thought his fears had been groundless.

Diffidently I asked Max between renewed outbursts of applause, "Did you understand the music?"

He believed he did, although in his enthusiastic review he was more circumspect. It did not behoove him, he wrote, "to make a technical judgment about the music. I think I may say that it does not — or at any rate only in a few places — attain the sovereign heights that distinguish great opera." Conscientiously, however, he tried to save the pieces, pointing up "lyrical, parodistic, and illustrative" virtues in Dessau's music, singling out for special praise the "Fishwife's Song" that "held the audience spellbound." Other critics also had good things to say.

But how could mere critics save a lamb from the slaughter when even the president of the German Democratic Republic failed? At a ranting Party postmortem that attacked *Lucullus* a week after the tryout Wilhelm Pieck the ardent theater-lover rose to ask, "Comrades, what if it is *we* who are in error?" He was quickly snowed under, and at the next Party conference on formalism Dessau was pilloried by an overwhelming majority as one who "confused, disoriented, paralyzed, and debilitated the progressive forces of society."

Brecht was not attacked for his libretto; only the title and a few lines had to be given more force, they said, and he professed (slyly?) the most heartfelt gratitude for the criticisms; but who could read Brecht's mind? Ulbricht, in any case, saw the devil in him and had quite another bone to pick. He had been saving it for an appropriate occasion ever since the revival of Brecht's play *Mother* two months earlier (not to be confused with *Mother Courage*). Although based on Gorky's novel it had been stripped à la *Proletkult* and the WPA's *Living Newspaper* to the bare bones of a lesson on revolution, which in 1951 was a red rag to bullnecked Ulbricht. Revolution had played no role in the creation of the GDR. Its socialism was a gift horse into whose mouth the populace was forbidden to look, so to preach it at this juncture when consolidation was in order, that is consolidation of Ulbricht's power, sounded to him and his merry men like counterrevolution.

He had marshaled the most erudite intellectual stooges in his stable to outsmart the playwright, but Brecht had a way about him that made halfway intelligent stooges extremely nervous. No sooner had one of them hesitantly raised a stick at Brecht than he was falling all over himself to proffer a bouquet.

A Politburo member named Oelssner, proudly disclaiming any knowledge of art, which entitled him to kick it around like a tin can, at first stormed, "Is this true realism? Are typical figures presented here in a typical environment? This isn't theater at all, but a cross between *Proletkult* and Meyerhold!"

Wsevelod Meyerhold, a Jew, brilliant director of all Soviet theater for nineteen years, praised as an "iconoclast of accepted norms," was arrested in 1939 and executed a year later, the charge being formalism.

Did Oelssner suddenly realize what name, what terror he was conjuring? Was he warned by a certain look on Brecht's face? At once he called himself to order, flattering from his high horse, "If only a man as talented as Brecht would write a logically composed *play*, what a magnificent work he might give us!"

One critic, a middle-aged baby kangaroo who felt safest in the Party's pocket, couldn't help praising *Mother*, which despite Brecht's alarming theories of theater as a function of criticism and not an arena of histrionics and tear-jerking, "appealed to all that was human in us."

Enter disgustedly as deus ex machina the all-round theater mediocrity and air bag Hans Rodenberg, for whom all this was much too woolly. He condescended, "A brilliant dialectician. But his materialism must be examined for vulgar elements." Rodenberg was so ridiculously vain as to be jealous of Brecht, as if any comparison between them were thinkable. He was also too basically dense to realize how fast his thin jet of spittle would blow back and dribble down his own coarse face. Brecht, he pointed out, had not enjoyed the advantages of exile in Moscow as he, Rodenberg, had. Therefore more time should be granted the poor misguided fellow to develop in a "right" direction, "more time than I would have been granted. But," Rodenberg concluded, smugly snide, "the final judgment on Brecht will have to be postponed until we see how much *more* time he needs to discover our own period in history!" Ho ho, he must have thought: Touché! Touché!

I can imagine Brecht's wry smile. Who could write a play about the GDR? If anyone, Brecht, but as the British actress Fiona Shaw observed, "A play starts when the cataclysm has already occurred." Brecht would not live long enough to see the cataclysm from which such a play could have taken its point of departure. His seemingly easy verbal victories over a Party whose long-term aims he supported were more stressful than a heart already torn by love gambles could stand.

On the GDR's birthday in October, an occasion for important awards, Brecht got one of the National Prizes. Was this an appreciation of his latest pithy plea for peace, addressed to the writers and artists of all Germany?

> Great Carthage waged three wars. It was still powerful after the first, still habitable after the second. It could no longer be found after the third.

Or was the prize just an anodyne in advance? Five days later *The Condemnation of Lucullus* — this was the opera's revised and now more than apt title — reopened to a handpicked audience and was then closed for good, allegedly on the recommendation of a musicologists' triumvirate.

From founding to foundering the GDR was organized like a monarchy, said Gregor Gysi, son of a one-time friend of ours, in a public discussion. "Favor alternated with harshness. Civil rights were unheard of."

Gregor was Dee's age, his baby name Gogy, and I had had the sorry distinction of stepping on and smashing to smithereens the tiniest doll from the inside of his hand-carved Russian matreshka set; it had been indistinguishable from the complicated pattern of his parents' living-room rug. I confessed this to the grown-up Gogy, a lawyer, and to my distress — I still felt guilty — he eyed me more intently than I would have expected, and said — himself still grieved — "*You* were the one who did that?"

By the time he reached adulthood Gregor had had ample opportunity to observe how his charming father Klaus, a born diplomat, wit, and well-versed Marxist (he even impressed Bill Blake) rose to higher and higher posts, fell, rose again, dropped friends who might embarrass him, fell again anyway, half rose like a punch-drunk boxer, sank, shrank gradually to half the man he had been, not even a charmer any more, in vain all his dodging and playing both ends against the middle.

Yet when the floor collapsed under the East German government and the Berlin wall burst open, Gregor at the crest of his career as a civil rights lawyer gave up his satisfying practice to head a new, independent communist party with a different name and no international connections. Hope sprang eternal.

And so it was with Max in the '50s. It may easily be imagined how the demented buffoonery of the formalism conference must have upset him, although — not having been invited — he was at least spared the live fulminations of Oelssner, Rodenberg, and the ogre Magritz, terror of the East German art world, formulator of the vicious resolution against Dessau. Yet strange to say, on a different plane of consciousness, Max could still demand in a tone of cheerful challenge, as he did once in my presence, "Where *are* all these radical manuscripts from young writers that our publishers supposedly suppress? Why doesn't Aufbau get to see any?"

Equally strangely I didn't even say, "What about self-censorship?" The departments in my brain seemed to have no access to one another. My left hand was happy while my right hand atrophied. I knew very well how acutely I myself suffered from self-censorship, I wrote to Christina naming it, asking her advice (to which she did not respond), and yet in the sparkle of an optimistic mood Max could be so delightful and look so assured and handsome that I felt he must know what he was talking about.

The reader may remember, if he is old enough, that in those days East Germany had not dreamed of building a Berlin wall. It was still striving for federation, a one-nation two-systems arrangement. West German Chancellor Konrad Adenauer had no intention of doing socialism that favor. His policy was to undermine and wipe it out.

This made those in the GDR who were committed to art as well as socialism all the more determined to defend both on socialist soil to the best of their ability. It was a question of honor, of conscience. For that reason the dogmatic taboos imposed on art were borne by most of its GDR practitioners as an unavoidable cross.

My poor Germany, torn and tattered
and cannot come together.

— HANNS EISLER
Johann Faustus

Until Hanns Eisler got the idea of writing his own opera, the libretto first, Max had never felt the noose of a Party lynching so close to his own throat. He had only been passed over when honors were distributed — pain enough, one might think, for such a deserving and sensitive man.

But in 1952, with that irrepressible optimism characteristic of pure Communist souls of the period, as blithely as if there had been no Orloff the year before, no formalism inquisition, no smashed *Lucullus*, Hanns had conceived a Faust with a new conflict: the well-meaning liberal's attraction to revolution and his dread of the personal consequences. And

Max had fallen in love with the witty, sometimes naughty libretto and rushed it to publication. It appeared early in 1953.

People unacquainted with Hanns were surprised that he could write a text. Some were naive enough to wonder why his best friend Brecht hadn't done the libretto for him, as if a full-grown story sprung from the mind of one genius could be transplanted into that of another. Besides it was Brecht, his brain already teeming to overflowing with play ideas, who could not do without a collaborator for the music, preferably Hanns; whereas Hanns up to this time, assuredly on projects not quite so ambitious as *Faustus*, had always managed on his own. It saddened him when he had to disappoint Brecht, but unasked he loved to set his friend's poems to music. This was pure pleasure, relaxation, homage.

With no singing voice, only vocal cords and a great heart, he would more or less croak these pieces, but with tender nuances that went straight to the heart as he banged the melody on his grand piano. Famous singers he coached understood from those endearing croaks and bangs (and the surprised joy or the commiseration on the composer's round, homely face) how they were meant to deliver the songs; but it was his own delivery that moved us to tears of inexpressible appreciation. Lucky us, to have been on earth in the same city at the same time as that uniquely endowed and lovable man.

To be sure, it is unusual for the composer of an opera to start with a libretto he himself writes, but the Faust brainstorm tempted Hanns Eisler, with his poetic nature and his profound knowledge of world literature and history, into a more hazardous literary plunge than he had ever yet taken. He was all too sensible of the shoals, and in his humility before Brecht's unattainable art he just this once avoided letting his friend all the way into the secret; he waited until the work felt so unshakable within himself that risking Brecht's critical eye seemed preferable to submitting the libretto unblessed to Max.

The protagonist of Eisler's *Faustus* was nothing like the aging, cloistered doctor of many sciences who realizes he has studied in vain and missed life itself, the figure it took Goethe all his days to reinvent from medieval legend. In his old age he had added a part 2, seldom played, in which the contract with Mephisto is made null and void, for Faust has turned into the sage with an immense grasp who was really Johann Wolfgang von Goethe in his eighties.

Eisler's libretto introduces us as the curtain rises to a former scholar, still young, lingering nostalgically over books that once inspired but now only accuse him. Weirdly the Bible opens of itself at the Book of Job. "Horrible, let me not read it," he shudders, and hastens for comfort to a volume of Thomas Münzer. Dreamily he reads aloud

> You will be sold like cattle. Serfs as you have been, now you would be slaves. Begin the good fight while it is yet day! Bestir yourselves!

"Oh Münzer," groans Faustus, torn between uprightness and self-love.

With hindsight it seems amazing that neither Hanns nor Max nor even Brecht, the sharpest politically, could have failed to foresee what nightmare for Hanns, what perverse imp, would rush out of any unusually shaped bottle marked FAUST if uncorked by the ever-dithering dodos of the SED. They saw a new Faust as not only superfluous but as a piece of unpardonable effrontery, a bad boy's pissing on the German national monument Goethe, a heresy heinous as sniggering at Karl Marx. They attacked it with such malevolent intent that it dealt Hanns one of those deadly blows that at first seem to leave the victim intact, but eat away at heart and marrow like a slow poison.

It appears that Brecht examined the work principally from a dramaturgical point of view, and for the time being kept his reservations to himself. He felt strongly that tragedy and satire do not mix; for Hanns did regard his *Faustus* as a tragedy, but as he told Hans Bunge, recording angel of the whole Brecht circle, he "took tragedy lightly," interlarding it with fun.

According to biographer Mittenzwei, Brecht's first impression was of "an omnium-gatherum of style elements" joined together solely by his friend's skill at montage. On reflection, however, it seemed to him that with the music, the staging, and all those imponderables that develop in the course of rehearsal, contradictory style elements might be minimized. So he made only practical suggestions regarding arrangement and offered Hanns a verse or two of his own for the concluding "Confessio," a long poem in which Faustus bewails his sins. Hanns was delighted with this bonus, but Brecht must have kicked himself afterward for so fatally overlooking what should have been obvious.

In their right minds many of the Party intellectuals who subjected Hanns to a three-week grilling at the Academy of Arts were aware that new Faust versions were an old story, that Goethe's had not been the first, nor had Marlowe's before him, that both had been preceded and followed by innumerable others including the latest, Thomas Mann's *Doctor Faustus* novel, and the earliest, a medieval puppet play which was Hanns Eisler's model; but other factors were involved in the discussion that turned normally stacked brains into hysteria-soaked mush.

Hanns Eisler's variant, set in the period of the Peasant Wars, portrays an intellectual of peasant stock who for the sake of cheap and easy personal success takes no part in the mass rising of his class. After its leader, his idol Thomas Münzer, is martyred, his roiling conscience reminds him again and again of his betrayal, but self-deception is the leitmotif of the piece. It is not so much the devil's tinsel trickery as his own shame that brings him to damnation in the end.

Why did the Party find this so objectionable? To begin with, the Peasant Wars were a sore point with Ulbricht because that first German revolution had been a lost revolution and because Marx and Engels had seen in its annihilating defeat a prime cause of what they termed "the German *Misere*"; this meant an exhaustion of revolutionary energy, a hopelessness deepened by the devastation of the Thirty Years' War, whose upshot was the failure of every future insurrection in Germany. The last had been the quickly crushed organization of German Soviets in 1919 that brought about a wishy-washy Weimar Republic and the Nazi barbarism that swept it away.

As if this tactlessness were not enough, an Austrian friend of Hanns (the nerve of him! an Austrian butting in!) fatefully misreading Hanns's intentions, praised him in Germany's most prestigious intellectual magazine *Sinn und Form* for making his Faustus a typification of that same odious "German *Misere*." Still worse, the East German publication was edited by Peter Huchel, long an irritant to the Party with his supercilious indifference to Zhdanov pronouncements and the ease with which he won distinguished writers and thinkers of both East and West as contributors. His aura made it almost impossible to fire him.

It didn't help that Hanns had never given up his Austrian passport. This had long been resented.

"An Anti-Faust!" the Academicians raved.

"Anti-patriotic, antinational, subversive," echoed the Party press. Motivated by "abysmal pessimism, alienated from the masses!" Ascribing to "the people," that imaginary sacred cow, "a coarse, debasing, low-comedy type of speech! Stirring up filth for its own sake! Mocking the entire history of German thought!"

Opportunists and zealots were only a few of those who took part in the Academy's three once-a-week hearings. Many people Hanns had respected, friends pained by having to hurt him, wielded a well-meaning polemic against the libretto, which in combination with the official vilifications struck Hanns like an avalanche of rocks out of the blue. He sat there too stunned at first to say anything in his own defense.

What particularly incensed the fanatics was the complaint of Faustus about the dullness of "humanist" Germany, a mischievous allusion to the monotony of daily life in the GDR (even the stupidest fanatics could understand that, they themselves were bored), contrasted with the dazzling immorality of a country Hanns called "Atlanta," an alias for the United States.

> Faustus: Back again, back, alas, I found our homeland gray
> and cold again, confined and stale the dirty alleys
> of my birthplace. How glad I was to leave it! Now
> again it has me in its talons.
> Why am I here?
> Thinking on what is past I do not call it good.
> And yet — Atlanta, how gloriously shines thy sun!

Was this not a hint that despite his interrogation by the House Un-American Activities Committee Hanns Eisler wished himself back in corrupt Hollywood? And what kind of zany idea was it to introduce the medieval yet suspiciously contemporary Hanswurst as a guzzling, gourmandizing, amoral, anti-intellectual clown? Did *Goethe* stoop to using a clown? Certainly not!

"I would laugh if we had the wrong religion," grins Hanswurst at one point. One can imagine what suspicions were touched off in the thicker skulls by that crack.

At the second hearing Brecht rode into the ring like a knight in shining armor, raised his visor, and read out twelve terse "theses" he had been preparing, which for a few minutes reduced the hysteria to a torn balloon. Losing their thread, the more obstinate attackers pretended respect for Brecht, mumbling that his theses would require study; but they were soon shouting all over again, and as the hubbub threatened to drown the whole session in chaos Becher stepped in.

Hanns, said Becher, had experienced in his own person [he didn't have to emphasize that Hanns was Jewish] one of the worst periods of

German *Misere* in centuries and had seen all too clearly the helplessness of the German spirit. "Why is it," he challenged one of Hanns's most furious attackers, "that this 'glorious, shining, unique' German culture of which you speak allowed a Hitler to come to power and cannot even now get Hitler out of its system?"

Such a frank utterance of unpopular home truths was not what most of us would have expected from Becher.

Becher had a soft spot for Hanns, having worked with him on the GDR anthem "Arisen out of Ruins" and a few eminently singable "new folk songs" intended to instill some national pride into disillusioned German youth. Feeling the mantle of poet laureate on his shoulders, even though such a title had never been officially conferred, Becher continued to believe himself immune to Party disapproval. As the person closest to the absent Ulbricht in that room, he may have considered it his responsibility to squelch idiots who disgraced the SED's image.

"And why, may I ask," rhetorically thundered the inevitable Hans Rodenberg, "does such a person as the Aufbau editor make no contribution to this discussion?"

"That was Max Schroeder!" called out some helpful nit, as if Rodenberg didn't know. Max was not there. Nonpracticing artists were not members of the Academy.

"I have no idea what editor may have gone over the book," Rodenberg countered peevishly. "I merely note that here he is silent." Never one for shorter speeches when he could pull them out like taffy, he blustered, "This is an anonymity which is not necessary."

As one who had made himself so indispensable in Moscow that he could hang on there for three years after the war ended, Rodenberg indulged himself in the spite against West exiles which was actually envy. While he had nobly sacrificed himself to starve and freeze with "the great Soviet people," fine gentleman like Hanns and Max had lived it up in the fleshpots of "Atlanta."

Max must have been shattered when he heard of the merciless lambasting Hanns had taken. At the last of the three Academy hearings, a week before the June 17 rebellion, he listened for some time before rising to say his piece. His first words were urbane and affectionate, a reaching out to

Hanns. Then he said that his own "precipitate endorsement" of *Johann Faustus* had "only done his friend a disservice."

These words and all the rest of a relentless self-castigation caused me agony when in 1991 the minutes taken by Hans Bunge were finally published. Another two years passed before I learned that not Max alone but Janka and all the editors had been mad about the libretto and that the decision to publish had been a collective one. Yet no one could have stopped Max as editor-in-chief from taking the whole responsibility on himself. Janka's uncharacteristic silence at that hearing seems to confirm this.

The hearing was in the afternoon. In the morning the Aufbau mountain had labored for hours and brought forth only the mouse of a recantation's clumsy first draft, an "omnium-gatherum" if ever I saw one, containing even such shameful locutions as "cosmopolitan" and "formalistic."

Max read it off three pages of a yellow carbon copy that I eventually found folded up in the *Johann Faustus* book, with a few last-minute corrections in his jagged handwriting. A yellow-paper copy of Brecht's twelve theses was folded up along with the Aufbau draft.

But Hanns, when Max had finished reading this miserable collective "confessio," said graciously, "I thank you, dear Max. Many of your points are identical with the ones Brecht raised. We can almost handle both at the same time, so I suggest we just go back to his. One will always return to Brecht's formulations." Could a man in deep trouble have fibbed more forbearingly than that?

Whereupon Brecht offered to state in one simple sentence how Hanns's libretto had affected himself. "It strengthened my confidence in the mission of the German workers and the intellectuals allied with them," he said without batting an eye.

Only after this unparalleled piece of chutzpah, which no one dared contradict, did he speak of "failings" in the work: The discussion had shown that "in its present form" the libretto "wasn't getting across to everyone," and Hanns would have to draw his own conclusions from the fact.

One day Max came home despondent and told me that Hanns had gone back to Vienna, the city of his childhood and youth.

"Not to *stay*?"

"Who knows," he said, and retired into his study, where I was not welcome unless invited.

He could not have begun to tell me what went on at the Academy or the depths of his own despair.

In a radio talk years afterward Hanns' ex-wife Lou disclosed that when in 1953 Hanns arrived in Vienna "his life-force was broken, his almost proverbial *élan vital* shaken to its foundations. But Vienna had nothing to offer him; he longed for the GDR. Under socialism, he felt, he could hope to work his way through hidebound pettiness and intolerance, but he would not go back without having made his standpoint clear to the SED's Central Committee."

Five months passed in Vienna while he wrote one draft letter after another. He did not, in the long letter that finally satisfied him, strew any ashes on his head, only perfunctorily mentioned "serious errors" on his part without specifying what sort, and apologized for any "inconvenience" he might have caused the Party.

"You must understand, Comrades," he addressed the great stone face as if it were an actual thinking being,

> that an artist's total production is many-sided, and that every composer, in addition to works that are immediately understood, must also produce more complicated ones in order to advance art. . . .
>
> Probably it is part of an artist's nature to react with intense sensitivity to external influences. You may consider it weakness, but I require an atmosphere of good will, of trust and friendly criticism, to be capable of artistic endeavor. Naturally criticism is necessary to test art against the needs of society, but not such criticism as crushes all enthusiasm, diminishes the artist's reputation, and undermines his self-confidence as a human being. . . .
>
> Since the Faustus attack I find that I have lost all heart to compose. I have reached a state of depression deeper than almost any I can remember.

Party replies were not usual. He can hardly have expected one.

He came back to the GDR, but never wrote the music for *Johann Faustus*. What might have become a fascinating opera full of surprises had been criminally aborted.

A postscript: during the Academy hearings Ulbricht, Pieck, and Grotewohl were in Moscow going through a nightmare of their own. If anyone had blabbed, not only would the inquisition of Hanns Eisler have been dropped like a hot brick, the GDR itself might have been wiped off the map thirty-six years sooner.

Details of the secret might never have emerged if ND — a very different ND after the GDR actually did collapse — had not thought of interviewing on his deathbed former Politburo member Hermann Axen (the one Max called "a behind with ears") about what really happened in Moscow early in June 1953; for the trusted Axen had been in the leaders' entourage too, in his usual subaltern capacity.

Only then was the SED delegation informed that on Stalin's death three months earlier, Lavrenti Beria had become chief of the Commission on Germany and was now prepared to dump socialism in the GDR in order to mollify West Germany and NATO. If this was not done, he said, a hot war would be inevitable.

Vladimir Semyonov, only just named "High Commissioner of the USSR in Germany" (Germany, not "the GDR"), handed Axen a coded urgent message signed by Ulbright and Grotewohl (Pieck being in hospital, perhaps from shock), to be carried to Berlin at once. It instructed all SED adjutants to cease their propaganda for socialism and start publishing material that called for a united Germany on terms acceptable to the West. Horrified, Axen delayed going to Berlin until Semyonov pressured him so menacingly that he obeyed.

> ND: Was the message really signed by Ulbricht and Grotewohl?
>
> Axen: It was. They had been convinced or forced in Moscow to accept this line. Though shortly afterward things took a different turn. About a fortnight later Beria was replaced and the instructions to Berlin rescinded. That was why I was demoted to second secretary of the Berlin leadership.
>
> ND: So you were made the goat.
>
> Axen: The demotion was not given publicity. My name wasn't even mentioned. At the next plenary session of the Central Committee I made a self-critical speech

stating that I had acted wrongly, that as a Communist
I should have done my own thinking about the
matter.

ND: If you had done that you would have been called to
account in the same way.

Axen: True. No matter what I did would have been wrong.
If I had refused Moscow's bidding I'd have had my
head torn off.

When Stalin died I happened to be in a fancy hotel in the Harz Mountains where Max had sent me to recuperate from a lingering pleurisy. It was
early March, 1953, the fifth being the official death date released by TASS.

For all we knew he might already have been dead for days or weeks,
but nobody dreamed that such seemingly senseless falsifications were
possible, nor did it greatly interest the *bessere Leute* ("finer type people")
in the Heinrich Heine Hotel what story some committee might have
concocted to give the Generalissimo's unappetizing demise the most dignified and noble appearance possible.

After the embalmers got through with his remains, which I saw with
my own eyes three years later in the Red Square mausoleum (if those really were his remains), he looked great and brand-new, just like in Soviet
films, whereas poor Lenin had been allowed to shrink to a shocking caricature, like a macaque monkey's tiny dead uncle with makeup on.

The news of Josef Stalin's death inevitably caused a certain stir
among the guests of the Heinrich Heine Hotel, predominantly profes-
sional-class government pets who were needed so badly in their various
fields that they didn't have to join the Party. I saw no evidence of grief.
The broad, thickly carpeted staircase between the entrance foyer and the
first floor of the former baronial mansion was full of people heading for
the telephones on the mezzanine to hear further details from town or
just exchange exclamations.

My own feeling was a kind of numbness, as if I had bumped my head
against something, but not very hard. I thought of Max, who I knew
would be as unhappy now as he had been when Franklin D. Roosevelt
died. Vaguely I reproached myself: where would we all be now if Stalin
hadn't pushed back the Nazis?

I knew only that the loss of Lenin was the one that hurt me. He was
real to me through his tender, almost motherly concern for the ailing

Gorky's well-being when they met for the first time at a Social Democratic congress in damp London (Gorky reported this) and also through the answers his widow Krupskaya gave to a questionnaire from the Soviet Institute for Brain Research on Ilyich's daily habits, characteristic gestures, and favorite leisure activities.

Credible portraits of a good Stalin had never existed. There were only the adulatory salaams and brainwashed testimonials of Soviet writers and film producers who viewed the man and his pipe, his mustachios, his bemedaled chest and his much touted fatherly wisdom from a distance so vast that the graven image got lost in the telescope.

On Stalin Allee, built in imitation of Moscow's grand white-tiled Gorky Street, it had seemed appropriate to East Berlin's architects to have some sort of Stalin statue erected. This must have been an afterthought, however, and not an essential feature of the boulevard's original plan, because it ended up in front of the small, gray, homely Construction Workers' Cultural Center, which had no more style than a factory outbuilding. The Center was set back about fifty yards from the sidewalk so as not to insult too blatantly the panorama of gleaming white facades on either side. (Jokers likened the panorama to an inside-out bathroom.)

For similar reasons the Stalin statue was not placed immediately in front of the Cultural eyesore but close to the sidewalk where, although barely larger than life-size (as if the sculptor had found himself running out of granite — the GDR was always running out of something), it could nevertheless be seen from a window two blocks away on the same side of the boulevard, if one hung out far enough.

I know this because, improbable as it may seem, I who never hung out of windows was hanging out of mine to greet a particularly beautiful dawn and sniff the fresh air of an early spring Sunday when (I swear on my honor as a lucky newspaper amateur) I saw the Stalin statue being surreptitiously lifted from its pedestal and loaded onto a truck while the Allee dwellers slept off their Saturday night and there was no danger of West cameramen gleefully photographing one of the more embarrassing moments in GDR history: several years after the Khrushchev exposé of Stalin's true character the SED had finally decided to abandon the one-time theologian and rename his avenue Karl Marx Allee.

But at the time of his death, there being no more impressive monument to him in the East German capital, mourners including our friend and neighbor Harry had flocked to this undistinguished likeness and stood without speakers or flowers (there were never flowers to be had in March) and wept.

"I sobbed," Harry confessed to me a year or so later.

Before that it would have been impossible for Harry to say anything so private to me.

Since the awkward collision in 1952 we had been a bit stiff with one another, although Gillian with her clever tact always contrived to keep the surface of our neighborly foursome smooth and light, as if nothing had ever happened and nothing could happen. Yet for reasons she herself surely failed to grasp she was still daring it to happen, nagging it to happen. While I confided more and more of my frustrations with an increasingly inscrutable Max, she was repeating as many details to Harry as would inflame him with a desperate ambition to console me. The person who finally told me this was in a position to know.

As for Max himself, his pained preoccupation with Party stupidities prevented his noticing anything that might have gone on, or not gone on, between the house across the road and ours.

One of the most flagrant stupidities had been the cancellation of ration cards for small shopkeepers, as if they were speculators and made of money. The ruling had been issued the month before the June 17 uprising, and was one of its principal contributing causes.

I was in Copenhagen translating at a Women's Federation congress when this happened. No one told us technical staff the news from Berlin, but the functionaries of the GDR's women's league were certainly informed and couldn't have cared less. What got their dander up was Danes. Any Danes. In Gedser, the ferry landing opposite German Sassnitz, they were scandalized to discover that the natives used no glass curtains — only scrubbed their window panes to dazzling, practically an invitation to passersby to peer in!

While my colleagues and I were enthralled with the charming, handsome chaps detailed to decorate the congress hall and during breaks show us a bit of Copenhagen, a capital of such stunning good taste that I wept to leave it, the official East German women's brigade armored with unsightly fat, and their overbearing president, whose nape like a tree stump (I once sat behind her on a bus) would have baffled a guillotine, apparently hated every minute they had to waste in Denmark; for as they stampeded down the gangplank on returning to the GDR they cried out emotionally to one another, *"Daheim, Kinder, daheim!"* This meant "Thank goodness, dearies, back on our own home soil!" — where the Party was always right and one got real food, not outlandish little samples of God knew what, called Smorga-something. They would soon find, however, that their real food was rapidly disappearing.

Because whatever Nazi conditioning the struggling neighborhood shopkeepers of the GDR might have concealed behind bland, customer-friendly smiles, they constituted an indispensable distribution network, the penultimate link in the production-consumption chain. Naturally, with the cancellation of their ration cards, it broke down forthwith, and wives of government leaders had to scream at their fat-headed husbands that there was no place left to honor their own ration cards.

"I don't see how we can go to the seaside this year," Max said after the shit hit the fan on June 17. His spirits were already at lowest ebb since the Hanns Eisler affair. So low that he could never tell me what it had done to him.

"You're wrong," I said.

Vacations were not frivolity, they were the only chance for us to repair the rents in our relationship, the only time when the mists in his driven head seemed to clear and he would recall what I and Dee meant to him. I pleaded against the crazy notion that self-punishment and punishment of one's family were a Communist soldier's duty. I reminded Max that Dee was a chronic victim of flu and that I was still tottery despite the two weeks granted me in the Harz.

He wavered, and after a while gave in and assured me that on the coming Monday he would reserve a three-bed room for August in Ahrenshoop.

And it actually came to pass that in August we set out for the Baltic in one of Aufbau's ancient chauffeur-driven BMWs.

There was a Kulturbund shack at the edge of the fishing village where members registered, got the address of their *Quartier*, and paid the vacation tax. Walter and Ellis, a couple we used to see frequently when we all lived in Friedenau, happened to be standing about in front and hailed us joyously. They accompanied us inside while Max groped in various bulging pockets to find the reservation slip.

But it emerged that he had none. With the best of intentions, careening along on two wheels, he had neglected to ask Fräulein Schmidt to take care of the details.

Walter's jolly face fell. Max looked unutterably dashed, helpless, and confused. There was no such thing as a fisher cottage that still had accommodations. The *Kurhaus* was full up. Every available space, even lean-tos and former chicken coops had been commandeered by the Kulturbund. Nobody had canceled. We would simply have to get back into the car and drive home.

"Rot!" said Ellis with a vigor that amazed me. She was a quiet, retiring woman who usually stood half a pace behind her adored husband and waited for him to take the lead. *She* knew where there was a room. "Come outside," she said, fuming at the idea that the editor-in-chief of Germany's largest publishing house should be turned away like some mendicant and mortified before his wife and child.

There really was a *Quartier* never used by anybody, including the man for whom it was permanently reserved, President of the Kulturbund Johannes R. Becher. It went to waste month after month, year after year, on the upper floor of a villa, just in case he might be in the mood to splash in icy waves and then, on coming out, be forced dripping wet to behave affably to people he didn't wish to know better.

The lower floor was occupied for the moment by Becher's toady Abusch (pronounced *Ah*-bush), a Kulturbund functionary who had been removed from his post as an untrustworthy West exile, then reinstated after a year through Becher's powerful influence. He and his wife and little girl were at home, just changing for supper at the *Kurhaus*. Ellis, Walter, and Max, but especially Ellis, inveighed against bullheaded iron regulations that only promoted waste until Abusch, whose sole happiness seemed to be the honor of serving Becher, at last broke down. "On condition that you clear out if he comes," Abusch quavered. But of course, said Max.

He was still sleeping peacefully at eleven next morning in an immense room with three exposures when Dee and I, equipped for the beach, were accosted by Abusch on the doorstep. "Wake him up!" Abusch yelped. "Becher's on his way!"

"I can't wake up that exhausted man," I said. "Let him sleep out." And we proceeded to the beach with our basket of towels and toys, ignoring the cries that followed us down the path and grew fainter. The dignity of an umbrella-bearer to the Mikado prevented Abusch actually pursuing us, and he dared not wake Max himself.

While we were digging our wind shelter, Becher arrived, heard out the sniveling apologies awaiting him at the villa, took refuge on the

Kurhaus verandah, where he smoldered red in the face (as tickled witnesses told us) and after half an hour made the only possible decision for an Olympian who has driven six hours from the capital only to learn that his virgin sheets have been forever defiled. He left orders that we be provided with quarters befitting mortals, and then drove like a madman out of Ahrenshoop, casting up clouds of sandy dirt that hid his route.

We got a nice little room with white furniture and a one-exposure view of the dunes, and were delighted with it. Silly to ask how this was possible when there were no accommodations.

Abusch, curiously enough, seemed to forget or forgive my unwillingness to drag Max out of Becher's bed. Possibly, I thought, he saw me as a loyal, old-fashioned helpmeet like his own wife, and unlike that impudent American playgirl Alma to whom nothing was sacred. In fact he once asked me quite paternally whether I was "being taken care of." I hadn't the dimmest idea what he was talking about, so I obligingly said yes. He said he was glad, and walked on.

Neither Max, who tended to give most people the benefit of any doubt, nor I who from the first wrote off Abusch as a nullity, could have imagined him as the "perfect sweetheart of a bastard" recalled by Professor Hans Mayer in a talk show after the GDR fell apart. He disclosed how Abusch had connived in a plot to get *Sinn und Form*'s editor Peter Huchel out of the way in order to take the job himself.

Mayer was Germany's most illustrious lecturer and writer on German literature in the '50s. His classes at Karl Marx University in Leipzig were such a drawing card for disciples from both parts of Germany that the Party (of which he was not a member) harassed him until, on a permitted visit to the West, he decided he would be better off remaining there.

The plot against Huchel probably served a double purpose: it was conceived just before the Hanns Eisler hearings, which would explain why no remarks by Huchel are recorded in the minutes taken by Bunge.

The unsuspecting Huchel was sent on what appeared to be a privileged junket to speak with writers in Moscow. At once Abusch appropriated his desk in the Academy and wrote in Huchel's name a self-criticism with which to start off the coming issue.

Getting wind of this in time, Brecht went to the Academy, just happened to meet Abusch on the marble staircase, grabbed him by the lapels, shook him, and shouted, "You turd, what right have you in the Academy?"

"I said that wouldn't work," Becher is reported to have told Abusch glumly. It was Becher himself who had installed Huchel in the job for literary reasons, indifferent to the fact that politically his appointee was at best a fellow traveler.

The contributions Abusch had thrown out of the coming issue were hastily restored at the printer's and the ridiculous mea culpa Huchel would sooner have died than written was destroyed. Nauseated when he heard the story, Huchel wanted to quit, but Brecht talked him out of it. "You've got to defend your emporium just as I defend mine," said Brecht. "The Berliner Ensemble and *Sinn und Form* are the GDR's best advertisements."

There were people in the Party who realized this and saw that Huchel was left in comparative peace for a few more years.

How could the same Becher who so boldly stood up for Hanns Eisler against Party attackers continue to tolerate a creep like Abusch as his right-hand man? Was it only to repay the years of devotion that culminated in the drooling monograph *Johannes R. Becher, Poet of the Nation and of Peace* which Aufbau had to publish the same year as *Johann Faustus*? Could it not also have been because Becher, working on an equally fulsome biography of Walter Ulbricht, knew in his heart that he was no less craven? Had he really given tacit or even explicit support to the usurping of Peter Huchel's chair?

A psychiatrist might point out that there had never been any "sane Becher," but always a tormented, vacillating coward whose load of guilt started building long before he learned of Stalin's crimes and tried not to think about them. It was his own deeds from an early age that he could no more forget than the world can rid itself of atomic waste. The foulest of these was probably an adolescent suicide pact with a prostitute, in which he managed to kill the young girl with one shot, but to fire three times at himself so inefficiently that a hospital soon had him back on his feet. He even wrote a confessional poem that describes the incident with such morbid nostalgia that the stomach turns. His father was sufficiently influential to get the murder charge dismissed on grounds of temporary insanity.

He did keep trying to commit suicide. In the Soviet Union, after his third failed attempt, Georgi Dimitroff asked the other exiled German writers to help their colleague overcome his chronic depression. Despite the man's weaknesses Dimitroff believed he could be a decisive good influence in postwar Germany.

Abusch automatically endorsed this estimate as long as Becher sat on top of the pile, but detached himself from the unequal friendship the moment his idol fell from grace. This ensured his own rise to a position of Party prestige from which he could and did snub the Poet of the Nation and of Peace and help embitter his former protector's last months on earth.

It was Becher's lifelong delusions of grandeur that ultimately blinded him to danger from an ego even more swollen than his own. But had not the wily, grudge-cherishing Ulbricht encouraged these delusions? Had he not let Becher get away with the most staggering impertinence at the stock-taking Party congress after June 17, and nevertheless in 1954 appointed him the GDR's first Minister of Culture?

"I'll tell you what 'absurd' is," Becher had swaggered at that congress, "'absurd' is when the Central Committee describes the lacy fountains and cascades at the Aero Circus as 'formalistic.' A joke's a joke, but my God, what kind of people are these! We need a mental hospital for the Party where its functionaries can get their brains cleaned out!"

It is impossible that such remarks were not gleefully repeated in the Kulturbund dining room, or that Ulbricht was kept in the dark about any sniggers at his expense.

Meanwhile, when the Party's hated censorship bureau (known euphemistically as the "Arts Commission") was replaced by Becher's ministry, most of the artists truly believed that June 17 had shown Ulbricht the writing on the wall and that an era of greater freedom was opening. Max was thrilled. It irritated him — alas, I irritated him more and more — that my only reaction was a disgusted "What can that big phony accomplish?"

For one thing, Max reproved me, his appointment would encourage our profoundly depressed sculptor friend Gustl, among others, to remain in the GDR.

As it happened, Gustl was to become still more depressed. No doubt at Becher's urging, the Party bestowed on the aesthete and bon vivant Gustl a commission for which he was not equipped, that of sculpturing a Marx-Engels monument. He had never read a line by either Marx or Engels and only knew that Marx's face was the once encased by a woolly bush of hair and beard, whereas that of Engels was more or less shaven. He asked learned friends such as Ernst Bloch the philosopher (whose book *Das Prinzip Hoffnung* [The Principle of Hope] would soon be roundly condemned by the SED as un-Marxist), what he should read first.

It was generally agreed that *The Communist Manifesto* would fill the bill, the only trouble being that you couldn't tell which of the pair had written what parts, and it made no difference anyway when it came to sculpting Marx and Engels as individuals and not as two indistinguishable hunks of granite.

Party-approved biographical material was about as inspiring as a McGuffey Reader. The real thing, Yvonne Kapp's two-volume life of Eleanor Marx, which threw the first blazing light on Marx, Engels, and their whole circle, was still years away. So poor Gustl, one of the finest sculptors in twentieth-century Germany, made one meaningless clay sketch after another — of Marx seated and Engels standing just behind him, of both standing woodenly side by side, et cetera, until in the end the whole project landed on Arnold Zweig's back porch, a final maquette which makes the two miniature figures on a discarded side table look so beggarly that in Engels' palm, upturned in a gesture of elucidation, Zweig had placed a Hungarian forint, then worth a seventh of an East mark.

The holiday that temporarily rid Ahrenshoop of Becher was our first together whose beneficial effects on Max's health and mine were of short duration.

We couldn't claim that we had been tied down by our enchanting child, who was always being borrowed by friends and taken to the nudist beach, allowing us maximum rest and freedom. Yet only a month after our homecoming I collapsed over my desk at the Federation while reaching for a dictionary. It was a sort of faint in which I was conscious but unable to move. An ambulance was called, and I was rushed to Buch, a borough whose pine forests and tonic air recommended it as a hospital center.

After six weeks in bed, taking tiny silver pills which turned out to be tranquilizers — the first I had ever had — and warm baths administered by a tactful blind man who brushed me under water with a soft brush, then a brisker one, the station doctor told me I had "only vegetative *Dystonie*" and could now be discharged.

"What is vegetative *Dystonie*?" I asked.

She was a sweet-looking young woman in her early thirties who resembled a robin with her dainty little beak and round brown eyes. She sat down at the foot of the bed and gazed at me earnestly.

"It means you have nothing organic," she said.

"And those needly pains in the heart?"

"Only functional. But if you don't solve your personal problems they will become organic."

I had not confided in her. It hadn't occurred to me, although my heartaches begged to be told.

My mother couldn't walk any more. Dad in his seventies carried her to the bathroom until he got a hernia and had to pay a registered nurse to live in while he was hospitalized. Now he was looking for one of those ghastly institutions called "homes" for the incurable, one he could afford; and John without his sister was bearing the whole burden of helpless, miserable witness.

I couldn't even give our parents the joy of seeing Dee for a few weeks, the real Dee, not just photos, because when I appealed to police headquarters downtown for an exit and reentry visa I was told that while I of course had double citizenship, the "makeshift" identity document issued in Friedenau in 1948 to ensure me a coal ration was proof of my being "first and foremost a German" who had no more right than any other German in the GDR to travel to the West.

I a German? Close to vomiting I hurled at Max, "They kidnap people! They make up the law as they go along! They tell me I sold my birthright for a few briquettes!" He put an arm around me and soothed, "Write to Norden."

He believed that just because a "comrade" had drunk our coffee a few times he would use his influence on our behalf. Did Norden even *have* influence, icy Norden who used to pretend not to notice when I came home during an editorial meeting of the *German American*?

He was now a member of the Politburo, where as a West exile he had to mind his p's and q's, but doubtless did so with never a wince. Still, I composed the letter and Max improved and hand-delivered it to the doorman at Party headquarters, which were just around the corner from Aufbau. Naturally no answer ever came.

I missed John so horribly that I dared not dwell on it. I missed Helen, her face from a Phoenician frieze, her lightning perceptions. No more letters came from her, either because they were confiscated or because, fearing that they would be, she simply stopped writing. The electrocution that year of Julius and Ethel Rosenberg, Communists, convicted of smuggling atomic secrets to the Soviet Union, may have served as a final warning to her.

I missed the Jewish faces everywhere that made New York so homey to me. I missed the black, brown, Latin and other foreign faces I used to see in the subway, faces of hard-working human beings who despite fatigue never bumped indifferently into other people the way people-resenting Germans did, but slithered with instinctive agility in and out of the crush hurrying underneath Times Square between the Bronx-Brooklyn lines and the shuttle.

I missed Manhattan's cluster of proud skyscrapers between the East and North rivers, their upper windows flashing red at sunrise and sunset. I longed for the public libraries whose books I could read with simple pleasure and no cumbersome dictionary. I wanted a long, never-ending gaze at "our lordly Hudson hardly flowing," as Paul Goodman called it, in the poem ending "Be quiet, heart! home! home!"

"I wouldn't know where to begin," I told the station doctor.

Her face grew stern. Only I could figure out where to begin, she said, and when I had done so, the sooner the better; I might have to change my life radically.

I understood then that I had had a nervous breakdown and that there was nothing I could do about it.

Max broke down differently.

As long as we had lived together he never once took to his bed on account of an ailment, he never caught flu or so much as a sniffle, he read his eyes bleary but got no headaches, had a heartbeat good for a hundred years at the same steady pace, and a digestion that might have served as a model of normalcy for medical students. He must have had first-rate genes. Still, the toughest person feels rotten sometimes. To show it would have been beneath Max's dignity. Something in his teasing smile when I was too exhausted to get up on a Saturday morning and he brought a breakfast tray to the bed seemed to say, "You wouldn't just be malingering, would you?"

But at some point in 1953, probably while I was in hospital and he wouldn't have to decide to tell me or not tell me, he who owned no boat and had no time even to want a boat, joined a boat club on the Dahme River for its bar privileges.

The only other place in our neighborhood that served alcoholic drinks was Hanffs Ruh, but to get there meant going along the short remaining stretch of asphalt-covered road on the sunset side of the Grünbergs' house and attracting the attention of the alert missus. The last two Colony families on that road minded their own business, but might have been surprised, perhaps saddened, if they happened to notice Max passing all alone into the pine wood and then returning none too steadily an hour or so later.

Not that such considerations necessarily influenced him. I knew less and less about what influenced him. The boat club was certainly much nearer, a short walk past intelligentsia dwellings whose occupants were strangers to us, and across the trolley tracks to the Dahme.

Before 1953, when in the warmer months Max would emerge from his study between three and four of a Sunday afternoon and suggest a walk, I gladly seized the rare opportunity to have him all to myself. The only desirable direction for a walk was through the wood past Hanffs Ruh to a meadow half ringed by trees with tremulous, twinkling leaves — a subject for Corot. A bit farther on was the frog pond, a favorite haunt of the children, above which blue dragonflies could stand in the air absolutely still if they wished. Once I discovered pure white lilies among the green pads and waded in and picked one, carefully draping its long winding stem round and round my wrist. I was not aware that taking a pond-lily was an ecology crime and that I could have been prosecuted if a forester had caught me. But one never saw foresters back then in Grünau; there it was still the hordes of crows that ruled.

The lily was the only contribution I ever made to Max's usually empty flower window. I worshiped it as it gently closed at dusk, and was thankful in the morning to see it had opened again and was still perfect, despite the unworthy tin basin in which it was kept with no sustenance but water from a faucet. Eight mornings later I found it still asleep in its own satin shroud. With a sinking heart I remembered that our lives were equally limited. They only seemed longer; nor were they likely to end with such fastidious refinement.

The only trouble with those Sunday walks with Max was that they invariably ended at Hanffs Ruh. But because they were so few and far between I was surprised each time he said, as if only reminded by the sight of the weathered house with the long tables and occupied benches out front and the sign FAMILIES MAY BREW COFFEE HERE, "Hey, why don't we have a schnapps or whatever?" He might add jovially, a favorite expression of his, "Why should *we* live like dogs?" We would go inside to the dark bar, which was the atmosphere my old bohemian preferred, and stay so long that by the time we started for home it had grown dark outside as well, and the last flowered bosoms and bulging beer-bellies were dragging away overtired offspring who got a whack if they whined.

I don't think Hanffs Ruh sold pocket-sized bottles. The boat club did. I used to find the empties hidden behind books when I was maidless and had to dust Max's study myself. The sight depressed me.

Formerly he had bought a normal fifth downtown. As we sat in our two secondhand armchairs he offered me as much as I liked; only I drank a great deal more than I liked, in order to prevent his draining the bottle too fast. It was bad for me, the quantity gave me no pleasure; but the frantic race was worse for him because the threshold between his feeling cheered and becoming stupefied was gradually sinking.

He did not drink when he had to edit, write, or read manuscripts, he was far too disciplined, and that was the difference between him and an alcoholic. He only smoked immoderately. He would come out of his study cold sober at about 10 P.M., the time of day when his brain functioned best and he was most apt to give me an enthusiastic lecture on some literary topic, never noticing (partly astigmatism, partly his zeal to educate me) that I could hardly keep my eyes open and was covering my allergic nose with a handkerchief. Annoyed sinuses had forced me to stop smoking, and I missed it, especially the first cigarette of the day when I used to sit down at the typewriter believing that those whiffs beckoned the muse. The temptation to smoke was defeated with difficulty, which was why I tried not to interfere with Max's habit. If I did occasionally mention that his smoke was bothering me, he put out the cigarette and lit another almost at once without realizing it.

The lecture completed, he would say, "I'll just take a turn in the fresh air for a few minutes." Usually he did come back in a little while. Lying in bed and hearing his throat rasp and correct itself in the road outside I felt reassured; he was near, life was whole.

Sometimes Max seemed to me an elf deposited by Puck in his mother's womb as a joke on the Hansa aristocracy (although, as I had yet to learn, aristocrats can be charmed by their own changelings. It was official socialism that felt affronted, suspecting that a being at once so worldly and unworldly as Max would sooner or later slip from its control).

"You have elf ears," I told him — it was true — and he seemed more pleased than not. But to whom or what should a misplaced elf turn for comfort when his *Wahlverwandte* — a Goethe word meaning a relative not by blood but by affinity — proved to be the uncomprehending p-p-pest Hans Meyer said I was?

How could a marriage straitjacket, the same pattern, the identical shoddy for every couple (never mind what hopeful name they gave it) not split into tatters when two sets of needs started pulling in opposite directions? But such tatters hold, such tatters bind. Even when totally unraveled — blown away, mere threads clinging here to a naked branch, there losing themselves in the shifting forest floor — those nearly obliterated relics of a marital warp or woof are the ties that bind, that enslave, that madden.

It would be almost unbelievable if Max had never once regretted choosing me above Rosl after he found her again in Germany and was so "very much attracted," as he wrote at the time. Her inbred humility, her perception from below of a man's fragility and hurt were the medicine he needed; there had never been a would-be boy in her. But Max, androgynous himself, had been powerfully drawn to the boy-girl who whistled on the stairs of 3 Horatio Street and looked — to him, at any rate — so fetching in a uniform with a peaked cap, man-tailored shirt and four-in-hand necktie. He must have imagined in me the strength I imagined in him. I supposed that most men were stronger than women, and not only physically. Max I considered especially strong, brave, yes, indomitable after the dangers he had faced down and the escapes he had managed with the instinctive accuracy of a boy vaulting over a fence.

A night's sleep no longer dispelled his fatigue, but he thought he was concealing this. Loving to cook for friends, he had always done it with aplomb and perfect timing, but increasingly it made him so anxious that he drank in the kitchen to steady his nerves while preparing the meal. He was quite unaware, as he brought the last fragrant bowl to the table and with a thick tongue wished *guten Appetit*, that a foolish smile was flickering over his wonderful Gothic features like a candle guttering out.

The meal never suffered, only Max's friends did. They ached for him when his head suddenly drooped over his concave chest and stayed drooped. He no longer followed the gallantly labored conversation. He forgot about eating. At last, to spare him the necessity of remaining upright with so much effort, our guests saw no other recourse than to depart long before dessert, apologizing as gracefully as they could. This roused him to lift his head and in a loud, proud tone order me, "See them to the gate!" — as if without his instructions I would not have shown that much elementary courtesy.

The repetition of this sorry scene, always ending with Max's resentful guilt toward me, at last pained Gustl and Luise so intolerably — she was almost crying — that on the way to the gate, begging my forgiveness, they said they could not go through with such a scene again. I told Max about this afterward, and for a long time he invited no one to dinner.

However uneventful a marriage may seem to outsiders, it is so dense with drama that despite all clues, sporadic entries in notebooks, recovered letters, lucky flashes of memory, I cannot put together what drifted through and around me and Max in any dependable sequence. If I try to pin down causes they evaporate and the pin twists into a question mark. Monogamous relationships that survive have passed through countless meteorological changes within a larger climate, which itself appears steady only because its changes are so gradual.

For my part, long periods of gloom were forgotten the moment the sun came out. Actual words of abuse from Max (he had to be drunk) were remembered next morning, although not by him. On the third day I knew something ugly had been said, but I didn't know what and I let well enough alone.

A fine-weather interlude with long-lasting effects was the visit of Jean Effel, a popular French cartoonist who drew for *Humanité* and brightened our lives with his charm and his book, *La Création de l'Homme* (The Creation of Man), which Aufbau had taken on board. Although not a children's book, its cartoons and captions appealed to the wise child in everyone. It starred God looking like George Bernard Shaw in a white nightie.

We had explained the whole of the French edition to Dee, so that when Jean at last arrived in Grünau and asked what he might draw just for her she was able to reply without hesitation, "A good devil!" He was nonplussed, and so was I. I hadn't realized that she might identify Eden with our own modest garden. When God was mixing a thick coagulation of Adam ingredients with a broad spatula and the devil sneered "First the mud, then the muddle!" she probably wondered why such a nasty creature was allowed in.

But Jean quickly recovered and drew the most benevolent fallen Lucifer imaginable, placing his then well-known circular signature underneath.

As a deeply satisfying memory, Jean Effel remained with all three of us forever. Soon after his departure, Yves Montand's songs on a phonograph record arrived at Aufbau (Jean knew that otherwise we would never get the package) and were played over and over again. This was followed, also care of Aufbau, by a subscription to *Elle* magazine, whose fashion pages (like material in any Western magazine) were considered much too seditious for the GDR. Gillian and I pored over that first copy of *Elle* as if it were the first excitement in our lives, and were soon sporting models cleverly copied by Frau Braun from the illustrations.

Max's evenings were taken up by the Jean Effel book for weeks. He and Christine Hoeppener, one of Aufbau's best translators, found that two heads were better than one for transposing French witticisms into a completely different culture complex.

She had been Klaus Gysi's longtime sweetheart, peach-skinned, even-tempered, incredibly good-natured, and gifted with a sense of humor which at that juncture she needed all the more, having lost her amusing, irreplaceable lover to a married, not particularly young or pretty woman with five children.

Since humor alone could hardly compensate for such a deflating loss, Frau Hoeppener started to hit the bottle. I believe she had been fond of her dram even before the heartbreak, and this made her and the boat-club member Max the more compatible in hilariously translating French captions into German. If he was still a bit tipsy when he came home late from her downtown apartment, he was also merry and pleased to find me awake — when I was; for those were the nights when I didn't lie awake imagining him struck by a hit-and-run driver and bleeding in a gutter somewhere.

One morning before going to work Max forgot the indispensable and never-before-forgotten briefcase lying on the foyer table. It contained everything he would be needing for his various conferences all day, and he missed it the moment he finished the sociable cigarette he always smoked with the driver, but by then it was too late to go back. It must have been a day full of frustration which not even his resourceful Fräulein Schmidt could avert, and it resulted in his getting himself arrested on the way home.

Sheer absurdity, one might think, wonderful material for one of his friend Kantorowicz's life-of-the-party anecdotes, but to Max an indignity so corrosive on top of all his other shocks and defeats that it acted on him like a daily drop of arsenic in his food.

When the crows wakened me to the sight of an empty pillow next to mine I shot upright in panic. I don't know how long I remained rigid, waiting, before at last a sort of cough became audible from the road. It was a weak, despairing cough not followed by any proprietary urination into the bushes. Maybe, I thought, it had grown too light for that. Soon I heard him moving about in the kitchen making himself something to eat, but he nevertheless looked as distraught when he came upstairs as if his head had been spun round on his shoulders until it fell off and been put back any which way by a Samaritan in a hurry.

As if with the last breath left in his lungs, he told me he had been held in a lockup all night. A cop had noticed his *Spiegel*, he explained. Then he sat down on his side of the bed, bending forward as if to fumble with shoelaces. It seemed he was not going to tell me any more details, but next day he told me just a few expurgated ones.

The *Spiegel*, a news weekly modeled on *Time* magazine, was one of West Germany's snidest and most effective weapons against socialism. Naturally it was prohibited in the GDR. There were grudging dispensations for enterprises that required up-to-date reports on literature, the arts, and for that matter everything else, and Aufbau's sole copy was passed from hand to hand to be read overnight by editorial staff. Needless to say, one didn't go about brandishing it in people's faces.

That night happened to be Max's turn, but a Party meeting after working hours dragged on so long that the chauffeurs went off duty and he had to take himself and his *Spiegel* home by S-Bahn. Someone lent him a wide-meshed shopping net to carry it in, not thinking to remind him, "Wrap it up in something," because anyone knew enough to hide contraband, and the *Spiegel* was as glossy and slippery and obvious through the meshes as a fresh-caught fish. So as Max, lost in thought, emerged from Grünau's brightly lit S-*Bahn* exit his elbow was seized by a "People's Policeman" who must have been delirious with moral triumph over a crime so shamelessly flaunted.

We had always regarded the "People's Police" with a certain affection. Firstly because the word "People's" suggested that they belonged to us, the people. Secondly because they were known to be Party members, each and every one of them, which implied that they had principles. Thirdly because being unarmed like London's bobbies, although for a different reason, they could scarcely be expected to hurt or humiliate anyone. In fact the impotence that kept them shut up in barracks on June 17 had made them appear rather foolish, but foolish was better than brutal. One day Germany might again be trusted as a civilized nation. Meanwhile we could thank our lucky stars for Soviet tanks.

But Max's arrest demonstrated that an able-bodied cop needed no gun to take into custody a frail, weary man whose only defense was to explain with patient courtesy, as comrade to comrade, the prerogatives of publishing houses. Strong-arm tactics were probably more gratifying anyway to the officious dolt who hustled Max through the streets like some stumblebum to an empty station house, never relaxing his iron grip until with one heave (at any rate this is my reconstruction of the incident) he flung Max into the unoccupied cell like a sack of potatoes before leaving him alone, uncharged, hungry, thirsty, and without even the homework he had to bring back next morning — provided he ever got out of the cell. No sound penetrated to it. Hours passed.

The cop meanwhile (it stands to reason) must have spent all that time laboring undisturbed through sophisticated innuendoes that amounted to a foreign language — but when would he ever get hold of another *Spiegel*? Toward morning he phoned headquarters, read the data on Max's identity card to a superior officer, held the wire for ages while somebody rummaged in files, and was finally told to let the prisoner go. Whether with or without the *Spiegel* I have forgotten.

Such educated guesses about a suburban arrest could not possibly have been made in the GDR in 1953. The worst I imagined was poor Max sitting outraged and exhausted in a cell I didn't even picture as dirty. I didn't imagine the mildest violence or wonder why, when the comrade cop could see the *Spiegel* in the shopping net, he took no cognizance of the equally obvious Party badge on his prisoner's lapel.

Max had been in so many jails and concentration camps in France, Switzerland, Morocco that he had lost count, but never heart. This experience was in a different category. It was child's play compared to what others suffered in socialist internment, but it did afford a peephole into the unthinkable. One might, for example, have concluded from it that the Party membership of People's Policemen had nothing to do with principles, but was imposed on them as a condition for acceptance in a relatively prestigious unskilled job. This was perfectly true, but if anyone ventured to entertain such a thought he did not utter it. Utterance, even to one's nearest and dearest, approached the sin committed "only" in one's heart.

That autumn Aufbau had portrait photos made of its executives, perhaps for a yearbook. When one day I came across a copy of Max's, marked 1953, I wondered how I could have failed at the time to notice how shockingly his face had changed from the passport-size photo dated 1947, the year his new life in Berlin began with little more than his own devout optimism to keep him going. He sent me that one while I was still in New York, and I had seen: this is a man who has found his place in the world. He was so happy he wasn't even gaunt.

The innocent choirboy lips were no longer to be seen on the 1953 portrait. The mouth was diminished, embittered, the eyes suspicious, as if in the humble photographer with his routine promptings — "Could you lift your chin a little more? Could you look toward that clock on the wall?" — Max had seen still another stooge acting on dubious instructions.

It was toward the end of 1953 that Max seemed to forget entirely who I was. His splendid forehead might have been battlements and his eyes manned holes in the castle masonry for all I could read what was in there from my side of the moat. He, however, could tell by my obtuse questions that I diagnosed a simplistic ball-and-chain syndrome in himself as the cause of our growing rift. He "didn't love me any more."

In Colette's novel *Naissance du Jour* someone says, "But she isn't difficult to know. She gives the impression of shunning mystery as though it were a microbe." Reading this I recognized myself, and felt stabbed. Being open did not necessarily make me a more satisfactory companion. The spade I called a spade could be felt as a lash. "I'm not your whipping boy!" Max had shouted more than once. Choosing what I thought a favorable moment I pestered timidly, "Do you consider our marriage over? Are we no longer living together, but simply side by side in the same house?"

He was silent for a while, then replied from a great distance, "I can't answer that right now."

"When could you?"

After a longer pause, which I thought would never end (I was waiting patiently), he said, "I don't know."

Just as he didn't know how to answer, I didn't know how to leave uncertainties hanging in air. Cards on the table, slip slap. Neither did I understand as yet the blessing of being left alone. There were not only personality and class differences between us, but sixteen years.

"An incubus then I thought her." That line from *Trial by Jury* comes to mind when I recall how, on an *S-Bahn* platform where we had to change trains, Max kept wandering away from me as if he no longer knew we were going somewhere together. Worse — as if I were some obstrusive stranger trying to make his acquaintance. I remember pathetically following after him, not too close to annoy him even more, wondering if I shouldn't just jump on board the next train back to Grünau. I hadn't the faintest idea what I had done to make myself so abhorrent.

It is inaccurate to suggest that Max could really have forgotten me. He remembered well enough the resolute young woman I had been in New York, a rod and a staff to him; and if I broke rod and staff over his head for the drinking that led to vague pawings and sentimental blather in place of lovemaking he came to understand why. Only: where was that prize of a girl now? How could she of all people become a prey to vapors, oblivious as an amnesiac to her own potential? A person so persistently pining for love testimonials could only freeze him to a dignified avoidance.

I had become a public embarrassment as well, snoozing during a production of Schiller's *Wallenstein* which everyone called brilliant. (Musty German history, how it bored me!)

But even at the opening of Brecht's updated *Caucasian Chalk Circle* I slept through the last part and missed Ernst Busch as Azdak, a character who had not hitherto appeared. This wily, self-appointed judge with holes in his underwear (he exhibits them) goes King Solomon one better, finding for the lower class: he awards the child to a peasant girl who rescued, loved, and protected it, rather than to its own haughty mother, wife of the Governor, who abandoned it in its babyhood and only wants it back as heir to the meanwhile deceased Governor's lands.

The storyteller informs the audience that after this judgment Azdak was seen no more, but that the people of Grusinia did not forget him. He enjoins all who listen to obey the wise, saying of Grusinia's forefathers "that what exists belongs to those who cherish it, the children to the motherly, wagons to good drivers, and the valley to those who water it. . . ."

Applause wakened me.

To have fallen asleep just as the dénouement unfolded seemed to Max unforgivable, an insult to the incomparable Ernst Busch, an *Armutszeugnis* (evidence of inborn inferiority or lack of *Kinderstube*, the good manners one should have learned at home). I had missed the whole point and best and funniest part of the play. Never again would there be such an Azdak, for Brecht had modeled him on his sardonic friend Ernst, one of the great singers and actors of that or any period. His voice could produce a sort of tender snarl that went straight to one's marrow.

I suppose this lapse, as Max saw it, was comparable to that of a time traveler with a seat in the Lords' Loge of the Globe Theatre in 1603, who, tired from the long trip, starts nodding just as the immortal Richard Burbage steps forward to speak Hamlet's best known soliloquy. To be or not to be mentally present after eight hours at the office, to sleep perchance to snore, that was the question.

Käthe had urged me over and over again to become English editor of the Federation's monthly magazine, which meant working full-time, and if I was maidless or ill a Federation chauffeur would bring me the work and take away what I had finished. More money yes, an editor's salary, no not quite, but neither would I be an editor; the title was just another of Käthe's transparent ruses to make people consent to be made fools of. It was the Secretariat bullied by Zhdenka that decided what went into the magazine, keeping its spotlight on horrifying atrocities against women and children in the poorest backward countries and excluding, as if by accident, any discussion of the humiliating position of all women in a man's world.

But I gave in and started working full-time after Max seemed to get fed up with bills as a sort of unreasonable interference with decent human intentions. The last straw was when he handed me a hundred marks "toward the coal bill," which amounted to three hundred, saying irritably that he was short of funds.

If nothing else insulted friendship, the joint domestic economy of unequals would. Our coal cost more than money. To order those stinking brown-coal briquettes (coke came from the Ruhr in West Germany, only it didn't come, was too costly) I had to walk a mile through the woods and across *S-Bahn* tracks to the nearest coal man, who had no phone, and the mile back, thereby losing three hours of potential writing time. Now that we had central heating Max never made fires anymore, except in the handsome tile stove he had ordered for the living room. It was I who tended the coke furnace in the cellar which refused to digest brown coal, and I who rushed about the house opening windows to let out the poisonous fumes it farted.

"You just got a bonus of two thousand marks," I pointed out as mildly as I could.

"I have debts!" he exploded, furious that I knew something he hadn't told me. What sort of debts could he have, I wondered.

I asked.

"None of your business!" he shouted.

Only one thing seemed to bind him to me any more, my writing, but why was I so undisciplined? He would not countenance a wasteful structuring of my days. No maid? Then let the dust pile up! Not enough money? Did I need that much money? The coal man and other pests could wait! Didn't I myself jeer at some of the "Party Chinese" I had to translate? Writers wrote!

And I flinched, painfully knowing that writers wrote, and that if I let housewifery and motherhood and base necessity deter me, then I never would be one.

Loyal, however much he seethed with undigested resentments which he could not analyze, Max never ceased to fight for my writing, and the least I could do in his opinion was produce it. He was incensed when the railroad book came back from Volk & Welt with a letter complaining that it ignored the role of Earl Browder in the women's fight for seniority rights. Why not the role of De Gaulle, Rothschild, Marco Polo?

He had reluctantly agreed when I warned against publication by Aufbau. Malicious people might indeed mutter, "If the husband doesn't publish what she writes, no one else will bother with it." And sure enough, here was the malice not even from people who might feel unfairly treated, but from Volk & Welt, the publisher that held the main concession for foreign authors.

Or was this rejection, in fact, one more gratuitous tit-for-tat from an aggrieved author, a Colony neighbor whose wife's English-language paperbacks had become a department of Volk & Welt? Was their revenge to be a lifelong preoccupation? But it didn't occur to me at the time that being under Volk & Welt's roof, and an American herself, Gertrude would be the first person whose opinion they sought. This certainly passed through Max's mind, but he had the discretion not to mention it and make things still more painful.

He only forbade me to enter into any argument about the rejection. What could I tell Volk & Welt that they would believe, benighted as they were? That the American Communist Party had ignored "women's matters," as Elizabeth Gurley Flynn contemptuously dismissed our problems? That Browder himself, then a mere dot on the American political landscape and now not even that visible, reacted quite cynically when told that the Party had fired a perfectly able woman editor in order to give one of its male pets her job?

No no, the thing to do was have Anna Seghers read the book and write a report on it for Aufbau.

No one but Max would have dreamed of asking such a favor of Anna, and there was no one else in the world for whom she would have done it. Still, not even for him whose judgment was the one editorial criterion she totally respected, would she have sinned against her schedule to spin pleasant half-truths. She told me once that all the rest of a day went wrong when she hadn't started mining her inspiration first thing in the morning and kept at it until the vein was exhausted. But to my amazement, and perhaps her own, she sacrificed hours for the good deed, and for the first time beamed on me.

The one person connected with Aufbau who disagreed with Anna's estimate was Erich Wendt, and this was the cause of our other tiff.

As Erich could not set aside the opinion of a state icon, he concentrated his irritation on me when we chanced to meet in the lobby of the Club. He refused to accept my unvarnished portrayals of American women as fair or true to life. He could not have read far enough to discover that the young women who remained on the railroad throughout the war and to the bitter end — a period as long as a college education — came to understand other women as they never had before, women they at first disdained (as they disdained themselves without knowing it) or, in the moral jungle of their sexist environment, had feared as competitors. The shaming sense of inferiority had left them. They had grown to appreciate themselves for what they really were, had begun — just before they were all fired — to identify, as the men did, with the romance of railroading in a land three thousand miles broad from ocean to ocean.

Erich was appalled by my showing that women can be so deformed by the denial of status that duplicity becomes their way of life. Was this socialist realism, was this "typical"? Was it not sheer perversity on my part to foist such repellent images on readers in need of role models?

Ralph Waldo Emerson wrote in the nineteenth century that if American women ever got the vote, all polling places would be decorated with flowers. He extolled them for filling every vase to the brim with roses, so that the whole house became redolent of perfume. He visualized women as always being in a house, a good sort of house, not the kind that might at best, because of poverty, be redolent of cabbage; but let us not hold this one limitation against a man who bestowed so much philosophical wealth on both sexes. Women, he wrote touchingly, "unloose our tongues and we speak, anoint our eyes and we see."

Dear man, if he could have lived in our century and discovered how many of us were out of the house and yet woefully still tied to it hand and foot, he would have remained our advocate with all the fervor of his pure soul.

Erich was Emerson in reverse, insisting on an idealization that excused him from taking women seriously. "Erich isn't like that," his gentle, yielding Lotteken had pleaded when I called him down for a grossness that betrayed his real opinion of our sex. He truly was not "like that" to the sweet flower he had further ennobled with his surname. He only demanded that the rest of us "raise" ourselves to a standard that would keep us down.

And a day would come when a certain look, a certain jarring inflection in his voice made me understand that for him even Anna Seghers was just another female whose opinions could be shrugged off. It was after the sentencing of Walter Janka to five years solitary confinement for high treason, a horror which Erich found quite easy to accept, whereas Anna was so wrought up, Erich told us with a sneer, that she wept on his shoulder.

But that day was a long way off, two or three years beyond the period when coping with a wife who argued had become an unbearable ordeal for Max. His impatience took on a new dimension when all at once he perceived me as a lax and irresponsible mother. He was mortified when we had guests to Sunday dinner and his child contributed an opinion of her own to the general conversation. After his friends had gone he upbraided me severely. Such forward behavior should have been nipped in the bud.

Astonished, crestfallen, I objected that she had only spoken once. "They didn't mind her tiny four-year-old peeps," I said. "They only smiled and went on talking."

"Bad enough," cut in a heavy father I didn't recognize. "They have manners," he was saying, "but who is to teach *her* any?"

"What should I have done?"

"Sent her from the table," he said promptly. He actually added, "Children should be seen and not heard!"

Was he possessed, I wondered? Was a dybbuk speaking out of his mouth? It wasn't as if she had been showing off, which would have been odious, but even a cherished family dog is indulged when it believes, as Dee did, that it too is a human being. Did Max really think it proper to send from the table in disgrace the bright, sensitive little girl so much like himself? To hurt her, humiliate her, turn her trivial misstep — if it was a misstep — into a bad dream?

He had never been disgraced before guests by his parents. The problem couldn't even arise in a mansion with trained servants. When company came to dinner he and Thea were seated in another room at a "pussycats' table," which (he had told me long ago, laughing) they thought a delightful dispensation. There they could be as wise or as silly as they liked, could giggle, make funny faces, and repeat in jokey baby talk their favorite challenge , "*Fiß bis Du patzt!*" — meaning "Fuff (stuff) till you bufft (bust)!" And the two of them had each other for solidarity. Dee had only us.

I'm the one he wants to punish, I thought.

He forbade me to take Dee to Buch for a routine nasal operation meant to stop her frequent colds and prevent any more deep coughs and middle-ear inflammations. It had been recommended by a respected pediatrician, but he didn't care who recommended it. His childhood asthma had started when he was five years old, the very day after such an operation. It had gone away, but suppose Dee's didn't? Some parents, he raged, meaning not only his own but me, subjected helpless infants to the knife just because some stupid medical fad had not once and for all been condemned. I got the doctor to phone and try to soothe his fears, but he shouted at her too. I waited a few weeks but at last took the child out to Buch, praying she wouldn't tell Max, but of course she did. She bubbled over, relating every detail in her own special style, starting in the middle and working alternately forward and backward.

Max mastered himself and joked with her about the operation, but gave me a look of implacable enmity such as I had seen only once before on his face — the time when he told me of his first New Year's Eve in

Lübeck after exile. Evidently he regarded my "disobedience" as a betrayal on a par with his mother's when she refused to open the last hoarded bottle of wine for her long lost "dear, dear boy." Was I now to be lumped with that ghastly woman? Would I too never be forgiven?

A sad event brought us together for a time. Max came home late, unintentionally waking me, and I noticed although his back was turned that he was covering his eyes with one arm and breathing in a strange way. "What's wrong?" I asked. After a moment's resistance he sobbed, "Our good old Puma died." He turned to me and I took him in my arms.

The only other mourner at the funeral in West Berlin was Kantorowicz's ex-wife Friedl, one of the Pagels' last surviving friends, and we three went home with Pagy afterward for the postfuneral collation usual in Germany. The absence of Puma made the apartment look as if no one lived there any more, and was so unbearable that Pagy told a joke. The gist of it was that on a cold winter's day a man returns from his wife's funeral tightly clutching the urn, but the icy sidewalk has become so perilous that he can hardly move for fear of falling and losing the ashes. When he can no longer feel his nose or toes he yells in desperation, "Shit on piety!" and strews just enough ashes at a time in front of his feet to get home without slipping once.

We burst into relieved laughter, including Pagy as he wiped his old eyes, and I think we all felt Puma looking lovingly down through the ceiling from her throne of honor in Elysium. A fifth person present, an elderly woman with a widowed look who had prepared coffee and cake and laid the table before our return from the cemetery, made as seemly a face as she could. Pagy addressed her as Eva, but did not introduce her. He told several more jokes.

To our surprise the woman had also set a place for herself. The quintessence of obtuse refinement, she apparently felt a need to demonstrate indispensability as one who knows how to preside with grace and charm over the table of a personage. During a pause which she considered awkward she jumped into the breach like an elephant, intoning so many meaningless sentences on a single exhalation (some sort of yoga exercise?) that having no breath left she lengthily and noisily drew in all the air around her, much of which belonged by rights to the rest of us. Those repeated and interminable inhalations were so unnerving that we sat frozen in suspense lest the next sentence, unable to wait so long, fatally clog her windpipe.

The following week we received a note from Pagy telling us he had married Eva. Doubtless she had made him a proposal that seemed to him, in his despair, a halfway reasonable solution to his immediate problem. She would clean the office and the apartment, cook, and generally look after him, asking nothing but the resplendent title of *Frau Doktor*.

Max seemed unable to find time for Pagy after that. "Why don't you at least phone him?" "I'll go next week," Max would say. It made me angry. Who or what could be more important than Pagy, the best friend of both of us?

It was he who, finding me in the kitchen in tears over the dishwashing when I had no help, had taught me the simple way of doing it without hot running water, detergents, or a second sink for rinsing. He had seen everything at a glance, the enormous heavy pot on the stove just coming to a boil for the second time, the mess in the sink, the mess beside the sink, and the fact that my desolation was really caused by being a displaced person. He gently explained that if I put everything in the sink at once, one pot of boiling water would do the whole job.

My visiting him alone would have seemed strange, and been hurtful; fond of me though he was, Max was the one he needed, who knew him through and through. "Go," I urged, and Max meant to go.

Then Pagy, having just set down his breakfast cup of coffee for a moment, died in his chair opposite Eva from her inhalations, exhalations, and incorrigible presiding.

I refused to go to the funeral. "*He* won't see whether we're there or not!" I shouted. Max went alone.

I was wrong. We would have seen each other there. We needed to weep together at that grave. As it was, not only had Max abandoned Pagy in his misery, but I had judged and abandoned Max.

Whether the downs prevailed over the ups or vice versa, Max never failed to invite me to first nights or any other interesting function for which he automatically received two tickets.

I wondered why. He didn't love me, he only tolerated me, I thought. But I knew by then that this was not a subject I could broach with him. He would have seen it as a tasteless provocation, beastly, unnecessary.

So I went with him when Frau Grenzius, an old lady I had met in a queue, was able to babysit. I dressed as smartly as possible, playing my part, glad when Max looked refreshed, thinking resignedly that these public occasions were the typical veneer married people glued over their conflicts. It might even help us imagine for a moment that everything was fine, that tomorrow life would return to normal; but the ice was thin.

At the Academy of Arts after an abstruse lecture in clumsily convoluted German by the Hungarian literature philosopher György Lukács — I understood absolutely nothing — Max realized it had been silly to drag me there, and tried to make it up by suggesting *"Jause"* at the nearby Hotel Neva. The funny word for snack reminded me — he knew it would — of our first holidays at the Baltic when even sprats washed up on the beach seemed a gourmet treat; and knowing he was remembering this too I walked lightheartedly by his side.

But as we entered the dining room whom should we discover but Lukács again, at a table with some Academy intellectuals. As he was one of Aufbau's most highly prized authors, as well as a personal friend, Max excused himself to me in the center aisle. "I'll be right back," he said.

They greeted him warmly. One took a vacant chair from another table for him, which he declined, obviously on my account, for they all glanced over for a moment at the woman standing in the center aisle with her coat on; but Max, unable to tear himself from the guru's stimulating talk, also kept standing where he was, while waiters hurried past me with loaded trays, trying not to jostle me but clearly irritated with me for blocking traffic like bales fallen off a truck.

I could sit in the lobby, I realized after awhile, and headed there, consumed by the shame of the unwanted, remembering the time in the *S-Bahn* station when I couldn't even summon enough gumption to board the next Grünau train while Max's back was turned. On a desperate impulse, my heart in turmoil, I strode right through the lobby, out the door, and up Friedrich Straße to the *S-Bahn* station.

If I had had any place to go but home I would have gone there, gloating, "Let him wonder where I went! Let him call the police! Let him call the morgue!"

No, of course I was not emancipated. Believing passionately in the natural equality of the sexes is not a form of emancipation. A woman who knows what she is worth has an air of sovereignty that makes it impossible to exclude her.

For the same reason that yin implies yang, Max was not emancipated either. He got to our bedroom half an hour after I did, exuding hostility. I was reading.

"What did you do that for?" he demanded, but as the question was rhetorical I made no reply. He started undressing.

I noticed over the top of my book that he was dropping his dirty socks on the floor. Nothing new, he always did that, but this time I asked, with no special emphasis, who was to bend down and pick them up. It was probably the words "bend down" that caught his attention and made him mutter, "I don't tell you to do it."

"Who is to do it?"

"Leave them there."

"For how long?"

He said nothing and got into bed on his side, staying as close to the edge as possible. I went to the bathroom and on coming back inadvertently and ever so slightly bumped against him. Our old brass bed had never been king-size and now seemed not only to have shrunk, but to be (this fits the case) taking sides, though I don't know whose. With both legs Max indignantly protested against my invasion of his reserve, the cover flew up, down and sideways, and a foot connected with my shin. I can't say that it actually hurt or that it was meant as a kick; it was more like what a child does in wild self-defense against an attacking sibling.

But while Max's kick was probably not deliberate it did make a point, so I took my pillow, found a sheet and a blanket, and lay down on the imitation Biedermeier sofa in the room where I did my writing. It was one of Max's finds in the Aufbau attic, with a once polished, now dull and scratched walnut facing double-curved across the top like Buddha's upper lip. The overstuffed back bulged, but the seat was long enough for my height and I managed to rest quite comfortably on it.

"I think I have a maid for you," Max told me merrily. He had found her at the boat club, where she was helping out the proprietress at the bar.

Frau Jogel (pronounced Yogel), not a Berliner but a good mixer newly arrived from Thuringia's green hills, not much of a drinker, not a person attracted to boating, had nevertheless found the trail from her ex-employers' door at the other end of Grünau to the club on Regatta Straße, where with hoarse sobs and floods of tears she shared her melodramatic history with everyone she served and anyone who stopped to listen.

"Frau Jogel is crying again," Dee used to comment with disinterested cool, but it wasn't true that Frau Jogel only cried. She could laugh at the same time. She was a diversion, a happening.

The way Frau Jogel had lost her last job as a maid, actually her first job of any kind although she was forty-seven, was that her cavalier of the evening put her house key on his own keyring as a safer place than her shallow skirt pocket; only it wasn't safer because on bringing her home he detached the wrong key, out of tipsiness or because there was no night-light over her employers' door. He only discovered the mix-up when he couldn't get into his own furnished room somewhere near Alexander Platz.

Two mornings later Max's chauffeur called for her and her baggage. Was this the Queen of Sheba? Where were the camels? We stood open-mouthed at the spectacle of only two people, Jogel and the chauffeur, who managed to look like a procession, she loaded with dozens of dresses, sets of lingerie, suits and coats, and the astonished chauffeur not knowing what kind of face to make, carrying valises and armfuls of hats, footwear and household linens, stomping one behind the other up the stairs and down again as fast as they could to get more stuff from the car, until at last a collection of worldly goods that beggared our few effects had been deposited in her cubbyhole. We had to move the normal-size closet into the cellar and buy her a double one, upon which her valises and other gear were piled.

"I wasn't letting *them* get their hands on it," Frau Jogel said with satisfaction, meaning her father's deceased brother's widow and other relatives in Thuringia.

She was the daughter of a prosperous peasant who had forced her, when young, to marry a mean little runt half her size because his acres adjoined theirs. She bore the runt a harelipped and otherwise ill-favored son whom she hated, but later gave birth to a handsome son from the seed of Osbert, a carpenter, the real man of her life, who matched her in hugeness and high spirits but could never, as she expressed it like a dime novel, be hers. They had to meet in hotel rooms, seldom enough, because he too was married. Once they swapped clothes in the hotel room and laughed so much that they could hardly do anything else. She was mad about Osbert's son.

Out there she could never have sued for divorce; that was why she came to Berlin. Little by little in the dead of night she and Osbert smuggled all her belongings to a disused barn on the road to Trusetal. "We'll meet again," they swore, both crying, hardly believing it, and she went off in the truck driven by a pal of his to seek freedom and maybe even a good life without Osbert, before it was too late.

Every Sunday she prepared the same midday meal, not a feast, but edible, as in a mediocre restaurant where one had expected worse. Once she even told a story at the table which quite won Max over, about how her mother bought their farmhand a mustache-trainer for Christmas the day he shaved off the mustache.

After washing up she would go downtown to search out some likely-looking man. Between 9 and 10 P.M. she would return, either bitterly disappointed, angry, red-eyed, or elated beyond reason. "I'll tell you all tomorrow," she would promise in a whisper.

"I told him mine and he told me his," she used to say mournfully, referring to their hard-luck stories, then she would burst into guffaws that exposed the full horseshoe of her upper teeth as she remembered a comic effect, or sob and wipe away tears as the tragedy of all humankind became vivid to her again.

When the man had been a Beau Brummell, her ideal, she would gush, "But above all" — as if at any moment she would faint dead away with rapture — "the wardrobe! The *ward*robe!" she would moan again, and describe every item of it down to the pattern of his necktie.

In principle, however, she was out for something finer. A judge, for example. A man of impeccable respectability. If the wardrobe was right she would immediately assume this.

It must be said that Frau Jogel was exceedingly homely. She was not just big and fleshy, she had gargantuan breasts, belly, and rear, and lips like those of an immense carp. I thought of those lonely women Gillian collected, still with fading traces of prettiness. *They* never found anyone. How did Frau Jogel do it?

I finally asked. "I walk slowly around the whole pub from table to table," she said. She swayed with dignity round and round our living room, and I saw for the first time that she had an amazingly graceful, light-footed, feminine walk. With her fish pout almost covering the prominent teeth and a look of neutral unconcern on her face she would glance from table to table until she saw one where a lone man was sitting. When she felt certain that he was the best catch in the place she stopped and fixed him with her pale blue eyes for several seconds. She demonstrated the look. It was appallingly expressionless rather than brazen.

"I never smile," she emphasized.

She would then walk away slowly, gracefully, light-footedly to any unoccupied table, sit down, and signal to the waiter. Usually before she even got a chance to order coffee the man she had mesmerized came over.

"They always come over," she said.

"Always?"

"Always."

Max was unfailingly polite to Frau Jogel, so when she proclaimed out of a clear sky, "Your husband is a pill!" I was so startled that I broke up laughing. I knew I ought to have rebuked her in some stuffy way.

"What's a fun-loving live wire like you doing with *him?*" she orated, though she didn't really say "fun-loving" or "live wire," she said "*lebenslustig*," whose marriage-ad suggestiveness is untranslatable. "What's funny?" she complained. "You're going to waste! There's a fellow at the boat club, I told him about you —"

"Good lord."

"I can fix you up with him," she pursued eagerly, "he'll be just what the doctor ordered. He said name the hour and the place and he'll meet you there."

"Forget it, but thanks, Frau Jogel. That wouldn't be my line at all."

"You can't mean —"

"I do."

It was during that period that the government committee which owned or managed the Intelligentsia Colony got tired of waiting for Max to pay for the tile stove and red brick fireplace he had so buoyantly ordered when we moved in. It sent the bailiff to collect our pound of flesh, that is, as much movable furniture as would equal the cost of stove and fireplace, plus the accrued interest which had been raised with each relentless dunning letter.

In this situation Frau Jogel came through like the Royal Canadian Mounties. While I could only retail Max's arguments, sarcastically challenging the bailiff to paste his cuckoos onto the tile stove and the fireplace if they were so valuable, she sprang in front of every piece of furniture he approached, spreading her arms wide and shamelessly shouting, "This is mine, not theirs!"

Confused by my heckling and her leaping about, the bailiff bent down and lifted a corner of the long-haired white rug only to hear Frau Jogel roar, "That's mine!"

He was becoming frustrated and angry. To his mind no one could be more reasonable and understanding than a bailiff. He hadn't come with moving men and a truck to take our precious things away, all he wanted was to paste cuckoos (woe betide us if we peeled or scrubbed them off!) and tell us how much time we were granted to pay up. (Not much. Enough time had passed.) But this harpy with the oily dustrag in her hand was driving him mad by intercepting him wherever he turned.

"How can all this belong to the maid?" he demanded.

"Who's a maid!" she shouted. "When I came here to help my cousins I had to bring everything I owned. *They* had nothing," she asserted contemptuously. "I wouldn't have a bed to sleep in if I hadn't brought mine!"

He changed his tack, walked firmly into Max's study and proceeded to paste cuckoos on the bookshelves and a few of the larger books. Here even Frau Jogel fell silent, and I watched with a sinking heart as a cuckoo claimed Max's capacious office desk. It was not an antique such as Frau Jogel might conceivably have owned.

Upstairs, however, when he tried to enter her room, the first he saw, she again blocked his way with arms spread wide, bellowing, "All this is *mine!*"

He pasted a cuckoo on our secondhand brass bed, then went back downstairs with us anxiously hastening after him. Heading straight for the living-room drapes, whose little woven workmen Dee still fingered lovingly when she came home from kindergarten, he pasted a cuckoo on each of the two voluminous panels. Again Frau Jogel hesitated; how could she have brought drapes that so perfectly fitted the space?

I went to an attorney recommended by a girl I had met at a congress in Geneva. He was her husband. Legal advice cost nothing in the GDR; it was like the free medical care, except that one did pay if the attorney had to conduct correspondence or take a case to court.

"You have no case. Your husband will have to pay," he advised me with a weary smile that suggested we were either incredibly naive or too cunning by half.

The bailiff incident marked the zenith of an anarchically democratic, generally good-natured employer-maid relationship, after which I think Max and I were both too preoccupied to notice its inevitable deterioration.

One evening as I was coming home from work, a familiar figure appeared in the road just at the place before one turned a corner and saw our house to the right and to the left the one where Harry and Gillian lived.

The familiar figure was Harry.

What was he doing all alone in the road as if hiding from the eyes of his own house? He was waiting for me, waylaying me. He took a step toward me, lest I misunderstand and think he was there only accidentally.

Something in him was pitched so high that he was above and beyond himself. Taking another step toward me he said my name like the beginning of a prayer. He said it again in a voice I can always recall, deep, resonant, rich, and dark.

Memory of a voice is not always given us. I well remember sayings of Max that impressed me, but not the voice that carried them. I see his face light up with laughter, but the laughter's timbre is lost. Although audible enough, his organ of speech was a will-o'-the-wisp. I took in its unpretentiously expressed wisdoms or a bit of salty gossip he couldn't wait to share, but no tone was preserved for the future.

Now out of the gloaming (my mother used to laugh at that word — "roaming in the gloaming," she used to jeer — but no other suggests those moments when night slowly absorbs dusk while still leaving outlines visible) Harry pleaded as if there were no danger that anyone might take note of him or me.

True, the danger was slight. The inhabitants of the only two dwellings between the streetcar stop and the Colony, old residents of Grünau, were as unreal to us as we were to them. They lived in small and humble discolored stucco houses, side by side, within earshot of the squealing streetcars that connected our neighborhood with the S-Bahn. Occasionally toward nightfall I saw a man in shorts, rotund as Humpty Dumpty, watering with an unnecessarily long and heavy hose the mean strip of grass which separated his house from the road. The few pansies, then roses, then asters on the strip were policed by a garden gnome in a slightly chipped red and green suit and a hard red nightcap.

The month was May.

In that dim road between streetcar stop and Colony I scented spring for the first time since I gave up cigarettes, although without recognizing the exquisite odors for what they were; they must have seemed to me a part of the delirium caused by Harry's beguiling turn of phrase. His declaration concluded with an envoi that contained a half-apologetic smile, as if to say he knew how foolishly theatrical this must sound: "Rescue me! Oh, my darling, rescue me. . . ." He was crushing my right arm and this time instead of slapping him I went up in flames. Two years had passed.

"We must talk," he urged, and already knew when and where. He did mean talk. He had an agenda.

A week later at four in the afternoon I saw him on an *S-Bahn* platform rushing toward me as if a typhoon were at his back. The name of the station, on a different line from Grünau's, translates as Wallowpuddle Heath. Neither of us had ever disembarked there and we didn't know a soul in the neighborhood, which was why he had chosen it. His face came so abruptly near that the confused kiss of greeting seemed all nose, himself unfamiliar, frightening, ugly. Did I know this apparition?

The sky was gray. We descended a long staircase to a thoroughfare that looked bleak and depopulated, and walked three or four blocks to a not particularly inviting park entrance. Neglected by the East Berlin municipality, Wallowpuddle Heath looked tatty, but for Harry it had the magic of Shakespeare's Forest of Arden.

He now became confident, explaining with contagious ebullience facts of life which I thought every adult knew, but it seemed there was much more and he was going to introduce me to it as soon as we could get a hotel room.

Utilitarian as this may sound after the emotions he so stirringly described in the road (for instance, "When I think of you the earth moves under my feet" and a stammered "You look so — so noble. . . .") his practicality did not put me off; on the contrary it both amused me and made me soar, and I sang him a couple of American folk songs that I loved and thought anyone must love, especially a musician. He seemed carried away by them, or by me; he was in no condition to distinguish which was which. A young man in a trance passed by whom he recognized with shock as one of his students, but no one else apart from ourselves seemed attracted to Wallowpuddle Heath that afternoon. The student didn't seem to notice anything at all; maybe he was composing in his head.

The other point on Harry's agenda was that Gillian must not be hurt. "That goes without saying," I assured him. "I knew you would feel that way," he said, "otherwise I couldn't have hoped." We swore never to tell, and he clasped me to him. "Oh, you're so thin, darling," he exclaimed in horror, and I echoed in a sort of groan, "Rescue me. . . ."

But it was not easy to find a date on the calendar about which Harry could convincingly lie. It was harder still for people with an East Berlin address to get an East Berlin hotel room. The better hotels were reserved for contacts of GDR industry, politics, and the arts, and for the few Western tourists not discouraged by the GDR's bad press abroad. Otherwise a reception clerk inspecting one's identity papers would accuse, "But you're from *here*!" The clerk's look meant, "You have a perfectly good bed at home, *we* know what you're up to!" — "we" being the hotel in cahoots with the secret service.

How did Harry have knowledge of this difficulty with hotels? A close friend embroiled in a love affair of his own might have laughed about it to him; but I didn't even wonder.

In any case he managed a gilt-edged excuse for defeating official prudery and preventing suspicion at home, though it meant a two-week wait before an international music congress opened in Saxony. Harry had to go there anyway, and wanted to. What he didn't have to do except for my sake, was return a day earlier.

The wait was racking.

It was convenient for both of us that we lived so far from the center of town. When I told the clerk at the Hotel Neva that I would be translating in Unter den Linden the following Thursday at a conference that would last until midnight, yet had to be fresh and slept out when it resumed first thing Friday morning she believed me. I suppose I had that lean and hungry "noble" look so admired by Harry and doubtless caused by the attempt to put a brave face on deprivation. And from the moment my room was reserved I must have looked ever nobler, wasting away from obstreperous desire, nervous tension, continuous sweating, and in the last few days an inability to get any food down.

My other problem was to think of a confederate who on the fateful Thursday would go to the hotel in time and leave a sealed note for Harry, telling him in code what my room number was. Although deeply shocked, the dear, unassuming boss of the translation pool agreed to do it, and I'm sure she kept the secret. "Many thanks for letting me see your very interesting manuscript," the note said. "My only criticism relates to the passage I already noted on page 308, but we can discuss this at your convenience. All the best!"

Room 308 looked rosy by lamplight, and so did I in my bath, although I had lost at least ten pounds. I left the room door almost invisibly ajar, only locking the bathroom, but as 8 P.M. drew near I kept my ears attuned to the first, faintest sound of Harry's arrival.

"Come in!" I called. He tried the bathroom door.

"No, you must wait!"

"I can't!"

"I'm nearly ready!"

Steam followed me out of the bathroom as I emerged in a new white slip. Like the high hum of many telephone poles, everything was singing around me.

The first food I got down in a week was ham sandwiches and apples that Harry brilliantly produced from a briefcase at about two in the morning. I was astounded at his foresight. "Where did you *get* all this?"

"On the train. I knew we would need it," he preened, and he had every right to preen. No Lobster Newburg at the Savarin in Penn Station ever provided more satisfying sustenance. I had not known that people got hungry from lovemaking.

Friday at the office passed in a haze. Thank God there had been no conference. Saturday morning I woke up only to brush my teeth and go back to bed. There at least I had time to review the night at the Neva. I played and replayed it, lying on my back like drowned Ophelia floating flower-bedecked amidst the ripples, but living, living! Oh 308, heavenly room number!

"I've brought you something small and appetizing," said Max, and put a tray down on the dresser. "Dee and I have eaten," he said. "I put her to bed for her nap."

"You're good!"

"Enjoy it," he said, and went downstairs. Through the rose canopy that still enclosed me I heard his typewriter clacking.

I didn't know yet, but he too was in a state of bliss, writing his first pure literature in years. It had begun as a short tribute for Lion Feuchtwanger's seventieth birthday, recalling the time they and other German writers had been held during the winter of 1939–40 in Les Milles concentration camp near Aix-en-Provence. Of itself it grew into a longer and longer memoir, accounting for an angelic mood that lingered in him for months.

On Sunday morning Gillian knocked at our door. "You all up?" she greeted me in her crisp, bright way. "The old man says shouldn't we all go for a family walk before lunch?"

Terror-stricken, playing for time, I apologized, "Max is working."

They had never suggested a family walk.

"Of course Max is working, it's Sunday, isn't it?" she laughed. "Oh, we didn't expect to lure *him* out. We just thought the children might like to visit the frog pond in this lovely weather." She had already gone straight through to the garden and was calling from the terrace, "Dee! Tommy! Come along to the frog pond!" Delighted, they left their game, and Tommy fetched his father.

In the pine wood the children ran and skipped ahead, but it took all my willpower to keep up with the casual, halting stroll of my neighbors. When we passed the pines opposite Hanffs Ruh, where Harry and I had agreed to meet two hours after sundown in a week's time my lungs couldn't seem to process the delicious air. Getting through the thick green grass of the Corot meadow was as difficult as walking through water, but it didn't seem to impede Harry or Gillian. As I fell farther and farther behind I saw Harry put an arm around Gillian's shoulders, an arm I knew as brown, silky, and curiously short for a man so tall. The sight struck me like a bullet and I sank into the grass as if boneless, dead but not dead enough.

Dear God, I prayed, let them not turn around and see this, and God having nothing better to do let them amble on, knitting and purling one of their habitual self-extending dialogues like the sock that a James Thurber woman absentmindedly continued until it became a whole woolen husband. Biblical jealousy "cruel as the grave, whose coals of fire have a most vehement flame" had leveled me to the ground for the first time in my life, and I vowed to myself never again to admit that barbaric poison to my blood. Anything was better than this. Anything.

Still I must have pulled myself together fairly soon, because when I caught up with them a time warp later they hadn't noticed I was missing. From there on my memory blacks out; I know nothing more of that excruciating walk.

My next meeting with Harry was not among the uncomfortable pine needles, cones, and twigs of the forest floor but in a rather crummy hotel he was immensely proud of having "discovered," although he had passed by without noticing it dozens of times. For himself he booked a room; I just happened to be in the lobby. In the cramped dining room, feverish with longing, we forced ourselves to consume something like meat with floppy potatoes and mealy canned peas. The few other diners looked like out-of-towners too tired to wonder about anyone else sitting there, but Harry gave them credit for X-ray perceptions. "They can see we only want to make love," he whispered.

On the inside of the room door, whose number I had no need to note, hung a sign listing the inventory in case of theft: 2 beds, 2 night tables, 1 ashtray, 2 chairs, 1 closet, 1 rug.

"What's the difference if it's ugly?" Harry coaxed. "We don't care." He didn't. After awhile I didn't either. We talked about having a whole glorious week together somewhere, but how? Oh, *how?*

I had forgotten what Gillian told me once, that if Harry were ever "unfaithful" she would know immediately.

On one of those June evenings during the annual unseasonable "sheep's cold" (sheep in Germany cannot be shorn until it is past) Max made a fire in the fireplace, and the four of us were deployed around its irresistible crackling and flaring, falling under its spell, content just to gaze. At any rate three of us were, when Gillian at her most vivacious broke into our reveries to say, "Harry, do tell them the joke we heard the other night!" "Which one?" "You know. The rabbi joke." He didn't seem eager to tell it. It was too old, everyone had heard it, he said. "*We* never heard it," she said.

"I'm not sure I could reconstruct it. Why don't *you* tell it?"

"Come on, Harry, you know how I ruin every joke!"

The thing was becoming an issue, so rather than appear churlish Harry gave in, avoiding my eyes and laughing shamefacedly.

With the first few words I felt my hair stand on end.

A husband tormented by desire for the wife of a neighbor goes to his rabbi for advice. The rabbi warns, "Sleeping with a neighbor's wife is like sitting on a hot brick. Control yourself for a week, then come back and we'll discuss it again." The husband returns a few days later. "Rebbe," he says, "you're wrong if you think sleeping with a neighbor's wife is like sitting on a hot brick. I tried it. There's no comparison!"

We all managed to laugh more or less heartily. God knows what Max thought.

I remembered the time ages ago when Gillian reproved me for not keeping my husband on a halter. Now I saw what she meant when she told me she "managed" her marriage. But did she actually know what she was managing when she put Harry through that cruel test?

Once Max invited so many friends to dinner that we had to pull out the table and insert two extra leaves. We hadn't enough cutlery, so I ran across the road. Gillian was busy in the kitchen; it was Harry who let me in. "It's only Edith," he called out. "They want to borrow some cutlery. Don't trouble, I'll get it!"

She pushed open the hatchway between kitchen and living room, and seeing him eagerly fumble great handfuls of knives, forks and spoons out of a drawer snapped, "Not the *good* silver, for heaven's sake!" He hastened to put it back again, and pulled out a different drawer.

Snapping about silver in my presence was a degree more disturbing than forcing him to tell a joke while she watched his face and mine. She came into the living room. "We never use that stuff ourselves," she said to me. "It's such a nuisance to clean." "We don't mind what it's made of, the main thing is nobody gets splinters in their mouth," I joked, and Harry laughed, but Gillian was in no mood for levity. Eying him, eying me, she burst out, "The two of you make me feel like the flaming sword that keeps you apart!"

This was terrible, unanswerable. "Please, Gillian," I said, helpless.

I couldn't bear to see her suffer. In a stolen moment I told Harry that the affair must stop. "I know you're right," he said humbly. And it stopped therewith.

I did regret that we never got the dream week together somewhere that we so badly needed. At any rate, I needed it. To know one another in the non-Biblical sense as well, friends talking the hours away from sunup to sundown — how lovely that would have been, I thought.

One day as I was coming home late from work a sort of miracle happened. It was on the part of the road where in May Harry had waylaid me. What seemed a vision connected with a bright rent in the darkness above the trees was probably nothing visual, but the intimation of a path to all origins. I stood rooted on it, sentient, blessed, clinging to the moment as to a dream just before waking; only a dream inexorably fades, whereas the sensation of belonging to a living cosmos remained. Why have a regret? No, no, I was thankful.

For us the affair had stopped, but not for Gillian.

Although normally a respecter of my anxiously hoarded writing time, she appeared without notice in the den upstairs on a Saturday morning. "Can't be helped, cock," she said. "I know it's *verboten*."

"Take a seat," I said, and she went over to the old sofa and launched on maneuvers similar to those of beaters at a hunt. I was no match for them.

She looked poorly. As she passed to the sofa I saw across the nape of her neck a shocking red rash that spoke its own language. Her skin had always been perfect. Had she cut off those charming honey-colored curls in order to treat the rash? Maybe she had changed her hairdo long ago and I hadn't even noticed.

Her misery tortured me more than the traps she set. She wanted certainty, even bad certainty, although without a clue as to what this might cost her. Wouldn't it be better, I thought — but what did I know! — to put an end to the roller coaster of suspicions that were making her ill? Shouldn't I tell her the thinnest possible sliver of truth wrapped in cotton wool?

"It did happen once, and that was the end of it," I said abruptly. "It meant nothing to him."

"Oh! That was very nice for *him*, wasn't it!" she cried, all sympathy and solidarity against the selfish sods of this world.

A couple of days later I found a note from her slipped under the front door. It said, "I think it would be better if we didn't meet for the next while."

Living across the street from one another became agony. The children noticed nothing and went on playing together like the brother and sister they had become as babies, but if Gillian saw me in the street she looked the other way. It made my heart heavier than I would have believed. Harry didn't have to see me in the street. Either he left his house by car or he returned to it in a car, getting out at the gate and never looking back as he walked the path to his door.

At the beginning of the "next while" I witnessed from our bedroom window a conversation between Harry and Gillian in their garden. At that distance it was a dumb show, but she was evidently giving him what the British call "stick" and he was standing before her with bowed head. Why was such a humiliating scene being enacted outside the house where I might just happen to observe it? I felt ashamed for Harry, hanging his head like that instead of standing up for himself. But who could guess what she had made of that thin, thin sliver of truth in its useless cotton wool, and how much had she managed, on the strength of it, to worm out of that poor credulous hostage to conventional matrimony? Everything, no doubt.

There was no way I could keep Max in the dark about the ruptured relationship with our neighbors. I told him simply, "Gillian and Harry aren't speaking to me any more. We quarreled."

After a moment he said thoughtfully, "Really!" He asked no questions. I could tell he was sorry for me.

For himself he must have felt relieved. Many things pointed to it. There was a general lightening of the atmosphere in our home. Gillian and he had never really taken to one another, and doubts had long since crept into his initial respect for Harry, one of the music triumvirate who cooperated in the *Lucullus* ban. Of which, by the way, Max never told me. Nor did he tell me then. He read me parts of the memoir he was writing, and said Janka was so impressed that he had offered him a six-month furlough to develop it into a novel. "But you'll do it," I urged anxiously, though without much hope. I could see that although mightily pleased he was going to say no. "*I'll* support us if it takes longer," I cried. "Please do it!" He patted my head and repeated that like Theodor Fontane he would start writing novels at sixty, and not before.

I didn't see Harry close up until a cold, damp day that autumn when we nearly collided in Grünau station. I was coming home from a nose doctor who had drained the sinus cavity and warned me to keep the area warm when I went outside. I was raising a corner of my shawl to that cheek when Harry rushed past me within inches on his way to the trains. Under the brim of a black fedora (what a thing to wear, it was like a sight in a dream) his face was distorted with hatred. For whom, if not me? He appeared not to have seen me, but how was this possible? Could the corner of a shawl against my cheek make me invisible to him of all people? My heart ached unspeakably.

Instead of reducing Gillian's suffering I had managed on a moment's impulse to intensify it and into the bargain break a promise. Because Harry had known in advance what awaited him if I told, he assumed I must also know. I knew too late. She would never stop giving him "stick." He would never forgive me.

- 348 -

As time passed the heartache dulled. A kind of indifference took its place. The house across the way became a stage set made of painted cloth stretched over frames. Of its inhabitants only Tommy remained real. The other two might have been waxworks like the fake people with their immobile faces at Mme. Tussaud's, except that — there was something astonishing about it — they could walk.

PART VII

What comes to us is what we've come to.
What wears us out is what we took along.

— GEORG MAURER
Ghost Train

August 5, 1956
Max has a pretty bad case of TB. Last week discovered blood on
his pillowcase and handkerchiefs and rushed him to nearest
doctor. He must enter a hospital at once for an indefinite period.

August 8, 1956
Brought Max out to Buch this afternoon. I'm worn out and
shocked through and through, terribly sad.

August 14, 1956
Brecht died.

S TRICKEN MYSELF AND TERRIFIED of the effect Brecht's death would have on Max, I sat up most of the night pouring out my feelings in a letter to Charles Humboldt, editor of *Mainstream* in New York, with whom I had been corresponding. He had suggested I write a Berlin Letter for the magazine when anything interesting came up, but this letter was purely personal. I knew Charles from *Daily Worker* days when I was an editor and he a young contributor.

"Last Thursday," I wrote, "when Brecht heard about Max's illness he sent a note telling him to spare himself, to cut out overwork, to concentrate on getting well, and sent a bottle of champagne to cheer him. . . .

On Sunday August 12th in the literary supplement of *Neues Deutschland* there appeared an old poem Brecht had written in 1919, "O Falladah, die Du hangest!" [. . . that you should be hanging there!] Falladah was the loyal talking horse from Grimm's fairy tale "The Goose Girl," beheaded to prevent his telling the truth about her identity; but his head nailed to the city gate could still talk and was overheard in converse with his grieving charge, an unrecognized princess.

Poems by Brecht never appeared in a periodical without his wish, and his wish always had some purpose. I have translated it in haste, should you care to print it with an obituary. I stuck close to the sense and the feeling, but had to sacrifice the rhyme. . . .

Charles, another idealist ruining his health in struggles with bullying blockheads, used the whole letter as the magazine's obit. It filled a page. He also published Brecht's last word to the wise.

> *O Falladah!*
> *I pulled my load despite my weakness.*
> *I got as far as Frankfurter Road.*
> *There I was just thinking, Oh dear!*
> *This weakness! If I let myself go,*
> *It could happen that I break down . . .*
> *Ten minutes later only my bones*
> *Were left lying in the street.*
>
> *Because hardly had I broken down*
> *(The drayman ran to the telephone)*
> *Than hungry people rushed out of houses*
> *To grab themselves a pound of meat,*
> *Tore the flesh off my bones with knives,*
> *And there I was, still living,*
> *I wasn't even finished dying.*
>
> *But I knew them from before, the people!*
> *Why, they brought me sacks to keep the flies off,*
> *Gave me stale bread and even told the drayman*
> *To treat me gently.*
> *So friendly then, and now so vicious to me!*

As if they suddenly had been transformed. Oh,
What had happened to them?

And I wondered, what kind of chill
Must have come over the people?
Who beat them so unmercifully
That now their very hearts are frozen?
Oh help them, please! And do it soon!
Or something may happen to you
That you never thought was possible.

On August 15, weary from lack of sleep, sick at heart, in the gut, and in the brain all the way to the TB clinic, a trip of nearly two hours by *S-Bahn* and bus, I was afraid I would lose control of my excretory organs, afraid I would faint, afraid I would slide off my seat into the aisle and make a spectacle of myself, afraid that Brecht's death presaged Max's. Fear wrung me out like a wet towel.

I strained away from it. Hadn't great progress been made in combating TB? Everyone knew the disease was virtually wiped out in the GDR. Every six months all employees were sent by their firms to have lung X rays made, and until recently Max had not played truant. For some reason he had missed the latest examination, and at once guiltily confessed this when I showed him the blood; but what of that? Wasn't the main thing the medical profession's skill in curing the disease?

Was it? The X ray made after I found the blood still hung before my eyes. It showed a "large cavity," as the Grünau doctor called it. Even we could recognize in those confusing shadows on the film that about an eighth of the lung was already destroyed. We were both shattered, and Max looked badly frightened. How could this have happened in only six months? It was terrible to think how long the process might have been going on inside him. Were the X-ray assistants for those examinations of employees just slobs? Were the radiologists who were supposed to check on them really reliable? Employment was assured in the GDR, and this made many people complacent, some cynical. To get a slob fired meant miles of red tape and endless tussles with trade union functionaries. In the end the slob was usually kept on.

*　*　*

The iron gates of the clinic were still locked at a few minutes before 3 P.M., but the crowd of relatives and friends pressed forward whenever a man squeezed through who might have the key. On the inside the patients were also pressing forward, wearing — like babies — "blue for boys and pink for girls," the men in striped pajamas that made me think of concentration camps and the women wearing light wrappers over their hospital-issue nightgowns.

Only Max, tall, rosy, and smiling as he waved at me through the bars of the grating, was dressed in normal street clothes, as if discharged and expecting me to take him home as soon as the gates opened.

He hasn't been told about Brecht, I thought.

All the same, life streamed back into me at the sight of him. Max was my life, it appeared. I had never quite grasped this fact before, but I began to know it then.

He had been told. He was writing something between a soliloquy and a graveside address, an evocation of Brecht, all he knew and felt about the man summed up in spare, epigrammatic sentences suddenly interrupted by the cry, "O evil month of August! Brought clouds, took away our sun!" It ends, "His greatness was not the kind that crushes. It was the touching greatness of the newly born. Lift it in your arms and you hold the world."

It had not been ignorance of the tragedy that made him so serene when we met at the gate, nor had it been a performance for my benefit. It was the ritual of every true artist's expression of pain when (scarcely knowing how) he places it in a perspective that rescues him from despair.

Every time I traveled to the hospital I died all the way out there and returned home calm, reassured, strong, and happy. Max was fine, actually gaining weight, his face filling out a little. They hadn't yet found any of the so-called moths, a jesting designation for those bacteria one pictures eating away a lung like an old woolen garment forgotten in the closet. Frau Dr. von Veith, the station physician, assured him that they didn't always show themselves so readily; this was well known, she said, and he should continue saving his valuable sputum in the little brown containers provided by the lab.

My calm, however, lasted no longer than the day when I had last seen Max. The only time I wasn't sick with fear on the way to him was one memorably sunny Sunday when Dee, home from camp, was able to come along. Just by being her father's daughter and delighting in every kind of festivity she gave me the support I had meant to give her, and which she didn't need. She could hardly wait to see her exciting Papa and help open the basket of goodies we had packed to compensate him for badly cooked meals and ourselves for having to live without him.

"Hello, Popsky!" she cried out, beaming, as she spied him through the gate. It was I who had invented the spoofy pet name, but she had seized on it with enthusiasm.

The hospital had tremendous grounds, even a whole forest of its own, which kept the air fresh but was not suitable for sitting down to *Jause*. So, walking not too fast — Max admitted that he could breathe better at a slow pace — we three meandered into the meadow between forest and hospital buildings and soon found a patch of welcoming greensward where we could enjoy our picnic with no audience to gape at the bilingual fiddle-faddle of three sillies.

Where then were the other patients and relatives? No signs warned them to keep off the grass, but as orderly Germans most of them stayed on paved paths or settled on benches beneath trees just outside the two-story brick stations where the sick were housed, exchanging family news and health reports (such as they were). Even visitors who at home had bored them out of their wits were an excitement on visiting days. I noticed male patients (not women, for some reason) who, having no company from the real world, strayed aimless and forlorn in the vicinity of their own "*kraal*," then disappeared.

"Probably to smoke an illegal fag in the toilet," Max remarked, as if he himself were quite indifferent to cigarettes. I had not yet heard that the hospital wisely allowed five smokes a day to keep addicts from desperation. "Illegal" meant only in excess of five.

It was amazing how well Max became by being ill. The pressure of duties and conscience had been lifted from him. He expanded, he read for pleasure. With delight he noted on his large writing pad a paragraph out of Stendhal's *Armance*:

> A famous physician in the last century was once called to the bedside of a nobleman to whom he was quite close. After a lengthy examination of the patient, during which he maintained absolute silence, he suddenly burst out with joyous enthusiasm, "Oh, Monsieur Marquis, this is a disease lost since hoary antiquity! Glassy mucous congestion! A marvelous disease, and above all fatal! Oh, I have rediscovered it! I have rediscovered it!"

On a day when it looked like rain and confined us to one of those benches under a tree, Max read me a passage from Elsa Triolet's novel *Das rote Pferd* (The Red Horse). It ran,

> Which reminds me of a young whilom friend of mine. I had come to inform her of somebody's death, and she was quite astounded by it. "What!" she said. "He's dead? But he was so stupid!" Don't you find this "but" extraordinary? Death, that redoubtable affair, so terrifying, so monstrous, so solemn, within reach of the first nitwit that comes along!

And we were both tickled. Delicious, those macabre tweaks that make mortals laugh over mortality!

Max was not only on a French novels kick. He took a lively interest in the nature of TB, borrowed a book from Dr. von Veith, and copied out of it, "Peculiarities of the TB patient: Nervous irritability, aggressiveness, disturbed sleep, sexual behavior [this was not elucidated] and often his lack of insight into his own disease." To this Max appended an observation of his own: For the first six weeks his roommate W. had chafed constantly against the loss of his accustomed routine, thereby making himself even sicker, "until it struck him that I had adjusted myself at once, i.e., in his eyes was behaving as if nothing had changed in my life (although in this respect I had profited by my experience of prisons and concentration camps)."

He seemed to have accepted his TB as one more adventure in a dangerous life, and he had no intention of succumbing to it. TB patients are kept busier than most, and he had never before bothered with a diary, but he somehow found time to make a thoughtful and witty record of his experiences with that hospital and its personalities, the resident chaplain, the barber, Oldenburg the Lumpen-Proletarian, the Bow-Wow zealous to report on fellow-patients' trespasses, Alfred the Spit Collector who had been pronounced cured in 1951 but stayed on, tolerated because he had no home and didn't mind collecting spit.

Mornings were given over to doctors' visits, tests, streptomycin or penicillin injections in the hindquarters (dreaded if a notoriously ham-handed nurse appeared with her tray of equipment), and "hanging from the drip." The drip alone could take up to two hours while PAS was guided into the bloodstream drop by drop from an overhead apparatus. During this procedure the patient had to lie perfectly still, lest the needle wobble in the vein at the inside of the elbow. The daily period of lying down cot beside cot on the veranda was divided into two three-hour spells. In the second of these rest periods silence was strictly enforced. After that, dressed like a civilized human being, Max went out for a walk in the woods, breathing as deeply as he could.

So it may have been during the silent period that he managed to write his diary, propped against a pillow and with his knees up as a slanting desk for the hard-backed pad. When his secretary visited he gave her the new pages to type and put away for safekeeping. That I knew nothing of this does not necessarily mean it was a secret. Dee, too, from an early age displayed that self-sufficiency that keeps its own counsel, requiring neither confidantes nor approval, whereas I had run to my mother with every trifling new discovery or achievement.

Once he recorded:

> Visiting day. The gate opens. Enter a slender blond girl, sixteen, a smooth curl at the right side of her forehead. She walks smartly up to a boy (seventeen probably), also blond, hair brushed back, the nose rather sharper but the family resemblance unmistakable. Their hands meet like a railroad coupler, their eyes more shyly. She says, "Good day, brother mine, how goes it?" And both are holding back tears. Embarrassed by the emotion that can neither be repressed nor any better expressed than by this purposely chosen greeting, part of their game as chicks, forgotten, now resurrected.
>
> Hansel and Gretel.

When I was unable to visit Max because of household burdens and Dee's need of me when she came home from school, I sent one of his devoted friends and I wrote letters, such as

> Dear Sweetie, I'm thinking about you all the time while I work. I'm getting the English of "A Man's Job" [the railroad book] polished up to give François Monod [a publisher] before he returns to Paris and I'm translating his wife's novel about the hydrogen bomb as fast I can to send Charles, along with my own book. But I see you and feel you in my heart all the time. I had a small lying-down rest period in a deck chair in the garden today, imitating you, with blanket and pillow and book. I'm going to continue it every afternoon, in lieu of the vacation we missed. I admire you, Max, I must try to be more like you — courageous, strong-willed.

But I soon saw that despite his fortitude all was not well with him. Suddenly one visiting day he was so depressed that he could not hide it, and on the return trip to Grünau I was wretched.

To himself he expressed it this way:

> As with every vacation, punctually at the end of three weeks the blues set in. Three weeks of well-regulated living in wholesome surroundings are enough. Then, inexorably, comes the morning after the night before.
>
> Today I feel ill for the first time since being in hospital. Kind letters, visitors, love tokens, cannot cheer me. I dread the prospect before me. Summer is already autumnal, autumn will be wintry. Dr. von Veith says she wishes she had found the tubercles by now — as if I had been deliberately hiding them. That was all I needed to hear.

As if I had read this entry, a rampant anxiety began making inroads on the heart that pined for his well-being, rousing it to defenses that jabbed needles into the region around it and boded no good. What would become of Dee if we both went down? Only the translation of Martine Monod's clever, slick *Die Wolke* gave me peace from the instant I sat down to it until the alarm rang, signaling that Dee would soon be home.

I shared Martine's sanguine conviction that this romance for not-too-sophisticated readers would move enough people to make a government stop its nuclear experiments. The title referred to that innocent-looking cloud from which white flakes that looked like snow had gently fallen on Japanese fishermen returning to port with their catch. The one whose name became known, Kuboyama, had died a slow, grueling death from the contact of those flakes with his skin; but since few people in the West cared overmuch about a poor Japanese fisherman, Martine had invented an American heiress on a yachting trip in the same Pacific waters to share his fate and make the point. Beautiful, young, charming and in love, meaning no harm to anyone, the happy girl stands at the railing, gazes in wonder at snowflakes falling in summer, and holds up her lips to taste their benison.

Except for a few colloquialisms which I had asked Martine to explain, I finished the job by the end of September and then collapsed, as I had done once before in the Federation. Ann, my Dutch ex-colleague who lived at the other end of Grünau and had two little girls close to Dee's age, took her in for as long as I would be in hospital.

It was not in faraway Buch. From Max's hospital the village of Mahlow was even farther away, in the quiet Brandenburg countryside near Potsdam, but it had been recommended by one of his protégés. The poet Franz Fühmann, whose black and bitter insight into the making of fairy tales made me shiver with appreciation, had gone to Mahlow after a bad heart attack for which he was too young, and had come home tranquil.

Although a branch of East Berlin's famous old dirty-looking Charité, this place resembled an exclusive hotel for the sick, although most of the patients were as humble as Max's hospital mates. It specialized in a nature and water cure famous since the nineteenth century in Germany, and it treated — among other ailments — my bugbear "vegetative *Dystonie.*"

I didn't know any of this when I set out. My mind utterly empty, I sank into a downy bed in a single room, saw a tree of some kind through the window opposite, and hoped no one would make me get up again. No one did. I was allowed to lie there inanimate in the silence for a long time before a sweet nurse came in and took my history.

Meanwhile at Max's hospital, a new head doctor fluoroscoped him thoroughly and ordered the TB therapy discontinued. A bronchoscopy was scheduled to find out what his illness really was. Max noted:

Farewell, TB halo and crown of thorns. It appears, as was originally surmised, to be "only" an abscess. I spat blood and water for nearly three months, and nary a moth made its appearance. I've lost my moth investment. Basically it may only be a carbuncle — if not like Oldenburg's on his ass, then on a lung.

I gradually got used to the idea that the lung patient is both irascible and fatalistic. But how about the lung *abscess* patient? Which characteristics am I to assume under this heading, and which are pardonable?

So everything and nothing has changed.

Not quite yet. I still have to deliver sputum seven times next week for analysis. In normal life Germans wish someone luck by spitting three times into a corner. I must now spit seven times into a bottle. For better or worse?

Overcast sky. Still no new diagnosis. But coughing, asthma, blood in the sputum again (suddenly appearing and after a penicillin shot disappearing). As if you had set forth like Columbus to find India and then steered into the nearest emergency harbor. You ought to be happy over what you've been spared, but you aren't because. . .

Because what? Something fishy is going on in your body. All is dark.

October was slipping toward November. My own chances of leaving hospital looked dim. Letters flew back and forth between Mahlow and Buch, and if Max had ever seriously doubted that he was the most precious person on earth for me, those doubts must have been set at rest.

"Today I asked for a day's furlough to visit you, and I got it for next Tuesday," he wrote me on October 19. "I don't know exactly what hour I will be out there, probably between 11 and 12 o'clock . . . I am longing for the day. Would they let you go out with me to some neighborhood restaurant? I think that would be good therapy." He ended the letter with the tender English-German verbal caress his parents taught him when he was put to bed in his crib: "Sleep you well in your *Bettgestell*." In a sudden burst of optimism he wrote me the next day, "If not earlier I am sure we will be together at home by Christmas."

Of course Oberarzt Camrat gave permission. (An *Oberarzt* was second in the medical hierarchy of a department.) Due to accidental gerrymandering of the occupation borders, this doctor could live physically and intellectually in the West, yet work in an East German village only a mile from his home. His methods, halfway between Kneipp and Freud, might have seemed to the GDR's Health Ministry nutty if not absolutely heretical, but he was protected by his boss in the Charité, a *Chefarzt* (top of the hierarchy), and could exercise full authority in his own little backwater. I was very lucky to have landed in his care.

Max was wearing the chestnut brown suede cap I had bought him in China, the last country I visited as a Federation translator, and the only socialist country whose still glowing revolution bolstered my belief instead of making me worry that idiots would destroy the whole dream. Max was mad about that peaked cap with the suede button on top, not only because it was so becoming but because it seemed to prove that even a socialist economy could produce elegance.

Despite the ordeal of the bronchoscopy the week before, when a small piece of the ailing lung had been cut out for examination, he looked happy again as we got into the back seat of the Aufbau car. "To Schönefeld Airport," he told the driver, as one might cry out, "To freedom!" adding, "The food there is supposed to be very good." "Ah," said the driver, and shifted into third while we began exchanging our impressions of the latest thundercloud overhanging the political scene in the GDR.

Max knew more than I did about what was going on in the world outside hospitals, but that wasn't saying much. His best-informed visitors could only speculate as to causes and effects in Hungary, from which vague rumblings, something about an uprising, had been heard.

Excitedly I interrupted, "I was so angry with *Neues Deutschland*, I wrote them a letter. One day they carried an item announcing that the trouble in Budapest was over, the streets were now calm. Trouble, what trouble? Believe me, I read the paper thoroughly and there hadn't been a word about trouble in Budapest. Did you see that stupid polemic against some speech by Tito in Pula? Where the hell is Pula, what was the occasion? They hadn't published the speech they were attacking, so what were we supposed to think? We were supposed to feel guilty about having missed something important, not reading the paper attentively enough — the usual trick!"

"What did your letter say?" Max asked.

"I told them off," I said. "I told them they were insulting the readers' intelligence with their evasions."

"Have you sent the letter?"

"Oh yes."

"Good thing we're both in hospital," he said mildly.

Naturally I was aware that as an American I had a certain *Narrenfreiheit* when I wrote protesting letters. I also realized that Max did not enjoy that "freedom granted to fools." What neither of us realized was how perilously close Max was, hair's-breadth close, to a terrible political crackdown on him. He might well have said, "For God's sake, do you want to get us in trouble?" — but he never did that. He dauntlessly improved my German, added weight to my arguments, often sped the letters faster to their destinations by mailing them himself downtown.

In contrast to my former protest letters, however, this latest one was so short and snappy that no diplomatic locutions could have made it palatable. By its very nature it was a punch in the eye, and if the German was crude that at least made clear that Max was innocent of it.

From our seats in the Schönefeld restaurant we nostalgically watched planes with various insignia take off. I remembered the tears in Max's eyes when I came home from China via Moscow with all sorts of stories and a cornucopia of presents. "We must save money so we can see China together next year," I said. "It might take two years," Max replied with a smile. What an impossible lark, a couple flying abroad just for pleasure! One had to be *sent*, that is, *one* might be sent, but never one plus spouse. In any case the airport food was as good as people claimed, if not quite Neva standard.

I asked about the results of the bronchoscopy, which he had passed over so lightly in a letter. "The new *Chefarzt* is sure now that it isn't TB, more likely an abscess," Max said. "Plus chronic bronchial infection, which is no news. They're still studying the piece of lung."

His tone had been noncommittal, but a pall fell with this suggestion of medical impotence. I could see by the way he glanced at wine being poured at a neighboring table that he wanted nothing so much as to get good and drunk. The driver was smoking a cigarette at his table across the room, and I was sure Max had a pack in his inside pocket. If so he didn't reach for it. I myself would have loved a cigarette after coffee, but it was easier for me to refrain; I had never even inhaled.

Max paid and signaled to the driver, who briskly went out to the car while we followed at Max's pace.

I was thinking sadly that our little holiday was already over, I would be driven back to Mahlow and he from there to Buch, but he surprised me. "Let's get you a new wedding ring," he said. In the rush to pack and leave New York in 1947 when a berth on a safer ship unexpectedly became available I had forgotten the ring I kept in a box of rose petals.

"After that we can visit our house," Max added, as if on the spur of the moment. I was overwhelmed.

When a house has not been lived in, even for a few weeks, it relapses on itself. It sinks into a reverie and time departs from it. The owners, by not using it, have grown irrelevant, and the house tells them so when they have the temerity to return. With a yawn and closed eyes, stirring vaguely like the dragon Fafner in *Siegfried* who groans in his bass voice, "Let me sle-e-e-ep!" the house was grumbling, although under its breath, its musty breath, "Not *you* again?"

The untenanted foyer had no color. The little round white table looked gray from being forgotten. The tall bookcase which had never stood quite straight now seemed to slump against its wall by the kitchen where no one cooked. Only we had color and were real, tremulously real, longing with such intensity for the restoration of our life together that we stood in that memory of a foyer clinging to one another and unable to let go. The kiss in the doorway had moved inside, a longer one than for many years.

"Let's not go back to hospitals," I murmured. "It will mean we're sick, but here we'll be well!"

"Later we'll be here and well," he said.

In a letter newly taking me into his confidence he wrote,

Yes, I got to Buch with my teeth, coat, glasses and cap, lucky fellow that I am. In the Neva I met Olga Gábor and Janka. Later the Kantors came. No one knew any more details about Hungary. Olga was planning to go back to Budapest on Thursday, but had to stay in Berlin, as I was told on the phone yesterday.

Thank God the Poles were wise and courageous enough to prevent such a mess. [He meant the invasion of Hungary by Soviet troops, which ND by then was presenting as a rescue of the grateful populace from counterrevolution.] As far as I understand, the Hungarians had made the typical mistake of putting a small unpopular man, Gerö, in the place of a big unpopular man, Rakosy, so that the situation got critical all over the country. Now Gerö is out, but the price seems very high.

I must try to get hold of the London *Daily Worker* regularly (thanks for sending that copy back) because our papers become more and more abominable every day. To think that even Rosl's husband, a man with some brains, is so deceived about the Polish events! It's sickening how sectarianism takes possession of people like a fever. It's hard to resist, I know that myself.

Terrible to see that our people will not learn a thing, either from the Polish or the Hungarian events. It's ghastly. ["Our people" was a euphemism for the SED.]

His wrath grew as the days passed. "I am furious about the slanderous, misleading reports on Hungary," he wrote me. "They're trying to put the blame on the writers now." This must have referred to the deportation of Georg Lukács to Romania and the hysterical attacks in *Neues Deutschland* on those who worried about what might be happening to him.

During the second week of November, Max was transferred to a shining new clinic in Buch where he had a private room and even a bathroom shared with only one other patient. An operation was scheduled.

"That's a first-rate place," Dr. Camrat assured me. "What exactly is wrong with your husband's lung?"

"An abscess," I said.

"What kind of abscess?"

I didn't know. It was news to me that there was more than one kind. I pictured an abscess as something roundish, a smeary yellow-pink, and about the size of a plum.

The doctor was looking intently into my eyes as if to understand just how much I might know or suspect. I knew little and suspected nothing. "Why don't you go and visit him?" he suggested.

"You'd let me?"

"It would do you good."

"But how would I get there?"

"You could take the *S-Bahn*."

"I could?"

I, weak as a cat? During my daily half-hour (compulsory) walk I had never glimpsed or known of a Mahlow Station. It must have been miles away and I would have to change trains here there and everywhere. As for the brand-new Rössle Clinic, how far would that be from the station, and how would I find the strength to repeat the whole marathon after barely an hour's visit with Max?

I didn't say any of this, I was ashamed.

"You can do it," said Camrat, reading my eyes.

So I went next day and was overjoyed to see for myself how well-off Max was in his spotlessly clean new room, and why he was so enchanted by the picture on the ceiling above his pillow. He had written me about it.

Bodo Uhse recalled making thoughtless fun of that picture the first time he entered the room. It was a circle enclosing pretty flowers and a few birdies perched on the rim of a well, as if planned for a child patient. Bodo quoted Max's gentle reproof: "When one lies here it's a comfort to have something like this before one's eyes, a little altar of life. Those few tendrils . . . they'll keep growing. I imagine a young greenwood coming up behind them."

While I was there the nurse came in with Max's supper, placing on the small table a supper for me too. How immensely kind, what a wonderful haven this was! How lucky we were with our hospitals! The one hour grew into two, nobody scolded in that civilized place, and I got back to my own bed at 10 P.M. bone-weary but triumphant as if I had climbed the Matterhorn. The next day I had a charley horse, but no heart pains, and soon afterward I was discharged.

I needed money, but could not bear to discuss such mundane ugliness with a sick man. Quite easily I found a part-time job translating for a news agency, which also distracted me from constant worry about Max.

The day of Max's operation approximately coincided with the arrest on November twenty-ninth of Wolfgang Harich, his highly prized editor for philosophy and Marxism, the former child prodigy who once naively asked me whether the Garden of Eden I had painted on a closet door was Early Christian. He could have been kidding, but I don't think so. I was an older woman and as his boss's wife, a *Respektsperson* for young Wolfgang.

Naiveté may be a function of inordinate conceit. It was this quality, along with an unappeasable craving for admiration, that eventually ruined Harich, and not him alone; for he talked.

At thirty-three, an age when most people have attained a degree of common sense, that zany of academe ran about telling anyone and everyone that it was time for Walter Ulbricht to step down. In Hamburg he hugely entertained the *Spiegel* directors with imitations of Ulbricht's ludicrous dialect, and confided his plan for a reformed socialism in the GDR. At the Social Democratic Party's "East Bureau" in West Berlin, an organization whose aim was to crack socialism's defenses, he asked for help in upsetting the Ulbricht regime and offered to speak over RIAS radio himself; he would appeal to the people of East Germany to remain calm when this happened. He helped organize a social gathering of certain Aufbau colleagues and their wives at Janka's house, suggesting that Janka also invite an old friend of his from Mexican exile, Merker by name, who might be interested in joining a reformed Politburo, perhaps even replacing Ulbricht.

Janka was agreeable. He called for Merker in his own car to make sure he came. It was a long way, and his friend was not in the best of health.

But the unfortunate Merker, who had thought he was going to a party, was appalled at the tone of the conversation. Had he walked into an open manhole? He had already been clouted with an eight-year sentence on false charges and only recently been freed after two years of grueling interrogation. It had led nowhere; he had done nothing except be a West exile and an acquaintance of Noel Field. All he wanted at this point was to lead a quiet life in the post granted him by the Party after his acquittal. It was not much of a post, but he was lucky to be alive. Something about him — his honesty no doubt — continued to make Walter Ulbricht feel threatened. Although not Jewish, Merker had written a passionately pro-Semitic article, worrying GDR authorities whose efforts to be neither anti nor pro (the latter would annoy the Soviet Union) kept them in a continuous bind.

People who thought Merker might have been the one to set up Harich could not imagine what he had already suffered in the pretrial basement of a political prison. The last thing he needed was to draw Ulbricht's vengeful attention to himself again. Figuratively speaking, he crept home as to a mousehole. Actually Janka, as promised, drove the frightened man home, where he tried to make himself as invisible as he could; but he was not to be spared.

Harich did not need to be set up, he did that for himself. Even the East Bureau had been leery of the glib talker with the subtle smile playing about his lips. According to his own evidence, the bureau put him off from one meeting to the next, each time with a different cagey representative.

His crowning foolishness was to go to Ulbricht, of all people, proud that the old spider waiting in his web for just such a fly had invited him in the most flattering terms to expound his interesting theories about the improvement of socialism. With an expression of avuncular indulgence Ulbricht listened for some time to the sense and nonsense that so lightly tripped from Wolfgang's tongue, then bade him good-bye with an "All the best!" *(allezz Güüde)* and telephoned his men to spring a long prepared trap. That same night Harich was picked up in the apartment of his mother.

Confronted with terrifying reality for the first time in his life, Harich named as instigators of a plot people who, like Janka, had considered their discussions only a springboard to wider discussions, gradually involving more and more people in a democratic and peaceful movement. At any rate, this is what can be gathered from Janka's autobiographical writings in later life. Certainly Harich had told neither him nor anyone else in the nucleus group about his foolhardy *Spiegel* and East Bureau adventures.

But in his zeal to appear a white-haired boy, he went on to implicate Aufbau colleagues who, he said, had "developed negative tendencies" after Khrushchev's disclosures on Stalin. These included Max. The more names he dragged in, Harich seemed to think, the shorter his sentence would be.

He even blamed the deceased Brecht for having had a subversive influence on him. He blamed Ernst Bloch, professor of philosophy in Leipzig, for "systematically working him up against Walter Ulbricht." (Bloch was then banished from the university.) He blamed Georg Lukács, whose works he edited for Aufbau, as having infected himself, Janka, and Max with the heresy of a road to socialism independent of the Soviet Union's. He declared that without Janka's "active encouragement" he would never have gone off the deep end as he did.

By the time of his trial in March 1957, however, he had cast aside the role of white-haired boy; his accusations of other people paled beside the blame he heaped, with curious relish, on himself. Having related every tiniest detail at the interrogations, but still lusting after the limelight, he swaggered, "Politically I was a runaway horse that could no longer be stopped by warning shouts. With those ideas in my head I simply bolted, and if I hadn't been arrested I would not now be ripe for the ten years which the Herr Attorney General recommends, but rather for the gallows; and therefore, in the interest of national safety and in my own quite personal interest, I want to express my heartfelt thanks for the State Security's vigilance."

He got the ten years, with reading and writing privileges for cooperating, and after eight of those years was released a white-haired man.

The Party had been interested in making capital of Harich's arrest, but not a whisper of Janka's a week afterward reached the general public. He might have dropped through a tunnel to the antipodes for all anyone outside the office knew. His name was not mentioned in the media of the GDR for months.

On December 7, however, someone from Aufbau was delegated to visit Max in the Rössle Clinic and inform him of what had taken place at the office the day before.

It appeared that the Ministry of the Interior had telephoned Janka in the morning to stay at his post and be ready to receive police who were coming with a search warrant. Janka was heard to shout furiously into the telephone that he was a busy man with more important things on his mind than some game of cops and robbers. Real cops and robbers turned up shortly to rifle files and leave offices a mess. Staff from all departments stood in silent horror in the hallways and on the stairs as their respected boss, gripped on either side by a secret-service officer, was hustled into the street. There he was handcuffed and taken away in a Green Minna (the German equivalent of a Black Maria).

Max was stunned to hear this report of high-handedness to the feared ministry. The madness of it! — although, alas, quite like the surly Janka of old with the chip on his shoulder in the period before he had been, as it were, knighted by the regard of the Thomas Mann family. Knowing of no other reason for the arrest, Max assumed that Janka's insolence alone must have provoked it.

He at once began composing a letter — in his frail state it took two weeks to complete — in which he urged his editorial staff to keep faith with Janka. "We cannot expect a halt to pending legal proceedings," he wrote, "but we may rest assured that in the not too distant future all misunderstandings will be cleared up. . . ."

This letter ended up in the archives. No one is left who would know whether it was ever seen by the addressees. Erich Wendt temporarily resumed the post of director, soon to be followed by Klaus Gysi.

There were no "legal proceedings."

Janka and three other men, strangers to him, were forced by guards to strip naked and stand erect in a brightly illuminated entrance hall with eyes unwaveringly fixed on the immense enlargement of a Stalin photo that took up a whole wall. Raging inwardly, Janka lowered his head for relief from the sight, when as in a bad dream he heard a familiar voice just behind him jeer, "Chin up!" He had not heard the voice for twenty years, but it was unforgettable.

It belonged to Mielke, a German NKVD (Soviet Secret Service from 1934–1946) officer who in Madrid was in charge of approving or rejecting German volunteers for the front. In contrast with the improvised attire of Loyalist fighting men, Mielke had worn a grotesquely gaudy operetta uniform and played Grand Duke, blowing clouds of cigar smoke across the great plateau of his desk into the faces of interviewees. He pronounced Janka unfit for the front and threatened, in case the young man persisted in being refractory, to send him — and Janka didn't even understand the allusion — to "Valencia," which referred to a prison where the Loyalists kept shady political figures. Calmly ignoring the strictures of a pug-faced fool, Janka walked out, and his conspicuous bravery and quick advancement had rankled in the spite-ridden agent ever since.

As the GDR's newly appointed minister of the interior, Mielke was at last in a position to get even. He could hold Janka under "investigatory arrest" for months and take personal charge of the interrogations. In the summer of 1957 Janka was sentenced to solitary confinement for five years and kept in cruel, unsanitary, and degrading conditions.

No one except Janka's wife, who dared not speak for fear of the consequences to him, herself and the children, could imagine into what a pit of horror he had been dropped; and even she could not possibly guess all. His whereabouts were a closely guarded secret as he was moved from one jail to another. Yet while the shutters were down on the GDR's media, the news inevitably trickled out to writers in the West. Without exact details, to be sure; but in the West ugly details of that sort had been generally known for a long time.

The GDR would not have dared throw a personality like Janka to the lions if Thomas Mann had still been living. Katya Mann pleaded for his release in a private message to Khrushchev. Erika Mann sent an eloquent and deeply felt petition to Johannes R. Becher. "I would hold my hand in fire for Walter Janka," she wrote. She asked to testify at his trial, but was not permitted. Nor was Leonhard Frank or anyone else allowed to be a witness for the defense.

Max never learned by how narrow a margin his illness saved him from — to say the least — cross-examinations in which witnesses, like Paul Merker at Janka's trial, are put through the mental torture of trying not to incriminate others while yet saving themselves.

The government of the GDR knew what was wrong with Max long before I did. If the Ministry of Culture had not made inquiries of the *Chefarzt* he would not — finally — have received a prize. It was not the National Prize of which he had once secretly dreamed, or the equally prestigious Fatherland Order of Merit — both of these carrying with them fairly grand five-figure sums of money. It was the relatively unassuming Lessing Prize for which only literati were eligible, but which for that very reason deeply gratified Max. Lessing, author of a famous parable play about the human equality of Jews, Christians, and Muslims, was the German literary figure Max revered second only to Goethe.

The prize ceremony took place in the hospital room, the bed surrounded by Bodo, the doctor, the doleful Eeyore woman (an interchangeable chip that any institution could use), Günther Caspar, Max's stand-in at Aufbau — the same editor who substituted for Bodo during his bout with TB — the Deputy Minister of Culture Abusch, masses of flowers, and myself.

Max was too weak to sit up, but he had written a short speech. Lying back against his pillows, he read it with as much voice as he could muster. His glasses seemed dimmed, I could barely make out his eyes. Even Dr. Matthes had a little homily prepared. It was as we were leaving that Abusch asked me in the corridor whether I was "provided for" and I vaguely said yes. I had never thought about it.

For some time after the operation Max had been listless. He had had no appetite and was unable to stand on his feet without assistance. His leg muscles were nearly atrophied from too many injections. Suddenly he began to improve. The prize, the chemotherapy, two blood transfusions, the physiotherapist who helped him learn to walk again, and his own renewed determination, all must have played a part. He savored his meals, put on weight, regained hope.

Nevertheless Dr. Matthes telephoned me in late spring to say I should come to his office before my next visit with Max. He didn't hint at a reason, but that was tantamount to telling me. Alone in the house, a "little helper" having just gone home, I laid the receiver on the cradle and began to scream, screamed and screamed at the top of my voice like a peasant woman finding the rigid, blood-soaked body of her son.

This was the moment when marriage as an institution for which I never had much respect powdered away completely, leaving only Max and me.

Avoiding the word cancer, Dr. Matthes said Max had a type of tumor that could not be controlled. "But don't tell him," he cautioned. "He doesn't want to know. Let him enjoy the short time he has left." "What must I do when I see the end coming?" I asked. "Be brave," said Matthes.

He told Max that his bed was now required by a really sick person, the eighty-five-year-old mother of the *Chefarzt*. Surely he wouldn't mind continuing his convalescence at home? Mind? He was all aglow as he stepped out of the Aufbau car, and Dee was joyous.

A lovely pastoral summer stretched before us in which I lived for the day and thought no further. A white hospital bed with an adjustable head-end was set up in Max's study, but weather permitting he spent most of his time on a deck chair in the garden. Every day I asked him which friend he would like to see, and the friends made sure to come. They kept him alive.

Most often he asked for the poet Paul Wiens, who was so easily available in a Colony house just around the corner. A charming young man formerly on Max's staff, but now a freelance translator, he could juggle his time as he pleased, particularly since his wife had contracted TB and had to be sent to the mountains. Part of Paul's childhood had been spent in Mauthausen concentration camp. "I'm one-sixth Jewish," he joked. While other survivors of Nazi camps seldom escaped some inner crackup, the only obvious mark Mauthausen had left on Paul was rotting teeth.

He let them go on rotting, so great was his fear of dentists, but his blackish smile captivated just the same. "Just dropped in for some blather," he would say when he appeared unasked, and immediately gaiety entered the house. The two men would sit down to a game of chess, or just chew the fat. He was a great consolation.

One day when I came home from work I found Max in the kitchen cooking. My lord, the excitement! A few days later I phoned from downtown, "I saw real pheasants for eleven marks apiece! Do you know what to do with them?" Of course he knew. "Get one, and some sour cream," he said. All he did (as far as I could observe) was pluck it, fill it with sour cream, and put it into the oven. After this exquisite dining experience he remarked, "I've decided I can go to the office one afternoon a week from now on." A car was duly provided.

The one terrible shadow to fall across that summer was the trial of Walter Janka toward the end of July. Janka's old friends among the official invited guests in the courtroom were baffled by his obstinate refusal to say anything in his own defense except four words he kept repeating: "I emphatically deny that." Why resort to such a ploy if he was innocent, some wondered. Why not shout the truth, accuse his accusers? They had no conception of what can be learned in the oubliettes of a supposedly socialist Interior Ministry.

The manner of his arrest and the indignities he had endured from the moment he was pushed through the prison door had taught him that here he was not dealing with people who could be considered comrades. One difference between himself and Harich was that Janka never for a moment, either before or after his arrest, believed he had done anything contrary to Marxist principles. To a man brought up by Communist parents, the designation Comrade with a capital C was sacred, but in this prison he saw it trampled into muck. Through the nearly eight months of pretrial grilling he had thought constantly about how he should behave on the day of his trial and what words he must use to deprive this gang of any chance to pervert a meaning.

From the dock he saw the distress of uncomprehending friends, but could not ease it. He saw Brecht's widow Helene Weigel trying to signal encouragement, saw her go ashen when the sentence of five years was pronounced. He saw Anna Seghers bow her head in shame and despair.

Surely she, of all people, knew he had not dabbled in counterrevolution. She who, with Becher, had unwittingly helped get him into this mess by asking him to drive to Budapest and like a Scarlet Pimpernel in modern dress capture Lukács from danger (Ulbricht put the kibosh on that) — Anna, in any case, might have jumped up and cried out, "If he is at fault we are all at fault!" Might have, could not, had lived too long on nervous tiptoe.

A month later Kantorowicz, then a well-paid professor of Recent German Literature, went to West Berlin and requested "protection, permission to remain, and civil rights in the part of my Fatherland which is secure." It was easy to go West in those days before the wall was built, especially if one had a certain renown and didn't mind groveling a bit. "That piece of shit!" Max burst out when someone brought the news of his old friend's cap-in-hand radio speech. It had been broadcast over all West German stations.

Max was coughing blood again, although by no means every day, when the sunburst of the year occurred and made the whole world look better.

Early in September Christina Stead and Bill Blake at last arrived for their long-deferred visit. By this time Bill had accumulated over twenty thousand non-convertible East marks in Aufbau royalties, from his Civil War novel *The Copperheads* and a lesser but tender story called *Evergreen* about love between two elderly German immigrants in New York. Bill was now sixty-three, Chris fifty-five.

Both of them exhausted by poverty that had lasted too long, they urgently needed medical attention as well as clothes to replace their baggy and mended ones. To avoid any possible political difficulties they had given a West Berlin address on the visa application, that of Walburga's Aunt Agnes, who felt honored by the favor we asked.

They spent the first several days of their visit in Grünau, beautiful, dreamlike days for me. The logistics were no problem. To spare himself the climb, Max always slept downstairs in his hospital bed, which meant that they could have ours. I, not inappropriately, moved into the maid's room.

Dee was pleased to have such amusing company in the slant-roofed chamber next to hers. "She's like wild honey," Christina said. "Why didn't you ever tell me about her?" Of course I had told Christina story after story, but I treasured the wild-honey image ever after, like a gold locket hidden inside my blouse.

It was the greatest conceivable privilege to see Christina's strong, subtle face every morning at breakfast, florid as if from bursting good health; in reality, as we soon learned, a signal of frighteningly high blood pressure; Bill's ivory pallor was the same as always. In *For Love Alone* Chris had described him as "a black and white man." Now the black eyes were rusty, the thinning hair mixed with gray, but the youthful jokes kept bubbling up as if neither he nor Chris had a care. The reason they both looked so marvelous, so unbeaten, so truly free from worry, was that for once they were in a country that treated them like royalty and not as has-beens who must bow and scrape for every crumb of grudgingly bestowed publishing hack work.

But what had *we* to be proud of? We ached with the ignominy of having achieved nothing for Christina in all these years. In the GDR only Bill could reap the credit he deserved, while the genius to whom he was married was seen as a mere wife, courteously smiling. If she had written only *The Man Who Loved Children*, a stunning Greek tragedy, and *For Love Alone*, she should have made enough money in worldwide publication to keep them both for the rest of their lives.

Admittedly, the maddening babytalk improvised by *The Man Who . . .* would be hard to translate, although not impossible. But *For Love Alone* was a classic as straightforward as anything by Thackeray or Fielding. Richer, to be sure. Max and I (how many times!) went over title after title of her extraordinary works, only to see again and again how futile each fresh hope was. Stories that enthralled us would be rejected out of hand by GDR censors. Christina was not uninterested in Party concerns, quite the contrary, but these had not been reflected in her works to date, nor would she join.

She was Bill's fellow traveler, no one else's.

And that was just one aspect of the problem.

The idea of woman as a hero denied her chance was not particularly popular in Germany. I say hero advisedly. A heroine is a step lower and usually only a literary figure, beautiful if possible, whereas a hero in the body and soul of a woman is something so formidable that the Teutonic man's world instinctively refuses the representation, preferring not to know what is meant.

After Chris and Bill had completed their business and social rounds in Berlin they took a train to the Harz Mountains to relax and eat well for a fortnight at the Heinrich Heine Hotel, where we joined them for two red-letter days of talking and walking. We stayed on the more level mountain paths near the hotel, but Max once actually walked to the highest point of the half-timbered city of Quedlinburg to admire the view. Certainly the pure air and perhaps even more the pleasure of such company had something to do with the miracle, but when we got back to Berlin and he insisted he could now take on an additional afternoon a week at Aufbau, why should his opinion not have been trusted? What did doctors know?

Our guests went on to Leipzig, where friends had arranged for every kind of medical examination, and they returned to London more or less relieved of uncertainty. Bill had only been worn out and tormented by his inability to keep Christina in the circumstances she deserved; his eyes were weak, but he was not ill, not yet. Sadly Bad Tölz, recommended as the ideal spa for Christina's high blood pressure, was in West Germany and financially out of bounds for all of us.

One day in November Max pushed his luck too far. Instead of taking the Aufbau car home after work he phoned to tell me he was going to a P.E.N. meeting. After it he sat in the Press Club café drinking with a few of the writers. Of course he told me nothing about that part of the evening. Someone else did, although not at the time. He cannot have drunk very much, for he was able to let himself in quietly and go to bed unassisted, but when I looked into his room next morning I found him unable to get up. The P.E.N. meeting had been one activity too many, I thought.

Yet the sight of him lying so inert in his hospital bed, seeing but not even greeting me, made me understand that there was no sense in asking which friend I should invite that day. It was I who needed to see a friend. I phoned my news agency, gave indefinite notice, went round to the house of Paul Wiens, and burst into tears the moment he opened the door.

No no, he soothed, how could I think such a thing? It was an abscess. It took time for an abscess to be resorbed. "They tell him that," I sobbed.

"He'll be himself again tomorrow, you'll see," said Paul. "I'll keep in touch."

He did not keep in touch.

Curiously, Max did not seem to notice the loss of his amusing chess partner. He forgot chess. From time to time he asked me to phone one of his older friends.

He grew impatient when the television set ordered for him was delayed. His Lessing Prize had paid for it, but regardless of who paid in that country only the powerful — at least some ministry — could actually get their hands on it. I asked Aufbau to prod the Ministry of Culture, and eventually the thing did arrive, black and high and hideous and apparently made of solid lead. Two big bruisers wrestled it out of a truck and into a corner of the living room. It was not a color TV. I don't think we were aware that color TV existed.

Max surveyed it with satisfaction. He would put on his bathrobe and slippers, and taking along his small glazed earthenware jug, which resembled the sputum containers in Buch, would say quite cheerfully, "Just going to the *Kintopp*," a joke word for cinema, like "moom-pitchas," and would sit down before the monstrosity to watch second-rate entertainment and West commercials calculated to destroy East morale. Could anyone really believe that a slosh of Swish and one deft twirl of a mop would reflect enraptured faces in a kitchen floor? "Why not," said Max tolerantly, and we sat bemused while the novelty lasted.

He was often cheerful, especially after I unfolded the wood and canvas cot I had used for sunbathing back in Friedenau. I set it up on the other side of the fireplace from his hospital bed, and stopped sleeping upstairs. The cot was surprisingly comfortable when padded with a summer quilt. "I'm a bone ghost," Max observed good-naturedly after noticing his changed appearance in the lavatory mirror.

We chatted from bed to bed. He remembered the Thurber cartoon in which the wife impatiently tells the distracted husband, "All right, have it your way, you heard a seal bark!" — and there really is a seal behind their bed. Max barked like a seal, and I barked back. We were like children naughtily talking instead of going to sleep after our parents turned out the light.

But when I began to cough in a way that sounded just like his cough he became stern. "Pull yourself together, *Mädchen*," he said. "I can cope with my own sickness, but I can't cope with yours." I was ashamed, forced back the coughs.

Pain started, not in his lung but in the left shoulder. The Grünau doctor, who called me "*gnädige Frau*" because I lived in a villa, now permitted morphine pills, but they made Max sleep too much. He rebelled against this stupid daytime sleeping; he wanted to live to the utmost as long as he was alive. "Take them away," he whispered. His voice was almost gone. He had stopped eating.

I dreamed that I saw him walking across a flat roof (no part of our roof was flat), both arms stretched to clutch with all his might an enormous pane of glass the size of a picture window. I was frantic, he would fall off and kill himself, and I woke up.

The meaning was obvious, but why the enormous pane of glass? Then I remembered a discovery of Freud. The unconscious, without a clue to spelling, murmurs a comment which produces a picture: Max was *bearing his pain* as he advanced toward death. God knows he was the bravest man I ever knew.

On New Year's Eve Dee demanded a party. "Last year we had false noses," she accused. "What did you do with the false noses?" She was nine years old, smart and sensitive, yet managed not to see what she dared not believe.

The pain in Max's shoulder had spread into his back and was so intense that now he was glad of the morphine pills. I realized that it was time to send Dee back to Ann's. But in packing we had forgotten something, and she came home a few days later to get it. First she hastened into Max's room, and saw all at once what a child is better off not seeing. Shyly, uncertainly, but with all her courage she said, "Hello, Popsky," and my heart broke.

When had she last used that pet name? Wasn't it on the sunny Sunday when we took the basket of goodies to the TB hospital and picnicked with Max in the grass?

Gustl felt the need to make a portrait. He brought charcoal and a large pad and sketched one Max after another. He could reproduce his model with unerring speed — and guts.

"Let me see," said Max in a voice just above a whisper. Gustl looked at me as if for permission. How could he let Max see these frightful images? "Come," said Max, "show me."

Gustl showed him the last, worst, best one, and Max gazed a long time, carried away by a connoisseur's admiration. At first he said, "I'm not going to tell you what I think," but after a few moments, unable to take his eyes from the sharp black strokes, he pronounced, *"Toll. . ."* Terrific. What did it matter whose likeness this portrait happened to be!

I slept upstairs again, otherwise I would have got no sleep at all. On waking one morning I wrote a poem about Max. Actually it wrote itself, I could find nothing to fix. It could be read at his grave, I thought; it had only to be translated into German. In the misery that enclosed us like dense fog I had scarcely thought of Paul Wiens, an ingenious translator, but now I rang his number. No one was at home. I tried in the afternoon, in the evening, the next morning. I didn't even know whom to ask where he might be, as we had no friends in common.

Suddenly the name Bärchen sprang to my mind, Little Bear, a friendly soul I had met once at the Wienses, wife of a writer with whom Paul had collaborated on a film. The surname came to me and I found them in the phone book. "Oh yes," she said, "didn't you know he moved into a furnished room downtown? It was weeks ago. He couldn't stand being alone in that house any longer."

I was seized by a bitter, unjust rage. He had not run away from his empty house, but from Max's final ordeal. He hadn't even phoned at Christmas-time.

It took me years to review this incident and wonder why a child alumnus of concentration camp should have been expected to bear a burden I myself could not bear.

Max drifted in and out of coma. I could tell when he feebly thrashed and groaned that he was having a bad dream, and I was able to suggest it away, stroking his forehead and softly saying, "It's only a dream, it isn't real." Then he would quiet down and sleep.

Forgetting the dingle-bell I gave him and unable to call out, he would shape the word "medicine" with his lips only. I set the alarm for the moment his last dose of morphine would lose its effect, but fearing this might happen sooner I kept running in to check.

At dawn in the first week of January I stood at the gate and noticed Stefan Heym jogging in my direction. I hadn't known he jogged, and so early! I had to respect such self-discipline. "How's Max?" he asked. "Bad," I said. "I'm waiting for the doctor." He paused helplessly, wanting to say something, not knowing how, then jogged away toward the pine wood. I had never before seen compassion in his eyes. I was amazed.

It was a nuisance for a doctor with a regular practice to be on emergency call, but there were so many doctors that it didn't happen too often to any one of them. The one who came that morning was about forty and looked impassively grave. I opened the second door to Max's room, the one from the foyer, but was so exhausted that I didn't follow. I sank down on the stairs to wait. The heaving, gurgling breaths became peaceful; the doctor must have given him something.

"It's the *Agonie*," he said as he came out. I had never heard that word. It sounded like agony, but that wasn't the meaning. It meant the last throes, but Max's heart was so powerful that it ignored last throes, it beat steadily on like the heart of a young man.

Later that day as I entered his room he did a strange, seemingly mad thing, perhaps to evade the end he sensed coming at him from behind. He vaulted forward from his pillows in an access of incredible energy and would have hurtled across the foot of the bed and crashed to the floor if I had not grasped him and with all my remaining strength pushed him back. I don't know where I got that strength, I was utterly drained; and he hated me for it — I saw the hatred in his eyes. I had prevented his escape from death, and that was not all I had done. I had connived in the abscess lie!

But hate, mercifully for us both, was only one of many different clouds that passed across his consciousness. A metastasis in the brain must have slipped from one neuron to another, changing his moods and memories. Once when I said goodnight and kissed him, saying "That's a kiss," he showed me he understood by pursing his lips to receive another, and turned back a corner of his blanket as if to invite me in.

Then the morphine stopped working and I phoned the doctor whose sole parting advice had been "Be brave." Suddenly he knew something practical: there was a visiting nurse in every district. He gave me a telephone number.

The nurse came early in the evening, bringing her husband, which surprised me. They were as un-German as could be, their surname had an ending like "aitis" or "okat," suggesting one of the eastern regions colonized by Prussia. The couple were soft-spoken and kind. She washed Max tenderly and gave him an injection stronger than the pills that no longer worked. Her husband helped her, although mainly by his presence. Thinking back on that evening I often wondered whether angels hadn't been sent to us.

"He'll sleep through the night now," she said. "If you need us please call no matter what hour. Don't worry," she added. "You must sleep too. Go to bed and sleep as long as you can."

I did as I was told, slept deeply, then as if a pistol had gone off was wide awake and looked at the clock. It wasn't morning, it was only 10 P.M.

I rushed downstairs and it seemed to me in Max's doorway as if I heard a breath. Just one breath. I waited for the next breath, but none came. His face was perfectly calm. I pressed my ear to his heart. It was all over.

When the phone by my bed rang early next afternoon it was Gertrude Heym, inviting me to a meal. I was very grateful and very, very hungry, but too fagged out to rise.

"We'll bring it to you," she said, and they came up the stairs with everything required. That spaghetti with the succulent meat sauce Gertrude had cooked was unforgettable. They brought dishes and cutlery for themselves too, eating at my bedside. They could not have been kinder.

A couple of days later Mildred Olsen paid what she considered a condolence call. I told her about the Heyms' good deed and how deeply it had moved me.

"See?" she triumphed. "Didn't I always tell you they were nice?"

I tried to make clear what had gone wrong between us and the Heyms, not dreaming that a condolence caller would run from my doorstep to theirs and regale them with her own warped understanding of what I had said. Stefan never spoke to me again.

Gertrude, however, gradually relented as her heart disease worsened and Stefan's impatient weariness of her hurt more and more. She no longer automatically endorsed his every judgment. One day in the road she told me she was "on the death list," trying to make it sound like a joke, but her voice quavered and her lips trembled, The last time we spoke was on the phone: she had heard I was going to America and wanted to wish me "the pot of gold at the end of the rainbow" when I got there.

Getting there was not so easy.

It was not even easy, while endlessly waiting, to swap our way out of the Colony house with its expensive upkeep and aching memories.

The Eeyore woman, now representing the Colony management, told me I could swap only with a member of the nomenclatura, but at the moment they knew of no one suitable. Then one day the director of the State Opera arrived with an architect, and without asking permission or so much as greeting me, tramped around the garden as if it were already his, measuring the outside wall of Max's study with a view to building an extension. Herr P., formerly a member of the Nazi Party, had been forgiven for some reason, though not by me, and I blew up at the Eeyore woman.

Astounded at my getting so angry over a trifle she tried to soothe me. They had a lovely, brand-new apartment for us downtown, she said, just built, not quite finished, but I could look at it as soon as I pleased. She referred to it as a "folk apartment," *folk* being a Nazi euphemism that made the little hairs on my arms and legs stiffen. It was applied only to things that were cheap because inferior, but good enough for such nonentities as proles, widows, and orphans. I took one look at the skimpy dump, advertised for a social heavyweight who needed a house, and immediately heard from a family of five too big for their apartment in Stalin Allee. Dee was excited. To her Stalin Allee was the height of glamour.

The driver of the moving van had room for us both up front, and we rode out of the Colony of the Intelligentsia without a regret or a backward look.

In late June 1958, taking along my old expired green passport, still beautiful to me, I embarked on a long, long ride in the *U-Bahn* to the American Consulate in West Berlin and asked the gentleman in charge to issue me a new passport that would include Dee. He gave me a form which he advised me to fill out at home because of its length; I could come back with it next week. But when I unfolded it in my kitchen I saw that it had nothing to do with passports. Its name was AW-585, "Questionnaire and Application for Registration."

What did that mean? Registration as or for what? I was furious, if not entirely surprised by this dirty trick, but wrote the consul courteously that if he had no form applicable to my case I could make a sworn, notarized statement that I had done nothing to expatriate myself, that is, not voted in a foreign election, been a member of a foreign political party, or worked for a foreign government. I asked him how many passport pictures of myself with Dee would be required and gave him my telephone number.

He didn't use it, so I finally phoned the consulate and was told that the man in charge was on holiday. True, it was summer, so I waited until August, asked somebody else how many passport pictures I would need, and went back to West Berlin. At the consulate the cad in charge blithely admitted having given me an incorrect form and handed me the right one. I filled it out then and there and watched him slip it into an envelope with the photos. He said I would hear from him.

I didn't, of course, and when I returned in September with murder in my heart he demanded that I bring an affidavit from some East Berlin authority confirming that I had really and truly never ever voted in Germany. How such negative information could be tracked down nobody knew, and I was shunted from one office to another until I reached a borough president. This lot were as stupid as the consul was dastardly.

"The German Democratic Republic," the borough president told me, "is under no obligation to give affidavits on its own (yes, "its own"!) citizens." No use begging and pleading that my mother was incurably ill, hadn't seen me for twelve years and might die any day. No use repeating this once again to the consul, who in March 1959 sent me an entirely new kind of form which was already filled out; all I had to do was sign it, the only trouble being that it was not filled out accurately. It incriminated me with the lie that I had not been employed since my residence in Germany. Why shouldn't I have been? Thousands of Americans are employed abroad.

The form further stated snidely that I "do not pay the American income tax." How could I? East Germany had no currency relations with the United States. It was impossible even to figure out how many East marks equaled a dollar.

The third lie: "I intend to return to the United States permanently to reside immediately." Desirable as this might have seemed, how could I foresee whether, when I got there, I would be able to make a living for myself and my child? I would have to look around. I was forty-three.

My beloved brother then retained Leonard Boudin, the lawyer who during the Cold War became famous for cutting through passport sabotage. His services cost a pretty penny, but John somehow scraped it together and on November 20, 1959 Boudin wrote a curt letter to the State Department, threatening that if his client continued to be subjected to this cruel runaround he would recommend "the institution of a lawsuit based on the conduct of the American Consul in Berlin."

Whereupon, presto change-o, the Consulate telephoned me to come for my passport. One of the sourpussed ladies who worked there in their best clothes and costume jewelry opened a desk drawer and reluctantly handed it over.

John felt sure it had lain in that desk drawer for months, all signed and sealed in Washington, while Mother yearned for Dee and me. And died.

★ ★ ★

Dad sent us the plane tickets, looking forward to a dear little granddaughter who would comfort his loss and a daughter prepared to spend three months keeping house for him.

Poor Dad.

At the airport he and John could only wave and send us radiant smiles from a gallery while we, below, were being processed. At last on the same level, it was love at first sight between Dee and her thrilled grandfather. In me there was shock and sadness when I saw how twelve years of the hustle to support a wife and three small children had made inroads on John's dear face. Dad's age hardly showed, which was astonishing after Mother's years of heartbreaking illness. No doubt the joy of seeing that longed-for first grandchild had rejuvenated him. But he made no attempt to conceal his dismay at the appearance of an unexpectedly middle-aged daughter.

"Why, your face is covered with warts and excrescences!" he reproached me. As an English teacher, although retired, his daily vocabulary was still quite choice. He must have meant a few little moles which I always had, except that they probably looked cuter when I was young.

The real trouble started when Dee, full of trust in the fond old man whose hand she was holding, pointed at some ordinary, harmless-looking male in a hat and coat and asked, "Grampa, is that a capitalist?"

Dad's happy face shaded over. "Not that I know of," he said. He seemed to stiffen from head to toe.

But she would not give up. Just as one expects to see lions or camels in different parts of Africa, in a capitalist country there must be at least a few recognizable capitalists wherever one goes. I don't know what she pictured. Nothing, apparently, for she pointed hopefully at another ordinary individual carrying an undistinguished suitcase and asked, "Is *that* a capitalist?" "I'm sure I have no idea," Dad said, trying not to sound annoyed. He had never knowingly seen a capitalist, although he had quite a few extremely rich relatives of whom he was proud. I suppose he was thinking, "Poor brainwashed child! Well, give her a chance, she'll come round. . . ."

As soon as she had slept off her jet lag Dad took her to the nearest super-market. At first she was shaken, but by the time they arrived home with their bundles she was able to enthuse, "We *must* get this kind of store in the GDR! And we *will* get it," she proclaimed. "At the end of the seven-year plan things will look quite different in our part of Berlin!" Dad listened with a wry smile. Give her time, give her time!

He had a two-room flat with kitchen and bath on the eighth floor of a pleasant pink brick apartment house, part of a project built by the Met-ropolitan Life Insurance Company for its customers. The elevator was dreamily noiseless, not like the one in Stalin Allee that clanged and banged all day. This one's doors knew just when to open and close by themselves, and they were not the kind that bump the arm of a person getting in at the last minute. A last minute was impossible with such an in-telligent elevator. The whole neighborhood was on the comfortable side without being rich, and due to the landlord's relationship to insurance-holders like Dad, the rent was not prohibitive.

He gladly gave us the bedroom. There was no other possibility. He and Mother had disposed of the double bed I remembered and bought twin beds for old-age comfort, but now that we occupied them he had to sleep on the old chaise longue in the living room, with a chair at the end for his extra length. He said he didn't mind, and I'm sure this was true. He minded other things.

At eleven a child is not quite a child any more, nor yet a grown-up. A man selling Fuller Brushes or some such thing rang our bell; I declined with thanks and shut the door, but Dee was as scared as I used to be when I woke up from a bad dream and ran to my parents' bedroom. "That was an FBI man," she insisted. "Of course he was, didn't you see how mean his eyes looked?" Then she thought she saw him in the street. "It's that FBI man! He's following us!" Maybe an FBI man really was snooping around to see what we were up to; if so he must have been bitterly disappointed.

We had arrived in time for Dee to be enrolled in the nearby elemen-tary school for the term beginning February first. The principal received us in her office most cordially. I explained that while Dee's spoken Eng-lish was nearly perfect and she easily read English, her spelling was a mess. "That's all right," the principal said. "We'll put her in the dumb class where it won't matter." Immediately she turned to Dee with a warm, motherly look. "I can see you're bright," she said. "Don't feel badly about being in the dumb class. By next term your spelling will be so much better that we can put you in the smart class where you belong." Dee smiled sweetly, harboring unsweet thoughts. When we were out of the principal's office she said, "Dumb class, smart class — how must kids feel when they're told they're in a dumb class? What a disgusting system!"

After a week in the dumb class she told me indignantly, "Those kids are not dumb, not in the least!"

They were certainly sweet. When we met any of her schoolmates in the neighborhood they always smiled touchingly and called out, "Hello, Dee!" and she would call back, "Hello, Charlie, hello, Sue!" How different from Berlin, where schoolmates meeting in the street were so inhibited that all they could utter was "*Na*, Werner?" "*Na*, Inge?" in gruff tones, hardly lifting their eyes from the pavement. Working-class Germans seemed to feel comfortable only within the family. The parents had no circle of close friends, only relatives, and there was no prescribed etiquette for dealing with "strange" children. One's own children were not encouraged to bring a schoolmate home.

Once a boy in Dee's class asked Miss McCue, "Why don't whales sink to the bottom of the sea when they're so heavy?" and Miss McCue replied with an endearing smile that she was sure God took care of that.

Dee related this incident at supper in the kitchen. "How can people learn anything in this country?" she demanded. "How could I become a natural scientist here when God is the answer to everything? In the assembly there's God in the songs. When we pledge allegiance we have to say 'one nation under God'!"

The whale story did sound as if Miss McCue was the dumb one in the class. "But Dee, such an answer from a teacher isn't normal," I said. "You can't judge a whole school system by one teacher."

Dad was smiling, embarrassed. He made no comment.

In our borrowed bedroom I told Dee in a low voice that she must not make cracks about God in Grampa's apartment. "He believes in God. Don't hurt his feelings."

Every week he gave her twenty-five cents, with which she could treat herself to chewing gum, candy, tiny souvenirs, Donald Duck comic books and the like, and she was quite content with this allowance. She knew that Dad's pension was relatively modest and that he augmented it by working for his nephew-in-law in the garment district, writing business letters and with his irresistible charm showing customers the new line. She knew that he gave me a really handsome allowance for her American clothes and mine. Out of decency she ate "only" three bananas a day, otherwise she might have eaten six. She watched animated cartoons on Dad's color TV until her eyes became glassy, but made sneering faces at the commercials.

"How will you ever exist in Berlin again?" I kidded her. "You hate the chewing gum and there aren't any TV comics, let alone bananas. Except at Christmas."

She said matter-of-factly, "I'll tell you, Mommy, in three months I'll have enough chewing gum and comics and bananas to last the rest of my life."

Then she caught a flu so vicious that it looked as if there would be no rest of her life. If it hadn't been for my cousin Nat, a pediatrician whose practice was just around the corner, she might very well have died; she was not inured to the local bacteria and was faint from throwing up everything she ate. Nat put her on a regimen of pure cola (not coke) from the pharmacy, the only nourishment her stomach tolerated. The fever went down somewhat, but hovered between 102° and 103° Fahrenheit.

Providentially the Winter Olympics were being held in Squaw Valley, and for the first time a GDR ski jumper was to compete, Dee's hero Helmut Recknagel. I turned on the TV and suggested I make her a bed on the chaise longue so that she could watch; but from the darkened bedroom a barely audible voice said only, "You watch it, Mommy. You tell me what happened." I was terrified, I prayed, never in my life had I kept track of scores with such intensity. *Recknagel won!* I shouted.

"I knew he would," she said in her normal voice, and gave a long, eloquent sigh. "That was the best medicine I ever had," she said, and fell asleep like a breast-fed baby. Improbable? But true. . . .

With the return of Dee's energy she began getting on Dad's nerves again. When we watched TV together and saw the Sharpeville shootings in South Africa she said, "Those whites should all be pushed into the sea." Dad pointed out that there were also good white people in South Africa. "Would you want good people, innocent people to be pushed into the sea?" he asked.

"Let them get out now, or they will be," said Dee.

I could see him thinking, "A little girl like that, hard as nails!" He could not grasp the fact that she was not exactly little, although she did still think it fun to make cutouts.

Dad grabbed away the scissors because she might let snippets of paper fall on the floor. He snatched the fruit juice bottle from her when she tried to fill her glass, fearing she would spill juice on the tablecloth.

John's little girl might have spilled it, but she was only four. Dad had never recognized that babies become children, children adolescents, adolescents adults, and worst of all they form their own opinions and stick up for them come hell or high water.

Nevertheless he began talking about a larger apartment in which we could all be comfortable. I thought about it, although it was hardly an ideal plan.

Dad wasn't easy. He continued trying to bring me up, hoping that something might come of me yet. He was chary of praising me — I might become big-headed. When the steak or the lamb chops turned out as well as Mother's, and I, still childishly longing for a crumb of his recognition asked, "Satisfied, Dad?" he niggled, "Well, it was a good cut of meat." Just once he was so surprised to see me carefully scraping the last smears off the butter paper that despite himself he approved, "I like that, Edith. Thrift is a rare virtue nowadays." He didn't realize that I had learned habits from the scarcity in postwar Germany that I would not get over as long as I lived.

"You could easily become a teacher in New York," he mused. "You do have the equivalent of a B.A. You might have to take a refresher course, but I don't see how they could turn you down. Especially with your knowledge of German."

Dee saw me listening to Dad's siren song, being tempted, considering. Oh, New York! Uninhibited New York! I wasn't myself without it. How lovely it had been these last couple of months being in the swim like other New Yorkers, jabbering with customers on either side of me at the drugstore, and with the counterman, while having a snack or a soda.

"*I* can't live here," Dee said. She had begun to cry.

"But you told me you like New York," I said. "I thought you were happy here."

"As a tourist! But not forever! All my friends are in Berlin!"

"You'll make new friends."

"Not *such* friends!" she sobbed, and I knew what she meant. She was weeping stormily.

Eleven is not six. Had *I* found "*such* friends" in Germany as Helen, Deborah, Gina? Never. I had found stopgaps, like Gillian, for whom I too was a stopgap.

Max was a strong presence in me. He always would be. He was saying in me, "You can't do to her what you did to yourself."

Should I subject our child to incurable homesickness such as I had suffered for years, never being really well? Should she be punished for my leap into the unknown when I left New York in 1947?

Max was saying, "What right have you to deprive her of the socialism for which so many people died or went into exile? It may be imperfect, but something can be made of it."

I listened, and a violent struggle went on inside me.

The Cunard Steamship Company's embarkation check dated April 6, 1960, noted, "Tourist Class, Queen Mary, embarkation hours 10 A.M. to 1 P.M."

At 10 A.M. I was in Nat's office, bent double from a severe pain under the heart. It was not from the heart, he said. It seemed to be a cramp in the diaphragm. He tried to massage it away; he did not succeed. "It will go away by itself," he assured me, but I still had it in the taxi and on the gangplank, walking into the ship like a spastic. Dad was waving from the wharf, smiling broadly, not sorry to be on his own again.

We put our luggage down in a cabin shared with a quiet Belgian mother and young daughter; then Dee scampered away to explore her first ocean liner (it would soon be retired) while I went to the infirmary. There too a doctor tried to massage the cramp away, failed, and gave me an injection to make me sleep for an hour. When I awoke I could return upright to our cabin, where Dee was eagerly waiting to tell me her adventures. She had met the whole Viennese Boys' Choir in the swimming pool! "And you, Mommy?"

One day on deck we saw another ocean liner passing ours in the opposite direction. The two liners hooted the customary nautical greeting as passengers waved handkerchiefs, took pictures, peered through binoculars. Was Alma on board that ship? When we got back to Berlin I was told she had just left her clumsily philandering Bodo forever and taken the two boys, his and Jim Agee's, back to the United States.

It had always been a wonder to me how lightly Alma could step from country to country, lightly leave friendships behind, never suffer homesickness. She was rootless as a mushroom. Yet the self-dramatizing good-time girl had been wonderful to me and Dee after Max died. She insisted that we accompany her and Bodo's delicate son Stefan on a ski holiday in Oberhof and be distracted from our grief. It worked for Dee. She learned to ski in an hour, and the next day kept up with experienced adults on a ski hike that lasted from early morning to suppertime. How proud she was when they praised her to me! In Oberhof I shed tears over Max's death for the first time, and Alma congratulated me, "Thank God, I thought you'd never cry!" It was Alma, too, who looked over the apartment in Stalin Allee where other people's deserted little rooms made me feel a stranger, and said, meaning it, "Oh, I'm so glad you got this place! It's perfect!" — after which I was able to accept and live in it.

It was a jolt that now I had lost her too, a passing ship, the never-quite-friend who unexpectedly stood by me when I needed someone.

July 26, 1962

As I woke up this morning I became conscious that something deeply disturbing had happened.

I had run into Walburga in the street, and she had told me of seeing Max. She often saw him, she said. Although in poor health he was nevertheless managing to keep his head above water with a small photography studio in West Berlin. She laughed ruefully: His photo of her hadn't turned out too well; but it wasn't actually bad. She took it out of her bag to show me, chattering gaily as if her maidenly existence were one long round of amusement. My heart stopped. A mere ex-neighbor knew more about Max than his wife did! He was alive! — and hadn't I really known it all along? Hadn't I, knowing it, simply let him disappear from sight, sick as he was, let him go under while all my unworthy thoughts were of my own survival in a country where without him I was lost? Shattered, I begged Walburga to give me the address of that studio in West Berlin. Groping for pencil and paper I awoke to the clang-banging of the elevator outside my apartment door in Stalinallee.

One day, but not in a dream, the real Walburga telephoned me. She had received a large package containing an unframed, rolled-up oil portrait of Max wrapped in brown paper and tied with string. There were no stamps on the package, so Walburga paid the postman. Inside was a note saying that the sender, Till Hienz, hadn't had a pfennig to spare and that the portrait was meant for me. It couldn't be sent direct because the West German post office was forbidden to send fine art to East Germany. Mutual friends had given her our old Friedenau address and Walburga's name.

Till was Max's first love, whom he had meant to marry if he ever managed to return from exile; and she had waited for him. A weaver of Gobelins who seldom found a customer, Till lived in a trailer where there was no space to hang a painting, and now that Max was gone why should not his widow and his child have it? Walburga would not hear of being reimbursed for the postage by a friend who earned only East marks; I remonstrated in vain. Good old Walburga. Noble Till.

By rights, I thought, the life-size picture belonged in Aufbau's entrance hall as a memorial to its irreplaceable editor-in-chief. I had it framed and invited Klaus Gysi, then the director, to view it and tell me what he thought. He did look at it for a couple of minutes before rushing away. Then I found the perfect place beside our old brass bed and was thankful that shifty Klaus had spurned my offer by pretending to forget all about it. (Who knew but what suspicions linking Max with the Harich plot mightn't yet implicate *him!*)

Dee sat down on the foot of the bed and gazing up at Max said, "Now we're all together again!"

The portrait had been painted in the famous art colony Worpswede when Max was about thirty years old, but it made him ageless — he was the Max with whom we were familiar. I would seat myself opposite, as if in a pew, looking over at the face that was so acutely intelligent, so inaccessible to pettiness, and with a sensitivity so sage, and consult him about knotty problems even after I became older than he had been when he died.

The exact day of the turnabout escaped my attention. In fact several years passed before it struck me that this man would regard me with deference rather than desire if we were now to meet for the first time. Yet the traits apparent in the picture must at thirty have been fully developed when the painter made them more visible by not too precisely rendering the outer man.

The widow's peak that crowned his brow is very slightly off center. The short and stubby fingers are made extremely long and bony; probably the painter did them between sittings, imagining that long bony fingers were the kind a long bony man must have. The fingers of the right hand are longer again than the left fingers, which loosely hold a cigarette whose ash will fall in a moment on the always crumpled jacket. The eyes are seen as enlarged by his glasses, round and dark as an icon's, but the artist had left out the glasses.

To the person I have become the portrait reveals an extraordinary quality of those eyes: youth. A kind of opacity was not simply optical helplessness, it was the blindfold which would come off in maturity and concentrate the alertness of the gaze.

I pause in my writing and discover through the window a friendly well-lighted moon looking in. How thoughtful! As if Max had suggested, "Go, see how she is doing!"

Acknowledgments

All German epigraphs, poetry, and prose quoted in this book were translated into English by the author and with generous permission from heirs and publishers who hold the rights. These were: Franziska Kugelmann (epigraph part 1); Barbara Brecht-Schall (epigraph part 2); S. Fischer Verlag, Frankfurt am Main (epigraph part 3); and Eva Maurer (epigraph part 7).

I am deeply grateful to new friends and old who helped in the preparation of the manuscript, flatly refusing any remuneration. Their enthusiasm buoyed me up and any criticisms had a salutary effect. Regine Schmitz made the clean copy on her computer while perfectionist husband Manfred checked every page. Elga Abramowitz took time off despite an overload of translation work to read all seven parts with an eye to cutting what could be sacrificed. Valuable photographs were loaned without fee by the Berlin Academy of Arts Hanns Eisler Archive; others were donated by filmmaker Werner Schweizer of Zürich, whose documentary *Noel Field, der erfundene Spion* (The Imaginary Spy) cleared Field and his wife of accusations that they had ever been agents, let alone double agents.

But to not mention Hans Bunge, a brave man I wish I had met personally, would be worse than unfair, for without him none of those of us who lived through the indignities inflicted on artists in East Germany would have learned what was really said during the cruel three-week inquisition of composer Hanns Eisler which led to the stillbirth of his planned opera *Johann Faustus*. Bunge agonized over this tragedy. His documentation in book form reads like some play in *Inferno*, but constitues the actual minutes of the proceedings.

How he got hold of them is a mystery, for he himself could hardly be present. He was persona non grata to the Party, which had seen to it that he got no work for years. Only after the East German government fell in 1989 could the documentation be taken to a publisher. It came out in 1991, after Hans Bunge's death.

Author's Note on Sources

1) Werner Mittenzwei, *Das Leben des Bertolt Brecht*, Aufbau Verlag, Berlin, 1986. Volume IIin particular backs up my reporting on the bullying of artists and writers. For example, it was Mittenzwei whose mischievous remark about Walter Ulbricht I quoted: "Art was taken so seriously by him that both artists and public could lose all pleasure in it." It was also Mittenzwei who, having attended a Party conference at the opera house where the Brecht-Dessau opera *The Trial of Lucullus* had had its "tryout" and promptly been banned, quoted President Wilhelm Pieck (a theater lover) as protesting, "Comrades, what if it is *we* who are in error?" (This in turn is backed up by a book review in *Die Berliner Zeitung*, "The Trial of an Opera" on May 16, 1995, edited by Joachim Lucchesi, publisher BasisDruck Verlag, Berlin.)

2) Hans Bunge, *Die Debatte um Hanns Eisler's* Johann Faustus, *a Documentation*, BasisDruck Verlag, Berlin, 1991. In his preface Bunge emphasized that the rights to the many contributions were held by the various contributors. The most important part of the book is the minutes of three hearings in the East Berlin Academy of Arts on three successive Wednesday afternoons ending on June 10, 1953. Bunge related in his preface that he was fortunate enough to "get hold of" the minutes and that the "procedure was secret."

3) Brecht's *Arbeitsjournal* (Working Diary) published by Suhrkamp Verlag, Frankfurt am Main, 1973. Two volumes. In the second I found his impressions of Anna Seghers when they met in Paris after exile on November 4, 1947.

4) *Das Herrnstadt-Dokument,* edited and with a contribution by Nadja Stulz Herrnstadt (daughter), written by Rudolf Herrnstadt himself. This tragic account was published by Rowohlt Taschenbuch Verlag in Reinbek bei Hamburg, 1990.

5) "Kollege Zschau und Kollege Brumme," a sensational long article by Rudolf Herrnstadt that appeared in *Neues Deutschland* on October 14, 1951. (I have a Xerox of it.) Kollege means colleague, and there is a hint of sarcasm in its use, also in the invented surnames Zschau and Brumme.

6) *Der Fall Rudolf Herrnstadt,* by Helmut Müller-Enbergs, Links-Druck-Verlag-GmbH, 1991. Another view of the tragedy.

7) *Catalogue of an Exhibition* in the Märkisches Museum, Berlin, in 1993, featuring paintings by Horst Strempel. The name of the exhibition was "Im Labyrinth des kalten Kriegs" (In the Labyrinth of the Cold War). I also used an article of much later date in *Neues Deutschland,* November 8, 1993, by Hermann Raum, who wrote that this exhibition showed "how rapidly and rabidly the revolution in those years (the 1940s and 1950s) devoured its most eager children in the arts. Although there were hundreds of individual cases of this conflict, Strempel's life and work can be read as a typically horrible example."

The catalogue itself is a mine of political information by historians and art experts. (The use of the word "revolution" in Raum's article harks back to the title of Wolfgang Leonhard's bitter book *The Revolution Dismisses its Children,* published by Kiepenheuer & Witsch, Cologne, 1955. I would prefer a freer translation of the title, *"kicks out* its children.")

8) Walter Janka's autobiography *Spuren eines Lebens* (Traces of a Life), published by Rowohlt-Berlin Verlag GmbH in April 1991. I have this book to thank for all the facts about Janka's life which are included in *Love in Exile.* It is also a good source of information on the accusations and self-recriminations in court of the young man, Wolfgang Harich, whose treachery sent Janka to solitary confinement for years. *Neues Deutschland* and *Sonntag* corroborated this information.

Selected Index

A NOTE ON THE AUTHOR

EDITH ANDERSON'S short story collection and a chronicle of her railroad work during the second world war were
published in Germany. She has lived in Berlin since 1947.

A NOTE ON THE BOOK

The text for this book was composed by Steerforth Press
using a digital version of Electra, a typeface designed in 1935
by William Addison Dwiggins. Electra has been a standard
book typeface since its release because of its evenness of design and high legibility. All Steerforth books are printed on
acid free papers and this book was bound with traditional
smythe sewing by BookPress of Brattleboro, Vermont.